WISDOM FOR TODAY ALONG RECOVERY LANE

DAILY READINGS FOR PERSONS IN RECOVERY THAT ARE USING THE TWELVE STEP PROGRAM

John S.

PRIMIX

PUBLISHING

THE WRITE CHOICE

Primix Publishing
East Brunswick Office Evolution
1 Tower Center Boulevard, Ste 1510
East Brunswick, NJ 08816
www.primixpublishing.com
Phone: 1-800-538-5788

Published by Primix Publishing: 03/06/2025

ISBN: 979-8-89194-408-4(sc)
ISBN: 979-8-89194-409-1(e)

Library of Congress Control Number: 2025901627

From the Author

As the creator of these daily readings, I have provided a means that may assist you in the recovery process. Recovery is most likely the hardest thing you will ever do. The readings you find here can help. *I believe <u>you are worth it!</u>*

I am a Certified Alcohol & Drug Abuse Counselor, having worked in the field of addiction medicine since 1982. I am also an Advanced Certified Relapse Prevention Specialist. I have worked with a variety of patients – adults, adolescents, professionals, minorities, chronically relapsed persons and those with dual diagnosis. I have worked in a variety of treatment settings – inpatient, partial hospitalization, intensive outpatient and continuing care. I have worked as a counselor, supervisor, trainer, director and consultant in the USA and Sweden. I am myself a recovering person.

Sometimes people ask me what I do, and I say, "I am a builder, and I teach people about recovery from addiction." When they hear this, they often give me strange looks. Yet this response is most certainly true. "Oh, I see, you teach people how to recover from addiction," they respond. And I say, "No, I teach people to let themselves recover!" "What do you mean by teaching people to let themselves recover?"

I reply, "I believe all people can recover from addictive disease, but some people just get in the way of their own recovery. Anyone can build a house of cards, anyone can nail together some boards and call it a shelter; but in order to build a strong recovery, you must know how to read a blueprint, be able to follow a plan, know how to use the resources that are available, and finally, how to finish it all off. Some people just can't seem to let anyone else help in constructing their recovery."

"What do you mean a builder?" they add. "I am indeed a builder. I built a recovery program for myself, or maybe I should say that I allowed a recovery program to be built, with the help of a Great Contractor, and I assist others in their daily walk of recovery. "I have come to believe that this Great Contractor is a source of power and wisdom I can rely on. So I let this Great Contractor continue to advise me about the building projects with which I am involved.

If this sounds spiritual, it is. All I ask is that you keep an open mind to find your own Great Contractor, and let him help you build a strong recovery program.

And so I build. I have built a wonderful family. I have built some very good addiction treatment programs, and I have helped others to find out how to let them build recovery into their life. All this and more was only possible and accomplished with the help of others and my Great Contractor.

I hope that you build a fine house, with a strong foundation, straight walls, a unique floor plan, and a roof that doesn't leak with the program you are working. I pray that these devotions will be a helpful tool in your construction project.

John S.

* * * *

Preface

How to use *Wisdom for Today*

Finding recovery and holding on to it is a gift of working the program presented to us in the Twelve Step program. Each of us has traveled a different path to arrive in a place where we are able to face up to the reality of addiction in our life, and each of us must travel a path to find recovery. This book may be used in a variety of ways:

❖ As a Reference Book

Wisdom for Today can be used as a reference book to assist you in understanding the Twelve Steps, the principles of a recovery program, and the "stuck points" that may complicate your recovery process. As you read the book, you may find there are particular topics or statements that "push your buttons" or challenge your thoughts or beliefs. I would encourage you to highlight these sections and talk with others about these concepts. I encourage you to search out other sources of information and to seek clarification on the issues that this book may bring to the surface for you.

❖ As a Guide Book

Wisdom for Today can serve as a guide in your daily mediation. I hope you will use this book to search more deeply into yourself. Hopefully it will inspire you to reach for a deeper meaning and lead you to enhance your recovery. May this book serve as a compass in finding your way.

❖ As a Recovery Tool

Wisdom for Today may challenge you to a new honesty and may assist you to a renewed openness, and it may help you discover the courage that exists within yourself. This book may bring clarity, and it may cause you to discover more questions that need answers. Hopefully, it will help you to find a deeper meaning in your life.

Additionally you can use this book as a way of "passing it on" and giving it away. I hope it leads to many good conversations with others as you act as a teacher, a sponsor or a friend.

❖ As a Change Agent

Wisdom for Today may just have one or two pearls of wisdom that can serve as a catalyst for change in your life and enhance recovery in your life. It may help you to accept the brokenness that exists in all addicts and alcoholics and find ways to fix or improve your functioning. Hopefully it will help you to grow spiritually.

❖ The Goal

To find the happiness we all seek, the peace of mind we all desire and to better understand the possibilities that exist in recovery.

*   *   *   *

Acknowledgements

To Curly J., my sponsor, and my home group that held my hand and guided me along the path I want to express my deepest gratitude. This miracle called recovery would not have been possible without your help.

To the counselors and doctors that have provided me with a roadmap to insight and encouraged me to find the answers I needed, your wisdom has inspired me along my journey.

Special Acknowledgements

To my parents who put up with all my insanity during my active addiction but always let me know that I have been loved. You have assisted me in the celebrations, joys and struggles of ongoing recovery and helped me to find wisdom along the way. Special thanks are given for your patience and willingness to assist me in this effort.

To my family, especially my children, you have taught me the need to seek wisdom and helped me find courage when I needed it most. You have increased my self acceptance and taught me humility. Without your love I am not sure I would have found the energy to keep going.

Also, I want to thank all my colleagues in the field of addiction treatment that have helped me find productive ways to help others find recovery. Your wisdom has also inspired me in many ways and helped me to find effective ways to help others.

* * * *

Dedication

And finally, I want to thank the myriad of clients with whom I worked that have trusted me to guide them in their pursuit of recovery. It has been wisdom that was revealed in working with each of you that inspired many of the pages of this book

* * * *

Wisdom for Today   Jan 1

I'm tired. Some days I just don't feel like I have the energy to go on. It is at times like this that I trust that God will lead me to a place of rest. Just like a river runs dirty after a storm, I know that my life also ran dirty after the storm of addiction. Yet over time as the river continues to flow, it is cleansed. This is true in my life. God does not promise that storms won't come back into our lives, but He sees to it that the river of life runs clean again. The water does not always rage; it does calm down and flows peacefully again. Do I trust that God will bring me to a place of peace and serenity as long as I walk with Him?

Meditations for the Heart

When I was stuck out in the rapids of addiction, I just wanted to find a way out. I kept bouncing off the rocks and thought for sure I would drown. It seemed that no matter how hard I would swim that I would never get out of the rapids. It was not until I called out for help and realized that I could not get out of the rapids by myself that I then found hope. The Twelve Step program threw me a rope and began to pull me back to shore. Do I trust that God will give me the strength to hold on to the rope?

Petitions to my Higher Power

God,

Sometimes I just want to give up, even though I know I am being pulled back to shore. I grow tired and weak. God, give me the strength to hold on so that I may rest a while when I get to shore. Help me to realize that my work is not done even when I get out of the river.

Amen.

* * * *

Wisdom for Today   Jan 2

When I was busy getting high or wasted, whether at the bar or at a using buddy's place, I was constantly worried about running out. I always had to keep the "fridge" filled with cold beer. I could never let my "stash" run out. I always had to have "more." It became a way of life for me.

The Twelve Step program is not so different. It too is a way of life. Each of us uses the principles of the program in different ways, but with the same purpose. Some of us use quiet time and meditation, some use meetings and sponsors, some use Twelve Step social functions with the intent of learning a new way to live – clean and sober. One thing that we can't forget is that we need to be refilled constantly. Do I use the program to get refilled?

1

Meditations for the Heart

Prayer was a very difficult thing for me in early recovery. It was something I had to grow into. Then my sponsor told me it was simply "talking to a friend." That was something I could do. A true friend was somebody that was willing to listen, someone who cared, and someone who would give me guidance. A true friend would look out for me and would pick me up if I stumbled. A true friend would point out the stumbling blocks along the way. Is my Higher Power my true friend?

Petitions to my Higher Power

God,

There are times that my tank runs on empty. Remind me to continue to refill my recovery engine when I need to. Be my friend as I walk through this day and guide me along the way.

Amen.

* * * *

Wisdom for Today   Jan 3

When I was active in my addiction, I did not take care of myself physically, mentally or spiritually. Frequently I did not eat enough or ate the wrong things. I never got any exercise other than lifting a "cold one." Mentally I played lots of games. I made many assumptions that were wrong. I was constantly busy figuring out what my next lie would have to be. My whole belief system was messed up. And spiritually, I had simply given up all hope. I was convinced that "God" did not exist or had forgotten about me, when in truth it was I who had forgotten about Him. I had become as useless as a lump of clay. Am I taking better care of myself physically, mentally and spiritually?

Meditations for the Heart

Just like a lump of clay, I am shapeless and formless when I walk into the doors of the Twelve Step program. Through the handiwork and care of sponsors, other recovering addicts and alcoholics, my life began to shape up. My "Higher Power" also worked hard to craft me to a new usefulness. I was "fired" in the kiln of the Twelve Steps. I was glazed in the principles of honesty, openness and willingness and fired again. Today I can see that I have become a "new vessel," one that can be used for good in this world. Can I see the beginnings of usefulness in my life?

Petitions to my Higher Power

God,

Today I want to be of service to others and of service to You. Help me to accept Your will in my life. Mold me, shape me and use me for good in this world today.
Amen.

✳ ✳ ✳ ✳

Wisdom for Today   Jan 4

In early recovery it is vitally important to keep our faculties about us. If we don't stay alert, we may not recognize that we are in trouble until it is too late. It is all too easy to overextend ourselves, trying to get the quick fix. There were many problems I faced in early recovery. I felt driven to try and resolve them right away. I wanted immediate gratification.

I found myself working extra hours trying to dig out of my financial mess. I found myself agreeing to do things to which I should have said, "No." I thought that keeping busy was the answer. However, I soon found myself out on a limb and very tired. When I got overtired, I couldn't think straight. My recovery was at risk. Fortunately I had the program reminding me to slow down. "Easy does it," "HALT," "Let go and let God" were the slogans being repeated over and over again. Am I willing to slow down and focus on self-preservation? Do I know that getting overtired is not good for me?

Meditations for the Heart

Understanding that recovery is a process that occurs over time is a concept I cannot afford to ignore. I didn't become an alcoholic or addict overnight. I certainly can't expect to fix all my problems overnight. Learning to slow down and rest along the road to recovery is important for my health. Now that I have some time under my belt, I can see that slowing down actually helped me to resolve my problems quicker, in part, because the fix lasted. Am I willing to trust God's plan for me? Do I understand that He will lead me in His time frame?

Petitions to my Higher Power
God,

Today let me do only those things that are necessary. Help me to know when to stop and rest. Renew my strength, and let me know I am secure in recovery when I follow Your will for my life. Let me focus on what is important today.
Amen.

✳ ✳ ✳ ✳

"*We admitted.*" (*Alcoholics Anonymous,* Fourth Edition Page 59) The first two words of Step One are most important. The longer that I have been clean and sober, the more I realize that this was not something I could have done on my own. Looking back, I had made many, many attempts to change, control and quit on my own. Each of these attempts ultimately led to failure, and I was back in the insanity of my addiction. It was not until I was ready to stop doing it my way that things changed. I needed the help of others. I had to become "we."

Have I admitted that I am addicted? Have I stopped trying to run the show my way? Am I convinced that my way doesn't work? Is there any doubt left that says, "Someday I will be able to drink or use again?" Admitting that I was powerless was not an easy task. It meant a radical shift in my thinking. Fortunately, being powerless was not the same thing as being helpless. I did not choose to become addicted or alcoholic. I just wanted to be like everyone else and have a good time. But once I admitted that I had this illness, I had to take responsibility for recovery. Have I accepted the responsibility of recovery?

Meditations for the Heart

It's all good. This must be my roadmap for today. It is easy to get caught up in the "tunnel vision" that recovery is awful or too hard. Do I believe that God cares for me and will provide what I need for this day? When I believe this, I can see that God is with me at all times. I can begin to see that even in my most difficult times in recovery that He will give me what I need to deal with the problems I face. And this certainly is good.

As I walk through this day, I can stop along the way and see His grace. I can see those times when He places people in my life to give me direction, encouragement and wisdom. I can choose to be grateful for each miracle I experience. Do I trust that God walks with me each step of the way?

Petitions to my Higher Power

God,

One step at a time I must walk though this day. I admit I need guidance along the way. God, help me to follow Your will for me. Step by step You show me the way. I have to "walk the walk," but You show the way. When I stumble along the way, God, pick me up so that I may continue on this path. Amen.

* * * *

What are the building blocks of our program? Honesty, fellowship, faith in our Higher Power and caring are a few I have found important. We can never fully attain these goals. Yet these are the things we need to build on if we are to be successful in recovery. Honesty is where it all starts. We must find honesty with our addiction. If we continue to lie to ourselves about having this disease, we stand no chance of getting better. We each surrounded ourselves with people to support our addiction and need to surround ourselves with the fellowship that supports recovery.

Learning to have faith that God can and will do for us what we can't do on our own is an important factor in the quality of our recovery. It makes the difference between being miserable and sober and content and clean. And finally, learning to really care for others and for ourselves is what working the steps is all about. Am I including these building blocks in the foundation of my recovery?

Meditations for the Heart

Knock and the door will be opened. I believe that my Higher Power is always ready to help me. When I feel as if my life is in stormy times, I know that there is a safe haven to which I can go; and the door will always be opened for me. God helps me to find peace in the storm. He grants me the courage to deal with the struggles I have. I am sure that His help is always there. He anticipates my needs even before I ask. The fact that I survived my addiction is ample evidence for me of His anticipating my needs. God was surely looking out for me as I was not looking out for myself. Do I see that God anticipates my needs?

Petitions to my Higher Power

God,

Today I walk in the confidence that You are always ready to help me. I trust that You will give me what I need for this day. Help me today to strengthen the building blocks in the foundation of my recovery.

Amen.

*   *   *   *

Freedom is a concept that is too often difficult to grasp. I believe that too many addicts and alcoholics see freedom as meaning "no strings attached." Certainly, when we were using, our view of freedom was distorted. We thought we were free to choose to use alcohol or drugs whenever we wanted.

But this kind of freedom led to our bondage. Our disease imprisoned us. Addiction took control of our will. We were no longer able to make free choices. We had to use.

Freedom in recovery comes with a price. There is a string attached. Freedom in recovery requires responsibility. We may not be responsible for becoming addicted. Certainly none of us chose to be alcoholic or drug addicted, but we must choose to be responsible for our recovery. We are required to do "the next right thing" if we are to maintain our recovery program. We must be responsible and go to meetings, use our sponsors and work the steps. The freedom that recovery offers comes only with this string attached. Am I willing to be responsible for my recovery in order to find freedom?

Meditations for the Heart

Making the choice to be free is not something we can do all by ourselves. My will always wants to choose the wrong way to freedom. My will wants to find the easier, softer way. I believe that our will gets short-circuited in addiction. I believe addiction fries the circuits of the will. It is only by the grace of God that we are able to again choose the responsible path. Step Two talks of being restored to sanity. Do I recognize that my "Higher Power" is the only hope I have for being restored? Do I see that my circuitry needs to be rewired in order for me to make responsible choices that will lead me to freedom?

Petitions to my Higher Power

God,

Too many times I have tried to do it my way and failed. Help me to see that my only hope is through You. Help me to choose the responsible path to freedom in recovery. Help me to see that my way will not work and that I must rely on You to lead me to freedom.

Amen.

* * * *

Wisdom for Today   Jan 8

We all traveled different paths to arrive at the door of opportunity that recovery offers. The same is true regarding our concept of "*God as we understand Him.*" (*Alcoholics Anonymous,* Fourth Edition Page 59) Many of us claimed to believe and have faith when we were active in our addiction, but our behavior did not match our words. We may have asked for God's help, but we did not accept it when His hand reached out to offer help. As we enter the Twelve Step program, we all start in different places with regard to our spiritual faith. Yet one thing is sure -- we all need to grow in this area. Some of us can crawl, others walk and still others may be able to spiritually run right from the start. Do I realize that I need to grow spiritually if I am to succeed at abstinence?

Meditations for the Heart

Our journey toward spiritual health often begins in a place of weakness. Yet it is in this place of weakness that we are most receptive to grow in faith. The program offers plenty of evidence that it works. We can see that many before us have used the steps to grow and stay in recovery. Faith begins with a willingness to accept this reality and begin to trust that the steps indeed can lead us out of insanity. Opening ourselves to the concept of "God as we understand Him" can indeed be where we find hope in the middle of hopelessness. Do I recognize that I can no longer be my own Higher Power? Am I willing to open myself to the spiritual principles of the program?

Petitions to my Higher Power

God,

It seems strange to call out to You this way. I always looked for a quick fix. Help me today to be open to the spiritual principles of the program. Increase my willingness to have faith.

Amen.

* * * *

Wisdom for Today   Jan 9

When I was active in my addiction, I thought I was having fun and that life was good. As my disease progressed, I began to experience all the harmful consequences associated with my drinking and using. Early in my recovery life was not a lot of fun. It seemed as if my whole life had been taken away from me. I had a hard time seeing that what was actually happening was that I was finally getting my life back. I kept going to meeting after meeting, and little by little I found my life and myself again. There were times I could laugh again. I found myself being able to look others and myself in the face again. I found that I no longer felt like I was on the wrong side of the tracks. It didn't happen all at once, but over time I found meaning in my life again. Do I believe that the program can bring meaning back into my life?

Meditations for the Heart

I will search after the Divine Spirit in life and trust that God will bring meaning back into my life. I will search to improve my conscious contact with God, as I understand Him. For in doing this, I know that I will find the answers I am looking for. I know that when I search after this Higher Purpose, I find not only what I am looking for; but I also find what I need. Am I willing to search for God's will for me?

Petitions to my Higher Power

God,

Today let me laugh and find enjoyment in the simple gifts that the program provides. Help me to remain forever grateful for each day I am given back in recovery. Help me to see that even my bad days now are far better than when I was wasted.

Amen.

* * * *

Wisdom for Today   Jan 10

I believe that each of us has an inner desire to be loved. We want others to care for us, often times secretly. We want to know that others will be there and reach out to us when we are in need. With addiction to alcohol or drugs, often times this inner desire gets skewed. We look to alcohol or drugs to fulfill this inner desire. In the height of my addiction I looked to drugs and alcohol for comfort, love and to satisfy my inner desires.

In recovery I need to recognize how easy it is to misplace this desire for love. It is easy to misplace this desire on to things, people and even my Higher Power in unhealthy ways. If I am honest with myself, and others and even God, as I understand Him, I can find healthy ways to accept love. I do not need to try and manipulate the process to satisfy my inner desire. Am I still trying to manipulate others or God into accepting me?

Meditations for the Heart

Perhaps one of the best ways to assure that I am not trying to manipulate is to learn how to love myself. I need to realize and accept that I am valuable and worthy of love. I do this by loving myself. This means that I care enough about myself to correct myself when I am wrong, just like a father corrects his children when they do things that are hurtful, dishonest or manipulative. This is an act of self-love in a healthy way. Step Ten teaches us to admit our wrongs. Do I see that I wrong myself when I try to hide or manipulate others?

8

Petitions to my Higher Power
God,

Someone once told me, "God don't make junk." Help me value myself as You value and love me. Help me to recognize and accept love from others in the program. Help me not to try and manipulate to satisfy my inner desire for love. Give me courage for this day.
Amen.

* * *

Wisdom for Today   **Jan 11**

I can remember thinking, "What am I doing here?" I really didn't see how going to meetings was going to help. I would go and sit around, not say much and hope the "magic" would work. When it became apparent that just sitting around wasn't going to work, I realized I had to put it into action. That meant going to meetings regularly, sharing my story, talking about the problems I faced along the way and helping others. As I began to become more involved and put as much energy into my recovery as I did drinking and using, I soon began to leave meetings feeling better. No longer was I leaving grumpy and dissatisfied with life, but I was happy. Something was working. Am I giving of myself, my time, energy and effort at meetings?

Meditations for the Heart

I remember building "forts" as a child. Sometimes I made them with an old blanket that I draped over a table. Later I made them out of sticks and limbs I found in to forest. Inside my fort I always felt safe. The program is a lot like that. If we build a secure foundation, strong walls and a roof that doesn't leak, we feel safe. Through active participation at meetings, talking with a sponsor and listening to the winners, I found the building blocks to help me feel safe in recovery. Real security came with knowing that as long as I remained active in the fellowship and worked the steps, I would find that the promises were there for me. Am I working to make my recovery secure?

Petitions to my Higher Power
God,

Today show me the building blocks I need to use in my life. Help me to have faith that You will guide my steps. Let me listen to Your directions along the way. Let me experience the miracle of life today.
Amen.

Wisdom for Today   *Jan 12*

It took me a while to understand that I came into the Twelve Step program, not to learn how to stop drinking and using, but to learn a new way of living. I had quit dozens of times but could not figure out how to stay "quit." The Twelve Step program was not going to teach me how to quit. It would, however, teach me how to stay clean and sober. I had to stop lying to others and myself about my disease. I had to learn to rely on a Power greater than myself. I had to change my lifestyle, my thinking and my behavior.

I did not learn this by going to just a few meetings. I had to go to meetings frequently at first. I needed to do this not only to learn a new way of living but also because I needed time just to let my brain come out of the fog. I generally do not go to meetings as often anymore, but I still increase the frequency of my meetings when I need to do so. I am not advocating going to meetings infrequently, rather using meetings effectively. I also urge all addicts to do something each and every day to support recovery. Step work, daily readings, prayer and meditation, talking with your sponsor are just a few of the options. Am I willing to invest in my recovery each and every day?

Meditations for the Heart

I want my will to be in line with my Higher Power. I want to be on a parallel track and to follow His will for me in all that I do. I want to be happy and healthy again. In order to do this, I need to set my thinking and desires on a different path. I must be willing and open to follow the suggestions of the program. I need to "come to believe" that God can and will do for me that which I cannot do by myself. Am I willing to do that which will help and not hinder my spiritual growth?

Petitions to my Higher Power

God,

Today help me not to be a block to my recovery but to be willing to do what is necessary for my spiritual growth. Help me to believe that You can and will do for me that which I cannot do on my own. Help me to be willing to invest in my recovery today and everyday. Give me an attitude of gratitude today.

Amen.

* * * *

"I want it now!" These words are familiar to all addicts and alcoholics. Early in my recovery process I struggled a lot with impatience. I wanted everything to return to "normal" now. But the reality is that a new life cannot be built overnight. It takes time. It takes work, and it takes patience. Just because I was clean and sober did not necessarily mean that my addictive thinking stopped. Learning to think and do recovery takes time. It has to be practiced. It is too easy to get back into our old ways of thinking and behavior. That is why we must practice. Building a new life takes time, but it can be done if we follow the suggestions of the program. Am I practicing clean and sober thinking?

Meditations for the Heart

Faith is a gift from our Higher Power. In response to our prayers, we are given this gift. Faith and hope come from our willingness to trust God and the program. If I keep doing what I need to do each day, and if I practice the principles of the program, I receive these gifts. This does not mean I won't have struggles or problems along the way. We will always have problems. It does mean that I will find the strength and the wisdom along the way to deal with these problems in recovery. The more faith I have the easier life becomes. Am I willing to pray for a stronger faith?

Petitions to my Higher Power

God,

Today I need your help just as I do each day. Walk with and give me the gift of faith. Strengthen me for the times I struggle and help me to think with a clear mind.

Amen.

* * * *

As I have walked through life in the program, I have learned many things. Perhaps one of the more important things that I have learned is that there are two kinds of Wisdom. There is spiritual wisdom. This is the wisdom we gain when we seek to improve our conscious contact with God and His will for us. Learning to recognize that God is active in our lives and that He gives us direction is also a part of this wisdom.

Secondly, there is practical wisdom. This is the wisdom regarding the choices we make regarding our behavior. Practical wisdom tells us not to drink or use that which is poison to our lives. Practical wisdom tells us what is healthy. Practical wisdom pushes us to care for ourselves.

Meditations for the Heart

I have so many choices. What is the next right thing to do? Which way do I turn? To whom can I turn for help? When should I proceed? Where should I go? This is where the wisdom, both spiritual and practical, comes into play. What questions do I have in my life today that need answers? Am I seeking wisdom in my search for answers and direction? Do I trust the answers that I get?

Petitions to my Higher Power

God,

I know that you are willing to guide me along the path of recovery. Help me to listen for direction. Bring people into my life that can teach me the wisdom of the program. Grant that the choices I make lead me in a healthy direction. Amen.

* * * *

Wisdom for Today   Jan 15

At first it was so much fun. It was exciting, and I was on top of the world. But over time as my drinking and drug use progressed, I began to experience more and more problems. For a long time I could explain away the problems or I could blame the problems on something other than my use. My dependence on drugs and alcohol became more and more evident as the consequences provided more and more evidence that I had a problem. Despite all this, I kept on going; and my use became an obsession. I had lost all control.

In the Twelve Step program I had to face the truth; I was addicted. I stopped drinking and using, yet my life did not return to immediate happiness. Just because I had stopped using didn't mean my problems disappeared. I still had much to change. This is where the steps and guidance from those people who had been there helped. Little by little I changed. Today I know I still have work to do. Recovery continues one day at a time. Am I willing to use the steps and the fellowship to help me change the things I can?

Meditations for the Heart

Today I will be calm and know that each day presents new challenges and new rewards. I will be calm because I know and trust that the promises are real and that I can have each of them if I do the work and follow my Higher

Power's direction. Sometimes I hear people say that God is in the driver's seat. I don't follow that logic. I am the one who has to walk the walk. I am the one who must be responsible for my recovery. I am the one that needs to be in the driver's seat. But I do want God to read the road map and show me the way. Am I doing all that I must do to be responsible for my recovery? Do I ask God for direction along the way?

Petitions to my Higher Power

God,

Today help me to stay focused on the tasks at hand. Encourage me to follow the steps to recovery. Tell me when to turn and when to stop. Let me know if I need to take an alternate route. Give me the patience not to get frustrated with the process, and help me to trust that You are always there to help me when I need it.

Amen.

* * *

Wisdom for Today   Jan 16

It was indeed a heavy load that I carried around because of my drinking and drug use. The dishonesty, guilt and shame all piled up into a tremendous burden. Addiction turned me into a liar. In order to get what I wanted, I would con, manipulate and lie. I lived in constant fear of being found out. I lived constantly trying to hide from others and myself.

When I walked into the Twelve Step program, my dishonesty did not just vanish because I stopped using. I still wanted to hide. But I found acceptance in the eyes of those people sitting around the tables. I listened to others whose story was like mine. I heard people talk openly and honestly. I wanted what they had. I could see the freedom that honesty provided. I found out that I did not have to hide anymore. Have I gotten rid of the heavy load that dishonesty and addiction provide?

Meditation for the Heart

As fear, worry, deceit and lying slipped away, I found new spiritual principles filling my life; and with them came serenity and peace of mind. Old ways sometimes die hard and are quick to come back. It is easy to slip back into dishonesty, but I can never afford to lie to myself about my addiction. I am an alcoholic and an addict. I must rely on the guidance from my Higher Power and find the courage to remain true to myself and to my Higher Power. It is the only way to find freedom. Do I let dishonesty enslave my heart and mind?

Petitions to my Higher Power
God,

Today let me be honest and truthful in all that I do. When fear grabs my heart, help me to find courage to speak in truth. When I want to run and hide, let me seek Your guidance. Lead me to freedom.
Amen.

*　*　*　*

Wisdom for Today   *Jan 17*

What an incredible beating alcohol and drugs put me through! Waking up in the morning with my head feeling three sizes too big, jumpy nerves and nausea, pounding headaches - all were a part of the physical beating. Then there was the mental punishment. The worry, anxiety, fear seemed constant. The remorse, regret and guilt were constant companions. The shame of realizing what I had done to the people I cared about and the inability of being able to even look at myself in the mirror were all a part of the mental pain I claimed because of my use. Then came the loss of freedom and the loss of dreams and even the loss of self in the spiritual demise that addiction provided.

It was an awful beating that alcohol and drugs provided. The physical, mental and spiritual devastation was complete. Yet the insanity of the disease told me that next time would be different. But it was not. My family told me to get out. They had had enough. Am I convinced that I am beaten? Am I ready to give up?

Meditations for the Heart

When you reach the point of defeat, you are left with no choice but to give up. But this brings on the question of what or who can help me if I cannot help myself. When I sought the path of the Divine Spirit, it meant that everything in my life suddenly had to change direction. I could no longer continue on the path I was on. The reversal of direction was not easy. My body had to heal physically, my mind needed time to clear and I had to admit that I was not God. This new path seemed very rocky at first, and I had no idea where it would lead. But I had to stay the course because I knew where the other path I was on would end up - total destruction of my life. Soon I found that this new path led me to something I did not expect - peace of mind and hope. No one said it would be easy, but it was simple -- follow the principles of the program. Do I see that this new path can only bring me good?

Petitions to my Higher Power
God,

Today guide me along this new path. Help me to hold onto the hand that recovery offers, and lead me to a place of peace. Help me to heal physically, mentally and spiritually. Give me the gift of hope in this new way of living. Give me the courage and strength to stay on this path and not go back to the one that led to my destruction.
Amen.

∗ ∗ ∗ ∗

Wisdom for Today   **Jan 18**

I will never be able to figure out how much money I wasted on alcohol and drugs. The sad part is that I was not just wasting my money, but money that rightfully should have been spent on my family. Getting wasted really wasted a lot more than just me. The financial burden I had put upon my family was tremendous. Over and over I would ask immediate and extended family to bail me out of a jam. Eventually I found there was little I could do to regain their trust, and asking them for more money was not possible. This led to a growing desperation and more use. The insanity continued.

I was not able to dig my way out just because I stopped using. It took time and staying connected to the program. Frequently I was tempted to take on extra work to pay the bills, but going to meetings was the only way I could stay clean and sober. If I didn't stay clean and sober, I knew I never would get out of the mess. Am I willing to be patient for financial answers? Am I being responsible with the resources I have?

Meditations for the Heart

My future is in the hands of God. I still need to do the footwork if I am to find a way out of the mess addiction created in my life. I must take responsibility for my recovery and seek wisdom from others in the decisions I face. One thing I have learned is that each day can be about progress. Sometimes it is not always easy to see. One day I woke up, and many of the problems I had were gone. This did not mean I had no problems, just better ones - in most instances. And the problems that weren't better, I could handle more constructively. Are the problems I am facing today better than the problems I had? Do I trust that God can and will help me with each problem I face?

Petitions to my Higher Power
God,

Today help me face each problem I have with hope. Let me feel assured that by following the principles of the program that the promises of recovery can indeed happen in my life. Help me not to be discouraged but to walk with the knowledge that You walk with me.
Amen.

* * * *

Wisdom for Today *Jan 19*

My drinking and drugging kept leading me from one dead end to another. Despite all the signs along the way, I kept up this vicious circle and kept coming back to the same dead end. This was the insanity of my illness; I couldn't learn from my drinking and drug using experience. Despite all the consequences of my use, I kept going on making the same mistakes over and over. I refused to accept the evidence. I couldn't face the truth. I wouldn't even consider that there might be a way out of the insanity.

In part I continued this insanity because I could not believe or hope for anything better. This false pride and my inability to be honest kept me trapped. The program offered me something different, a road that led somewhere. When I first started going to meetings, I was not an instant convert. But over time I saw others making their way out of the insanity. They were no different than I, and they were making it. Finally I had hope that life was not a dead end. Am I spinning in circles and going down dead ends?

Meditations for the Heart

I sometimes sit and realize the gifts I have gotten along this new path and sit in awesome wonder. None of the wonderful things that have happened are because of what I have done. They are the gifts of recovery. Life still has its problems, and some of them can be difficult, but I rest assured that God will do for me what I cannot do for myself. He gives me strength for my journey. I still have to walk the walk each and every day. Yet I know that I will find the answers I need if I just follow God's will for me. Am I willing to let God be my guide today?

Petitions to my Higher Power

God,

Help me stay on the narrow path. Guide me and direct me to the next right thing. Help me to be open to Your will for me, and give me the strength and courage to follow where You lead me.
Amen.

* * *

Wisdom for Today — *Jan 20*

I relied on drinking and drugging for a lot of things. It was the only way I knew how to have a good time. It gave me the "rush" and excitement I craved. It seemed to break down walls and give me the courage to talk with others. If I was hurting physically or mentally, I looked to my addiction to cure my ills. If I had a bad day on the job or was in trouble with my spouse and the whole world seemed against me, I would seek comfort in my addiction. I just felt better if I was wasted. I looked to drinking and my drugs to solve all my problems. I relied on my addiction for all my answers. Have I stopped relying on my addiction?

Meditations for the Heart

To give up my reliance on drinking and drugging, I had to surrender. This was the only way out of the insanity. Surrender is the foundation on which all solid recovery programs are built. Surrender must be complete and not conditional, or it is not really surrender. But what was I surrendering to? Was I simply admitting defeat? Well, no! I also had to find something else to rely on, because I surely could not rely on myself. Whenever I tried my way, it did not work. The AA Big Book pointed the way, "That one is God; may you find Him now." (*Alcoholics Anonymous*, Fourth Edition Page 59) Am I willing to surrender to the care and love of a Higher Power, as I understand Him?

Petitions to my Higher Power

God,

I give up. I have nowhere else to turn but to You. Help me to see that in surrender I am giving my will and my life over to Your care. Help me to stay on the path – "just for today."

Amen.

* * *

Wisdom for Today — *Jan 21*

Early in my recovery process I was frequently tempted to put myself in high-risk situations. I wanted to see old friends. I was lonely. I wanted to have a good time. I was bored. I would get angry, or I would find myself living in the pain. I even found myself making things worse and sabotaging my recovery. I would relapse back into old behaviors. It didn't take long for me to figure out that just because I stopped drinking and using did not mean I was cured. I was still behaving like an alcoholic and an addict.

I also had a lot of evidence that I could not trust my judgment. I was impulsive and always wanted to act without thinking things through. In times like this I needed others that I could trust to help me. I needed help to make healthy decisions. I found this help at meetings. I was my own worst enemy, and it would take time to learn how to be my own friend. I had to learn to truly care for myself. Being honest and talking about what was really going on in my life at meetings did help me to learn the things that did not come naturally to me. Am I willing to be honest and ask for help when I need it?

Meditations for the Heart

Being very self-centered makes it hard to ask others for help. I perceived this as a sign of weakness. Asking for help meant I was not successful in managing my own life. I had to admit that my life was unmanageable. Then my sponsor asked me a question, "If you cut yourself, would you stitch yourself up; or would you go to the emergency room?" His question was valid. I certainly would not do something I didn't know how to do, and I certainly didn't know how to stay clean and sober. I needed help, and I had to ask for help when I needed it. Fortunately God put people in my life that I could turn to for help. I learned from those who had a few more twenty-four hours than I did. I got the guidance I needed. Am I too proud to ask for help when I need it?

Petitions to my Higher Power
God,

Today let me be humble and not proud and arrogant. Let me be willing to ask for help when I need it. Give me the courage to do the footwork necessary to change the things I can. Help me learn how to really care for myself and make healthy decisions.
Amen.

* * * *

Wisdom for Today   Jan 22
Living in a dead-end life happened because I refused to be honest with others and myself. I always had to be on the run to avoid the truth of my addiction. I didn't want to give up my alcohol or drugs. I didn't want to admit that I was out of control. I didn't want to give up my anger and resentments. I didn't want to give up my selfishness. I didn't want to give up my way of thinking.

All this led me to a place where my drinking and using were truly threatening my life and all that I valued. Still no matter how severe the consequence, I couldn't bring myself to admit that I was whipped. If I was ever going to find a way out of the insanity, I had to change my thinking. I had to give up and surrender. I had to admit I was and always will be addicted. Have I changed my thinking?

Meditations for the Heart

Life without limits is possible in the program, for my Higher Power is not limited in what He can do for me. This does not mean that I can run wild and have no guidelines to follow; but it does mean that with the words, "He can," my life can be limitless. There is such freedom in surrender. Yes, this is paradoxical; but it is how it works. Giving up control and letting go is the only way out. Those first steps on the road to recovery are not easy. In fact, it is the hardest thing I have ever done. Still it is a simple thing to say, "I can't." And then the recovery process begins. Do I really believe "I can't?" Do I believe that "He can?"

Petitions to my Higher Power

God,

The vision of what my life will be is not always clear. Help me to trust that Your vision for me is limitless. Help me to take just one step at a time on this journey. Thank You for the freedom You provide me in surrender. Amen.

* * * *

Wisdom for Today   Jan 23

In the beginning, all I wanted to do was to stop the insanity of my drinking and using. I felt so helpless and hopeless; I didn't see a way out. I had to find someone or something I could rely on, as I had plenty of evidence I couldn't trust myself. I found the answer in the voices of those who sat around the tables at meetings. I found that I could rely on a Power outside of myself. I found out that I was not God. Before long I didn't just want to be clean and sober, but I wanted to stay that way.

Learning a new way of living was not easy, but the program provided some simple guidelines. When I was in my insanity of addiction, I relied on an artificial method of finding excitement in my life. Through the program I found that I could find happiness in the simple pleasures of life. I could get a kick out of life without drugs or alcohol. I no longer needed an artificial means to happiness as I was finding happiness in the simple everyday events in my life. I could laugh again. I could live through the difficulties and come out okay. I could give and receive love again. Is my outlook changing?

Meditations for the Heart

Gratitude is an attitude that I must have each and every day. I must remember to thank God and others even on the difficult days. Often times I find strength I didn't even know I had. I know now that this is a gift of grace. God does for me what I cannot do for myself. It is easy to develop tunnel vision and only focus on the things that are going wrong or the things that continue to be problematic. At times like this I must open my eyes to see the things that are going right. I need to look for those things that have changed in my life and understand that I am still a work in progress. God is not finished with me yet. I need to be grateful for all that He has done. Do I take time to live in gratitude?

Petitions to my Higher Power

God,

Today help me to focus on all the problems I no longer have. Help me to see that You are helping me to solve those problems that remain. Let me see the opportunities that You provide for change in my life and take advantage of these opportunities. Walk with me as I walk through this day.

Amen.

* * * *

Wisdom for Today   Jan 24

One of the times that I struggle most is when I am sick or have physical pain. When I don't feel well and am having a hard time just doing the basic tasks of the day, it is easy to fall into some big traps. The first trap is a desire for immediate relief. I want out of the place in which I am even if it is only temporary. This is dangerous thinking for the alcoholic or addict. The other trap is the "poor me" syndrome. Feeling sorry for myself is equally dangerous. The final trap is isolation. I don't want to be around anyone when I am not feeling well. I tend to get short with my patience and short with my anger. I just want relief.

Fortunately, the program has taught me some valuable lessons. The first is delayed gratification. Some things just have to be worked for. This is true with physical recovery. I have to work harder at being responsible and harder at being patient. Illness is a temporary condition. It will pass. The same is true of pain. Having had to endure the struggles of physical rehabilitation, I know this firsthand. I also know I must get out of isolation and "tell on my disease." If I start to get into stinking thinking, I have to call someone and tell on myself. Friends in recovery are quick to get me back on track. Am I willing to use the tools that the program offers me when I am sick or in pain?

Meditations for the Heart

"Keep it simple" is the slogan that has real meaning for me when I am sick or in pain. I have to go back and rely on the basics. I cannot afford to run to the drug store looking for a quick cure. It would be too easy to pick up something that might put my recovery at risk. This is why I have talked these things though with my doctor ahead of time, so I know which medications are safe for me and which ones aren't. I have to rely on the help of others. My sponsor is a good one to cheer me up. He will remind me of what taking care of me really means. Keep it simple! Don't be afraid to ask for help and guidance. Do I have a good plan in place should I become ill or injured?

Petitions to my Higher Power

God,

When I am not feeling well or in pain, help me to know I am not alone. Give me patience while my body heals. Help me to be responsible and to care for myself so that I can return to health. Keep me watchful for the traps that lie along the path, and help me avoid them.

Amen.

*   *   *   *

Wisdom for Today   Jan 25

When I was active in my addiction, my thinking was all messed up. Drinking and using seemed normal to me. I was capable of rationalizing and defending all my behaviors and decisions. When I entered the program, I had to learn a new way of thinking. I had to learn how to think straight. I had to learn how to look at life differently. This was not something I did on my own. I needed help from others. I needed to learn the "Wisdom to know the difference."

Wisdom was not something I had a lot of early on in recovery. I needed to rely on others in the program to give me feedback and suggestions. I had to learn that to do that which was healthy for me was the wise thing to do. Still today I need help sometimes to sort out what is healthy and wise for me. I thank God for the program and the people who have helped me along the way. Am I doing what is wise for me to do each day? Am I developing clean and sober thinking?

Meditations for the Heart

Sometimes I find that my day seems to be too busy. I have too much going on. I can even get overwhelmed. My sponsor used to remind me to breathe. It was his way of saying, "Slow down; easy does it." It was his way of reminding me to walk through the day knowing that God would only give me what I could handle. It was his way of saying to me that God would give me what I needed to make it through the day. Do I have confidence that God will give me what I need to make it through each day, each situation, and each breath?

Petitions to my Higher Power

God,

Today my plate seems full, and there are a lot of things I need to do. Help me to walk through this day without fear or worry. Help me to be wise in my thinking. Lead me to the people that will help me along the way. Give me the courage to ask for help when I need it.

Amen.

∗ ∗ ∗ ∗

Wisdom for Today   Jan 26

When I was using, I thought I was happy; but the truth was that I was not happy. A huge piece of this unhappiness was being cut off from others, particularly the people I loved. My addiction to alcohol and drugs formed a wall between me and the people I loved the most. My wife, my kids, my parents, my siblings -- all were held at a distance. I could have no real companionship or intimacy with the people I loved. It didn't matter how much or how often I tried to show them love, I just could not get close. My dishonesty, my guilt and the shame I carried around all formed bricks in a wall that did not allow me to be close. The result was terminal loneliness. I could not be in a real relationship with others or even myself as long as I maintained a relationship with the bottle or my drugs.

All this began to change when I entered the fellowship of the Twelve Step program. I began to feel a sense of belonging. I could risk honesty in my communication with others and found that I was accepted. This made it possible to begin being honest with the people I loved. There are still times that I want to run and hide in relationships with others. But it has gotten easier. There are still times I also want to avoid dealing with painful issues in my relationships with others. But the program and my friends in the fellowship give me the courage to face the pain and deal with reality. One thing I do know is that I no longer have to be lonely. Am I risking openness and honesty with the people with whom I need to be?

Meditations for the Heart

Sometimes it is important for me to go off to a quiet place and be in relationship with my Higher Power. God as I understand Him is a friend that cares for me no matter what. I have unconditional acceptance. I don't need to pretend, cover up or hide my brokenness. I am accepted for who I am. This does not mean I am not encouraged to change the things I can – quite the contrary. I go to the quiet place to find restoration, guidance and power. In relationship with God I find what I need for the day. I do not get what I need for a week or a month, but what I need for the day; and it is enough. In addiction I always wanted more; in recovery what I need is enough. This is one of the gifts of the program. I can rest assured that I will have enough courage, enough strength and enough wisdom for each day. Am I satisfied with enough, or am I still looking for more?

Petitions to my Higher Power

God,

Today I know You will walk with me and support me in all that I do. No problem will be too big, as I know in my heart I will have enough of whatever I need to deal with the problems I face. Continue to encourage me to be open and honest in my relationships with others. Help me to build bridges and not walls.

Amen.

* * *

Wisdom for Today   Jan 27

There is no doubt in my mind or my heart that drinking and drugging separated me from God. It really doesn't matter what your religious background is or if you claim to not know God, drinking and drugging creates separation from God. When chemical use becomes your Higher Power, you cannot have a relationship with God. You cannot serve two masters. When I was active in my addiction, I turned my life over to drugs and alcohol. I followed them blindly wherever they led me. One consequence after another did not deter my faith that somehow alcohol and drugs could fix my problems. The more I followed my addiction, the more separation I created between God and myself. There was this huge void in my life. There was guilt, shame and remorse. Why did I hurt so much?

When I entered the program, I heard the words, "God, as you understand Him." These were not the words I wanted to hear. At first I struggled with trusting God and did not want to believe that God could possibly care about me after all that I had done. Yet over time I opened myself up to the possibility that *"God could and would if He were sought."* (*Alcoholics Anonymous,* Fourth Edition Page 60) What I eventually found was a God of forgiveness and a God of acceptance. I began to see evidence that things were changing in my life, things that used to baffle me. I began to see that God was indeed active in my life and that He saved me from myself. Am I willing to open the door to the possibility that a Higher Power is working in my life?

Meditations for the Heart

Not every day in recovery is easy; problems still exist. Some days are down right hard to make it through. Still I need to believe that God will strengthen me for every battle I face. In my struggles I find that my faith is renewed and made stronger. Not everything turns out like I hope it will. I need to remember that I am following God's will for my life. This is not to say that God makes bad things happen to test me, but I must trust that God will give me what I need to face my struggles. Finding things for which I can be grateful in the middle of my struggles has helped me. Trusting that God does care about me has helped. What helps you to make it through the difficult times?

Petitions to my Higher Power

God,

Too often I do not even look for You in the midst of my struggles. Yet I am gently reminded that You are always there for me. So many times I can see that the people around me help me. How does this happen? Help me to see that You bring these people into my life for a reason. Help me to see that when others care for me, it is because of your Divine intervention.
Amen.

* * * *

Wisdom for Today   Jan 28

Alcohol and drugs took me to school, and the lessons were not easy to learn. Despite all the clues that I was in serious trouble, my addiction had a way of hiding the evidence. Denial is a way we defend ourselves from that which is painful. It is not something that is unique to addiction, but simply a part of life. Even in recovery I have had my struggles with denial. I have wanted to deny many of my character defects. I have wanted to deny many of the effects that alcohol and drugs continued to have on me long after I stopped drinking and using. Hiding from the truth was easier to do when I was using, and I'm glad I now recognize this. I have found that even the most painful struggles I have faced clean and sober can be survived. I have learned that I do not have to face these struggles alone.

The lessons learned in the school of addiction have to be unlearned. New ways of living life must be learned. Many of the lessons of recovery are not easy lessons either. Learning to surrender, learning to face self, learning how to repair the damage and learning how to live – all can be challenging. But these challenges do not need to be faced alone. There is help, and the instructors and teachers I find around the tables at Twelve Step meetings are more than willing to share their knowledge. Am I glad that I graduated from the school of addiction and now study in the school of recovery? You bet I am!

Meditations for the Heart

Life itself is a school, and the most important lessons I need to learn are the spiritual lessons. To be a good student I must be willing to listen. Learning to listen for God's voice in our life is not always easy. There have been many days when I would open myself up to listen and heard nothing but silence. Still, I had to keep trying. Little by little I began to hear that "still, small voice" in the middle of the chaos of my life. Over time it has become easier to listen for my Higher Power, and I am surprised at how often God reveals His will for me. I am amazed at the incredible sense of caring that God provides to me. At the time these things were happening, I did not always recognize them. Now I can look back and see many miracles that have happened in my life. Am I willing to listen for God's voice in my life?

Petitions to my Higher Power

God,

Today let me be an open book and ready to have You write Your message on my heart. Give me ears to hear that "still, small voice" in my head that is Your calling out to me. Give me courage to ask the teachers in the program for help. Make me a good student of life today.

Amen.

* * * *

Wisdom for Today   Jan 29

Worry takes so much energy. When I was drinking and using, I was always concerned about what tomorrow would bring. I had no idea what was going to happen. Would I end up in jail? Would I end up broke and living on

25

the street? Would I lose my job? Would I lose my family? All that energy going into tomorrow left little energy for the day in which I was living! Sometimes my worry would progress into fear and even hopelessness. I even entertained thoughts of ending my life when I felt so worthless. Guilt and shame were my constant companions.

Just because I stopped drinking and using did not bring an end to my worries. It was only when I really began to use the steps as a guide for my life that my worries started to diminish. I was able to begin to use my energy in today, and I started to see things change. Unfortunately, when things still go wrong, as they do in life, I can still find myself back in the old habit of worrying. This is when I have to go back to basics - the first three steps. I can't, He can, and I'll let Him. Turning my worries over to God has helped me tremendously. It has taken a lot of practice, but it has gotten easier over time. Am I willing to turn my fears and problems over to God? Am I ready to follow His direction for addressing these problems?

Meditations for the Heart

Life is not always easy. No one promised me it would be. However, how I respond to the situations that life presents me with is a choice. I can respond as an addict or an alcoholic would respond, or I can respond to each situation with wisdom. Wisdom is a gift from God. Wisdom can be learned. Usually, when I have a difficult problem I am facing, the first thing I need to do is seek out a quiet place and talk with God. In prayer I can find wisdom. The next thing I need to do is seek out advice and help from others in the program. I can learn wisdom from these people. Then I need to pray some more and make a decision as to the wise course of action to take. Finally, I must initiate action and evaluate the outcome. If it works, I don't try to fix it. If the problem still remains, I repeat the earlier steps until a solution is reached. Notice, I don't plan the outcome; I just follow the steps. Do I trust that God will give me the wisdom I need?

Petitions to my Higher Power
God,

Each day begins differently, and each day I face new challenges. Guide me to Your wisdom, and lead me to the people who can teach me wisdom. Help me to focus on just one day at a time, for I already know this is wise.
Amen.

* * * *

One room I spent too much time in during my addiction was the bathroom. Many times I found that I had too much to drink, or I had used too much of one of the drugs I secured. Then it was off to worship the porcelain god. The gut wrenching and the smell should have been enough to convince me that I should quit. Over and over I promised myself, "Never again!" But then it would start all over again. The mornings after were never any fun.

In recovery I now spend time in different rooms, the rooms where I am in fellowship with other recovering friends. The only time my gut hurts there is when I laugh so hard my sides hurt, and tears are rolling down my face. I guess that sometimes it is good to hurt like that. What's even better -- I can remember what was so funny the night before. Have the mornings after changed with recovery?

Meditations of the Heart

Early in recovery I felt like I was walking in darkness. I had no idea where the road would lead. But after a time on this path, I began to see a new light. Hope and faith in God brought brightness into my days. At first I didn't really understand from where the light was coming. But it was there for me nonetheless. As I got further into my recovery and began to help the newcomer, I saw the blinders they had on. That is when I realized that God's light had always been there for me but that in recovery God had been kind enough to remove the blinders from my eyes. Does a new light shine for you?

Petitions to my Higher Power

God,

Today I know that Your light is there for me even on the days that seem dark and overcast. Even when my problems seem most troubling, Your light shines. I know that as long as I follow the steps, Your light cannot disappear from my eyes again. Give me the strength today humbly to follow the Twelve Steps and stay in Your light.

Amen.

*   *   *   *

Wisdom for Today   Jan 31

When I wake up to a bright new morning and jump out of bed, I can be grateful that I am happy and not sick or disgusted with myself. Sobriety has given me many gifts, but none is more precious than peace of mind. I can get up in the morning confident that I haven't screwed up again. I can be sure that what I did last night won't get me in trouble today. I no longer look in the rear view mirror to see if I am being followed. When I was drinking and using, I always was looking back and trying to cover my tracks. Today because of recovery I don't have to do that anymore.

Yes, I still make mistakes and find that I am still wrong. But I no longer have to run from the past. I can own my mistakes and admit my wrongs. I make amends when needed and know that I now learn from my mistakes. I don't have to keep repeating my mistakes and trying to hide. Life is about progress now, not living in the past. Am I willing to admit when I am wrong?

Meditations for the Heart

I must rely on the guidance of my Higher Power. I must wait patiently, trusting and hoping for God to show me the way. God reveals His will in many different ways. Sometimes it is in the words that I hear spoken around the table at Twelve Step meetings. Other times I read words in books that reveal God's will. And still other times it is the words I hear "spoken" in my conscience. I just need to listen, and God will show me the way to a better life. Do I listen for the will of my Higher Power to be revealed?

Petitions to my Higher Power

God,

This is a new day; let me be glad in it. Let me give humble thanks for the way in which You constantly help me. Even when I feel lost, You let me know You are near. Increase in me the desire to listen for Your will for my life. Give me the courage to follow where You lead.

Amen.

* * * *

Wisdom for Today   Feb 1

Birthdays, holidays and anniversaries always seemed to be a time when I would get carried away. I didn't mean to get out of control; I just wanted to have a good time. It was a special day, and I deserved it. Invariably I would drink and use too much, and the special day was ruined. Even if I didn't embarrass myself too badly, I would have problems remembering the next day. The things that I could recall weren't always pretty. You would think that my behavior would have been the opposite. You would think I would have been on good behavior because these were special days. Yet this just was not the case.

Even in early recovery, I found that special days and holidays were sometimes difficult. I would once again get caught up in the euphoria that drugs and alcohol would promise. It became important for me to plan how I would deal with these special days ahead of time. Spending time with family that supported my recovery and spending time with my friends around the tables became an important component in my plans. Now I have learned how to really celebrate these special times in recovery, and am I grateful! Do I plan to take care of my recovery on special days?

Meditations for the Heart

Today, I celebrate new anniversaries -- Anniversaries of Recovery! There is something truly amazing about speaking up at a meeting and saying, "Yes, I have three months." It is more incredible to say one year, two years, ten years or more. I've been to some conventions and seen people celebrate 20, 30, 40, 50 or more years of being clean and sober. When you talk with these people and ask them how they did it, all of them tell you it is the program and a solid relationship with their Higher Power. What are you doing to make these special days happen in your life?

Petitions to my Higher Power

God,

Every day is special when it is lived clean and sober. Each day I receive is truly a gift from You. Let me treat this day as something special and enjoy the gift that it is. Help me daily to recommit myself to the Twelve Steps and to a stronger relationship with You.

Amen.

* * * *

Wisdom for Today   Feb 2

Each day I face new choices. Some of these choices are easy, and others are more difficult. I used to do a simple cost-benefit analysis to make my decisions. For the most part this worked fine. I simply needed to determine what a particular choice would cost me physically, emotionally, financially or socially. Next I would figure what the benefits would be and then do that which made more sense. I began to realize that this process did not always accomplish what I wanted it to achieve. Even when I thought the choices I made were good, I found out that they did not produce the desired results. Something was missing.

Too often I was leaving my Higher Power out of the equation. I was not evaluating the choices I faced in light of my values. When I started to make a conscious effort to include my values and the will of my Higher Power in my decision-making, then I found that I was at peace. I could live with my decisions and know that I had done what was best for me in each situation. I'm not saying this made choice making any easier, but it did make the choices clear. Do I pray for *"knowledge of His will"* (*Alcoholics Anonymous*, Fourth Edition Page 59) and the power to carry that out?

Meditations for the Heart

Learning to accept the struggles in life and realizing that God will walk with me in every struggle has made my life better. It is a matter of faith and reliance on my Higher Power. Trusting God to be there for me has not always been easy, nor has it always resulted in the outcome I would expect. Frequently I am surprised by the fact that the outcome was not at all what I had hoped for, but I have clear evidence that God gave me the strength and courage to deal with the struggle. I have found that often times I gain strength by simply admitting I am weak and need help. I guess that is why my sponsor kept telling me to, "Turn it over." Am I learning to "practice *these principles in all my affairs?"* (*Alcoholics Anonymous*, Fourth Edition Page 60)

Petitions to my Higher Power

God,

Each day brings new challenges and new triumphs. Help me to admit when I need help and to turn to those people that You lead me to for help. Give me a humble heart and mind, so that I may be grateful for the small and large triumphs I experience in my day. When I face new choices in life, let me turn to You first for help in making my decisions.

Amen.

* * * *

Wisdom for Today   Feb 3

I needed help, not just with my addiction, but with a lot of things. It was easy to admit my life was a mess, but it was a lot harder to clean up the mess. Unfortunately, I thought I got myself into this jam, and so it seemed to make sense that I thought I could get myself out of the jam I was in. It did not take too long for me to recognize that this was faulty thinking.

I needed to realize that I could not get on the path to recovery on my own. I had to understand that my best thinking had gotten me in this mess. I had to accept that my thinking was crazy; and since my thinking was not sound, I would have to rely on something else. This is where Step Two really helped me. I wasn't sure what I could rely on, but I came to believe in something other than myself. Do I believe that I need to rely on something other than myself?

Meditations for the Heart
Initially I was filled with doubt and confusion. Over time this was slowly replaced with a belief that God could and would do for me what I could not do on my own. This did not mean that I stopped trying, but it did mean I had to stop planning outcomes. I had to learn to trust my Higher Power and leave the results up to Him. I still find myself from time to time in the driver's seat which is okay, but I leave the map reading up to God. Do I let my Higher Power lead the way?

Petitions to my Higher Power
God,
Sometimes I seem to want to run the show my way. Please help me to accept Your direction in my life. Let me continue to work the program and seek my answers only from You.
Amen.

* * * *

Wisdom for Today   Feb 4
At first drugs and alcohol seemed to make the world brighter and more enjoyable. Then came the growing loss of control and unpredictability of my use. The morning after my escapades often brought feelings of depression and self-disgust. That feeling of exhilaration was replaced with a growing sense of darkness in my life. I was no longer getting a kick out of using, but was being kicked by my use.

In the program lights were turned back on for me. I slowly could see a new way of living. I began to experience a new feeling of satisfaction and self-esteem. I could look in the mirror with a new feeling of self-respect. Life started to be friendly again as I made new friends in the program. I could laugh again. The illusion of happiness gained through using was now real in recovery. Do I see that the pleasure I got out of using was not real? Am I gaining a sense of hope for truly brighter days in recovery?

Meditations for the Heart
In recovery I must practice acceptance, because a lack of acceptance will block the way. I need to look for good in others, those that I like and those

that push my buttons. All people have both good and bad qualities. All are children of God. I need to practice love towards all people because nothing unloving is done in the Spirit of God. If I am to walk with my Higher Power, I need to practice acceptance and love. In a Beatles' song there is a line of lyrics that goes, "And in the end, the love you make is equal to the love you take." Do I see that by practicing acceptance and love towards others that I will receive love and acceptance back?

Petitions to my Higher Power
God,

Today I need to find pleasure in the simple things of life. Help me to practice love and acceptance of others. Let me look for good in all of the people I meet. I pray that I may receive love and acceptance from others by giving it away to all people that cross my path today.
Amen.

* * * *

Wisdom for Today   Feb 5
On a dark and gloomy night, the lights of our old haunts can look very inviting. It is easy to get caught up in the memories of the good times we had. I would party until the wee hours of the morning. Drinking with friends, the camaraderie seemed so wonderful. It was my fantasies come true. But that was exactly the problem; it was fantasy and not reality. The night would end, and there was always the morning after. My wallet would be empty, and my head would be too full. Most of us have never seen the tavern the morning after with the smell of stale beer and cigarettes. There are a few of us who would frequent these establishments early in the day to stop the shakes in the morning.

When I was actively drinking and using drugs, I never thought about the next morning. I only focused on the night of partying ahead. I never thought about the consequences that might be awaiting me. This is what I must think about now. I must teach myself to think about the long view. When the lights of the tavern or the lights of my old using friends' houses seem to shine brightly, I must think about the morning after. I can't afford to think about the glitz and glamour of the fantasy life. I need to stay in reality - the reality that I can't drink or use. Have I stopped the "magical thinking" about the fantasy life?

Meditations for the Heart

One of the questions I used to ask myself a lot was, "Why me?" I didn't understand why I couldn't drink and use as other people. I couldn't understand why I kept putting others and myself at risk. I couldn't understand why I was different. As I began my recovery, I continued to ask myself this question, "Why me?" Then one day things changed for me. Rather than asking, "Why me, why can't I be like other people?" I began to ask, "Why me, why have I been given this opportunity for recovery?" Many addicts and alcoholics die of their disease. Why have I been selected to have another chance at life? My outlook changed as the question changed. I don't have the answer, but I believe that God must have a plan for me. God wants me to be useful for His purpose. Am I willing to believe that there is a purpose for me in recovery?

Petitions to my Higher Power

God,

Sometimes I still wonder and even question where You are leading me. Help me to trust and have faith that Your plans for me are good. Keep me willing to follow where You lead. Help me to keep a long-term view of drinking and drugging so that I don't ever forget the morning after.
Amen.

* * * *

Wisdom for Today   Feb 6

Man, I loved to party! I loved going out with my drinking buddies and buying them a round. I loved turning other people on. It made me feel important. But I wasn't doing any of them a favor. Most of the people I hung out with probably were alcoholic or addicted people just like me. Buying them a drink just helped them get drunk. Getting them high just enabled their addiction to progress. I wasn't really even doing it for them; I was doing it for my own selfish reasons. I needed people around me who would support and endorse my behavior.

When I joined the program, things changed. People genuinely cared and supported me in the changes I needed to make. As I put a few more twenty-four hours under my belt, I was able to return the favor. I was able to share my experience, strength and hope in order to help others. Sometimes I was doing this without even being aware that I was helping. Friends would come up to me after a meeting and say, "I could really relate to what you shared tonight." As time passed, I was able to become a sponsor to others in the program and could act as a guide through the steps. I was helping others in a genuine, unselfish way, just as I had been helped. Am I willing to help others in the program in an unselfish way? Do I give away what I have been given? This is the fellowship of the Twelve Step program.

Meditations for the Heart

You can't teach a child to learn how to really ride a two wheel bicycle if they refuse to take the training wheels off. It is a clear indication that they do not trust. Similarly, God cannot teach us if we do not trust. We have to let go of our fears and learn to trust our Higher Power. There are two roadblocks to trusting in our Higher Power. The first one is that we do not trust ourselves. We say, "I can't do that." We convince ourselves that we are not capable of accomplishing anything. The second roadblock happens when we say, "God won't be there for us when we need Him." Learning to trust that God cares for us is not always easy. But recovery can't happen if we hang onto our stubborn, self-defeating beliefs. It can't really happen if we refuse "to take the training wheels off." Do I trust that God will be by my side each step of the way in this new life I've been given?

Petitions to my Higher Power

God,

Today let me accept the help that is offered to me, and let me reach out to others by sharing my experience, strength and hope. When I get stubborn, remind me to trust. Teach me to use the steps in my life as a guide to solving my problems.

Amen.

* * * *

Wisdom for Today   Feb 7

All addicts and alcoholics in recovery will face times when cravings or urges to drink or use will come into our life. For most of us this tends to happen early on in our recovery attempts. This is when that "voice of addiction" screams the loudest. But, even if we make it through these times, we are not immune from having cravings or urges to use come back into our lives. There is little we can do to change our physical response to abstinence. Our brains simply tell us that we are hungry or thirsty. When we experience drug hunger or get thirsty for a drink, we must act wisely and use the tools we are given in the program. We have to tell on our disease; we need to reach out and call someone who understands and talk it through. It will pass. However, when we get caught up in magical thinking and euphoric recall, it is easy to set ourselves up to fail. When I think about drinking or using, that old "voice of addiction" reminds me of the good times. The fun I used to have and the camaraderie of my drinking buddies is what I want to focus on. This is dangerous!

I must train myself to remember the hard times and the consequences of my use. Rather than romancing the high, I must focus on the harm. I have to train myself to do that which seems unnatural to me. It is much easier to think about the good times rather than the bad times. Yet, I have learned that this must be my first defense. I must stop my "stinking thinking" and take action to protect myself from the voice of addiction that whispers in my ear. I need to see that the program can offer me everything that addiction did. I can find friends and laughter at meetings. I can find relief and real answers to my problems. I can find everything I need around the tables and on the phone talking with people who understand. Do I have a concrete plan in place to deal with cravings or urges?

Meditations for the Heart

I can start each day new. I no longer have to carry the past with me wherever I go. Each new breath I take is a gift from God. For this I must be grateful. I can choose to keep walking in shame, or I can accept the forgiveness that God offers. If God only gave forgiveness to "good" people, where is the need for it? I believe that my Higher Power gives me forgiveness when I ask for it. It is His grace that provides this gift. I also need to respect the gift that is offered through my genuine desire to change the things I can. Recovery does not demand perfection, only progress. I must look carefully at each of the choices I make and ask myself, "What does God want me to do?" I must choose wisely. I know I will never get it perfect, but I can improve each day and with each breath. Do I recognize that God can and will forgive me?

Petitions to my Higher Power
God,

Today I need to be reminded of Your will for me. With each breath I take and each choice I face today, remind me of Your presence. Give me the courage and wisdom to make healthy choices each step of the way. Help me to both ask for and accept Your forgiveness in my life.
Amen.

* * * *

Wisdom for Today   Feb 8
Somewhere along the way, I started to develop commonsense. This was not something I had when I was actively using alcohol and drugs. But in

35

recovery I began to learn that if I drank or used drugs, it ended in trouble. More importantly, commonsense told me that if I could no longer drink or use drugs, then the only alternative was sobriety. I found out that I could not simply switch from one drug to another. It was not a matter of stopping the liquor and only drinking beer. I simply had to stop everything. I wasn't addicted to just one and not the other. I was addicted to changing my reality in ways that destroyed me. Commonsense said I had to stop it all.

I learned other commonsense things as well in recovery. In order to stop my insanity, I had to do more than just stay clean and sober; I had to change my lifestyle. I had to be open to doing things differently. I had to be willing to change. I had to rely on a Power greater than I. My way didn't work. I had to find a new way of living. This is where the Twelve Steps came into play. These steps taught me how to live. Am I willing to learn commonsense?

Meditations for the Heart

Today as I look out my window, I see that the leaves are starting to change color. The air is crisp, and I am reminded of an important lesson. Soon the leaves will be gone, and the chill of winter will arrive. But now I have much to do if the trees are to bear fruit next year. Branches must be cut, and limbs pruned. The dead wood must be cut away, so that next spring new buds will bear fruit. Recovery is like this. If we are to have strong growth in the new spring of our life, we must prune away the dead wood. I had no idea how to do this effectively. I had to ask for help; I needed someone to show me how to do it properly, or I risked killing the tree completely. If I did nothing at all to the tree, there was a good chance that it would not bear any fruit in the coming year. Am I willing to cut away the dead wood in my life to bear fruit in the spring of my recovery? Am I willing to ask for help and to be shown how to do the job right? Do I realize I have to do this, not just once, but each year in order to keep growing?

Petitions to my Higher Power
God,

You walk with me in each season of my life. Help me to be willing to let You prune away the parts of my behavior that get in the way of new growth. Lead me to the people that can teach me commonsense. Help me to bear good fruit in the renewal of my life.
Amen.

* * * *

Trouble and more trouble were all I was getting from my alcohol and drug use. Yes, there were those brief moments when I would experience some relief from the insanity of my use; but trouble invariably followed. When I was using alcohol or drugs, problems would occur. When I wasn't using, I didn't feel right. I had to use just to feel normal. In spite of all the consequences and problems, I held onto the belief that somehow, someway, drugs and alcohol could bring me happiness.

I started to go to Twelve Step meetings. At first I looked at how I was different from everyone else. I wanted to find a reason that made me different from all "those" people. What I found was that I was different in only one way. They were happy, and I wasn't. I listened as person after person told of the problems they had experienced because of using. I listened as they told of how the program had helped them to resolve their problems. I watched them laugh, and I watched them speak of the triumphs they had in recovery. Do I want what the program offers? Do I believe that alcohol and drugs are poison for me?

Meditations for the Heart

"Throw me a rope, God. Get me out of this hole, and I promise I will be different." This kind of prayer never worked for me, because I always wanted a different kind of rope. I didn't want to accept the help that God was so freely willing to provide. In recovery I have learned that there are two ends to that rope. On one end is my willingness and faith to grab onto the rope and hold on for dear life. On the other end of the rope is God's power. I can come up with all kinds of reasons not to grab the rope or even let go of the rope, but it is only when I learn to trust that God indeed has the power to help me and wants to help me that rescue seems possible. Am I still trying to get out of that hole all by myself?

Petitions to my Higher Power

God,

Today I want to learn to trust in Your power to help me in my struggles. Teach me to trust and rely on Your power. Show me that I can't do this without Your help. Give me the strength I need to hold on to recovery today. Amen.

* * *

Sometimes life just isn't fair. When one problem after another seems to be piled on each other, it is easy to get frustrated, depressed or overwhelmed. It is easy to get caught up in the furious pace of trying to "fix" things or react in a way that makes you just want to give up. The road of recovery is not always an easy one. It's easy to go to meetings and complain that the program isn't working. This has happened to me on more than one occasion. When there are a lot of bumps and curves in the road, I can start to complain to my sponsor, or other recovering people, or friends and even God that it just isn't fair.

Fortunately, these people who care about me remind me that no one promised that life would be fair. No one says it has to be fair. I am reminded that in difficult times I will not always experience the outcome that I want, but I will always be given the strength to deal with whatever happens. I am reminded to look at my expectations. I am reminded to ask for God's will to be done in my life. Yes, I still need to do the footwork; but I also need to ask for help and direction. I am repeatedly amazed at what happens when I "let go and let God." Do I still want to control life? Do I still try to manipulate to get what I want?

Meditations for the Heart

Sometimes the emotions in response to life's struggles can get overwhelming. I can get wrapped up in sadness, self-pity, resentment and fear. When these powerful emotions rise to the surface and begin to determine how I respond to events in my life, I need to get out of my "gut" and get into my head. One of the slogans in the program is, " Think! Think! Think!" Yes, thinking can be dangerous for addicts and alcoholics, particularly when it becomes "stinking thinking." But this slogan reminds me to be wise. In the Serenity Prayer, we say the words, "the wisdom to know the difference." When emotions become crazy, it is vital for my existence to think wisely. It is the only way to make decisions that are healthy. I can't afford to let rage, or depression, or fear or self-pity make decisions for me. Do I know when and how to think wisely?

Petitions to my Higher Power

God,

As I walk through this day, keep me on the path of recovery. Help me to be wise in the decisions I face. Give me the strength I need to deal with the problems that come into my life. Give me wisdom to avoid making problems worse by reacting emotionally rather than responding intelligently.

Amen.

Wisdom for Today   Feb 11

There was no way that I ever would have learned how to stay clean and sober on my own. All I wanted to do was to get wasted. I wanted to drink and use more than anything else. If I ever was going to get into recovery and stay there, I had to learn to want something else more than I wanted to get high. I had no idea what it would be like to live life without drugs and alcohol. I thought it would be boring. I thought it would be painful. I thought it would be lonely. At first I know that it simply was faith that kept me clean and sober -- faith that there could be a better way to live my life. I don't think I really believed that I could be happy, but it had to be better than the self-destructive insanity that I was living in.

As I started to go to meetings, I saw over and over that the people there were happy. Yes, many of them still had problems; but they were happy. Slowly I began to want what they had. I wanted to find that inner peace, and I wanted to find out how they got it. I began to want recovery more than I wanted to get high. I began to want to go to meetings more than I wanted to go to the tavern. Soon I found that my life was going better. I no longer dreaded waking up in the morning. I actually began to look forward to the day. I looked forward to going to meetings. I began to enjoy the camaraderie of the fellowship. I felt like I belonged. I felt like people really cared about me. I also began to feel like God really cared about me. I began to really like what was happening to me, and I wanted to keep it more than I wanted to drink or use. Do I want recovery more than I want my addiction?

Meditations for the Heart

Impatience was something that followed me into recovery. I had walked though life in a very self-centered manner. My attitude was, "I want what I want, and I want it right now." Learning to wait was hard for me. I never liked standing in line, unless I was first in line. I never could wait till my next party time. I always wanted it now. My sponsor encouraged me to begin to pray for patience. Then one day it seemed as if everything that could go wrong did. Family problems, car problems and work problems all in the same day! That night I went to a meeting and told everyone there about the miserable day I had. I wanted my friends to feel sorry for me. As people around the tables began to comment, each of them talked about similar bad days and how the program helped them. Then this old-timer, sitting across from me, said, "It sounds like God gave you many opportunities today to practice patience." Not what I wanted to hear, but it was what I needed to hear! My impatience through the day made me miserable. It was me that had made things so bad, not the events of the day. Have I learned to be quietly patient?

Petitions to my Higher Power
God,

Some days I just want to throw in the towel. I feel like giving up. On the days that I struggle, remind me that You have a plan for me. Teach me to be patient and wait for Your will to be done in my life. Strengthen my faith each day that life in recovery will indeed make my life better. Give me that inner peace I seek.
Amen.

* * * *

Wisdom for Today
Feb 12

When I look back at my life when I was actively drinking and using drugs, I really have to wonder what I really wanted. What was it about my slavery to addiction that kept me coming back? It certainly wasn't the hospitals, or jail or the pain. I wonder sometimes why I even wanted that life at all. But when you are a slave, you do what your master commands. I turned my will and my life over to the care of alcohol and drugs. It was pure insanity. As a slave to addiction I had no power; I simply did what I had to do - get wasted. There was no other choice; at least I didn't think so.

Then one day I walked into a meeting. I expected to find more slaves who had been beaten by the disease. But to my surprise what I found were people just like me who had come to know freedom. They were free of the chains of addiction. It no longer had a hold on them. I couldn't understand how this could be. I kept going to meetings and seeing these people. Their freedom continued. I wanted to be free of the bondage as well. Finally in a moment of courageous fear, I asked, "How did you get free?" The answer was a real surprise: "I am only free for one day - one day at a time." Today I understand this answer, and each and every day I have to remember if I want to keep my freedom, I must be responsible for my recovery. Am I willing to be responsible for my freedom one day at a time?

Meditations for the Heart
My spiritual life must be centered on God. I must remain conscious of my desire to gain a closer relationship with my Higher Power and seek His will. I need to realize that this is my responsibility. Today I believe that God has always been there for me. He is always by my side. Yet even when He is so close, I can shut my eyes and not know He is there. I have to work

at improving my conscious contact with God. It is a part of what recovery is about. Recovery does not simply happen; it must be worked for. In the program you hear the slogan, "It works if you work it." Am I being responsible and working my program?

Petitions to my Higher Power
God,

Today I must be responsible for my recovery. I am glad that I only need to do this one day at a time. What I am most grateful for is knowing that I do not have to do this alone. I have You by my side, and I have many people in the program who will help me. Let me remember that it was You who loosed the bonds of addiction from me. Help me each day that I walk this path. Amen.

∗　∗　∗　∗

Wisdom for Today   Feb 13
Once in a while I can't help but think that I should be able to go back and drink or use again. After all, I have been clean and sober for a long time, and I know all about addiction and what to watch out for. But this kind of crazy thinking will only get me in trouble. I must remember that I am an alcoholic and an addict. It is important that I remind myself that I have a disease each day. I must remember all the times I tried to control my use but failed. I must remember that I can still fall back into the trap of denial.

Somewhere along the way I went too far. I went past the point of no return. I am not really sure when that happened, but I am convinced that I not only passed it but went far past it. I cannot ever go back. I need to remind myself that I already had enough and then some. I know that I cannot go back. My only choice is to move forward in recovery. Have I stopped looking back?

Meditations for the Heart
Somewhere along the line I read the poem called, "Footprints in the Sand." I was very impressed with this story because I suddenly realized the number of times that God carried me. By all rights I should have been dead. The number of close calls I had was astounding. But by the grace of God I walk though life today. Even in recovery I am amazed at how many times my Higher Power carries me through the difficult times and struggles I still face. Sometimes I forget just how close my Higher Power is. I need to remember that God is always near and freely gives me what I need. My job is only to improve my conscious contact with God, praying only for knowledge of His

41

will and the power to carry that out. Do I believe that a Higher Power will help me along the way?

Petitions to my Higher Power

God,

Sometimes I can still get mixed up with crazy thinking. Help me to recognize when I stray from the path of healthy thinking, and redirect me so I can continue on this path of recovery. Help me to recognize all the times that I am helped by Your power. Walk with me this day, for I never know when I will need Your help.

Amen.

* * * *

Wisdom for Today   Feb 14

It was like I had a one-track mind, like a speeding train that was always heading in the direction of self-destruction. Yes, I did a lot of things right -- I went to work, I played with the kids, I helped out around the house, but always in the back of my mind was getting wasted. Everything I did was solely for the purpose of being able to drink or drug. I became obsessed with altering my reality. I continued down the track until my train derailed. Each time my train crashed, it was not pretty; and each time it got worse. Still I would patch things back together and get right back on the same track. This was the insanity of my addiction -- doing the same thing over and over again expecting a different result.

In recovery I have learned that I do not need to get back on that train today. I do not have to be obsessed with changing my reality. I do not have to get wasted or destroy my life. The program has truly given me new choices. Yes, I can still try to use my old ways to solve problems; or I can use the steps and the principles of the program. I have learned that there is really very little in life that I do control, but I do control how I respond to life's situations and struggles. I can choose to respond with wisdom, or I can choose to respond with insanity. I do have a choice. Do I seek out wisdom in responding to life's struggles?

Meditations for the Heart

Each morning I try to start my day apart from the busy hustle and bustle of the day and spend time with God. It really is not so much the prayers I say that has created change in my life as much as simply spending time with God. It is this relationship that has led me down a path to wisdom. Simply put, seeking after God's will for me forces me to find wisdom. I used to think that

42

following God's will was hard. What I have found out is that following God's will actually makes life easier. I do not do this perfectly, and I still make plenty of mistakes, but I know in my heart that I have made tremendous progress over time. Am I taking quiet time to walk with my Higher Power each day?

Petitions to my Higher Power
God,

Today I seek Your will for my life. Help me to be quiet and listen for the wisdom that You will provide. Help me to think through life's struggles and see the choices I have. Give me the courage to choose to be healthy today. Amen.

* * * *

Wisdom for Today   Feb 15
How is it that we discover that we are alcoholics or addicts? Sometimes I wish it had been easier for me to figure that out for myself. It really would have been nice if I simply could have taken a simple blood test or something. But addiction is not that simple; it is more than physical. A blood test would only test for physical aspects of a disease. Addiction has psychological and social aspects, not to mention the spiritual deterioration. It took a while, but eventually I began to recognize just how mentally and socially impaired I had become. It took even longer to realize how spiritually bankrupt I was.

In recovery I began to realize how obsessed my thinking was and how self-absorbed I was. I had to begin to stop my preoccupation with drinking and drugging. I had to let my mind clear up and get out of the fog I was in. I had to learn to make changes in my life and begin to make new friends at meetings. Once my body and mind and social life started to straighten out, I then realized how important it would be for me to foster a relationship with a Higher Power. It was only in development of this relationship with "God, as I understand Him," that I began to be freed from fear. Do I realize that recovery is much more than physical?

Meditations for the Heart
If I am to really open myself to the Spiritual Realm, then I must rid myself of selfish ambition. I must open myself to being an instrument of God. God can and does work in and through people. I have seen this in the lives of people who have helped me the most along this path of recovery. What has really amazed me is that God works in and through me when I open myself up to His will. There have been many times when I am talking to others struggling to recover, and I am surprised to hear the words that come out of

43

my mouth. These words are not what I probably would have said, but they are the words that God would want me to say. God never ceases to show that He really does care about addicts and alcoholics. The evidence is the incredible number of people who are clean and sober today because of the grace of God. Do I open myself to be an instrument of God's work? Do I give back to the program?

Petitions to my Higher Power
God,

Today I ask that You remove any self-centeredness I have. Help me be open to Your will for my life, and give me the power to carry out Your will for me. Help me to be open to helping others and giving back to the program. Continue to amaze me each and every day.
Amen.

* * * *

Wisdom for Today   Feb 16
"You can't keep it, unless you give it away." This is a statement I have heard repeatedly at meetings, and yet it is something that all too often we forget. It is easy to get caught up in our own issues and forget that unless we help others, we will not gain what the program offers. I have found over and over again that when I reach out to a newcomer or someone who is in need that my difficulties seem much smaller. It is easier to establish and maintain an attitude of gratitude. It seems paradoxical that by helping others, I am really helping myself; but that is how it works.

When I get caught up in myself, I become more and more self-centered. I can become more angry and irritated. I can get into the self-pity trip. My pain and my fears seem bigger. However, when I reach out to others and share my experiences in recovery and using the steps, I am surprised to find that my life is easier. Often times I find that I am better able to self-assess and can choose wisely how best to proceed with my own problems simply because I tell others about my disease and my recovery. Do I take enough time to really reach out to others in the program?

Meditations for the Heart
Offering our experience to others is only half of the story. The other half is my willingness to reach out and ask for help when I need it. Probably the best definition of recovery I have ever heard goes like this, "You take your current set of problems and trade them in for a better set of problems; then you trade that set of problems in for a better set of problems." No one said

that recovery would ever mean I would be totally problem free, but I must admit that the problems I face now are certainly better than the ones I used to have. One thing is for sure, the steps can help me with whatever problem I face. I guess that is why Step Twelve ends with, "*and practice these principles in all our affairs.*" (*Alcoholics Anonymous,* Fourth Edition Page 60) Do I ask for help from others in the program when I need it?

Petitions to my Higher Power
God,

I really don't know what this day will bring my way. If this day provides me an opportunity to share my experiences with those in need, let me speak openly. If this day brings new problems, let me willingly ask for help. Amen.

* * * *

Wisdom for Today   Feb 17
If I ingest poison, it will make me sick and may even kill me. This is exactly what alcohol and drugs did to me. Drinking and using made me sick, and it almost killed me. In many ways I look back amazed that I made it through my active illness. Today I look at drugs and alcohol as a poison for me. It makes me sick. This is not to say that all drugs are bad, or even that alcohol is poison for everyone. I just know they are poison for me. This does not mean that I won't take a drug if my doctor prescribes it. It just means that I will be honest with my doctor about my addiction, so that I am not tempted to play games. I know for myself that I must tell on my disease; I can't hide it anymore. Addiction does not like being exposed.

As I stop and think about it, the same is true with each of the problems I have in my life. And this is what the steps teach us. We must tell on our disease and expose it to the light of the steps. This is why we do a Fourth and Fifth Step, to shed light on the exact nature of our wrongs. This is why we make amends and why we seek to improve our conscious contact with God. We need to shed light into our lives. Am I still stumbling in the dark?

Meditations for the Heart
Somehow I need to find a way to be closer to my Higher Power. The closer I get to the true Bread of Life, the more I am filled with an inner peace. The more I am in communion with my Higher Power, the stronger the relationship becomes. It was no different with my drugs. The more time I spent getting drunk or wasted, the stronger the relationship became. The bondage of addiction had me, and I couldn't escape. The program has changed all that

for me. Now I want to be closer and closer to my Higher Power. I want that freedom. Do I seek to improve my relationship with God daily?

Petitions to my Higher Power
God,

Today let me draw nearer to You. Give me the wisdom and willingness to seek You out in all that I do. Give me the courage to keep the light of the Twelve Steps burning brightly in my life. Help me to do the next right thing.

Amen.

* * * *

Wisdom for Today   Feb 18

Taking responsibility for my actions or my feelings – I seldomly did this in my addiction. Generally I tried to find someone or something else to blame. "I wouldn't be this way if…" or "It's all her fault…" I just couldn't seem to accept responsibility for anything. I would lie, or hide, or avoid or do just about anything to avoid saying that it was my responsibility. I certainly did not want to blame my problems on my addiction because then I might have to give it up. One relationship I was interested in protecting was my relationship with drugs and alcohol.

In recovery I have learned that I must take responsibility for my actions, behavior and feelings. There are still days when it would be much easier to blame someone else, but I can't afford to do this. I have to take responsibility, first and foremost, for my recovery. I am not staying clean and sober for anyone else other than me. I also must take responsibility for my actions and my feelings. Yes, I still get angry or afraid; but it is what I do with those feelings that is important. I can strike out at others or even get self-destructive. I can sit and pout or get into self-pity, or I can choose to deal with my feelings in healthier ways. I can blame or I can admit that I am human and make mistakes. Am I being responsible for my behavior and feelings today? Am I being responsible for my recovery?

Meditations for the Heart

Sometimes I just don't understand where the fear suddenly comes from, but I open my eyes, and it feels like monsters surround me. Those monsters all have names: worry, anxiety, judgment, condemnation and many others. Each of us has our own set of monsters, those things or people or situations we just dread dealing with. Life would be so much simpler if we did not have these monsters. However, life is not like that; everyone has these issues.

When my heart starts pounding and I get that lump in my throat, it is important for me to take a deep breath and remember that I am not alone. There are all those addicts and alcoholics that went before me and had to face the same monsters. There is my Higher Power who truly is my best friend. When I am surrounded by fear, I must remember I am not alone. I also must remember to think so that I do not act foolishly or impulsively. Do I know I am not alone?

Petitions to my Higher Power
God,

Today brings new challenges and even new rewards. Help me to make responsible choices for my recovery and myself. Remind me that I am not alone. Help me to trust that You will indeed help me in every situation I face. Keep me growing in my recovery, and let me bear good fruit.
Amen.

* * * *

Wisdom for Today   Feb 19
Sometimes when people ask me what my drug of choice was, I respond, "More!" The reality was that one was never enough; I always wanted more. One drink, one joint, one pile of white powder, one hit was never enough. One simply started the obsession for more. When I first tried to quit using, I thought that simply detoxing myself was all that I needed to do. If I could get through the physical craving, I would have it licked. I was wrong. The reality was that I quit hundreds of times, but I could never stay quit. That led me to my next mistake, a belief that if I just had enough willpower I could end the insanity. But even those times that I was really committed and wanted to stop using, I could not. The quick fix did not work.

These failures led me to a place of hopelessness. It never occurred to me to ask for help. Fortunately when I was directed to the program, I saw people who were just like me, only clean and sober. They had found a way to do something I could not do. They found a way to arrest their disease. They found the answer to a problem I needed to solve. I wanted what they had. So I kept going back to find out how they did it. Each of us takes a different path to arrive at the same door. The answers lie beyond that doorway to recovery. Yet each of us must choose whether or not we will walk through that door. Have I given up on trying to find a quick fix and accepted the need to work the steps?

47

Meditations for the Heart

Early on I found myself getting flustered a lot. It seemed that everything was going wrong, even though I had stopped drinking and using. I was continuing to experience the consequences of my disease. I was disappointed that my family and friends did not automatically trust me again. I was concerned because my finances seemed to get worse, even though I was not buying drugs and alcohol anymore. This is where the steps really started to work for me. I remember reading Step Two over and over. I listened at meetings and heard others talk about how their life did not calm down until they, "*let go absolutely.*" (*Alcoholics Anonymous,* Fourth Edition Page 58) I had to stop trusting myself to fix the problems and learn to trust in a Power Greater, who could restore me to sanity. As I started to do this, I found a deep inner sense of calm. The problems didn't automatically disappear, but they no longer bothered me in the same way. Do I believe that I can have that inner calmness even in the face of life's problems?

Petitions to my Higher Power

God,

You know that sometimes I slip back into old behavior and rely on myself. Each time I do this, I find that I lose that sense of inner calm. I lose the sense that You are in charge. Help me today to simply use what I know works. Take the problems that I face today, and walk with me along this pathway of recovery.

Amen.

* * * *

Wisdom for Today   Feb 20

Sometimes this disease just makes me angry. But then I think all addicts and alcoholics have a similar feeling. When I started out, drinking and drug use were my friends. I used to have a really good time with my friends. I would laugh, and I would dance. I thought I could conquer the world. I certainly felt like I was on top of the world most of the time. Then my friends started to betray me. Alcohol and drugs soon became my enemies. I really can't pinpoint the moment this started to happen, but I have a lot of evidence that indeed alcohol and drugs were out to hurt me -- and not just me, but also those around me. Now that I have been convinced that drinking and drugs are my enemy, I have only one choice. I must go about the work of staying clean and sober.

Even in recovery I still find myself at times angry at this disease. As I have walked through the steps, I have been given constant reminders of the betrayal I went through. My Fourth and Fifth Steps gave ample proof of the ravages of this disease. I have other reminders along the way. Character defects, making amends and practicing the principles of the steps in all my affairs - each has its own way of reminding me of the disease. Fortunately the program also teaches me things that help me to let go of my anger and teaches me how to heal from the wounds of betrayal. Am I using the steps to find healing in my life?

Meditations for the Heart

At first learning to rely on "God, as I understand Him," was not easy. Despite extensive religious training growing up, I found it hard to trust that *"God could and would if He were sought."* (*Alcoholics Anonymous,* Fourth Edition Page 60) Yet when it came right down to it, I had no other choice. My way just did not work. I had to risk trusting in a Higher Power. In some ways this was one of the most difficult things I had to do in recovery. Looking back, I am really glad I did take that risk. I can truly say that my life has not been the same since. It is absolutely wonderful to have a friend who will never betray me and never turn His back on my requests for help. I can say with confidence that God has become my best friend in recovery. Do I see that turning my will and my life to God, as I understand Him, will lead to a great friendship?

Petitions to my Higher Power

God,

Today let me not be consumed with anger or resentment. Fill me with gratitude as I walk through this day. Teach me to be open, honest and willing. And thanks for being my friend.

Amen.

* * * *

Wisdom for Today   Feb 21

I used to run a business to support my addiction. My business involved telling lots of lies, hiding out, scamming and manipulation. I had to work real hard to keep my business running. But I had to work hard so that I could keep drinking and drugging. I made an awful lot of people miserable running my business, not just myself. As my business progressed right along with my disease, I became willing to do anything to keep my business afloat.

In recovery I have a new business. Staying clean and sober is a full-time job. I go to meetings and talk with my sponsor as a part of my business of staying clean and sober. I work at the steps. I try to help other addicts and alcoholics as a part of my business. I spend time in prayer and meditation. And like any well-run business, I take inventory. I always want to remember what running the other business was like. I never want to forget that alcohol and drugs are my enemy, seeking to poison my life. Am I running my recovery business like I need to?

Meditations for the Heart

Sometimes even in recovery things get shaken up. When situations arise or problems seem to cause my emotions to run wild, it becomes very important for me to steal away and talk with my Higher Power. When my spirit is in a state of unrest, it is vital for me to again seek out that inner calm. There is only one place that I have always found that quietness in my soul - when I am in quiet conversation with God. Conversation means that I not only speak, but I also need to listen. In that quiet place I can again find the strength I need, and I can quiet the unrest in my heart. I can begin to think clearly again. Then when I have found that sense of inner calm, I need to talk with my sponsor or a close friend who can help me sort through what is going on in my life. This process has proven over and over again to help me get through the tough times. If I don't seek inner calm and talk with others, I risk opening the door for my enemies - alcohol and drugs - to come inside and play. Do I know what to do in times of unrest?

Petitions to my Higher Power

God,

Today let me walk confidently in the knowledge that the steps work. Let me use the principles of the program to help me when things get crazy and shaken up. When I call out to You in distress, help me to find that inner calm. Quiet my unrest and help me to seek out feedback from those people that I know will help me.

Amen.

* * * *

Wisdom for Today   Feb 22

Every once in a while it is important to sit back and think about all the good things that have happened as a result of recovery. At the top of the list has to be staying clean and sober. I am clean and sober today not because of something I did, but because of something that happened in my life. I never could have done this on my own, and it certainly is the most wonderful gift that recovery has given to me. None of the other gains would be possible without this gift. Certainly there are many other gifts that the program provides, but none is more precious than this.

Most of us in recovery have much for which to be grateful. Most of us have jobs that we probably would not have if we stayed active in our addiction. Most of us have families in which relationships were broken and rebuilt in the recovery process. Most of us have real friends, people who genuinely care about us. These friends stand ready to offer a helping hand when needed. Most of us have a new sense of self, who we are on the inside and what we value. These are the gifts of the program. Do I realize that I probably would have none of these things if I didn't have sobriety?

Meditations for the Heart

When life seems to be a mess, I find myself feeling like I am wandering in a desert. My first reaction is to try to find a way out of the desert. I want to run until everything around me is green again. I've tried to find my way out of the desert more than once in recovery. I just kept getting lost. What I have learned over time is that finding my way out of the mess is not important. What is important is finding my Higher Power in the mess. It is only when I seek out God that I am reminded of all that He has to offer me. I find peace and strength and answers when I seek out God. I am also reminded of all that I have gained in recovery. When my heart is calm and I have an attitude of gratitude, the desert seems to disappear. The problems I have suddenly feel manageable. Do I seek out God when my life is in distress?

Petitions to my Higher Power

God,

Today I see that I have much for which to be grateful. I know that none of this would be possible without Your Divine intervention. Help me always to remember to be grateful for what I have received in recovery. Teach me not to panic when life seems unmanageable. Help me to trust that You are always there to help me.

Amen.

* * * *

Wisdom for Today   Feb 23

When I was active in my addiction, I spent a lot of time in preparation. I spent time preoccupied with how I would get the money, with whom I would drink or use and where and when I would get high. It became a ritual to plan

51

my next drunk or party time. I was always thinking ahead and planning out the lies I would need to tell to cover up or hide my addiction. I always had to cover my tracks. Paranoia and fear were my companions.

In recovery things are not so different. I still spend time in preparation. Only now I am preparing myself for that critical moment when the thought of drinking or getting high returns to my thinking. This is just part of the reason I go to meetings. It helps me prepare. Recovery has taught me many other rituals, but these rituals are healthy. I spend time each morning preparing for the day by reading my daily meditations. I spend time working on the steps. I talk with others, who like myself, want to stay clean and sober. One thing that is different is that I don't spend time planning my next lie. I am no longer living in fear. Do I do the things that are needed to stay prepared?

Meditations for the Heart

Sometimes I wonder about all the prayers that are said that go unanswered simply because of impatience. Too often I see people, including myself, growing impatient with God. Our response is to grab the road map out of God's hands and take back control of the direction our lives should take. Sometimes it is very hard not to grow impatient. However, many times I have found that if I waited a little while longer, God will give me clear direction. I do not always get the answer I expect or the answer I want, but I find that I always get the answer I need. I don't always get the problem I have solved, but I find that I always get the strength I need to deal with the problem. Today I have learned that my Higher Power will answer my prayers. Do I wait patiently for God's answers to my prayers?

Petitions to my Higher Power
God,

Today let me spend time in preparation so that I am ready when that critical moment comes into my life. Let me be honest as I walk through this day. Help me to be patient and trust that You indeed will answer my prayers. Help me to be confident that You will give me the direction I need.
Amen.

* * * *

Wisdom for Today   Feb 24

It seems to me that all of us are faced with three choices when we look at the concept of God, as we understand Him. I do believe there is a significant variation within these three choices, but I have accepted that each of us in recovery really have only these three choices. The first choice is that there is a

God. The second choice is there is no god. And the third choice is, I am god. I think these are the choices we all face.

Looking at these choices, it is easy to see that I am not god. While it is true that I have gravitated to behaving this way at times, when I try and control the universe and make things go my way and in my time, I can see that I am not powerful enough to be god. I could choose to believe there is no god, but this would make me believe that the universe has no origin and simply rushes about going nowhere. That's practically impossible to believe. The last choice is to believe there is a God, who cares about all people. I have no problem believing in a higher power - alcohol and drugs certainly were more powerful than I. I turned my will and my life over to addiction and watched my life being destroyed. I have also seen many miracles at meetings - people who were just as beaten down as I was, who were freed from the bondage to this disease. Who did that? Do I believe there is a Higher Power that can and does restore addicts and alcoholics?

Meditations for the Heart

The spiritual life is filled with choices. Do I believe, am I willing to trust, will I wait, and can I let go are just a few of the choices. Each day brings new spiritual choices. The sad thing is that most of us don't take the time to see these choices. This refusal to see these choices paradoxically in and of itself is a choice. In every situation that I face and each day that I live, I have spiritual choices. Do I have to control this, or do I have to do this all by myself, or can I ask for help are a part of my days. I can choose to believe, and I can choose to look at life through spiritual eyes. Or I can walk blindly through my days. Do I look for ways to include spirituality in my decision making process?

Petitions to my Higher Power

God,

Too often I walk through my day with blinders on and refuse to see the whole picture that is life. Help me to take these blinders off and see the spiritual side of life as well. Let me find new ways to open my eyes as I walk through this day.

Amen.

* * * *

Wisdom for Today   Feb 25

I want to be alcohol and drug free for the rest of my days. For a long time I was not sure this would be possible. I always feared relapse. Somewhere along the road to recovery I discovered that this really was not up to me, and I am glad it is not. What I learned was that if I relied on myself, there would always be a risk for returning to addictive use. However, when I realized that if I left this up to God, I no longer needed to worry about or fear relapse. This did not mean that I could stop working the steps or going to meetings, but it did mean that if I surrendered to my Higher Power's will for me that I could be confident that He would not lead me back into addiction.

Instead I have been led on an incredible journey through the steps. Sometimes the path was rocky and steep, and the climb was hard. Sometimes I found that my life changed in remarkable ways, and I found new freedoms. Each step along the way, God has walked with me. Thus far, by the grace of God, I have not wanted to go back to the insanity. As time passes, I grow more and more confident that God is leading me on a path that does not involve relapse. This is not to say, it has been easy. In fact, I have had some very difficult challenges in recovery. Yet I am always led though these difficult times and find growing evidence that my Higher Power really does care for me. Am I turning over my will and my life to His care?

Meditations for the Heart

In the Big Book is a line that says, *"Half measures availed us nothing."* (*Alcoholics Anonymous,* Fourth Edition Page 59) There is no place this is truer than with our spiritual lives. I can put hours and hours of effort into working at change in my life. Yet if I ignore my spiritual development or only go halfway in my spiritual effort, all my work can fall apart. I learned this from old-timers in the program. I was told, "Never be afraid to ask God for help or for what you need." In recognizing some of my character defects, I found that they were not easy for me to let go. I could work and work at trying to change my behavior, and nothing would change. Then I would talk with my sponsor, and he would ask me if I had prayed for willingness to let go. I, of course, would say that I asked God to remove the defect. My sponsor again would ask if I prayed for willingness. When I finally would stop being stubborn and would listen, I realized that I had been praying for the wrong thing. I needed to be entirely ready to let go of this defect. There was a part of me that always wanted to hang on to my old behavior. Only in spiritual preparation did I become ready to let go. Do I prepare myself spiritually for change?

Petitions to my Higher Power
God,

Today help me to be open to spiritual development. Give me courage to use all measures necessary for change. Let me be willing to follow where You lead me. Let me always surrender my will and follow Your will for me. Amen.

* * *

Wisdom for Today

Perhaps the most important gift we receive from the program is the ability to form or renew our relationship with a Higher Power. We now have a Divine Principle that we can use to guide our life. I have learned again to trust in this leader that I call God. The pathway of recovery is not always easy. Life still has its problems, but I can now turn to this leader and ask for direction.

Some of us struggle with this spiritual concept. We want everything handed to us on a silver platter. We want to put God in the driver's seat and simply go along for the ride. God does not work like this. We have to walk the walk; He will not walk it for us. It is only when we rely on God for direction and strength but when we are willing to do the work that this spiritual principle will begin to work for us. Am I willing to do the work and rely on God for guidance and strength?

Meditations for the Heart

As a child, I recall playing a game called follow the leader. The point of the game was simply to follow and do what the leader was doing. I remember laughing out loud and having fun with all the other kids who played the game. Every so often we would change leaders, and there were times I would get a chance to lead. The Twelve Step program is much like this. When we come to the program, we are hungry for someone to show us the way. We spend time doing what we are shown by others who have been successful. We spend time learning and doing the steps. After we have learned how to play the game of recovery, we are given a chance to lead. We spend time with the newcomers. We begin to teach the principles. Whom do I follow on the path of recovery? Do I stick with the winners?

Petitions to my Higher Power

God,

Let me always remember to look to You for direction. Let me see that there are people in the program who can help show me the way. As I become more solid in my recovery, give me opportunities to lead newcomers along the path to recovery. Guide me in all that I do today.

Amen.

* * *

Wisdom for Today   *Feb 27*

When I first walked into a meeting, there were signs hanging on the wall. I'm not sure why I remember this because I spent most of my time staring at the floor. I was having a difficult time breathing. I was scared. I don't think I remember much more about the meeting itself. The thoughts in my head were racing, and I couldn't think straight. I remember a few people coming up to me after the meeting and welcoming me.

On the way out of the building, I remember looking at one of the signs. It said, "But for the Grace of God." I knew early on that I was alive only because of Divine Intervention. By all rights my drinking and drugging should have killed me. On more than one occasion it almost did. Even though I was till breathing, on the inside I felt dead. Was there a reason I was still breathing? Time has shown me that God has plans for me. I'm not always sure where He is leading me, but I have come to trust that His grace will lead me to a good place. Do I believe that a Power Greater than myself has plans for me?

Meditations for the Heart

One thing that surprised me was how easily everyone shared at meetings. I was not used to sharing anything unless I had a hidden agenda. And the things that were shared also surprised me. It was not just at the meetings; but I had many people in the program offering to share their time, or to give me a ride or even to buy me dinner. I was surprised by how easy it was for addicts and alcoholics to do this. Now I find that I am doing the same things. It is really amazing what happens when you begin to share with others. Sometimes you see changes, and at other times you do not, but what amazed me were the changes I saw in me. I became different by sharing and helping others.

Petitions to my Higher Power

God,

Today I will be given opportunities to share with others. Help me not to be selfish, but to give freely. I am grateful for all the people You sent my way to share their experience, strength and hope. Let me now give back what has been given to me.

Amen.

* * * *

Wisdom for Today   *Feb 28*

When I first came into the program, I really didn't want to stop drinking or using. What I wanted was to find a way to learn how to control my use. I wanted to find a way to get out of all the trouble I was in. However, as I attended more and more meetings, I slowly began to realize that drinking and drugging were not normal. I began to recognize that I couldn't control my use, because it controlled me. I began to understand that I no longer was able to choose to drink or not. Drinking and drugging were making all my choices for me. As I began honestly to look at my using career, it became evident that I was addicted to alcohol and drugs. I was powerless, and my life was out of my control.

This realization was overwhelming at first. I was scared, because if I couldn't control my life, who could? If I wasn't able to choose, what was I going to do? Yet in admitting that I was powerless, I soon discovered that I had only one choice left. If I couldn't stop on my own, then something or someone outside of myself was my only hope. I had religion shoved down my throat growing up. The thought of asking God for help seemed distasteful to me, but I really didn't have any other choice. So in utter defeat I reached out again to God for help, and am I glad I did. Trusting in a Power Greater than me was not easy. Yet, over time I was able to believe that God was indeed helping me. Has Step Two given me new hope?

Meditations for the Heart

Some days I am faced with new problems in recovery. It is easy to want to try to fix these problems all by myself. This invariably gets me back into trouble. I always have to go back to Step Two and admit that the only way I can deal with life is with the help of a Power Greater. When I get stubborn or prideful or arrogant, I loose perspective; and the solutions seem hidden to me. Yet when I open myself to humbly asking for God's help, I am always pointed in the direction of many possibilities. It becomes much easier to deal with life's problems when I have multiple answers and solutions from which to choose. Suddenly, my life becomes restored to sanity. Do I have sanity when I try to fix my life's problems all by myself?

Petitions to my Higher Power
God,

You know that sometimes I find it difficult to turn to You for direction. Help me to learn from those times when I become stubborn, or prideful or arrogant. Let me see that turning to You for help opens many doors for me and helps me choose solutions that will indeed help me with life's problems. Let me walk humbly with You today.
Amen.

* * * *

Telling your story can be a very important part of the recovery process. Each time I am asked to share my experience, strength and hopes, I am tempted to say, "No;" but I open my mouth and the word, "Yes," comes out. I am tempted to say, "No," because I don't think I will be able to help others; but that is not the point. The real reason to tell your story is to help yourself. It is a selfish program. I find as I go through my history, I am surprised to see how far I have come. I am also surprised by how far I still need to go. As I talk, I can still see areas of my life where I need to grow.

As I share my addiction and recovery history, I can see areas of my life where tremendous change has occurred. I can see that God indeed has been doing for me what I could not do for myself. Sometimes I recall some of my past behavior and realize that I still have amends to make, or I see there was a time when I really got off track. After the meeting, I usually have many other addicts or alcoholics come up to me and thank me for sharing. Often times they talk about how they could relate to both my struggles and my triumphs. I always thank them, because if it weren't for people just like them, the program would not exist. Am I grateful to have people like this in my life? Do I willingly share my story when asked?

Meditations for the Heart

The program offers a significant amount of literature that will instruct you about the Twelve Steps and the recovery process. I have found that reading about the program and the steps has been very beneficial for me. Each time I open a book, I find that I learn something new or reinforce something that I already knew. But where the real changes have come for me in my thinking or beliefs has been when I discuss what I have read. Using the Twelve Step program is a "we" process. If all I do is read about the program, it stays an "I" process. It has only been through this discussion that I have learned to challenge my misconceptions and increased my understanding. It is through talking with others that I have learned practical application of the steps and the principles of the program. It is in talking things through with others that I uncover my own denial and blind spots. Do I read program literature and discuss it with others regularly?

Petitions to my Higher Power

God,

Each day You provide me with more opportunities to learn about and apply the principles of the program. Help me to utilize these opportunities to grow in my understanding and application of the steps. Let me be open

to hearing others' opinions and beliefs. Give me wisdom to sort through this information and "take what works and leave the rest."
Amen.

* * * *

Wisdom for Today   Mar 1

Surrender is something I need to do each day as I start my day. I cannot afford to start my day saying to myself, "I'm in control." I have to remind myself each day that I am an alcoholic and an addict. I have to remind myself that this is a problem that I have turned over to God. I have to remind myself that I have surrendered to His will. It is important for me to do this because it reminds me that I have given my addiction problem over to God's hands, because it certainly does not belong in my hands.

I have to remind myself that it is in this act of surrender that I have given up the option to return to drinking and drugging. The act of surrender frees me so that I do not have to worry about relapse anymore. As long as I follow the will of my Higher Power, I can be confident that I will not return to my old ways. As I have walked down the path of recovery, I have found that there are many other problems that I have needed to turn over to God. Each time I do this, I find that I am led to a new place in my recovery process. Often times I am surprised by the outcomes to which my Higher Power leads me. Do I take the time to surrender anew each day?

Meditations for the Heart

I will try to grow a little each day; for if I am growing in my recovery, I am not wilting. In order to keep growing, I have to work the soil. I must keep the weeds of resentment, fear, and arrogance out of my garden. I must water the seeds of hope and honesty. I must seek out the light of openness and willingness. It is only when I work the steps and fertilize my recovery with meetings that I can be assured that my garden will grow. I continue to be amazed by the growth I have seen in myself and in others in the program. Each time I go to a meeting, I try to remind myself that the room is filled with miracles. What astounds me the most is that I can see that I am one of those walking miracles! Today I will look for the miracles that God creates in my life.

Petitions to my Higher Power

God,

Again this day I fully surrender my will and my life to You. Help me to be confident in the care that You provide. Help not only me this day but all

of the addicts and alcoholics who seek You out. Give me the tools I need to work in the garden today.
Amen.

∗   ∗   ∗

Wisdom for Today   Mar 2

Surrender is more than simply understanding that I can't run the show my way anymore. Understanding that I am an addict and an alcoholic and that my way doesn't work does not produce change. Insight, knowledge and understanding do nothing if I don't change my behavior. Surrender is something I must do behaviorally. Simply saying I give up is not enough. I must become willing, open and honest in my surrender to a Higher Power.

What this means is that I constantly must seek out advice and suggestions from others in the program and then evaluate each of the ideas I receive. I must ask myself, "What would God want me to do?" I must become willing to let go and follow the suggestions I get. When my behavior and thinking are in line with God's will for me, then I know that I have truly surrendered. Sometimes this means doing things and making choices that go against what I want. Yet what I want cannot be important if it goes against what my Higher Power would want for me. Does my behavior show that I have really surrendered?

Meditations for the Heart

Spirit power comes from spending quiet time in prayer and meditation. I always need to ask God, "What do you want me to do?" I need to listen to my head and heart to find this answer. When my head and heart both agree with what I know God would want me to do, then I know that I have the answer I need. Particularly early on in my recovery, I found that many of the answers I got were not the answers I wanted to hear. But if I was going to really surrender my will, I needed to put these answers into action. I have always been amazed when I do this. The outcome of surrender has always been positive for me. This does not mean the process was easy; in fact, often times it was very hard. But each time I let go and turn my will and my life over to the care of God, I find that I am made stronger. I find that I am able to handle the things that used to baffle me. Do I spend time each day seeking to be Spirit-powered?

Petitions to my Higher Power

God,

It is so easy for me to get off track when I don't listen for Your direction in my life? Today give me ears to hear Your "still, small voice" and the

willingness to follow Your instruction. Help me to understand that the only way that I can find freedom is to surrender to Your will.
Amen.

* * * *

Wisdom for Today   Mar 3

Surrendering our addictive living over to God does not mean we will never be tempted to drink or use again. Most of us, including me myself, have had times when we experience cravings or urges to use. Most of us have entertained thoughts of using again. In order to be ready for these times, it is important for us to be prepared. An important part of this preparation for me has been to get myself into the right frame of mind each day. Through prayer, meditation and reading, I find that I can keep my mind off of using and on recovery.

When I give my problems over to God, I no longer need to be fearful. I can build up my strength and be confident that God will help me in my struggle. As time passes, staying clean and sober gets easier and easier. It is important for me to stay centered in gratitude. I no longer have to live my life as I did before. Gratitude keeps me focused on what God is doing for me every day of my life. Do I see each day clean and sober as a gift?

Meditations for the Heart

Simply being rid of my desire for alcohol and drugs did not bring me happiness. There was much more to do. Eliminating selfish thinking and behavior was also needed. It was only when I stopped focusing on me and began to focus on "we" that a spark ignited in me. As I began to see that my Twelve Step groups were about helping each other, I began to understand that I had a responsibility to reach out and help others, just as I had been helped. This was difficult at first, because I was unsure of what to say. But as I began to see that all I needed to do was share my experiences and leave the rest up to God, I found that elusive happiness. Am I working to eliminate selfish thinking and behavior?

Petitions to my Higher Power
God,

Today is a gift from You, for I know that I cannot stay clean and sober on my own. Give me a willingness to accept the responsibility to carry the message to others. Help me to be free of selfish thinking and behavior. Let me seek out an attitude of gratitude today.
Amen.

* * * *

Wisdom for Today   Mar 4

Early in the recovery process I ran into a serious problem. There was this gift called recovery that God wanted to give me, but I wanted to earn it. I felt like after all the crazy and hurtful things I had done that I somehow had to earn this gift. I was working very hard at trying to work a "perfect" program so that I could say, "I deserve it." I was working hard at recovery and getting nowhere fast. This didn't last long because I got discouraged quickly. Why wasn't I getting the serenity and happiness that everyone else had?

Then I would go in the opposite direction. I began to feel like maybe I really didn't deserve this gift called recovery. Perhaps I was too bad. I snuck into meetings with my head hung low. I was bent over with this load of shame that I carried on my back. Accepting that I had a disease was relatively easy. There was lots of evidence. Learning to accept recovery was much harder. The reality was that I could not earn it. The reality was that I didn't deserve it. Yet God was offering it to me freely. All I had to do was accept it. God knew I was ready; it was me that was unsure. Do I accept this free gift called recovery?

Meditations for the Heart

Fear can be healthy, and it can be very destructive. Fear tells me not to spend time with people who are actively drinking and using drugs. Fear tells me not to walk in front of a bus cruising down the street. Fear tells me not to ingest poison. Healthy fear is based in commonsense. But there is also destructive fear. This fear tells me that I can't make the changes I need to make. Destructive fear tells me that I have to hide my faults. But most destructive is the fear that destroys hope. We cannot allow this kind of fear into our heart. The only way to do this is to replace this fear with love. When we carry the love of God in our heart and have faith that God, as our Higher Power, will indeed care for us, we have no room for destructive fear in our heart. Do I carry God and His love in my heart?

Petitions to my Higher Power

God,

Each time I think about what You have done for me, I am speechless. I did nothing to deserve recovery, and I did nothing to earn it. You provided it freely. Thank You for opening me up to accept this wonderful gift. Walk with me and let me carry Your love in my heart this day. Walk with me each and every day.

Amen.

* * * *

Once I turned my addiction over to God, I could begin to breathe easier, or at least I thought I could. But in turning things over and not running the show my way anymore, I soon discovered there was a catch. In turning over my will and my life to God's care, I needed to now cooperate with God. This meant asking for direction and then listening for the answer. So I would go to meetings and talk about the problems I was having in my life. I would get all kinds of stories from others and how they handled similar problems. I would visit with my sponsor and discuss the various options and suggestions I had heard at the meetings. Then I would pray. Soon I knew in my heart what it was that I was to do.

This was a problem. I didn't always like the answers and direction I was getting. Sometimes I even became angry at what my heart was telling me. Still, if I really was going to fully surrender, I could not argue but only follow the suggestions. To my surprise, I soon found myself getting better. My health improved. My thinking became clearer. My emotions settled down; and, best of all, the problems started to disappear. Something was happening to me. I was being transformed from an active alcoholic and addict into a recovering one. I even began to get brief glimpses of serenity. Do I cooperate with God's plans for me?

Meditations for the Heart

The spiritual aspects of the program must be learned. For me it was very much like learning to crawl and then learning to stand up. Next came taking my first steps and learning to walk the walk. There are even times now that I feel like I can even jog a little bit. Someday I hope to learn to run. My first prayers were very simple, things like, "God, help me, 'cuz I can't help myself." As I grew in my relationship with God, I found that each time I talk to Him it is a prayer. Sometimes I pray for strength. Sometimes I pray in gratitude. Sometimes I pray for wisdom, and still other times I pray for courage. As I continued to grow up spiritually and became less self-centered, I even began to pray for others. I know I still have much to learn spiritually, but I know I have many good teachers in the program. I also trust that God will continue to teach me along the way.

Petitions to my Higher Power
God,

Today I know that You will require much of me. I also know that it is my place to listen and follow. Help me to be a good listener. Give me willingness

to cooperate with You and follow where Your will takes me. Help me always to seek You out along the way.
Amen.

* * * *

Wisdom for Today   *Mar 6*

Quitting drinking and drugging was only the beginning of my recovery. I found out that I had to go to meetings for more than just abstinence from my addiction. I had to go to meetings in order to change my thinking and my behavior. My thinking was all messed up. I continued to behave like an addict. Just because I stopped drinking and using didn't mean that I was okay. I still found myself wanting to manipulate, lie and play all the games I played when I was using. If I was ever going to stay in recovery, I knew I had to change. I needed to be re-educated. This is what meetings were for. It was the only place I could get the education I needed to change my thinking and behavior.

Going to school was not easy for me. In recovery I found myself wanting to skip classes just like I did in high school and in college. I found myself not wanting to study or do my homework. Yet if I was going to cooperate with God, I had to go to meetings. I had to study the program literature, and I had to work the steps. Opening up and exposing my thinking was not easy. I was afraid that everyone would think I was crazy or judge me. This is not what happened. In the fellowship I found people who like me needed to change their thinking and behavior. I was not judged but accepted. Am I willing to expose my thinking to others in the program?

Meditations for the Heart

Early in recovery I was told, "It's not about quantity, but about quality." I was surprised by this remark. I had thought the goal was simply to put a lot of 24 hours together. I figured the person with the most time was the winner. I had heard the slogan, "Stick with the winners," and assumed that the winners were those with the most time. Then when I was talking with an old-timer, he told me that quality is what was important. I was beginning to string together several 24 hours, but I had no idea how to find quality in recovery. So I asked the old-timer, "How do I find quality?" He said, "Share the fellowship, stay Spirit-minded and learn the lessons." I was dumb-founded. I thought about what he said and had no idea where or how to begin. The next time I saw him at a meeting I asked him to be my sponsor. Do I have a good instructor for the classroom of recovery?

God,

There are so many lessons to be learned if I am to find this thing called quality. Help me to stay motivated and always curious. Let me keep asking questions, and thank You for the wonderful teachers in the program to whom You have introduced me. Today help me to be a good student.
Amen.

∗   ∗   ∗   ∗

Wisdom for Today   *Mar 7*

Turning our addiction over to God is not something we can do absolutely. If I were capable of an unwavering faith and could let go of my addiction completely, then I could "breathe easy." But the fact is that my faith is not complete, and I am not capable of turning it over to God absolutely. So I must always work at strengthening my faith and building my trust in God. I need to attack any reservations that I have in this regard because if I am not building myself up in my faith, then I am going to wind up relying on myself again. I cannot afford to rely on myself. I know where that road leads already.

To build up my faith I need to keep going to meetings and listen to other people share their struggles and triumphs. I need to share my own spiritual struggles. I need to reflect back on my journey in recovery. As I look back, I spend time looking for evidence that the hand of God has been there to point the way for me. It is much easier to trust in my Higher Power when I see so clearly that He indeed walks the path with me. I also see how often He has carried me; for many times along the journey, I have not been able to walk the walk. Fortunately God has been there to do for me what I could not do on my own. Do I work to build up my faith in my Higher Power?

Meditations for the Heart

Learning to "Keep It Simple" has not been easy. You see, I seem to enjoy complicating things. I do this in lots of different ways. Sometimes I just like to worry about tomorrow, and at other times I just get hung up regretting the past. In both cases I am not living in today. Sometimes I like to "awful-ize" and make life much worse than it actually is. At other times I seem to look at life through rose-colored glasses. Sometimes I complicate life by trying to think with my heart rather than my mind. This leaves me reacting to all my emotions rather than using commonsense. It is not easy to keep it simple; but if I can stay in today and live life the way my Higher Power would want me to, it gets easier. I have found out that if I live the way my Higher Power would want me to live, life is simple. Do I complicate my life rather than keeping it simple?

Petitions to my Higher Power
God,

Today let me live my life as You would want me to live. Help me to keep things simple. Give me the courage to continue to grow spiritually, and let me grow in faith.

Amen.

* * * *

Wisdom for Today   Mar 8
I can't take any credit for my sobriety at all. I didn't stop drinking or using drugs by virtue of my own willpower or by something I did. I had nothing to do with it. Every time I tried to quit on my own or control my use I eventually failed. Abstinence was not something I could achieve. Control was out of the question. My recovery is simply the result of the grace of God.

Surrender was my only option. I had to admit defeat and accept that I was helpless and powerless when it came to my addiction. It was only when I finally owned up to this reality and honestly prayed for help that a door was opened for me. My Higher Power then knew I was ready. I became willing to let go absolutely and give my life and my will over to God, as I understand Him. I can take no pride in achieving abstinence or recovery. It was not something I did, but it was something that was done for me. It was a free gift. Do I have a grateful heart for what has been done for me?

Meditations for the Heart
Learning to turn my life over was perhaps the most difficult part of the process of recovery for me. Learning that I needed to check a thing out with my Higher Power before I acted was not easy. Asking God for direction and then following the direction given me is not always easy. There are still times that I want to take back control. There are still times when I get willful or stubborn. Whenever I do this, I find that my life gets off track. I am repeatedly forced to go back to this basic step. It is through this process that I have been changed. Relying on His strength makes this change possible. The only way I can accomplish that progress is through, with and in God's power. Am I willing to walk with, work through and live in God's grace just for today?

Petitions to my Higher Power
God,

Each day I know I need to turn my will and my life over to Your care. Sometimes this is hard. Forgive me when I get stubborn, and help me to get back on track. Let me walk with You, work through You and live in Your grace today?
Amen.

* * * *

Wisdom for Today   Mar 9

Strength training requires regular workouts, lifting weights and exercise. Strength training in recovery isn't very different. If I want to strengthen my faith, I need to exercise it. I do this in a variety of different ways. I need to have regular workouts. This happens when I continually talk to my Higher Power. In prayer I talk to God and tell Him about my needs. I talk to Him about that for which I am grateful, and I talk about the help that I seek. I also need to lift up the heavy weights in my life - those problems, emotions and thinking I find especially heavy or troubling. I exercise my faith when I share openly at meetings. I trust that God will use my words to help others, but I also trust that He will use my words to help me as well.

When another addict or alcoholic approaches me, I recognize quickly that there is little I can offer except my experience, good and bad. When they come back and tell me that something I said helped them, I have to remind myself that it is not my words but how God is using them. I always thank these individuals not because of what they said, but because of the example that they give me that God does want to help addicts and alcoholics. Finally, after a good workout, I need to rest quietly and simply absorb what has happened. When I do this, I find that my faith has been strengthened. Do I exercise my faith?

Meditations for the Heart

Sometimes I am asked how to listen to God. There is no easy answer to this question. In part that's true because each addict or alcoholic understands God in his own way. For some individuals, G-O-D means Group of Drunks or Druggies. When this is the case, listening to G-O-D becomes listening to the group conscience of the program. In this case it is trust that God works in and through the fellowship. For others, G-O-D stands for Good Orderly Direction. In this case listening to what the mind knows is healthy leads us to God's voice. For some of us God is the One we came to know through our religious upbringing. In this case, I have found that listening as a little child listens to a caring parent helps me. I find answers in my heart and in my mind. As I have grown in my understanding of God, I have come to believe that all of these methods work. I guess He is what we need and talks to us in a way we can understand regardless of who we are. Do I hear God's voice in some way?

Petitions to my Higher Power
God,

In this day I know that I will be facing many different situations. Help me to exercise my faith regularly throughout the day. Let me carry the weights in my life to You and trust that You will lead me to the answers I need. Help me to listen for Your voice as I walk the path of recovery.
Amen.

* * * *

Wisdom for Today   Mar 10
With all the noise and confusion I have in my life, it is important for me to take time for quiet time each day. It is in these quiet times that I find my relationship with God, as I understand Him, is improved and maintained. It is in these quiet times that I learn to depend on my Higher Power. Then when I am caught up in the noise and confusion of my day, I find it is easier to turn back to God for help along the way. In these quiet times I can both talk to and listen to God. I can meditate on the things that are important and learn to stay focused.

It is so easy to get distracted when I don't take this time each day. For me it is something I do early in my day before the volume gets turned up. I also find that if I take time at the end of my day and reflect on how I was helped throughout the day, it is easier to have a grateful heart. When I find that I am being distracted away from what is important, I can stop for a few minutes of quiet reflection and get refocused. Do I seek out direction for what is most important in my life?

Meditations for the Heart
When seeking understanding of God, it is important to ask the right questions. It is easy to get caught up in asking ourselves, "What do I want God to be?" Perhaps a better question to ask is, "Am I open to let God reveal Himself to me?" God is who He is. To try and make God fit into a mold and be what we want is a silly attempt to try and control God. This is not to say that we cannot imagine the attributes that God has. Personally I find that it is easy for me now to see God as a friend. He cares and is also willing to be brutally honest with me. This has not always been my understanding, but one

I had to grow into. This growth only occurred when I was willing to be open to God's showing me who and what He is. Have I stopped trying to make God into what I want Him to be?

Petitions to my Higher Power
God,

Today as I start my day, let me think about You as a friend. Help me to be open to Your showing me how to grow in my faith. Let me remain focused on that which is important in my life. Help me to look to You in all that I do this day and to thank You for all that You do for me each day.
Amen.

* * * *

Wisdom for Today   Mar 11
In Step Three of the Twelve Step program we are asked to practice a simple principle – letting go. A story I heard once at a meeting illustrates this point beautifully. There were two men hired by a company to do manual labor. On the first day of the job, the foreman took the men outside and pointed to a large box of tools and told them to move the box to the storage shed. The two men looked at the box and walked over to it. Each one tried to pick up the box by himself, but neither man could do this. They thought about carrying the tools one at a time, but the foreman had wanted the job done quickly; so they finally agreed to help each other. They were able to accomplish the task quickly. Some people think the story should end here, but it does not.

After work the two men began their long walk home. One of the men commented that his back hurt from lifting the box of tools. He said, "That foreman should have never asked us to carry such a heavy load." The other man just smiled. After walking for almost two miles, the one man said that his back was really starting to hurt a lot. The other man just smiled. After walking for almost four miles, the man whose back was hurting said, "I don't think I can make it back to town; my back is killing me. You will have to go on without me." His friend looked at him and smiled and said, "Your back aches because you are still carrying the box. I let go hours ago when we put the box down." Do I really let go, or do I continue to carry the load?

Meditations for the Heart
At some point in time in our recovery we all must face this struggle. Old habits are hard to break. We surrender these old habits and behaviors to God and ask that He help us with the load. We must learn to let go and not keep carrying the heavy load in our lives. We cannot carry the load of addiction

69

ourselves. We must surrender this to our Higher Power. I believe that this process of letting go is harder than admitting that we have a problem. Yet it is in this step that we find freedom. Addiction is the only game in town that we win by giving up. Am I still trying to run the show my way?

Petitions to my Higher Power

God,

I am quick to go back and pick up the heavy load of addiction in my life. Help me to let go absolutely and entrust this heavy weight to You. Help me to stay focused on the freedom that comes with working the steps. Guide me along the path as I journey throughout this day.

Amen.

* * * *

Wisdom for Today   Mar 12

The Bible tells the story of the "Prodigal Son." In real life I lived this same story. I took my life and wasted it on insane living. Everything of any value to me was being destroyed by my addiction. Drinking and drugging led me down a path to destruction. After I had lost my family and my self-respect and anything that resembled hope, I had nowhere to turn. Everything was gone. "When he came to his senses, he said, I will go to my father." This is what an addict or an alcoholic does in the Twelve Step program. I had lost all hope; there was nowhere else to turn. I had to turn to a Power outside of myself.

Sometimes I wonder what caused me to turn to my senses. Somehow in the middle of my insanity, I turned back and looked for an answer. It was not inside of me. Everything I had tried didn't work. It had to be outside of me. I came to believe that I was not the answer. Sanity and wisdom returned. In defeat I found victory. In surrender I found hope and a way out. Have I stopped looking to myself for a way out?

Meditations for the Heart

"Keep it simple, stupid," is a slogan that teaches me that when we complicate life and lose sight of simplicity, I can take my troubles and blow them way out of proportion. I have found that simplicity is a way to unburden myself of heavy loads. When I face my problems honestly and carry them to my Higher Power, I find that I am rewarded with answers or directions for making my problems better. Believe me, it is not always easy to do this; but this simple concept does work. When I try to be my own Higher Power and run the show my way, my problems invariably get worse. When I retreat into denial or pretend that my problems don't exist, eventually they get worse. But when I surrender them to God and ask for His help, things change for the better. They don't always change the way I would expect, but change happens, and the problems do get better. Do I see the simplicity of surrender?

Petitions to my Higher Power

God,

Sometimes I still wander off the path of recovery. I don't drink or use, but I loose sight of the steps and keeping it simple. Each time I do this, things get crazy for me again. I am so grateful that I can turn back to You, God, over and over again to be led back to the path of recovery. Help me keep things simple today.

Amen.

* * * *

Wisdom for Today   Mar 13

The alcoholic and addict face many deaths throughout their using career. There is death of relationships, death of careers, death of dreams and in some cases physical death. There is death of our spiritual self and death of who we are. When I was drinking and using, I lost sight of the "real" me and walked around wearing this mask. In recovery I had to rid myself of this mask and once again find the real me. I can remember the day when the tears flowed, and I realized that all that was important to me was dead. I turned to a Higher Power for help, because I knew I could not help myself. I had to find a way to take the mask off and once again face reality.

In the old spiritual song, "Amazing Grace," there is a line that goes, "I once was lost, but now am found, was blind, but now I see." I did not see so well with the mask on. I had become lost. I had experienced many types of death in my life. In the Twelve Step program I found a way out. My life was restored. Once again I could breathe, and there was a new hope for me. In turning my life over to God, I found myself again. The real me was still there. It had been lost, but in surrender I found the real me again. Am I alive again because of the program?

Meditations for the Heart

Every breath I take is a gift. In working the program, I cannot ignore the spiritual aspects of my growth. I need to breathe in the Spirit, who will guide me in all that I do. God's will enables me to accomplish much, for there is little I can do on my own. If I do that which is the will of God, I know and can be confident that my day will be good. Even when problems do exist, when I breathe in this Spirit, I am assured of not being given more than I can handle. Life does not always go the way I would expect or even the way I want; but when I am working my program and have a strong spiritual foundation, I know that God will care for me. When I let my spirit be in harmony with God's Spirit, I trust that we will make wonderful music together. Do I work to keep my spirit in harmony with God's Spirit?

Petitions to my Higher Power
God,

Let me walk through this day with good sight. Help me to have no desire to put my mask back on. Let me not forget the deaths I have already experienced. Give me courage to live this new life in You and in every breath I take.

Amen.

* * * *

Wisdom for Today   Mar 14
In recovery the task is not to "get well," but getting well. There is no cure for our disease; it can only be arrested. Our ability to stop drinking and using is not determined by what we do, but by God's grace. However, our ability to stay clean and sober is in large part determined by our willingness to go to meetings, work the steps (all of them) and following where our Higher Power leads us. We have to walk the walk; God reads the road map. If I begin to think that some day I will be well and able to drink or use normally again, I am already in trouble. However, if I think about how to follow God's will for me and pray for power to carry out His wishes, then I will be on the path moving toward getting well. Recovery is about progress and not perfection.

The good news is that I only need to worry about this for twenty-four hours at a time. I know that the experience of thousands of addicts and alcoholics does not lie. Each of us that works a program can indeed make progress toward getting well. Sometimes this progress is slow and painful. At other times it happens so quickly that it seems as if our lives get completely turned upside down. Regardless of how the progress is made, it is still progress. The promises of the Twelve Step program await us all, but we must work for them with the help of our Higher Power. Am I working the program one day at a time?

Meditations for the Heart
It was a good thing that I was so stubborn when I was using. I would not let anything or anyone get in the way of my goal to get drunk or high. You may ask how this was a good thing. Certainly my drinking and drugging

72

simply destroyed everything in my life. It is not the using that I am talking about. It is the stubborn part. I knew deep in my heart that I had an ability to persevere. This has helped me a lot throughout all of my recovery process so far. I knew if I persevered in all that God guided me to do, I would end up on the right side of progress. There have been times when I grew tired or even felt like I wasn't getting anywhere. But if I remained persistent, then things started to change or improve. Sometimes the thing that I needed to be most persistent in was trusting my Higher Power. As long as I kept my hope in God, as I understand Him, I could not fail. Am I as stubborn about my recovery as I was about getting high?

Petitions to my Higher Power
God,

Today I want to be persistent in my journey. Help me to persevere in my endeavors to follow where You lead me. Give me strength to carry out the tasks set before me and help me remember I only need to do this one day at a time. Help me to keep my sights on the promises that the program offers and the promises that You offer me as well.

Amen.

* * * *

Wisdom for Today   Mar 15

It sure was a crazy ride I was on. The roller coaster of addiction took me up and threw me down. It spun me in circles and flipped me upside down. What made the ride crazy rather than exciting was the fact that I just couldn't get off the ride. It just kept going around and around. It became a hell on earth for me. I am not talking about all the bad things that happened or problems that occurred, but I am talking about the separation from God. While I was on this roller coaster, I never thought about my relationship with a Higher Power. Sure, like all addicts and alcoholics, I prayed, "God, if you get me out of this one, I will never do it again." But I really was not interested in what God's will for me was.

The reality was I couldn't get off the roller coaster, and only God could get me off the insane ride. I truly consider myself one of the fortunate ones. The AA Big Book says, *"There are such unfortunates. They seem to be born that way. But they, too, can get clean and sober, if they have the capacity to be honest."* (*Alcoholics Anonymous*, Fourth Edition Page 58) Everything changed for me when I admitted I couldn't get off the roller coaster. Nothing I did would make it stop. Only when I surrendered to a Power Greater than myself did

73

the insanity stop. Do I realize honestly that I am fortunate to be off the roller coaster of addiction?

Meditations for the Heart

There is an old prayer that begins, "Lord, make me an instrument of thy peace." In the program it is important for us to realize that we are simply instruments. In spiritual matters it is important for us to be the best instrument we can be. In my addiction, I kept trying to be the conductor leading the orchestra. The music I was making was awful. In recovery I need to be open to God's plan for me. I need to let Him choose the musical score, and I need to let Him choose how and when I will be played. As I go to meetings, I have seen hundreds and hundreds of alcoholics and addicts making wonderful music together. It is not my job to play every note, just to play my part. Do I work to be an instrument of my Higher Power's will for me?

Petitions to my Higher Power

God,

It all begins with honesty and willingness and openness. You have taught me over and over again that the only way I can make beautiful music is to become willing to let You direct and lead the orchestra. Help me to be a good instrument today.

Amen.

*　*　*　*

Wisdom for Today   Mar 16

Before deciding to quit completely, I felt like I had been caught in a steel trap. I was in a lot of pain because of the crises that occurred. That convinced me to look for help. I was angry that I had even stepped into this trap. I wanted to find someone or something to blame for setting the trap in the first place. But most of all I was scared, because I knew I couldn't open the jaws of this trap. Death seemed like a legitimate option. I didn't know where to turn for help.

I knew this was something that I could not do on my own. All I knew was that I wanted out of the trap. The program showed me a way out. First, I had to admit I couldn't get out of the trap. Then I had to believe that God could and would open the jaws of this steel trap. Then the steps led me through a time of healing and repair. And finally I had to learn how not to step into the trap again. I did not free myself, but was set free through the steps. Yet with this new freedom came much responsibility. I needed to follow

74

the suggestions of the program. Do I remain thankful for the new freedom I have in recovery?

Meditations for the Heart

I must have a singleness of purpose in spiritual matters. This is to seek out and follow the will of my Higher Power. In all that I do I must become willing to follow His lead. It is easy to get distracted from this singleness of purpose with things of the material world. But I cannot afford to be distracted because when I am, I put myself at risk. I start walking in places that I should not be. I start thinking in ways that will get me in trouble. I cannot allow "my addict" back out to play. I have been in the trap of active addiction and dare not risk stepping back into the jaws of that steel trap. The only way I know to do this is to have this singleness of purpose in my life. Am I learning just how important spirituality is in my recovery?

Petitions to my Higher Power

God,

Let me start this day in gratitude for the new freedom I have. Help me to take responsibility for working the steps in all that I do. Grant me this day spiritual wisdom to follow where I am led. Let me not be afraid to ask You for direction along the way.

Amen.

* * * *

Wisdom for Today   Mar 17

So the next question was an easy one. Now that I'm out of the trap, how do I make sure that I don't step back into it again? None of us can ever say that we will never fall back into that steel trap, but the program teaches us how to stay out of the trap of addiction one day at a time. By actively participating in regular meetings, I was able to develop relationships with other addicts and alcoholics just like me. In this fellowship I learned that each of us had fallen victim to the steel jaws of addiction. I was encouraged to share my story and talk about my struggles. I listened intently to others talk about how they used the steps to find and hang on to freedom. I learned over time that if I wanted to hang onto the gift of recovery, I would need to give it away.

So, even though I didn't know much, I began to talk about how the program was helping me. I began to share those stories of success and the stories of setbacks. The more I shared, the more I realized that I was changing. As I became aware of these changes, I wanted to thank everyone at meetings over and over again. Each time I did, I was redirected to my Higher Power and was told that was who I needed to thank. I was taken back by these comments, but what really surprised me was when members of the fellowship told me that they weren't trying to help me, but were trying to help themselves. That is when I finally understood the healthy, selfish part of the program. Do I believe that God wants me to take care of myself?

Meditations for the Heart

Sometimes I jokingly say, "I have had at least 16 seconds of serenity in my recovery, and not all at once." There haven't been long periods of time that I would call mountain top experiences - times when I am at peace with God, others and myself all at the same time. But I can say that as I grasped the spiritual aspects of the program, I began to have regular and even daily times when I was calm and knew that I was in a good place. This did not mean I was problem free; it just meant that for periods of time in my day I knew that God was watching out for me and making sure I had what I needed. It is almost like my soul finds a place to rest in the day even though I am surrounded by my problems. In this place of rest and security, I know that I can find calmness of spirit. Do I look for a place to rest in my Higher Power's arms?

Petitions to my Higher Power

God,

Sometimes, it is easy for me to get caught up in the race of life. Help me to know that I can always find a place of rest in You. Keep me open to the opportunities to carry the message to others, and help me to change my attitude from pride and selfishness to one of humility and gratitude. Help me today to carry the message, so that I might care for myself in a healthy way. Amen.

* * * *

Wisdom for Today   Mar 18

When I first came into the program, I was overwhelmed by the thought of never drinking or using drugs again. The thoughts of "forever" seemed like too much to handle. Fortunately, I learned quickly that all I needed to do was stay focused on today. There was nothing I could do about all the yesterdays, when I repeatedly failed to clean up my act. I also didn't need to worry about all the tomorrows, as they never happen. When tomorrow arrives, it will be today. All I needed to do was take it one day at a time.

In the early going, even one day was tough at times. Some days I struggled with cravings and the urge to use. Other days it was the confusing emotions that seemed to come out of nowhere. Sometimes my thinking was simply messed up. I struggled with giving up behaviors, people, things and places. The one thing I didn't struggle with was knowing that I was powerless; I had ample evidence that my life was unmanageable. My way didn't work. I really needed to rely on the fellowship to help me though those early struggles. I slowly began to put one 24-hour period after another together. Days became weeks, and weeks became months. Over time it has become easier to live life one day at a time. Do I work at staying in today, rather than trying to undo the past or live in the fantasy of tomorrow?

Meditations for the Heart

Persistent preparation is what the spiritual life in recovery is all about. I need constantly to work at preparing myself for the day by practicing the principles of the program. Persistent prayer is one way I try to prepare myself for the day ahead. My prayers change over time. Sometimes they are filled with requests for guidance. Other times I look for strength to handle my life in the moment. Sometimes it is about seeking willingness and other times about gratitude. But it is not just prayer that prepares me spiritually. I also need to put my program into action. I need to work the steps. I need to carry the message. You may ask for what I am preparing. Well, I am preparing for the promises – joy, peace, health, security, serenity and happiness. Anything is possible in the spiritual realm of recovery. Am I preparing my life for the promises of recovery?

Petitions to my Higher Power

God,

"Today" – this is a word I need to better understand. Help me to realize that all that is important for me in this life happens in today. Let me walk forward into this day with knowledge of Your will for me. Give me the strength I need to accomplish the tasks You set before me. Let me always work at preparing myself for the promises of recovery.

Amen.

* * * *

Wisdom for Today   *Mar 19*

When I first stopped drinking and using drugs, my whole being needed to focus on staying clean and sober. But it wasn't long before I began to hear some familiar voices from the past. Guilt, shame and remorse quickly came back into the picture. Fear also crept back into my life. These familiar voices used to whisper in my ear and give me reason for using. Now that I had stopped drinking and drugging, these same voices were back, only they were shouting at me. I was so ashamed of all the things I had done when I was wasted. I was afraid to look my family and friends in the eye. I felt guilty because of how I wronged them. My life had so much to regret.

Without the program I know I would have had no chance to stand up to these voices from the past. The program helped me to see that who I was as a person was not the same thing as what I had done. I began to see that God, as I understood Him, could and would forgive me. I began to see that I could forgive myself. I slowly learned that as long as I worked honestly to stay clean and sober, I could change how I felt about myself. More importantly, if I surrendered my will and followed the will of my Higher Power not only did my self-perception change, but the way other people looked at me would also change. Do I recognize that no matter how dark my life was, God can turn a new light on for me?

Meditations for the Heart

As I walk through this day and along the path of recovery, it is important that I realize that God walks with me. There is nothing that I think, do or say that my Higher Power does not know. When I feel fear, shame, guilt or remorse, I know that I am not alone. I can have no secrets from God. I cannot hide from His presence. It is easy to get wrapped up in trying to please others or to look good to the people with whom I interact every day. It is easy to try and conform my ways to the ways of the world around me. When I do this, I am not turning my will and my life over to the care of my Higher Power. Instead I am turning it over to the world around me. This is not something I can afford to do. I need to stay focused on His will for me and pray for the power to carry out His will. Do I realize I will only find lasting peace when I follow the will of my Higher Power?

Petitions to my Higher Power

God,

Today let me stay cognizant of Your presence. Help me to accept not only the gift of recovery that You provide, but also the gift of forgiveness. Help me to remember that no secrets can be hidden from You. Let me see that You see in secret but reward openly.

Amen.

* * *

Wisdom for Today   Mar 20

When things got their worst, I really felt hopeless. I spent time in worry about my future. Was I going to end up locked up somewhere? Would I end up in some mental hospital? Would I end up dead? Worry was such terrible mental torment. What was going to happen to me if I couldn't find a way out of the madness of addiction? I knew there was nothing I could do to find a way out on my own. It was a scary but simple choice. I could end it all in suicide, or I could ask for help.

In desperation I reached out for help and found that for which I was looking. In the program a new hope was born, and I actually began to believe that my life could turn out okay. The thing that still baffles me is the fact that I still find it difficult at times to ask for help. After years of evidence that asking for help works, I still find myself at times backing myself into a corner. Why is asking for help so hard? I think the answer to that question is different for each of us. Sometimes it is pride or arrogance. Sometimes it is simply foolishness or lack of commonsense. Sometimes it is fear of letting someone else know. Regardless of the reason, it is only when we come back to a place of surrender and honestly and humbly reach out that we find help. One day at a time my goal is to remember this. Do I still find it hard to ask for help?

Meditations for the Heart

One act of surrender is the act of obedience. When I walk though my day and ignore the directions that my Higher Power provides, I end up in trouble. When I follow the guidance I am given, I find that life goes much easier. In my addiction I always wanted to break the rules or at least bend them. I pretended that they did not apply to me. This is something I can't afford to do in recovery. It is too easy to get off the path of recovery if I do not obey the rules. Yes, I know that in the program you are told that there are no rules, only suggestions. But these suggestions are a matter of life and death. So whether you see them as rules or only suggestions, surrender involves the act of obedience. Sometimes I do not always like the suggestions I am given; yet in surrender I still need to be willing to follow the guidance I am given. Do I practice obedience, or do I want to still bend the rules?

Petitions to my Higher Power

God,

Help me stay open to all the suggestions I am given and recognize that Your direction comes to me though many different channels. Let me hear the words of Your guidance and be willing to obey and follow where You lead. Let me not forget that You care about me and will lead me to a good place. Amen.

* * * *

In the program I have learned many valuable lessons. Perhaps one of the most important is to let the future take care of itself. Everything works out well as long as I stay clean and sober and work my program. All I really need to focus on is today. I no longer need to worry about tomorrow. Now if this sounds like staying clean and sober means that I will never have problems in the future, this is not true. The problems I do have in recovery are certainly better than the problems I had when I was drinking and getting wasted. And any new problems I may experience in the future, I know that I have the tools to deal with them.

Each morning I wake up and start a new day, I can be grateful for the day I was just given. Any problem that I have, I can be grateful knowing that the steps and the fellowship can help me get through. This does not mean that every problem I have will be solved the way I would want; it just means that I know God will give me the strength and guidance to deal with any problem I experience. I know this to be true because I have had many difficult problems cross my desk in recovery. Time and time again, I find that I am given what I need to deal with these problems. Have I stopped worrying about tomorrow?

Meditations for the Heart

It's all good! This does not mean that everything is fundamentally good on the surface of things. What is does mean is that my Higher Power cares about me and that He has found a purpose for me in this life. I continue to be surprised by the ways that God leads me, and I am amazed at how He puts me to work. I have come to believe that God indeed has a plan for me. I do not always understand what this plan is when it is happening, but I am amazed when the plan not only works but also makes sense. Even when I have struggled in some difficult situations, I am given the strength to handle them. I learn from these struggles, and I share my stories, and I trust that God will use these stories to help others. I trust this because I know I have benefited from the stories of others. The world does not always make sense and often times are filled with pain, but one thing I am sure of is that His plan for me makes sense and ultimately will bring me peace and serenity. Am I willing to trust God's plan for me?

Petitions to my Higher Power

God,

I trust that You have a plan for me. Let me be willing to follow the directions I am given. Let me follow Your lead one day at a time. Today I will

walk down a pathway in my recovery. Help me to trust that this journey is
planned by You.
Amen.

*   *   *   *

Wisdom for Today   *Mar 22*

When I first walked through the doors of a meeting to get sober, I had
only one question on my mind, "Alright, so what do I need to do to stop
drinking and drugging?" I had no idea how to do this and even less of an
idea of where I would find the strength to do it. I was too afraid to ask this
question out loud, but somehow knew the answer was in that room. As I
looked around, I saw the faces of older members who had found the answer
to my question. Where did they get the answer? I listened to members speak
one after another and heard strength in their voices. Where did the strength
come from?

What did I have to do to get what they had? At the end of the meeting,
everyone chimed in, "It works if you work it; keep coming back." And so I
did -- kept coming back, that is. Slowly I began to realize that the source of
strength that each of these older members had come in different ways. Some
talked of the words of wisdom that their sponsor shared. Others talked of
the steps, and still others talked of the gift that had been given them by their
Higher Power. As days went by, I soon discovered that this strength I was
seeking comes in many ways. I needed to find what worked for me. Now
that I have a few 24 hours under my belt, I can see that the strength comes
from the same source. It just takes on lots of different faces. To quote the Big
Book, "*That one is God; may you find Him now.*" (*Alcoholics Anonymous,* Fourth
Edition Page 59) Do I see all the faces of God at meetings?

Meditations of the Heart

What needs do I have that God cannot fill? God can and does supply all
our needs. The fundamental needs of an addict or alcoholic are spiritual. We
can do nothing without the help of a Higher Power. Yes, over time in recovery
we regain our health, perhaps our families and jobs, our freedom and even a
sense of self-esteem. But none of these things are as important as our spiritual
well being. When I can take what I have learned and give it away, then I am
in a good place to receive what God has in His plans for me. Through this
simple act - caring for others, we learn how to care for ourselves. Through
sharing our struggles, defeats and triumphs, we gain strength. It is selfish. I do
this to help myself. Yet in this selfishness, I help others. In gaining strength,

81

I can do more for my family. I can be a better worker, and I can be a better person. And so it goes, the supply of my spiritual needs is met. God plans it that way. Am I willing to help others in order to help myself?

Petitions to my Higher Power
God,

Every day I have needs, and every day You show me how to fill them. I do not always get what I want, but I trust that You know what I need. Help me to use the strength I receive to share with and care about others. Let me follow You on the road to spiritual health.
Amen.

* * * *

Wisdom for Today   Mar 23
Strength comes to us through the fellowship. Simply being with so many other addicts and alcoholics who are making it brings me a sense of security. I remember suddenly feeling like I was not trying to do this thing called recovery – alone. As I would listen to speakers at open meetings, I would hear things I could relate to. It gave me a sense that I was not unique. Others just like me found the way. At closed meetings I would hear about everyday struggles and triumphs; but more importantly I witnessed recovery in action. Simply seeing others making it one day at a time gave me a sense of hope.

I began to get a sense of strength and hope as I had others come to me after meetings to share their genuine concerns about what was going on in my life. I also had others that would share with me that something I had said helped them. I was given permission to seek and find the answers that were right for me. I could choose a Higher Power that worked for me. I really began to get a sense that by talking with and listening to others I was becoming stronger. The hours became days, and the days became weeks. The 24-hours started to add up. Do I recognize that there is strength in being an active part of the fellowship?

Meditations for the Heart
As ancient armies marched into battle, the drummers would bang on their drums. The trumpeters would blast from their horns, and the soldiers would scream their battle cry. This provided a sense of unity and purpose - to gain victory over the oppressor. In recovery we need to have a battle cry as well. Mine has become, "God is with me, and He has all power." I have repeated these words often to myself in my battle with addiction. Even after I won a battle by establishing abstinence, I still scream out my battle cry as

I struggle with character defects or making amends or simply to strengthen my faith. I bang the drum when I talk openly about the steps and, "*How It Works.*" (*Alcoholics Anonymous*, Fourth Edition Page 58) I blast the trumpet each time I can say to others, "It works!" The war is not over, and I am sure there will be other battles to fight, but I know all I need to do is be the best soldier I can be. Am I being a good soldier in the army of those fighting for recovery?

Petitions to my Higher Power

God,

Today, I know that my strength will be renewed over and over again. As I interact with You as my Higher Power, and as I interact with the other soldiers who battle for recovery, keep me strong in the unity and purpose of the fellowship. Let me rely on the battle cry as my energy for ultimate victory. Amen.

* * * *

Wisdom for Today   Mar 24

It was like a light switch was suddenly turned on, and I could see just how messy my house had become. Early in the recovery process, I learned that honesty brought my addiction into this light. By sharing my story and all the troubles my addiction had led me into, I gained strength. By talking about the hospitals, jails and the demise of my family, I started the process of cleaning house. By sharing the money problems and all the foolish things I had done and talking about my suicidal behavior when I was wasted, I uncovered more and more of what had been hidden.

As I brought more and more of my life and addiction into the open, I gained both a sense of relief and a sense of strength. At first, I was worried that I would be judged and looked down on; but as I shared, I found more and more people that had experiences in common with me. I found out I was not alone. The strength I found in knowing this was very empowering. By witnessing my personal struggles and defeat at the hands of addiction, I became stronger. Do I recognize the strength I receive simply by sharing my story?

Meditations for the Heart

By sharing the events of my life as an addict and alcoholic, I managed to start the house cleaning. But I knew there was more dirt and clutter hiding in the closets and under the rugs in my home. Simply stopping drinking and drugging and sharing my story were not all that I needed to do. This surface cleaning was only the beginning. There still were all the secrets. If I was to move forward in my recovery, I needed more strength; and I needed more faith. I had my own understanding of the world. Everything fit into a nice, neat package. But when the light switch of honesty was turned on, I suddenly realized that my beliefs were limited. The truth was that there was much that I didn't understand or comprehend. There was much that I simply had to take on faith. Have I surrendered my old ways of thinking and accepted that I do not have all the answers?

Petitions to my Higher Power

God,

It has been amazing to me how this program works. By sharing all the ugly aspects of my addiction, You have made me stronger. By admitting my weakness, I have found strength and hope. By accepting that I am not god, I have been opened to accepting that You are God.

Amen.

* * * *

Wisdom for Today   Mar 25

Perhaps the best strength I have found in the program has come from trusting in a Power greater than I. Early in my life I had the concept of God introduced to me, and I had heard all the stories of God through all my involvement in organized religion. Yet, during all those addiction filled years, I somehow lost any relationship that I had with God. I saw people at meetings who repeatedly told me they could not define God for me or tell me how to rebuild this relationship. But what they didn't realize was that simply seeing their example and listening to their words taught me an awful lot about God, as I now understand Him. I could see how the Higher Power was helping these individuals. It helped me to believe that God wanted to help me.

Prayer was also something that I had little idea of how to do other than those I had memorized as a child. I began to recognize that if I wanted a personal relationship with God, I would need to talk with Him. And so I began, quite awkwardly at first, to stumble through very simple prayers. I began to talk about what was going on in my life and asking for direction. Unfortunately listening for the answer was often times even tougher. I spoke with others in the fellowship and asked what they did to listen to their Higher Power. I heard many different answers, but in hindsight this was good. It forced me to look for my own answers as to how to listen to God. Does my belief in a Power Greater than myself give me strength?

Meditations for the Heart

Developing skills takes practice. This is true also with spiritual skills. When I continually seek after God's will for me and I seek to follow His lead, I begin this process of spiritual development. At first it seemed that there was this huge wall between God and myself. But just as running water causes erosion, practice of spiritual principles slowly eroded that wall. I now realize that this wall was erected by my actions, beliefs and thinking when I was drinking and using. Today I can see that I did not take down this wall, but God in His love for me crumbled every stone in that wall. Today I need to be persistent in my spiritual development and never falter. I need to seek to go boldly forward and continue to be unafraid of where God will lead me. One thing I have learned is that if I seek to do His will and ask for power to carry this out, God will indeed care for me and lead me in a good direction. Am I developing my spiritual skills?

Petitions to my Higher Power

God,

I have come to recognize that my relationship with You is a personal one. Help me be open to improving my spiritual skills by continually bringing my concerns to You. Let me daily remember to give You thanks for all that You do in my life. Give me ears to listen to Your Divine wisdom.
Amen.

* * * *

Wisdom for Today   Mar 26

Strength comes from giving it away. I remember very early in my recovery process, I told my sponsor I wanted to help others. It was as if I was on fire to give away what I was receiving. Fortunately my sponsor very quietly told me to hang onto that feeling and save it for later. He knew that this fire inside of me could easily be extinguished. I did what my sponsor told me to do. I saved it for later and continued to concentrate on myself. Some time later I was at a meeting, and a newcomer walked in. My sponsor winked at me and told me to go and welcome him. I offered the newcomer a cup of coffee and proceeded to tell him about the time when I first came to a meeting. I could see he was scared, but what surprised me was that I could see myself in his eyes.

That night I learned a very important lesson. I learned that as I was trying to help this newcomer, my resolve to stay clean and sober grew stronger. I realized for the first time that I had something that I did not want to lose. The newcomer kept coming back for several weeks, and then I never saw

85

him again. At first I worried about him. I talked with my sponsor, feeling as though I had failed. Again there were words of wisdom that came from my sponsor's mouth. He said, "You are only responsible for carrying the message; you can't carry the other guy." He was right again and again. I learned that in helping others I am really helping myself. For the first time I think I really understood what the fellowship is really all about. We help others to help ourselves. Am I finding renewed strength by reaching out to help others?

Meditations for the Heart

Faith is a narrow path between God and you. This path only exists because God wants it there. Sometimes I have wondered why this path is so narrow. It is so easy to wander away from the path. I cannot explain why God wants the path this way. If I had all these answers, I would not need faith. And so I trust that God knows what He is doing. So my faith requires me to stay focused on this narrow path, so that I can maintain this walk with my Higher Power. In some ways it is not so different from when I was getting drunk or was using drugs. I had a singleness of vision. All I wanted then was to get high. It was a very narrow path. It is much the same now. All I want is a relationship with my Higher Power. So I walk a narrow path. Do I keep my vision on my relationship with God, as I understand Him?

Petitions to my Higher Power
God,

Each day You present me with new opportunities to build up my faith and renew my strength. When the time is right, lead me on a path to helping newcomers. Help me to keep my focus on the narrow path and walk hand in hand with You today.
Amen.

* * * *

Wisdom for Today   Mar 27

We also find strength in our failures. I know this sounds strange, but it is true. Throughout my recovery process, I have had a variety of setbacks and challenges in which I experienced failure. I am not talking about relapse, although this was a part of my experience, too. What I am talking about are the everyday failures we all experience. As I worked my way though the steps, I have fallen flat on my face on more than one occasion. As I struggled with my Fourth Step, I found it hard to be rigorously honest. In facing my character defects, I learned that some of them I liked and did not want to give them up, or I didn't know how. In making amends, I found some old resentments.

All along the way I have found periods of failure. Yet in these failures I also found the strength to try again and again until I found success. In each of these failures, I was forced to go back to my Higher Power and ask for help again, and each time I was given new strength.

Personally I have come to believe that life was not meant to be one success after another. It is filled with both success and failure. One thing I have learned is that I need to turn to God in both the times of success and the times of defeat. In my success I must be grateful to my Higher Power for showing me the way. In failure I am taken back to the essence of Step Three. I turn it over, and I am given the courage to try again. This spiritual principle is one of the wonders of life in recovery. If I entrust both my success and failures to my Higher Power, I am sure to come out okay in the long run. The strength that is gained is both from gratitude for what Our Higher Power does for us and for what we cannot do on our own. Wondrously our Higher Power even celebrates with us when we find success. Do I learn from my failures and ask God for strength to try again?

Meditations for the Heart

Where does this wonderful power and strength come from? Men conquer nations, and men become great leaders. Some people become very wealthy, and others become famous. But these things all pass. The power I am talking about is the power to conquer self. Within my being are an addict and alcoholic that is always trying to come out and take control again. Yet I can say that just for today, I do not need to let the addict out to play. I do not have to let the alcoholic take control again. God's power is the greatest power in the universe, and He is willing to share this wonderful power with me. It is free for the asking. Each time I ask, I am rewarded with one more victory in this life of recovery. Sometimes the victories are small, and other times it seems as though mountains have been moved for me. Do I see God's power working for me in my everyday life?

Petitions to my Higher Power
God,

I pray that I may open myself to the power that You provide. Give me courage to learn from my failures, and help me to find the power to conquer self. Let me turn to You for direction each step that I take on this pathway of recovery.

Amen.

* * * *

When I first walked through the doors of a meeting, I thought that is all it was - a meeting. What I didn't realize was that what I was really walking into was a new way of life. At first I simply thought I would learn how to stop my active addiction and that would be it. But it didn't take long to figure out that this was just the beginning. Today I am amazed at the changes I see happen in the lives of the people who adopt this way of living. Every so often I stop long enough to look at myself and see the changes that have happened in my life because of this program.

As I look back, I can see just how selfish I had become. Everything revolved around me and my desires. If things weren't going my way, I would con and manipulate to get what I wanted. When my way didn't work, I would get mad; or I would throw a temper tantrum. I acted just like a child. I would even isolate and sulk when nothing else would work. Just like a spoiled child, I had to have things my way. Sometimes my actions were very visible to those around me. I hurt a lot of people along the way. At other times I was sneakier, but always the goal was the same - to get things my way. Have I stopped trying to run the show my way?

Meditations for the Heart

As I began to let go of my old way of thinking and began to adopt a new way of life, I felt like I was missing something. I wasn't sure what it was at first, but soon realized that what I was missing was confidence. Then my sponsor told me that confidence is simply faith in that which is not seen. He asked me if I believed in a million dollars. I told him that I knew it existed. Then he asked me if I had ever seen a million dollars or held it in my hand. I, of course, said, "No." My sponsor responded, "But you believe in it even though you have never seen it." He went on to tell me that I could have all the confidence I ever wanted if I only believed in a Higher Power, who would provide me that confidence. He was right, because as I started to believe that I could have this gift, I indeed received it. My sponsor then cautioned me, you could only keep this confidence if you are willing to obey the directions of your Higher Power. A confidant faith and a willingness to follow my Higher Power have indeed created change in my life. Do I see that all successful living only happens in and with my Higher Power?

Petitions to my Higher Power

God,

I pray that I may follow Your lead along this path of recovery. Let me walk with You hand in hand each step of the way. Continue to provide me with confidence, as I still need it. Help me to remember always from where this confidence comes, and grant me willingness to obey Your will for me. Amen.

* * * *

Wisdom for Today   *Mar 29*

When I was active in my addiction, I was also very active in my being dishonest. I would lie to my family about where I was and what I was doing. I would lie to get money to buy drugs and alcohol. I would lie to my employer and call in sick. I would lie about my lies and would lie so that I could hide. I would lie to my friends, and I would lie to my children. Most of all, I lied to myself. It seemed that facing the reality of what I had become and also facing me were so distasteful that I would do anything to deceive myself and hide from the truth. There was a small part of me that somehow knew that I was damaged. I could not admit this to anyone, most of all I could not admit it to myself.

I got clean and sober, but to my surprise the lying did not automatically stop. "What do you mean be honest with my sponsor; how can I trust him? He's just another drunk." Developing a manner of living that demands rigorous honesty has been perhaps the hardest part of the recovery process for me. It was hard admitting to others and myself that I was an alcoholic and an addict. It was even harder to get honest about all my dark secrets. Dishonesty clearly was and still can be one of my biggest character defects. Learning to admit when I am wrong and learning that hiding only hurts me has not been easy. Fortunately recovery is about progress and not perfection. I have come a long way with my ability to be honest. But I also honestly know I am not done with this. Recovery is not so much about immediately being honest, but it is about becoming honest. Am I becoming more honest today than I was yesterday?

Meditations for the Heart

Each of us must face up to moments of truth -- times when we are confronted with the urge to lie, cover things up, misrepresent or just plain hide. The compulsion that an addict experiences when we want to lie is incredibly strong. Yet in these moments of truth, we can choose to do what is right. We can choose to do what our Higher Power would want us to do. Yes, sometimes this means that there will be consequences for our actions or behavior, but the consequence of dishonesty is much greater. All those things we have regained as a result of God's gift of recovery can be lost again. The trust we re-establish in recovery can be blown away by the winds of deceit. The self-respect we regain can be destroyed in the flood of dishonesty. The very essence of freedom can be lost in the chains of manipulation. This character defect, above all others, can make recovery disappear in a brief moment. It can fester like an infected sore for a long time until finally it brings death to all that is important to us. Am I working on becoming more and more honest with others and myself?

Petitions to my Higher Power
God,

Today I can see clearly how destructive dishonesty has been and still can be in my life. Help me to find the courage to do Your will when I face those moments of truth. Teach me the benefits and the wisdom that comes with honesty. Let me become willing to let go of this defect of character.
Amen.

*　*　*　*

Wisdom for Today   Mar 30
When I was active in my addiction, I had an ego a mile wide. Everything was about me and what I wanted. I had arrogance about life that somehow life owed me something. I acted as if I were more important than others. Certainly when it came to my family, I did not act in a loving or caring manner. I did what I wanted to do regardless of how my choices affected them. It was not that I didn't care or couldn't love my family, but I put my relationship with drugs and alcohol before my family. Even with my children, I acted as if their needs were not important. Most of all, I was not being loving toward myself. I cared only about satisfying one need – to get wasted night after night.

This arrogant ego of mine became a character defect. I cleaned up my act and stopped drinking and stopped using, yet I still had this ego problem. My ego would not allow me to make a mistake; I had to be perfect. I continued to blame others for my own shortcomings. I continued to put my needs and desires before others. As I continued to go to meetings, I began to listen and hear other addicts and alcoholics talk about similar problems. I heard others with more time under their belt talk about the freedom they gained in surrendering these defects. They talked of letting go of their desires and following after their Higher Power's will. I began to realize that this character defect stood in the way of my relationship with my own self, with others and with God. Do I let ego problems get in the way of my recovery?

Meditations for the Heart

Each of us has both an outer life and an inner life. There is the part of us that we show to the world, that part of us that is known to others. There is also the inner life; this is where we hide our crazy thinking, our mixed up emotions and our secrets. In recovery I need to open myself up and tell on my disease. I need to share how my thinking and emotions and secrets mess up my life. I need to develop a new inner life. This new inner life is one in which I am in communion with God. I need to seek after His will for me and seek after the courage and power to carry out His will for me. I need to go to this new inner world often to be renewed in my commitment to ongoing recovery. I need to do regular housecleaning of this new inner world. When I do this, it makes it possible to live in peace with the outer world. I am prepared to go to work, to interact with my family and to stay true to the tasks before me. Do I seek to expose my old crazy thinking, mixed up emotions and secrets so that I can develop a new inner world?

Petitions to my Higher Power

God,

Sometimes I do not want to clean house, but I know this must be done in order to have an effective relationship with You and others. I know that I can let my ego get in the way and act as if I am more important than others. Help me to accept myself, both my strengths and weaknesses, and learn to let go of my defects of character.

Amen.

* * *

Wisdom for Today   Mar 31

There are two kinds of fear in this world, healthy fear and unhealthy fear. Healthy fear tells you not to do something that will harm yourself, like grabbing onto live electrical wires. Unhealthy fear, on the other hand, distorts reason and distorts beliefs. Unhealthy fear can control every action you take. During my active addiction to alcohol and drugs, this unhealthy fear was a constant companion. Frequently this fear escalated into paranoia. This fear controlled me. I was not able to think clearly or make rational choices because of this fear. I began to believe that all people were bad and were out to get me. I felt trapped in this fear and could not do anything without first consulting my fears.

I stopped drinking and using, but fear had become a part of me. I did not feel I could trust others. People were willing to help me, but I actually

91

believed they wanted to harm me. Even at meetings I carried this mistrust. Even with family and friends who really cared for me, I found that fear of condemnation was still apart of me. This unhealthy fear had grown into a character defect. It was pervasive in my personality. I let fear run my life even in recovery. Have I let fear run my life?

Meditations for the Heart

Sometimes it becomes important to just keep things simple. My sponsor used to ask me a question, "Does it interfere with your breathing?" What he was asking about was the situation a matter of life or death. He told me that relapse could affect my breathing, and I needed to go to more meetings. It has only been in recent years that I have recognized that I need to keep things this simple in my spiritual life. Does it affect my spiritual breathing? Each day I need to take time to breathe in the Spirit. It is important that I slow down purposefully to breathe in the positive energy and the direction my Higher Power has to offer me. When I rush into the day without this time of quiet prayer and meditation, I find myself becoming short of spiritual breath. Rhythmically and evenly I need to breathe in what is offered to me freely. Do I take the time I need to breathe spiritually each day?

Petitions to my Higher Power

God,

Today I need to work on letting go of the grip I have on control. Let me rest comfortably in the assurance that You will lead me to health. Help me not to get wrapped up in fear and to simply trust You.

Amen.

*　*　*　*

Wisdom for Today   Apr 1

When I was active in my addiction, I developed all kinds of unrealistic expectations of others and myself. I expected my parents to bail me out of one jam after another. I expected my wife to put up with my insanity. I expected her to cover for me with my employer. I expected my kids to leave me alone when I wanted to get high or have a drink. I expected my using friends to turn me on even when I had my own secret stash. I expected my friends to buy me a cold beer when I was short of cash. My expectations of myself were no different. I expected no less than perfection. I had to be the perfect party animal. I had to be the perfect husband. I had to be the best drinker. I had to be the best father. All this left me feeling like a complete failure because there was no way I could ever measure up to my own expectations.

I stopped drinking and using, but my unrealistic expectations continued. I wanted my sponsor to bail me out of one jam after another. I expected my family to restore their trust in me immediately. I wanted my boss to pay me more money. I still expected my kids to leave me alone. My perfectionism didn't just disappear because I was clean and sober. In fact, all these unrealistic expectations had become another character defect. In my Fourth Step I was forced to begin to look at these defects. I began to see how I continued to self-sabotage the things that were important to me. There was no way I would ever be able to gain self-respect or the trust of others if I hung on to these old ideas and behaviors. Do I see how my expectations of others and myself have become self-destructive?

Meditations for the Heart

Each and every day provides us with an opportunity for progress. It is up to us to make the best use of these opportunities. It is not always easy to see the progress that we make. Each small step we take and each time we move forward in our recovery effort, we make progress. It all adds up, and over time the progress we make is realized. God sees this progress long before we do. He is there to direct our every step along the path to recovery. It is our Higher Power who presents us with the opportunities for self-improvement. Now we do have a choice: We can refuse to take advantage of these opportunities, or we can forge ahead confident that God is guiding our path. I have found it important to ask myself after meetings, "What is one thing I can do differently that will improve my recovery?" I do not believe God wants me to look for ten things or twenty things to change, only one step at a time. What opportunity have you been given today?

Petitions to my Higher Power

God,

This path of recovery has many twists and turns, yet it is always filled with opportunities for self-improvement. Today help me to let go of my unrealistic expectations of others. Help me also to see that perfectionism only hurts me. Help me to take each opportunity that is offered me and make the best use of each step I take.

Amen.

* * * *

Wisdom for Today   Apr 2

As my addiction progressed, I found that I became very careless. It got to the point that I didn't care about my family. I didn't care about my work. I didn't care about my friends. And I certainly didn't care about me. My ability to care about what was really important was drained out of me. I would try and put on a good show, but the reality was that I just didn't care. I was no longer using alcohol and drugs to have fun; I was using just to feel normal. I would wake up in the morning and be drawn right back to the insanity of my life. There just was no way out, and I didn't care anymore.

I got clean and sober, but my attitude had not changed. I still didn't care. I was just going through the motions. I would go to the meetings and say the right things, but I just didn't care. I had lost a lot because of my addiction, but I didn't care enough to try and get it back. My attitude was pervasive in my life. I really didn't care what my sponsor's advice was, because I really didn't care about me. This defect of character had to go if I ever was going to get clean and sober. I needed to learn how to care about myself again. I needed to learn to care about my life again. I needed to learn to care about others again. Have I started to care and be caring again?

Meditations for the Heart

God is all around us. His Spirit abounds in the universe. When I look back at my life, I am not sure when I began to care about myself again. It seems that there were many things standing in the way. Guilt, shame and self-hatred all served as blocks to caring. I went to meetings and heard it was a selfish program, but I didn't care enough to really try. Today I have come to believe that this willingness to begin to care for myself again is a gift from God. I know I would not have had any chance at recovery without this gift. Still, I have to do the footwork, which means that I need to care enough about myself to work the steps. It starts with very simple things like eating right and taking yourself to meetings. Do I recognize the need for the gift of self-care and then act upon it?

Petitions to my Higher Power

God,

I am so grateful that You cared about me when I could not care for myself. I am grateful You put people in my life to help me learn how to care for myself again. It has not always been easy, as there was so much self-hatred I needed to overcome. Yet You stuck with me and helped me find a way to care again. Teach me more about caring each day that I walk on this pathway to recovery.

Amen.

* * * *

94

During the final months of my addiction, I became very trustless. I no longer trusted my friends. I no longer trusted my family. I certainly had plenty of evidence that I could no longer trust myself. I no longer could even trust my using to help me escape the insanity of my life. I felt all alone. Then it all came crashing down. I walked in the house only to be thrown out. I had nowhere to turn. I trusted no one. I had hit bottom.

I believe that every addict or alcoholic experiences some crisis that finally wakes him or her up. I was no different. I got into the fellowship. I stopped drinking and getting high. But the fear of trusting others and the fear of trusting me did not go away. It had become a way of life. I'm not sure exactly when I decided to risk trusting again. Perhaps it was seeing others making it at meetings. Perhaps it was Divine intervention. Perhaps it was because I had no other choice. The risk I took was small. I asked for help; and to my surprise I was given not only help, but also friendship, encouragement and even trust. People started to trust me to come early and help set-up for meetings. I was asked to share my story. I was given trust even when I deserved none. Am I beginning to trust again?

Meditations for the Heart

When active in my addiction, I was a force for evil. I was dishonest. I had a false ego. I let fear run my life. I had unrealistic expectations. I became careless, and I trusted no one. All of these defects of character and more became pervasive in my life. They did not simply disappear because I stopped drinking and using. More work had to be done. My moral character had become twisted. I stopped the insanity, but I still needed to straighten up. In the Fourth Step I had to look at myself and see what I had become. I had to admit that much was broken. It was not an easy process honestly and fearlessly to inventory what I had become. Yet without this inventory I would not have known what my shortcomings were. This inventory allowed me to see what needed to change. It was not just my drinking and using that needed to change. I just had to stop drinking and using. I also needed to change. This is the miracle of recovery. It wasn't just changing the things I did; it was changing me from the inside out. I could not do this on my own, but I knew that my Higher Power would help me with this too. Am I willing to look for how I need to change who I am?

Petitions to my Higher Power

God,

Taking inventory is hard work. When I look at myself, I do not like all that I see. Guide me to become the person You want me to become. I know

that with your help, I will find the courage to change the things I can. Walk with me this day and show me the way to a new me.
Amen.

* * * *

Wisdom for Today   *Apr 4*

When I finally realized that I needed to change more than just my using, I was overwhelmed. I had no idea where to start. It seemed that my list of character defects was never ending. But as I listened at meetings and talked with my sponsor, things became more and more clear. The first thing I needed to do was learn how to care again. This was a complete reversal of direction for me. I had spent a lot of time behaving in very self-destructive behavior. I had so much self-hatred. My emotions were swimming around and all confused. Yet I knew that if I could not find a way to care about myself, then nothing else would change.

I had to start "simple" - just caring for myself physically. This meant beginning to eat right. It also meant becoming more physically active. It also meant getting enough sleep. This is where I had to start; and to my surprise, my life started to feel more manageable. Then I needed to learn how to take care of myself emotionally, and finally I needed to learn to care for myself spiritually. The changes I felt were not sudden or immense. Each day they came in very small steps of progress. Some days I did a better job than others. Sometimes it felt like I was backsliding. Over time I slowly began to realize that caring for me was something that seemed strange. It was selfish, but healthy. I also began to see that this was exactly what my Higher Power wanted me to do. Learning to care was the spark that would light a flame that would eventually lead me to learning how to care for others. Do I take care of myself physically, emotionally and spiritually?

Meditations for the Heart

"God don't make junk!" I'm not sure where I first saw these words, but I do remember when I first realized that these words applied to me. God made me who I am for a reason. He did not make me an addict or an alcoholic; this happened for other reasons. But He did make me for something. It was not to be on the bottom of the junk pile. In learning to live again, I needed to see my life though my Higher Power's eyes. I began to see that God's plans for me were much better than the plans I had for myself. All I needed to do was allow God to work His Spirit into my life. A seed of caring was planted, and I was given tools to nurture this seed. So I worked the garden, and God provided both the rain and sunshine to help this seed of self-care take root and grow. Do I see that God wants me to care for myself?

Petitions to my Higher Power
God,

I pray that I may let Your Spirit lead my life. I am so grateful for the care that You have given to me. It has helped me to see that I am not junk. Let me work diligently in the garden to nurture this seed of self-care. Help me understand that both Your sunshine and rain are needed to help this seed grow. Let me use the tools I have been provided to grow the wonderful garden of my life.

Amen.

∗　∗　∗

Wisdom for Today   Apr 5
Honesty was the next big hurdle for me. If I was going to change my character defects, I needed to adopt a manner of living that demanded rigorous honesty. The big problem was that I had no idea how to do this. I knew how to be sort-a, kind-a, maybe honest, but not rigorously honest. I began to read the stories of other addicts and alcoholics and saw that I was not alone. I talked about it in meetings and with my sponsor. I prayed that God would give me the courage to become honest. I knew I had to start somewhere, but where? Then one night as I sat in a meeting, I looked up and saw the slogans posted on the wall. I read the slogans one at a time. The answer I was looking for was right in front of me -"First Things First."

The place I had to start was by getting rigorously honest about my drinking and using. This meant that I could no longer glorify my drinking and drugging escapades. It also meant that I could no longer minimize the severity of my problem. I had to tell the truth, even if it was ugly. You see, as long as I could glorify my drinking and using, I could show off. If I minimized, I could keep hiding. The truth was not a pretty picture. I was a drunk. I was a dope fiend. I had all kinds of consequences directly and indirectly related to my addiction. I was powerless and unmanageable. So I began the process of telling the truth. I told my sponsor. I talked in meetings. Tears flowed from my eyes as I faced the truth, but I learned the saying was correct – "The truth shall set you free." Slowly I began to apply this principle to other areas of my life. I learned that I needed to do this in all areas of my life except when to do so would injure others. Have I begun the painful journey to honesty?

Meditation of the Heart

The first quality of greatness is service! I have a model of greatness that I interact with all the time. The AA Big Book says it best - *"that one is God; may you find Him now."* (*Alcoholics Anonymous,* Fourth Edition Page 59) I believe that God is the greatest of all servants. My Higher Power is always ready to listen and always ready to guide me through the storm. He willingly gives me His strength in all my endeavors. This is a free gift, but we have to ask for it. I also see this model of service at every meeting I attend, because God works in and through people. In order to achieve this greatness, we must become humble, accepting ourselves for whom and what we are. In this mindset of humility I reach out to offer a helping hand to others in need. I want this hand to be there for others just as it was there for me. Service work has many different faces. It is the backbone of our program, whether it is helping to set up before a meeting or going on a Twelve Step call. It does not matter what type of service we do, just that we do it. Am I willing to serve others in the program?

Petitions to my Higher Power

God,

Help me to face the world honestly and to face my own demons. Give me the courage needed for this day. Help me to cooperate in the acts of service that I am asked to do. Let me seek out these opportunities, and lead me to be useful and caring toward my fellowman.

Amen.

* * * *

Wisdom for Today   Apr 6

It is easy to get wrapped up in an attitude of self-depreciation. When we first enter recovery, it is easy to see all the negatives in our lives. As an addict or alcoholic it is easy to put ourselves down and beat ourselves up. The all or nothing attitude prevents us from seeing all the wonderful and good things that are also a part of who we are. If we see no good in ourselves, we cannot recognize the strengths that God has already given to us.

These gifts are a part of who we are. I can look back and see how hard I was on myself. I abused and battered myself with self-hatred. Then one day my sponsor asked me, "Does God make junk?" I had to realize that indeed, God had given me many gifts. I had to recognize that I had value. Do I value myself?

Meditations for the Heart

The more I looked at myself, the more I realized that I truly was a complex individual. There were the good, the bad and the ugly aspects to who I was. I needed to gain balance in seeing myself. When all I did was focus on the negative aspects of my being, I felt hopeless. I considered myself to be worthless. When I gained balance in my self-perception, I began to see many strengths that I could build on. I also began to find the courage to change the things I could. Do I have balance in how I view myself?

Petitions to my Higher Power

God,

Today help me gain a healthier perspective of myself. Let me recognize all the good that is in me. Let me see the gifts You provide. Give me courage to change the things I need to change.

Amen

* * * *

Wisdom for Today   Apr 7

When I was active in my addiction to alcohol and drugs, one thing I did not possess was the ability to be rational. I would avoid making decisions all the time (which strangely enough is a decision in and of itself), because I really had no clue about how to make a decision. Most of my actions were impulsive, without thought and made in reaction to an event or emotional response or in defensiveness. Being rational was something I just did not comprehend. Often times I lived by the motto, "If it feels good, do it." And often times as I lived this way, I really put others or myself at risk. Even when it came to making decisions about when or what to use to get high, I really wasn't making these decisions. My disease was making them for me.

Even early in the recovery process, I struggled with making decisions. I always seemed to leave a door open - "just in case." Even though I said I wanted to stop my using, I repeatedly relapsed, felt guilty and ashamed, would stop again and then start all over again. I was still on the merry-go-round of denial. It was not until I ruled out all my options, closed all the doors, got rid of all the excuses and made a decision to stop that I was able to really accept my powerlessness. In recovery I had to learn how to make rational decisions. It was rational to do that which was healthy. And so I began the journey toward becoming rational. It was rational to do things God's way rather than my way. My way didn't work. Many times I have had to look for rational answers to the problems of life, and each time I learn more. Have I started to be more rational?

99

Meditations for the Heart

The last line of the Serenity Prayer ends with, "and the wisdom to know the difference." But what is this thing called wisdom, and where do I find it? I was convinced early on in recovery that when someone would say the slogan, "Keep it simple, stupid," that I was indeed the stupid one they were talking about. Looking back, there was some truth to that; but the reality was that I had a lot of "smarts," just the wrong kind. I had street smarts but lacked commonsense. I behaved in foolish ways and did not possess the wisdom I needed. So I began to study and do research. I studied the program literature. I listened intently to others at meetings. They were the winners, and they had wisdom I did not have. I spent long hours doing "homework" with my sponsor. Little by little I began to pick up bits and pieces of wisdom that I could trust. Today I am not so "stupid" anymore, but I am wise enough to know that I can get that way again if I quit studying and researching what I need to do in ongoing recovery? Am I working to gain wisdom in the program?

Petitions to my Higher Power

God,

I have learned that wisdom can be gained if I am willing to do the footwork. I also know that true wisdom only comes from You, so continue to lead me to the places where I can gain the wisdom You want me to have. Help me to seek out the winners and learn from them the wisdom of a healthy life in recovery. As I walk through this day, help me to make rational decisions, closing the doors on irrational choices.

Amen.

* * * *

Wisdom for Today   Apr 8

Early in my recovery process I had to learn some hard lessons. One of the more difficult lessons was acceptance. It was not hard to accept the fact that I was an addict and alcoholic. It was hard learning to accept everything else. There was plenty of evidence that I could not control my use of alcohol or drugs. There was plenty of evidence that it had messed up my life. Accepting my addiction was easy. Learning to accept all the demands of recovery was another story. Learning to accept that I could no longer run the show was not going to be easy. I think surrender is hard for us all.

But what was really hard to accept was learning to accept others and myself. I had spent years acting like I owned the world. I took what I wanted.

I did what I wanted. I also had spent years feeling like I was the lowest form of slime on the bottom of the ocean. In recovery I had to learn how to accept myself for whom and what I was. I had to own all of me - the good, the bad and the ugly. There was an awful lot that I wanted to stay in denial about, but recovery would not let me do this. In order to accept myself, I would need to forgive myself for all the wrongs I had done. I also would have to stop acting like I was better than others or worse than others. I had to admit that I am just one drink away from a drunk, one fix away from getting wasted. I was no different than all the other drunks, junkies, cokers and freaks at the meetings. I was no better and no worse, just like others. Am I being accepting of others and myself?

Meditations of the Heart

Learning to accept one's own self is not an easy process in recovery. However, when you look at yourself through God's eyes, it becomes much easier. After all, being pulled from the pit of despair and insanity, God must have His reasons for that. God must see something in me that I could not see in myself. He must see that I fit into His plan somehow. If God sees this in me, who am I to deny what He sees? The really difficult part is holding onto that vision of what God sees. It is so easy to get wrapped up in the hustle and bustle of life and forget about God's vision for me. This is why I take time each morning to focus on God's plan for me. This is why it is important to seek His direction, so that I may hold onto His vision for me. What do I see when I look in God's mirror?

Petitions for the Heart

God,

Sometimes I try to be something or someone I am not. Sometimes I lose sight of Your will for me, yet You continue to guide me back to the path on which I am supposed to be. Certainly Your vision of me is not something that I easily comprehend. Help me to see glimpses of Your vision. Help me to see that I am worthwhile.

Amen.

* * * *

Wisdom for Today   Apr 9

Fear continued to interfere with my life even early in my recovery. This was not something that just disappeared when I stopped using. I needed to change this, and it meant that I had to discover something called courage. There was a problem though. I thought I didn't have any; or if I did, I certainly didn't know where to find it. Where would I find this, "Courage to change the things I can?" I had no idea. So I went to my sponsor and asked him, and I went to meetings and asked people there. I heard many different answers. I wasn't getting the easy answer I wanted. I was hoping it would happen if I did something, maybe if I worked the right step or said the right prayer. No such luck! Courage was not that easy.

Then one night I went to a meeting and blurted out the question, "What is courage?" There was this old-timer sitting across the room, who cleared his throat and said, "It is when you become willing to do something even though you are scared." At last! An answer that made sense! Courage was about willingness, not bravery or fearlessness. I could become willing to make the changes I needed to make. I knew that my Higher Power would help me. I knew that my sponsor and the fellowship would help me. Yes, I was scared to make the changes I needed to make - giving up people, places and things. I could even become willing to change my attitudes, behaviors and beliefs. I was scared to death of some of these changes but became willing to change anyway. I discovered the courage I needed already existed inside of me. I just had to find it. I also believe that this courage is a gift from none other than my Higher Power. Do I believe that I already have the courage I need inside of me?

Meditations for the Heart

Sometimes courage is needed immediately, and at other times much struggle must be given to find the willingness in the face of fear. One thing I learned quickly was that courage was an act of the heart. I could not think my way into courage. This was a problem, because the heart is filled with desire. Sometimes my heart wanted to run and hide from the truth or from need to change. Sometimes my heart desired to be lazy. And at other times it desired to avoid, manipulate or con my way out of the need for change. I do not know how to make the heart desire to be courageous. All I can say is that it becomes much easier knowing and trusting that God is right there with me. So, when I feel fear in my heart, I know it is time to talk to my Higher Power. Sometimes I have to talk to Him quickly to find the courage needed in the moment. Other times I must talk to Him often to find the courage to make it through the struggle. I have also learned that it is important not to give up, because often the courage comes when I feel the weakest. Do I know where to turn when I need to find courage?

Petitions to my Higher Power
God,

Sometimes I feel like my heart is all messed up. There are so many different messages I get because of my unhealthy desires. Help me this day to

seek after that which I know to be healthy, and give to me the courage I need along the way. Let me be watchful for the traps of the heart that can lead me backwards. Guide my steps with wisdom.
Amen.

* * * *

Wisdom for Today   Apr 10

Another quality of character that seemed to disappear with my addiction was the ability to trust. With increasing fear and doubt as my constant companions, I found it impossible to trust anyone or anything. It got to the point where I could not even trust drugs or alcohol to take me away from my misery. I stopped drinking and using, but my ability to trust had not returned. How was I supposed to trust a bunch of drunks to help me get clean and sober? And as for a Higher Power, my relationship with God was far in the past; I had no idea how to rekindle this relationship. Most of all I could no longer trust myself.

Trust was not easy to rebuild. The thought of taking off the mask that I wore was so frightening that I could not imagine living without it. Then one day in desperation, sitting alone in my room with tears streaming down my face, I cried, "God, help me!" To my surprise He did. I'm not even sure when I realized that I was being helped, and I'm not sure it really mattered. Like peeling layers of an onion away, one by one I let my defenses fall by the wayside. I began to open up, and I continued to ask for help. Soon I could see that that bunch of drunks really had my best interests at heart. I was being shown the way, not just to sobriety, but also to a new way of living. As I followed the suggestions of others, I also found increasing happiness. I even found that I could begin to trust myself again, because I was no longer out to destroy myself. Am I becoming more trusting?

Meditations for the Heart

Prayer is a way to communicate with my Higher Power. Yet as I walk through the day, I am often confronted with so many different things that it is easy to loose sight of keeping God in the center of my life. In recovery I find that the word serenity is a slippery thing. Sometimes I tease and say that I have experienced at least 16 seconds of serenity in my recovery and not all at once. Sadly this is not too far from accurate. I allow the material world to take center stage too often. However, when I am able to keep the spiritual world on center stage, I find that I have much more peace of mind and serenity.

As I have walked on this path called recovery, I have learned that practice does not make things perfect, but practice does allow for progress. So prayer is something I need to practice. My sponsor suggested I try using the Dr. Pepper method of practice. I looked puzzled, and he said, "On the old bottles of Dr. Pepper, you would see the numbers 10, 2, and 4." This was a suggestion of the times during the day to drink a bottle of Dr. Pepper. A marketing scheme turned sideways to help alcoholics and addicts! So I began to pray at 10, 2, and 4. I found that this practice helped and progress followed. So did more and more periods of serenity. Do I practice to improve my communication with my Higher Power?

Petitions to my Higher Power
God,

Help me this day to keep You central in my life. Let me not be distracted by the material world, but keep me focused on my spiritual life. Let me continue to risk trusting those who have walked this path before me. Most of all let me never stop trusting You.
Amen.

* * * *

Wisdom for Today   Apr 11
Another defect of character that I had to watch out for was inequality -- thinking that I was better than others or worse than others. Closely related was grandiosity, pretending that I was king of the world and all-powerful, in many ways pretending that I was god. This grandiosity also made me think that other people owed me. When I was actively drinking and using, I felt as if others should give me whatever I wanted. If I turned them on, I acted like I owned these individuals. This was particularly true of the women I dated. But even with my best using buddies, if I turned them on, I would act like I was king. I expected something in return. Even early in recovery I found myself judging others, looking for their faults, so that I could feel better about myself.

On the other hand there was shame, an attitude about myself that told me that I was a damaged product. I was less than others. Shame was pervasive in my belief system and had me convinced that I was a real loser. I was not worthy of anyone's care or concern. This was particularly true in my relationship with God. How could a Higher Power possibly care about someone as worthless as I was? In recovery it became necessary to learn about equality, that I was not better and no worse than anyone else. I was just like everyone else. I was human, capable of great mistakes, capable of great success. Regardless of success or failure, I was still a worthwhile human being. I needed to change my belief system and see that God cared about me not because I was worthy, but simply because He chooses to care about me - the good, the bad and the ugly. Am I making progress with equality?

Meditations for the Heart

The program is a fellowship of hope. This is not a hope that is overly optimistic and looks at the world through rose-colored glasses. It also is not a hope that is pessimistic that is doomed to fail. It is a fellowship of hope that is real and genuine. Ask those individuals who are making it about hope, and they respond, "Hope is the free gift of God that comes through surrender." It is not the profound success that people have in the program that gives us hope, nor is it the failures we experience that makes us turn to this hope. Hope is simply a free gift we receive that is most definitely real. Hope fills our hearts and strengthens us for the new day. Hope fills our hearts and brings both comfort and serenity. Hope brings security, and hope allows for each new breath. This is not something we receive in isolation, but it is given to us freely through our participation in the program. Have I found this gift called hope?

Petitions to my Higher Power

God,

Each day I am presented with the temptation to see myself as better than others or worse than others. Help me this day to fight this temptation and to see myself as You see me, for I know that You see me as Your child, equal and worthy. Let me grab onto this thing called hope and not let go, for in You and in following Your will I am given this gift - not because of my success or my failure, but simply because You choose to give this to me freely.

Amen.

* * * *

Wisdom for Today   Apr 12

Some people say there aren't any heroes anymore, but I know this is just not the case. Anyone who is engaged in battle and fights with courage certainly is a hero. I meet heroes all the time at meetings. These are the people who have fought the good fight against the disease of addiction. They all have demonstrated courage under fire, and all have come out of the battle a changed person. I say this because, when I first met these people, I thought they were just a bunch of drunks. But as I began to know these people, I was surprised to find them reaching out to me. They taught me the ways of recovery quite unselfishly. They had been through exactly what I had been through. They were more unselfish than I ever was.

As I spent time with these people, I began to think about myself less and a little more about other people. I began to share the things I had been taught with others. More and more often I was confronted with parts of my life that were still a mess. These same people continued to teach me all that they knew. I began to realize that I did not have to rely on myself to get clean and sober. I began to realize that through these people, I gained strength. These people continue to act in unselfish and heroic ways. They continue to teach, and I continue to learn. Am I now depending more on others and less on myself?

Meditations for the Heart

I remember the first time someone came up to me after a meeting and said, "I want to thank you for what you had to say tonight. It really hit home." I can't for the life of me remember what I had said, but I do remember looking into the eyes of the person who said this to me. Something about that look told me that I had honestly touched that individual in some way. I also remember going up to my sponsor and telling him. He said, "Now you finally understand service work." I guess I was really confused because I had always thought that setting up before a meeting or cleaning up afterwards was service work. So I asked my sponsor what he meant, and he smiled and said, "You see, serving others is about unselfishly sharing your experience, strength and hope." I thought about this for a long time. It made me more eager to share openly at meetings. There was so much so many different individuals had taught me, that I realized I needed to give back to the program and the people who had helped me so much. Do I give back what I have been given?

Petitions to my Higher Power

God,

Thank You for the many heroes You have placed in my life. They have made my walk along this path of recovery so much easier. I know now that it is You who gave them the words to say that have so impacted my life. I pray this day that You guide my words so that I may give back what I have been given. Amen.

✳ ✳ ✳ ✳

Wisdom for Today   Apr 13

Sometimes people ask me why they should go to meetings, and I respond, "Because you are not unique." I think this surprises them, but the truth is that Twelve Step programs work better than anything else out there. I should know. I think I tried just about everything else. I don't pretend to know what the magic is, but there is something about getting away from the self-centeredness, participating in the fellowship and relying on a Higher Power that really works. I suffered from terminal uniqueness for a long time, believing that I indeed needed a unique approach to recovery. None of them worked for me until I got into the program.

Now that I have been attending meetings for a while, I truly understand what they mean when they say, "We all traveled by many roads to arrive in this spot." Each of us indeed came to the program by our own path, yet each of us arrived at the same door. Not everyone chooses to walk through that door. I have seen many people arrive at this same door, two, three or four times, only to walk away. Some of them will get another chance, and others will never make it back. Do I still believe that I can do it on my own?

Meditations for the Heart

As for uniqueness, there is some truth in this. We all have our own individual personalities. Each of us has our own story. What is truly amazing is that God can speak to us all in a language we understand. I have watched as God turned my life around, unraveling the problems and straightening out my path. I have watched as others come into the program, each with a set of uniquely human problems. If they stick with it, God talks to them in a language they understand; and it works for them. This is a part of the miracle that is God. With such incredible diversity of peoples attending meetings, each with their own unique set of circumstances, it still works. God is the great interpreter for each of us. He makes it possible for us to use these tools and teaches us about a program of recovery. Do I see that God, as I understand Him, means that I will understand Him?

Petitions to my Higher Power

God,

In this day I know that You will interpret life in a way that makes it possible for me to understand. I know I have unique problems, and I am not like everyone else, but I also know that You have led me to a common meeting place to find the answers I need. Keep me in a right relationship with You, and help me to understand others so that I may help them, just as You have helped me.

Amen.

* * * *

107

None of us is perfect. In fact, we all have personality flaws. This is the case with me. I certainly had all kinds of reasons that I sought after the high that alcohol and drugs provided for me. Each of us had our own reasons to get messed up. Perhaps we were looking for a way to escape from the realities of our lives. For some of us it is that terrible feeling inside that we just aren't any good. Maybe it was because we didn't know how to make friends or were lonely. I know I had many conflicts inside, and I could not seem to find a way to fit in. Even when I was attempting to fit in, I still felt like I was on the outside. My drinking and drugging was a symptom of my personality flaws, and it was also the cause of some of these defects of character.

I stopped using all the time; my problem was that I couldn't find a way to stay sober. I couldn't until I found a way to deal with all the personality flaws that led me to drink and use. Simple abstinence was not the answer. It didn't solve anything. I had to find a new way of living. I had to find a new me. Recovery is about reshaping our lives. It is about finding our way along the path of recovery with all its twists and turns, bumps and bends. It is about change and changing some more. I'm not there yet, but I am happy with where God has led me thus far. Do I see that I am the one who needs to change?

Meditations for the Heart

Somewhere early in my recovery I realized that a seed had been planted in my life. A new life was growing inside of me. As that seed sprouted and grew, I continued to work the soil and see that the seed was nourished. I began to see wonderful changes occurring. I still needed to work the soil to keep the weeds from choking away this new life inside of me. I know that someday I will see the flower of this seed if I keep using the tools I have been given. But all I need worry about is today, and I really don't even have to worry about that anymore. I trust that God will take care of today for me if I let Him. Still sometimes I wonder, "Where did this seed come from in the first place? I did not plant it in my life." For me, I have come to believe that this seed was planted the moment I really worked Step Three. I did not realize it at the time, but God went to work right away. Do I value the seed that is planted in my life?

Petitions to my Higher Power
God,

Each day the seed in my life receives Your blessing. Sometimes this is in the form of sunshine, and at other times it is in the form of rain. Help me to realize that even when the thunderstorms of life occur, You are there to protect me and help me keep growing. Help me to grow into the flower you want me to be and stand with my brothers and sisters in recovery in the garden of life.

Amen.

* * * *

All those personality flaws and character defects do not need to last forever. I have seen many addicts and alcoholics find a way to solve these problems. I have certainly seen healing and change in my life. This is a process that takes time, and some of these characteristics are more resistant to change than others. I wasn't really sure just how to go about this change, but slowly over time three things occurred that brought about tremendous change in my life. What are these three things that happened you might ask. Well, let me see if I can describe the process and then tell you what happened.

First of all, I pulled myself together with a lot of help from my friends in the program. I had to be able to think straight in order to make the changes I needed to make. Where this change started was with personal honesty. I had to get honest with myself and with others. Not an easy process, but necessary if I was ever going to reclaim what I had lost - personal integrity! The second thing that occurred with the return of personal integrity was that I needed honestly to face my problems. I could no longer run from the truth. This is where the process of the Step Four inventory was so helpful. For the first time in a long time I could see where I really stood. This honest self-assessment showed me that I had strengths as well as weaknesses. Finally I could face the facts and not make excuses anymore for my behavior. This last step in the process brought me to a place of personal responsibility. Personal integrity, honest self-assessment, and personal responsibility were the things that recovery provided me and enabled changes to occur. Am I working to get these three gifts of recovery?

Meditations for the Heart

Why me? This is a question I have asked myself many times. I asked this when I was in trouble with my addiction to alcohol and drugs. I asked this question again early in recovery. Why me? Why did I have to get this disease? No one came to my school when I was growing up and asked me if I wanted to be an addict or an alcoholic when I grew up. I didn't volunteer for this disease saying, "Oh, please, I want to be a drunk." I asked the question again when I looked at all my character flaws and defects. I mean, wasn't it bad enough that I got this illness? Why did I have to suffer with these problems, too? After working with the steps for a while and finding a new sense of hope, I still asked the question, Why me? Why was I chosen to get a chance in recovery? Funny how the question changes with time! This in part is why the spiritual aspects of the program are so important. It allows God the opportunity to change the question. Do I see that I have been chosen and given a chance that many other addicts and alcoholics never get?

Petitions to my Higher Power
God,
    The path of recovery that You lead me on is not always easy. Many of the changes are hard. Still I know and trust that this is the right path and You will lead me each step of the way. Help me to work through all the issues I need to. Let me make needed changes, and grant me wisdom and courage along the way.
Amen.

* * * *

Wisdom for Today   *Apr 16*
    "Made a searching and fearless moral inventory." (*Alcoholics Anonymous,* Fourth Edition Page 59) When I got to the Fourth Step and read these words, I felt lost. I really didn't know where to begin or how to go about it; but being the good addict I was, I started by looking for the easier, softer way. I thought to myself, "What's so hard about admitting I'm a screw up?" I thought that was all there was to it, but my sponsor told me otherwise. He began to explain the process to me, and how I would need to write out this inventory. He told me that I would have to turn over every rock and see if there was any dirt under it. He told me there were many different Fourth Step guides, but the process was essentially the same. Suddenly I was no longer lost, but I was scared. I knew there was a lot of dirt under all those rocks.
    My sponsor helped me decide on which Fourth Step guide I would use; and then he suggested I spend a week in prayer asking for courage, strength and guidance before I began to write out this inventory. I was glad that my sponsor knew me so well. So I began the process of getting ready to complete this inventory. Uncovering all that I wished to keep hidden was not easy. Honestly facing all that I had done while drinking and drugging was very difficult, yet at the same time it was healing. When I got into this written inventory I was surprised to see some patterns of behavior, beliefs and errors in judgment. I could see how I hurt others and myself, all the anger and rage

that I was sitting on and all the losses. It was not a pretty picture. Do I see that I am only as sick as my secrets?

Meditations for the Heart
In reality I didn't want to do this inventory, but I knew that it needed to be done. Everything inside of me wanted nothing to do with this process. However, it was not up to me to decide this. I had to follow what my Higher Power's will directed me to do. Just like a child who hasn't cleaned his room and is made to clean it up, I knew my Higher Power expected me to clean house. In that week before I began to work on this inventory, I also found that my Higher Power would give me what I needed to help me through the process. It continues to amaze me that I rarely get what I want, but always get what I need. What surprised me even more was how I felt when I turned around and saw that my room was all picked up. Do I believe that my Higher Power will give me what I need?

Petitions to my Higher Power
God,
Taking inventory is not an easy process and is something that I would prefer not to do. Nobody likes to clean up a mess, especially me. Still I know that this is what You want me to do. So I ask You this day to remove any fear I may have. I ask You to help me to uncover all the secrets that keep me sick. Give me courage so that I might be responsible and clean every room, even the closets in my house.
Amen.

* * * *

Wisdom for Today   Apr 17
I once heard a story of a man who was down on his hands and knees in the grass outside of his house. A neighbor walked by and asked him what he was doing. The man replied, "Searching for my keys." So the neighbor got down on his hands and knees and helped the man search for the keys. After several minutes the neighbor asked, "Are you sure this is where you dropped your keys?" The man replied, "No, I lost them in the house." The neighbor looking shocked said, "Then why are we looking for them out here?" The man looked up and stated, "Because the light is better out here."

The man was correct. The light was better, but there was no way he would find his keys. In the Fourth Step we are asked to be searching. We have two choices. We can look for things in places where we have no chance of finding what we are looking for, or we can go back inside our house and turn the lights on. It is easy to complete Step Four if we look in all the wrong places; it is really more difficult to look and search where we need to look. I know that the best way is to look back over our past and examine our behavior, our motives, and look at the emotions that prompted our responses. I know it is hard to clean house, especially the closets that we keep our secrets in, yet this is what we need to do if we are to examine our moral thinking and behavior. Am I really willing to clean house and be searching?

Meditations for the Heart

God is our spotlight and shines brightly for us when we do this inventory. It is hard to look for things in the dark because we all have a tendency to fear what lurks or hides in the dark. Most of us have experienced this fear of the dark at some point in our life. The heart can play all kinds of tricks on us when we are in the dark; yet when the light is turned on, the fear disappears. The moment the light is turned on we feel reassured and safe. The same is true when we use God as our spotlight when doing this inventory. I know this does not make it easier to look at the dirt in our lives, but it does allow us to look at it and not be frightened or overwhelmed. Much of my Fourth Step work was very difficult and unpleasant, yet with God as my spotlight I was not afraid. Do I know that I need to carry the spotlight of God with me when I do my Fourth Step?

Petitions to my Higher Power

God,

There is so much darkness in my life as an addict and alcoholic. Opening up the closets and seeing the mess inside and dirt that has accumulated over the years is not pleasant. Help me by shining brightly for me as I go about the task of cleaning house. Let me not be afraid of shining Your light on my life.

Amen.

* * * *

Wisdom for Today   Apr 18

"A searching and fearless moral inventory..." (Alcoholics Anonymous, Fourth Edition Page 59) These are the instructions given us in Step Four, but that word "moral" troubled me. Just what was meant by this word? I guess I struggled with the meaning of this word because I had never thought of myself as moral. In fact, I needed to look up the meaning of this word in a dictionary because I had no concept of what was meant by moral. What I discovered was that morals are guiding principles of right and wrong. In my active addiction I guess I just didn't care if I was moral or not. What this step was asking me to look at was what was right and what was wrong with the principles of my life.

Finding what was wrong was going to be easy because there was so much wrong. The principle that guided my life in addiction was that of self-centeredness. Everything was about me. I did everything the way I wanted. It didn't matter whom I stepped on or how I accomplished the task of self-pleasure. I turned my life over to the care of alcohol and drugs. I watched them slowly destroy anything of value in my life. At least that is what I thought, but this step did not allow me to stop there. I also had to look for what was right in my life. This was the hard part, I judged myself so severely. But in searching through the rubble of my life, I did find that I indeed had some redeeming qualities. There was good in me after all. I did do some things right. Buried deep inside was another principle that guided me to do that which was right. It was buried so deep I had a hard time finding it. I had lost touch with the force in my life that guided my conscience to do what was good and right. Am I looking for both the right and wrong in my life?

Meditations for the Heart

Looking back at my life, it is easy to see that God was always there for me. He managed to protect me from the insanity of my illness and did not allow me totally to destroy my life. Even though there were times that I should have been dead, God kept me breathing. He saw the good that was buried under the rubble and saw in me what I could not see in myself. It was an act of grace that this occurred. I did nothing to deserve this grace, yet I was given another chance. Today I try to seek after God's will for me. I know this is what is right for me; and it is the principle I use to guide my decisions, my behavior, and my desires. I am nowhere near perfect and still fall on my face at times. The good news is that God is still there to pick me up and redirect me. Recovery is not about being perfect, but about the pursuit of progress. What are the principles that I am using to guide my life today?

Petitions to my Higher Power

God,

Today I do have a sense of what is right and what is wrong. Help me to develop my moral convictions to seek after Your will for me. Provide me with the power to carry out Your will. Let me seek out that which is healthy for me physically, emotionally and spiritually as I walk through this day.

Amen.

* * * *

One thing that surprised me with regards to completing my Fourth Step was the fact that I strengthened my faith. In Step Three, I had made a decision to turn my will and my life over to the care of God, as I understood Him. I trusted and had faith that my Higher Power would be able to walk me through the process of completing an inventory of myself. I did not expect that this process would actually strengthen my faith in God. I am certain that without my Higher Power leading me through the process, my fears would have taken over; and I would have been only willing to clean house superficially.

As a child I loved to climb trees. I would climb higher and higher until the branches were too thin to support my weight. Each time I would go higher in the tree, I trusted that the branches would support me, but eventually I would reach a point when I was unsure if the next branch would hold me. I found the opposite was true in doing my Fourth Step. It was as if the tree branches never got thinner. In fact the deeper I got into uncovering the truth, the more stable the branches became. I am not saying it was easy to uncover some of the secrets in my life, I just knew I was safe in doing so. Do I have faith that God is with me to support me in completing my Fourth Step?

Meditations for the Heart

Early in my recovery process, it was important for me to feel safe. I knew there were places and people I needed to avoid because my safety would be compromised. I also knew there were places and people with whom I could associate because it was safe. Meetings and recovering people helped make me feel safe, at least from the external pressures I felt. As I surrendered my life to the care of my Higher Power and walked through the steps, I found that I began to feel safe on the inside as well. This did not mean that I was immune to relapse or that I had been cured. It just meant that as long as I did what God wanted for me, my safety would not be compromised. It is important to find safety in the recovery process, but even more important to keep it once it is found. Do I seek safety in meetings and with others in recovery? Do I seek safety in a spiritual way?

Petitions to my Higher Power

God,

Thank You for keeping me safe as I walk through the steps. I know that the support I receive from others is a gift from You. Thank You for leading me to these people. You have taken me from a place of insecurity to a place of safety. Let me trust that as long as I walk with You, I will remain safe. Amen.

* * * *

Wisdom for Today *Apr 20*

In the world of addiction I became a slave. I sold my own soul into captivity. There I was, chained up in the bowels of a ship, journeying into the world of self-destruction. Day after day passed and I continued to live in bondage to my alcohol and drugs. I was not alone, for there were other slaves there in the belly of the ship. I watched as one after another was beaten. I, too, was beaten. I watched, and I saw the destruction of this disease take away all that was important to me. I watched as others died. I feared for my own life.

I look back and am amazed that somehow I was freed. The chains of addiction were loosened, and I was able to get a second chance in life. There is no doubt that I was scarred by the trauma of slavery. Just because I was freed did not mean that I was able to function normally. It would take some time for that to occur. The scars of my disease, those character defects, needed time to heal; but like all serious scars, a mark remains. I no longer bleed dishonesty, grandiosity, fear, unrealistic expectations, carelessness or self-centeredness. But each of these personality flaws is still a part of me, just like the marks left by a serious wound. So, I need to be on watch to make sure that these defects do not begin to ooze again. If and when they do, I must again do the things necessary to stop these defects from infecting my life again. I must ask for help from God and from my friends in recovery again and again to find the needed healing. Do I watch for my character defects to re-emerge?

Meditations for the Heart

Standing watch requires self-discipline. I need to be on guard and not fall asleep on my watch. I cannot afford to fall prey to a sneak attack or yield one point of what I have gained. Hatred, resentment, pride, lust, jealousy are but a few of the armies that can attack my camp. I need to remain a good soldier with self-discipline to stay alert. When I do see an attacker, I must sound the alarm by telling on my disease. By telling on my disease and by trusting my army for help, I can defeat any attacker. I cannot fight these battles on my own. I need help from my Higher Power and my support system. I must talk with my sponsor and at meetings and in prayer to find the best method to defeat these attackers. Am I working at self-discipline and remaining alert?

Petitions to my Higher Power

God,

Today I will stand watch for my character defects that come back to attack me again. Help me to be a good soldier with self-discipline and to remain alert. Let me sound the alarm if it is needed, and prevent me from selling my soul back into slavery.

Amen.

∗   ∗   ∗   ∗

Wisdom for Today *Apr 21*

Much like the slaves that were brought over to this country in the belly of a ship, when I walked into the doors of the Twelve Step program, I felt like I was in a different world. I was confused and scared. My brain was still cloudy from my last binge, and I didn't know what to expect. However, unlike the slaves when I got off the boat, I was free. This new freedom terrified me. I really didn't know what to expect, and I didn't really believe that I was free. I learned quickly though that with freedom also came responsibility. There was much work to be done if I was to survive in this new world. I had to learn a new language, and I had to figure out what the rules were. Fortunately these rules were well established and written out.

At the beginning of that first meeting, I heard words being read from a book, "*Rarely have we seen a person fail, who has thoroughly followed our path.*" (*Alcoholics Anonymous,* Fourth Edition Page 58) Where was this path and would the journey be difficult? I had no idea. I just knew it had to be better than being chained up in that slave ship of addiction. Each step I took along the way was not easy, just simple. I mean it was not complicated. First, I had to admit that I had been a slave to addiction and didn't know how to live in freedom. Then I had to believe that the path indeed leads to a better place, a place where my brain would no longer be cloudy; and I would be able to live in freedom responsibly. Next I had to agree to stick close to the guide who would lead the way and to agree to follow His every instruction if I wanted to get to this better place safely. This path was not easy, and I even saw some people turn around and go back to the ship wanting to be back in the chains, because it was familiar and known. Do I want to go back, or am I willing to continue the journey?

Meditations for the Heart

Arriving at Step Four, the path looked treacherous. I was not sure I wanted to continue, and I knew I didn't want to go back. I looked to my guide for help. He told me to move slowly along this part of the path and to look closely at the pitfalls along the way. I could see farther up the trail that there were others who had successfully made it and negotiated this part of the journey. The look on their faces told me it was not easy, but it was worth it. So I trusted my guide and moved carefully through the difficult path. As I moved through this part of the journey, I learned that all that depressed me, all that I feared and all that I was ashamed of were powerless to harm me as long as I followed my guide. Am I ready to follow my spiritual guide to a better place?

Petitions to my Higher Power
God,

Thank You for being my guide. Grant me courage in the difficult parts of this journey, and let me pass safely through this difficult path. Let me always look forward and not look back. Help me to take each step.
Amen.

* * * *

Wisdom for Today   Apr 22

As I went through the process of completing my Fourth Step, I found my heart very unsettled. A lot of different emotions spun around on the inside. I found myself becoming very angry at this disease and how it had ruined my life. I found myself disgusted with who and what I had become. I found that tears started to flow freely as the sadness of all the losses I had experienced were finally realized. I hurt for my family and what I had done to them. I felt overwhelmed at times by all of these different emotions that surfaced and were frozen deep inside me.

My denial had been enabling me not to look at myself. Now there was an incredible sense of shame that seemed to blanket me. Yet there was this small voice inside of me that said, "Do not be afraid!" As troubling as all this was, I knew that it was stuff I needed not only to face, but also to take ownership of it. Something told me that this was the road I needed to take to find my way out. Looking back, I now understand that my Higher Power was taking care of me in the process. Even though there were many parts of my life that I did not enjoy seeing, I was never given more than I could handle. Most of these unpleasant emotions would have given me every reason to drink or use in the past, but the thought of using never entered my mind. What did enter my mind was a desire to stop the insanity and rebuild my life. Do I understand how important it is to have the support of others in program and faith in my Higher Power, so that I can complete Step Four?

Meditations for the Heart

Pride shuts and locks the door to an open relationship with God. There are two keys that can be used to open this door, both the regular lock and the deadbolt. The first key is humility. When we swallow our pride and admit that we are not God and humbly ask for help and guidance, we turn the first key to unlocking the door. The second key to unlock the deadbolt is obedience. When we choose to follow the directions we are given in recovery and stop insisting that we can do it our way, the key is turned to unlock the door. When we find this humility and become obedient to the will of our Higher Power, the door opens to realizing God's love for us. We find peace, and we find joy in recovery. This spiritual concept is an essential stone in the foundation of recovery, and without a strong foundation our house will not stand. Am I building a solid foundation?

Petitions to My Higher Power
God,

Let me turn to You this day in humility and obedience, asking for direction and guidance. Let me know and experience Your love and joy in recovery. Let me find courage and willingness in my walk with You today. Help me build a solid foundation, so that this house of recovery may stand strong.

Amen.

* * * *

Wisdom for Today   Apr 23

Forgiveness is a difficult spiritual concept; yet it is essential to understand this concept to grasp the full meaning behind Step Five. As a young boy I would attend church each Sunday with my family. I learned of religious practices such as confession and absolution, but I really did not understand this spiritual concept of forgiveness. So here I was years later cloaked in a heavy blanket of shame, walking into a meeting with a recovering pastor to talk about doing my Fifth Step. I was about to tell God all that I had done wrong. I would admit this to myself and to another human being. My heart raced, and I am sure I was sweating even though it was quite cold outside.

How was I to tell God that I had fallen short? How was I to look at this person I was meeting with in the eye? The thought of forgiveness never entered my mind. I walked into the office and felt much like I did when I had been sent to the principal's office or when I stood before the judge. My breathing was heavy, and I stared at the floor. The church secretary told me it would a few minutes. I sat down, but wanted to run. This was when I remembered these words from the Bible, "Fear not." Fear indeed was trying to take control in my life in that moment; and so I took a deep breath and said to my Higher Power, "Walk with me and give me strength." Do I trust that God will indeed give me strength in my journey?

Meditations for the Heart
I wanted very much to be unburdened of that blanket of shame. I wanted to make the world a better place and happier, because I was in it. I wanted very much for the pain to go away, but I had no idea how to make this happen. But all this would change in the hours that followed; for I learned much about the role I had been playing as prosecutor, judge and jury in the coming hours. I would learn much about the concept of forgiveness – a forgiveness that was freely given to me by God and forgiveness I could grant myself. I would learn much about "not shutting the door on the past and not regretting the past." I would learn about wiping the slate clean and getting a fresh start. I gained a new appreciation of the statement, "but for the grace of God." Do I see that admitting my wrongs to God, to me, and another human being is the place that forgiveness begins?

Petitions to my Higher Power
God,
I need Your grace in my life. I know that I cannot earn this; for it a gift – a gift that You provide to me each day anew. It is a gift that indeed wipes the slate clean and gives me a new chance at life! Help me to accept this gift with a humble heart and to treasure what it means for me each and every day. Amen.

* * * *

Wisdom for Today   Apr 24
There is a saying that goes, "All good gifts come to those who wait." Well, waiting was not something that I was very good at; in fact, I was rather impatient. I can remember growing up as a child and being all excited because Christmas or my birthday was just around the corner. I knew that with these special days I would receive gifts. I was so anxious for the time to arrive that I couldn't wait. I was impatient. Between my impatience and anxiety, I would become irritable and often times would pick a fight with my brothers. In early recovery I was not much different. I continued to want what I wanted, and I wanted it right now. I completed my Fourth Step and wanted some instant reward, but there was none. I didn't want to wait.

I found myself clean and sober, yet still anxious and impatient. I had even listed these things in my Fourth Step. Why didn't they just go away? I found myself getting crabby at meetings and even wanting to pick fights with my sponsor. Wasn't it enough that I completed this inventory? I didn't really understand about what I was becoming angry. At a meeting one night, I was sitting there irritated. I was impatient. The topic for the meeting that night was patience. I sat and didn't even want to listen to what was being said. It came to my turn to talk, and I proceeded to tell everyone how bad my day was going. I whined and complained. Then after I had finished talking, an older and much wiser member of the fellowship looked at me and said, "It sounds like God has given you lots of opportunities to practice patience today." I wanted to get up and walk out of the meeting at that point. After the meeting ended, I talked to my sponsor, and he said, "Gifts come in all types of packages. We do not always see the gifts we receive." I thought about it, and he was right. God was giving me the opportunity to work on my defects. Today I am grateful to have been given such a wonderful gift. Do I see that many of the struggles I have are also opportunities and gifts?

Meditations for the Heart

Sometimes I find that it is important to look at things from a different angle to gain perspective. To see things more clearly, I find it helpful sometimes to imagine what the situation looks like from God's perspective. What I have discovered is that each and every need I have is an opportunity for my Higher Power. When I look at things this way, life looks very different. I can look at my needs and admit that often times I am powerless to meet them. I can turn to my Higher Power and ask for help. I then need to have faith that My Higher Power indeed will find a way to satisfy my needs. God then takes advantage of this opportunity. He provides me with ways to meet my needs. These are not always what I would expect them to be. Just as He provided me with opportunities to practice patience to learn more about my impatience, He also provides me with answers, resources and feedback from friends in the program to aid in my learning. Recovery is all about learning to live again. Do I look at things differently now?

Petitions to my Higher Power

God,

Give me wisdom and insight into all the ways that You gift me with opportunities for growth. Help me to take advantage of each of these opportunities, so that I might learn new ways to live life to its fullest. Help me to find things each day for which to be grateful, and help me to give credit where credit is due.

Amen.

* * * *

"Admitted to God, ourselves and to another human being the exact nature of our wrongs." (*Alcoholics Anonymous,* Fourth Edition Page 59) These words in Step Five made my very insides groan. To honestly say out loud the words so carefully written in Step Four and admit to God, myself and someone else who and what I was and what I had done and not done was a task I thought too great. Yet I knew that this step had been written for a reason. Very many that had gone before me had stated that they had found a new freedom in this step. So why was I so petrified by this task? The reality was that shame had me in its grasp. I stood broken and damaged and had no desire to complete this step.

I pondered for many days what the wisdom was behind this step and continued to be paralyzed. I could not even call the person that my sponsor suggested to me to arrange a meeting to discuss doing my Fifth Step. I didn't even want to talk to my sponsor about this. I went to a meeting I normally didn't attend hoping to find a way out. The chair of the meeting went through all of the opening rituals and then introduced the topic for the evening. He said, "Tonight I think we should talk about forgiveness." He went on to talk about his Fifth Step and how it had not only opened his eyes to the work he needed to do about his defects of character, but also how it opened the door to forgiving himself for all the wrongs he had committed. I was astounded. How was it that in this meeting I so rarely attended that this was the topic of the evening? God works in mysterious ways. The longer I stay clean and sober, the more I am convinced that there is no such thing as coincidence. Do I see how God works in and through the program?

Meditations for the Heart

Forgiveness was something I had heard about a lot in church growing up, but it was something that I really didn't understand. It was clear to me that this was a spiritual concept about which I needed to learn more. Perhaps this is why my sponsor had suggested I talk with a recovering pastor to do my Fifth Step. At any rate the next day after this meeting, I made a phone call to schedule a meeting; and indeed in the following weeks I did learn much about this spiritual concept. I also learned why it was not only important but necessary to keep my Higher Power in the center of my life. It was about balance. I had gotten so out of balance spiritually because of my addiction. Now I had to learn about balance. Do I understand the necessity of keeping my Higher Power in the center of my life?

Petitions to my Higher Power

God,

Standing before You has not always been easy. Too often I have wanted to run and hide because of my shame. I understand why it is so important

to keep You in the center of my life. If I do not trust You, whom can I trust? Walk with me this day and give me the willingness I need to live as You want me to live. Guide me each step of the way.
Amen.

∗　∗　∗　∗

Wisdom for Today — Apr 26

While forgiveness does indeed wipe the slate clean, it cannot undo the consequences of our actions. In completing my Fifth Step, I had to accept the fact that my actions while under the influence had certainly hurt a lot of different people including myself. Most of this hurt was not intentional. It simply was a consequence of my disease. When the drugs and alcohol were making my decisions for me, I said and did things I wish I hadn't. Even during the brief periods of time when I was not using, I said and did things of which I was not proud. I would have to pick up the pieces of my brokenness.

I had indeed made a lot of mistakes and wronged many people. My Higher Power knew this. I knew this, and now another person also knew this. It is God who in His grace provides grace and forgiveness. I also needed to learn how to forgive myself. This began with working on accepting me – the good, the bad and the ugly. It also was made possible by accepting that much of what occurred in my life was not by conscious choice. My addiction had made choices for me, choices that I would not have made if I were in my right mind. I also began to do repair work on the damage done. Perhaps what helped me most was to seek permission to forgive myself through prayer and meditation. Self-forgiveness is a process and not an event; it takes time. Have I forgiven myself?

Meditations for the Heart

There is an ancient myth about a bird of fire that rises from the ashes. The Phoenix was given new life. I likewise was given a new life in recovery. If I was going to rise from the ashes of my life, I needed to learn to forgive myself. The days of self-hatred, disgust and shame had to end. These attitudes needed to die. I needed to arise from the ashes of my life with a willingness to be obedient to my Higher Power's will and live a life of service and integrity. While I do not do this perfectly, and none of us can, I do strive for progress. Much like the Phoenix, I have experienced a resurrection and been given a new chance on life. Am I using this new chance on life to serve others and seek integrity in all that I do?

122

Petitions to my Higher Power

God,

Help me this day to seek after Your will and be willing to do that which is the right thing. Let me seek to follow Your direction in all that do. Let me this day find acceptance of who I am, Your forgiven child. Let me reach out to others in humble service.

Amen.

* * * *

Wisdom for Today   *Apr 27*

"At some of these we balked." (*Alcoholics Anonymous,* Fourth Edition Page 58) This line in the AA Big Book certainly described my feelings about doing a Fifth Step. I was like many addicts and alcoholics; I just wanted to find an easier, softer way. I mean after all, God already knew everything I had done wrong. Why did I have to talk to another human being about all the "yuk" in my Fourth Step? I was reluctant to discuss my shortcomings with someone else. I figured that as long as I was clean and sober and pointed my life in a new direction, I really didn't have to talk with anyone else.

But when I got honest with myself about the reason why I was balking about completing this step, it became clearer to me why I indeed needed to follow through. The reality was that I was guilt-ridden, ashamed and afraid. I was depressed. I knew these feelings would not go away by themselves. I also knew enough about the program to know that I probably wasn't the first addict or alcoholic to feel this way. I needed to trust that this step was a part of the process for a reason. I needed to trust that somehow this step would help me. I began to realize my need for others and that I would never get out of the isolation without carrying out this step, nor would I ever be able forever to hide the secrets. I knew the burdens I felt would never be lifted without completing this step. Do I trust the program works to relieve burdens?

Meditations for the Heart

Life certainly has its ups and downs; sometimes it can even spin around. I have learned the only healthy way to deal with this is to stay calm in the storm. Not something I was particularly good at when I was drinking and using! But the spiritual aspects and principles of the program can teach you to find this inner calm. I find that I can find that inner calm best when I spend time, even a few minutes, in quiet communion with my Higher Power. When I walk through the storms of life with this inner calm, I find I can get more accomplished. I find that worry does not enter into the picture. I find it easier to "stay in today." I am no good to others or myself when I get agitated, stressed out, angry or overwhelmed. I need to seek this inner calm in all that I do. Do I seek an inner calmness and things that are true and good for me?

Petitions to my Higher Power

God,

I know that I need to bring my burdens to You. Help me to be free to share these burdens with others also, so that I do not have to shoulder the load by myself. Teach me to seek after an inner calmness and to be true and good in all that I do this day. Give me courage to weather the storms of life, and help me to know that the sunny days of life do follow.

Amen.

* * * *

Wisdom for Today   Apr 28

When I looked at my life and sat down to tell someone else about the exact nature of my wrongs, I saw that there were very few major things that I had done wrong. But the list of little things that I had done wrong seemed endless. It was all these little things that really added up to the nature of my problems. I didn't just tell one lie; there were hundreds of them. Each one, in and of itself, didn't seem so bad; but the accumulated effect had been profound. I wasn't self-centered on just one occasion, nor did I let fear run my life just once. Each and every defect in my character was pervasive. It had been all these little things that had been so damaging.

In the same way, it has not been one huge event that provided me with a spiritual awakening. Lightning did not strike, and there has not been a bright light that suddenly came into my life. It has been all the little things that have really turned my life around. This is not to downplay what I have learned through crisis situations I have faced in recovery, because these tests have provided much learning as well. But it has been the little things – each time I tell the truth, each time I am of service to others, each time I have courage in the face of fear and many other events that have turned my life into something wonderful. Do I live in the moment from decision to decision looking to improve on the little things?

Meditations for the Heart

I used to believe in coincidence; but the longer I stay clean and sober, the more I believe that God has a plan for me. There are literally dozens and dozens of experiences I have had in recovery that I cannot simply write off

124

as coincidence. I have listened to story after story of others in recovery that makes me believe there is a Divine Spirit, who lives in those who are willing to have faith. I personally believe that the evidence of a spiritual existence is all around us. All we need do is open our eyes. Last night I listened to another alcoholic talk of one such burning bush experience. Much had gone awry in his life despite 1-1/2 years of clean time. He finally was ready to give up and walked into a bar to order a drink. He was dumbfounded when he looked and saw the bartender was a member of his home group. He talked with the bartender and chose not to relapse. Do I see evidence of Divine intervention in my life? Do I look for it in what I do every day?

Petitions to my Higher Power
God,

I have never been good at details of life. I am one who enjoys the forest but rarely takes the time to look at an individual tree. Help me to enjoy the beauty in the little things in life. Help me to trust that all of these little things add up to a life with which I can be happy. Help me to look for the artwork You complete each and every day of my life.
Amen.

* * * *

Wisdom for Today   Apr 29
Life is full of surprises. I never know what life has in store for me on any given day. There are days that life is difficult and filled with struggle. There are days that are filled with joy and happiness. There are days when I find fear creeping back into my life. There are days that do not seem special, and others that are turning points for me in my search for serenity. Regardless of what life brings my way, it is important for me to start each day the same way.

Each day when I arise, I take some quiet time to center myself and focus on what God wants me to do. It has proven to be one of the most valuable steps I take to protect my recovery. When I focus on God's will rather than my own will, I remove myself from the equation. What I mean is this: "The journey of my day + my will = potential for, if not, certain trouble," versus, "The journey of my day + God's will = a positive outcome." When I put God's will for me in the equation, I do not need to worry about the surprises life might bring. I know that God will guide me in the right direction and give me what I need to make it through any struggle. Do I still put my will into the equation of life?

Meditations for the Heart

Beginning my day with quiet time also provides me with a daily opportunity to ask for help. That has also been a good habit for me to get into. In accepting my limitations and acknowledging my on-going need for help, I practice humility. My sponsor always told me to practice the principles. For a long time I did not know what he meant, but was afraid to ask. In truth, I was not really afraid to ask, but afraid of the answer I might get. Finally I did ask, and he looked at me and said; "Now I know why they put the last 'S' in the AA acronym, K-I-S-S." It took me a little while to figure out he meant I was being stupid. He went on to say, "There is a big difference between reading a recipe and going out, buying the ingredients, putting them together in the correct measure and baking it. Practice means putting it into action." Do I practice what I need to do each day?

Petitions to my Higher Power

God,

This is a new day, and I do not yet know where the path will lead. Help me this day to start this journey with You by my side. Walk with me, and supply me with Your guidance along the way. Help me to know that You are always near.

Amen.

* * * *

Wisdom for Today   Apr 30

Admitting to God that indeed I had done much wrong in my life was no easy task. I had to get past this concept that God was a punishing God. I had learned this concept growing up. I could not get all those Bible stories out of my head where people were punished for the wrongs they had done. I was fearful that I also would be punished. Then the recovering pastor I was to do my Fifth Step with spoke up. I guess he could see the fear in my eyes. He suggested that we begin with a prayer. I figured fire and brimstone would likely follow. But I was wrong.

The prayer that was spoken was a Third Step prayer. It reminded me that I had made a decision to turn over my will and my life to the "care" of my Higher Power. "Turn it over to His care" – these words rang loudly in my ears as the pastor continued to pray. I am not sure that I heard anything else that he said. All I remember was a period of silence that followed the prayer. I looked up from the floor, took a deep breath and began to speak. Amazingly the words flowed from my mouth as I began to recount my past and what I had learned about myself in completing my Fourth Step. Do I trust that God will show me His care when I need it most?

Meditations for the Heart

In the presence of my Higher Power I can find safety, and I can find security. I used to turn to alcohol and drugs to cover up my insecurity. I never felt comfortable even in my own skin. It seemed as though I was always anxious. Yet in recovery I have discovered a new place to feel secure. I often times imagine myself walking down a path with God at my side. I believe that this is what the journey in recovery is all about. What is even more exciting is that God not only walks beside me, but also behind me and in front of me. He watches over me each step of the way. Have I found a safe place in the presence of God?

Petitions to my Higher Power

God,

I place my life in Your care. I know that You will walk with me on this journey called recovery. Give me courage always to walk with You. Let me seek out Your will for me this day, and grant me the power and strength I need to follow Your will. Let me know true security in and with You.

Amen.

* * * *

Wisdom for Today   May 1

Life is filled with lots of firsts. One thing I have learned in recovery is that my life cannot afford a first drink, pill or fix. I had my first drink already, and I don't want to go back. I don't think I really got to this point in my recovery until after I completed my Fifth Step. As difficult as it was to share my history with another human being, there was something almost magical about getting everything out in the open. It was very freeing. It was almost like the chains of bondage had been opened, and I could finally move on with my life. I didn't want to go back to the beginning anymore. I just wanted to move ahead.

I had reached a point in recovery where I could really accept the fact that I had a disease. I could see that because of my disease, I had behaved in ways I wished I had not. I could see all the mistakes and how I had wronged so many including myself. It was not a pretty picture. In spite of the ugliness that was behind me, I had reached a point where I could forgive myself. I could accept that much of what happened occurred as a consequence of my disease. I could look at myself in the mirror and believe that I was okay and that my Higher Power would help me put my life back together again. Have I forgiven myself?

Meditations for the Heart

I really had no idea what love was all about until I got into recovery. I know I had experienced love from others, but I didn't know how to give love to anyone. In recovery I began to look at others in the program as my brothers and sisters. We are all children of the same heavenly Father. I had to learn to think differently and to begin to reach out to others in a caring manner. I let go of my judgments, criticism and resentments. I didn't participate in gossip about others. Instead I worked on being patient and understanding. I began to develop a true compassion for others and worked at being helpful when I could. I found that when I did these things, I was actually helping myself. Have I begun the repair work of rebuilding my life?

Petitions to my Higher Power

God,

You have granted me a new freedom and a chance at rebuilding my life. Let me this day do the work necessary to put the pieces of my life back together again. I have no idea what my life may look like when I have finished the repair work I need to do, but I am willing to trust that You will lead me to that which is good. Help me this day to be compassionate and caring towards others, and let me always be patient.

Amen.

* * * *

Wisdom for Today   May 2

Step Five is like standing at the crossroads between our old way of living and the opportunity to begin living a new life. I remember when I first came into the program. I thought my life started all over again when I admitted my powerlessness and unmanageability. In some ways it did, but I continued to live my life without change except for abstinence from mood-altering chemicals.

In completing Step Five, I now had an opportunity to make significant changes in my life as well as begin the repair work I needed to do.

Completing Steps One through Five is a lot like taking out an insurance policy on recovery. While it is not a guarantee, these Steps certainly act as a strong insurance policy against relapse. If we are painstaking about this phase of our program, we will not wish to return. The remaining Steps are how we continue to pay our insurance premium. I really did not expect to get to a point where I no longer desired to get wasted or high. Now I can't imagine not paying my insurance premiums. Have I experienced the freedom that an honest Step Five brings?

Meditations for the Heart

Insurance brings a sense of security. It is not a false sense of security, because tragedy can strike; but there is a comfort in knowing that your recovery is protected. This is the security I felt when I accepted the gift of forgiveness that God offers. This is the sense of security I felt when I knew I was accepted by others in the program and when I could truly accept myself. Insurance does protect, but it does not mean that relapse can no longer occur. Indeed, if this were all that was needed, then there would only be Five Steps in the program. The founders of the Twelve Step program knew that there was more needed in order to stay clean and sober. In fact, they established seven more Steps. Am I resting on Step Five and not doing the repair work that is needed?

Petitions to my Higher Power

God,

You have provided me and thousands like me the Steps needed to escape from the bondage of addiction. For this I am grateful. Walk with me this day as I continue my journey in recovery. Let me experience the security that the program offers. Keep me motivated to experience the promises of the Twelve Steps.

Amen.

* * *

Wisdom for Today   May 3

There is a song that goes, "You can't always get what you want, you can't always get what you want, you can't always get what you want; but if you try, sometime you just might find you get what you need." This has certainly been the case for me in the program. In fact, I have come to accept that I have little or no control over the outcome. I am only responsible for the effort. When I look back at my drinking and my drug use, I rarely if ever got what I wanted. Sure, maybe in the beginning, I got high like I wanted; but it didn't take long for me to start chasing that ever-elusive high.

In recovery, however, I find that I get out of the program what I put into it. And if I put faith in a Higher Power into my program, I am amazed at how often I get what I need. Yes, I don't always get what I want; but I do get what I need. When I am faced with my own weakness, I am given strength

129

and patience. When I am faced with fear, I am given courage. When I am faced with truth, I am given choices for positive change. Am I putting what I need to into the program?

Meditations for the Heart

One of the things I needed most in early recovery was friends, friends who would be willing to be honest with me and who genuinely cared for me. I knew how to make using buddies, but I had no real idea how to make friends. If I was going to get what I needed, I had to become willing to put some effort into it. I had to become friendly if I was going to make friends. This meant that I would have to talk to others in the program and begin to show a genuine interest in their life. I would need to strive to be helpful to those who were near me. I needed to search for something in every person I met that I could like. I had to stop looking at how others were different than I was and start looking for similarities. I had to stop making judgments about others. I needed to work on accepting them for who they were. I found that when I started to treat others with respect, I began to respect myself more. I found that when I cared enough to be honest with others, I could be more honest with myself. Am I putting effort into getting what I need?

Petitions to my Higher Power

God,

You have given me this day all I need and continue to provide for my needs. Grant me strength to reach out to others and to put effort into getting what I need. Help me this day to see things in a new light and to take advantage of the opportunities for growth that You give to me. Help me to seek out Your will for me this day.

Amen.

* * * *

Wisdom for Today   May 4

There are days, and then there are days. This was a tough lesson to learn in early recovery. I would go for days and even weeks where life seemed to be heading in a good direction; then WHAM! – A bad day would hit me in the face. Sometimes it would be cravings or urges to drink or use that seemed to come out of nowhere. Other times it would be because I got into a fight with my spouse. Sometimes grief would just seem to creep into my day and slowly surround me. It really didn't matter what the reason was. I was suddenly in the middle of a struggle.

It was during these times that my character defects would like to come out and play. It was like trouble invited more trouble to the party. It was hard not to get back into my old behavior and use my old, unhealthy coping skills. This is when I would remember the words my sponsor gave to me, "Remember to breathe." He was referring to his conversations with me about only paying attention to things that could affect my breathing, in other words, things that could kill me. I knew that going back to my old ways of thinking, feeling and behaving would lead me back to using. I knew this could affect my breathing. So on bad days I would remember to breath and go back to the basics of recovery. Believe me, it was not perfect, but I am still breathing today. Do I know what to do when I am having a bad day?

Meditations for the Heart

"Going back to the basics," for me means using the slogans, prayer, meetings, phone calls and anything that works. On bad days I get knocked off center, so I go to a place that can help me get centered again. I close my eyes and take several deep breaths. I calm down and quietly go through the steps one at a time. I use what I need to use – admitting powerlessness and unmanageability, believing that God can restore sanity, turning it over, whatever it takes. I ask for help, and I reach out to others. I have seen this process work for me again and again. It doesn't change what is going on in my life, but it changes how I am looking at it. It changes me. So, I remember to breathe. What will I do to get myself back on track when I need to?

Petitions to my Higher Power

God,

I have come to realize that not every day is meant to be filled with sunshine. Help me to weather the storms in my life and use the tools that work. Sometimes when I grow fearful, it is like I stop breathing. Help me always to remember to breathe in Your Spirit and seek Your strength. Guide me this day, and lead me to the people I need in my life.

Amen.

* * * *

Wisdom for Today   May 5

"We will not regret the past, nor will we shut the door on it." (Alcoholics Anonymous, Fourth Edition. Page 83) This is the new freedom that Step Five provides. Completing Step Five allows you to stop regretting the past and at the same time still be able to look at it without disgust. This is not to say that I don't wish that many things I did while drinking and using drugs could have been avoided. But I can't undo the past; I can only work to repair the damage. I can only work to pay my recovery insurance premiums so that I do not relapse. Each time I attend a meeting and each time I spend in quiet meditation or prayer, I am making a payment on my insurance a policy I do not want to let lapse.

The founders of the program did two things that were absolutely brilliant, some say divinely inspired. First they wrote down the steps of recovery that they found worked. The next inspired thing they did was to number these steps. This shows me that once I have taken a good look at myself and shared this openly in Step Five, if I am to change, the change must begin with me. And so this is where the repair work was to begin. I was to make myself ready to have God do His work on me. This was to be the first of many premium payments I would need to make to insure my recovery. Am I willing to make all the necessary recovery insurance payments?

Meditations for the Heart

As I walked through the steps, I began to recognize that God was walking with me on this journey. In all my personal relationships, I began to see evidence of God working in my life to improve it. Over and over again I would see God guide and direct me. I was given opportunities for change. I was given strength, and I was given courage. I found myself doing things that I did not know I was capable of doing. Today I am convinced that each of the changes I have gone through on this journey have occurred only because God was leading me on this path. Seeing this evidence has only worked to strengthen my faith that my Higher Power is indeed caring for me. Do I believe that God is looking out for me and helping me along the way?

Petitions to my Higher Power

God,

You have guided me this far, and I now trust that You will continue to lead me to a better way of living my life. You have enabled one change after another in my life and in who I am. Let me continue to follow Your direction for my life.

Amen.

* * * *

Wisdom for Today   May 6

Quiet satisfaction is the best way to describe what I felt after completing my Fifth Step. There was this deep sense of calmness in my heart, knowing that God and another person both had listened to my disclosure and neither had rejected me. I also did not want to reject myself. I still did not like everything that I had talked about, but now it seemed less overwhelming. I had finished talking and was told by the recovering pastor that now that I had done my Fifth Step that it was time to be quiet and listen for God's response. We said a prayer together, and then I left his office and went and sat in the church for a while.

I sat there quietly and wondered about what God would have me do. It was as if the whole nature of my prayers had changed. I had spent months asking God for help and asking for guidance. I spent time asking for strength just to make it one hour at a time. Now, for the first time, sitting in the dark church, I was asking what God wanted me to do. I wasn't asking for something, I was asking how I could serve God. Not only was there an inner quietness, but also there was a satisfaction in knowing that I no longer needed to be self-centered. I could now begin to make changes in my life – in who I was – and became ready to do the needed repair work to put my life back in one piece. Have I begun to pray about what I can do for God?

Meditations for the Heart

From this point on, the path I was walking did not seem so difficult. There was a gentle rise as I walked forward. I had a sense that wonderful discoveries could now be made. My vision was clearer, and I now had something I had only glimpsed previously. I could see my hand in God's hand as I walked along this pathway to recovery. I could now see the power I had been given and how I had been kept safe throughout my life. I could now see that God had always been there with me, even in my addiction, and how He had protected me from too great harm. I could also see clearly that I needed to continue my journey through the steps and that I would learn new things every day. Has my sense of hope become stronger?

Petitions to my Higher Power

God,

I know that there will still be times when I need to call on You for strength. I know that You will satisfy my every need. Today let me serve You and do Your will. Let me reach out to others and share what I have been taught.

Amen.

* * * *

Wisdom for Today   *May 7*

There are a lot of little things that go into making recovery what it is, but all those little things add up over time. I'm not sure I could even begin to describe all the little things that go into it. I have just come to accept that when all of it is added up, life is good. This is not to say that there are no more problems, just better ones, or at least better ways to cope with the problems that come up in life. I have been fortunate enough to put together a good deal of time under my belt, but it has all been done one day at a time.

One of the more important little things is to find gratitude in recovery. I know for certain that gratitude was not present early in my recovery process. Yes, I was glad I had stopped drinking and using, but I was not happy right away. In fact, I was pretty miserable for a while. I'm not even sure when gratitude first came into the picture, but I know it was solidified when I completed Step Five. I became grateful for the inner calm and the quiet satisfaction I felt. I became grateful for the ability to forgive myself. I became grateful for the forgiveness I felt from my Higher Power. Have I begun to see the little things add up?

Meditations for the Heart

I came to a fork in the road of recovery when I completed Step Five. One path led nowhere because it was the path on which I see too many addicts and alcoholics stop. Too many times I have seen individuals finish Step Five and skip the repair work, jumping ahead to Step Ten, or even Twelve. This path seems to go nowhere because it just goes in circles. I know, because I walked on this path for a time. The other path leads on to Step Six, a process of preparation and letting go. I thought that the path that went nowhere would allow me some time to rest, but I found going in circles was not easy. I knew the other path would not be easy either, but at least it led somewhere. If I was going to hang onto that sense of gratitude, then the choice was simple. It was time to move on. Am I ready to move forward in my recovery?

Petitions to my Higher Power

God,

You never said this road would be easy, but the directions You provide are simple enough. Today I will be glad for the journey. I will seek out the things in my life for which I can be grateful, and I will acknowledge the gifts that I receive from You. Help me to make good and healthy choices today.
Amen.

* * * *

Wisdom for Today   *May 8*

One thing that completing my Fifth Step helped me with was in becoming humble. There was no more room for grandiosity or arrogance. There was no way to stand before my Higher Power and admit my wrongs with an arrogant heart. There was no way to stand before another person and tell my story and what I had done with my life and to the people I hurt and remain grandiose. Sharing my life history openly and honestly could only be done from a place of humility. At first glance, this does not exactly sound like a good thing.

But in retrospect, I personally believe that this was perhaps the best thing that could have happened to me. In this place of humility, I first discovered my inner most self. Even more importantly, I first discovered God, as I understand Him. What I mean is that I really moved from a place of simple faith that perhaps God could help me to a place where I had a personal relationship with God. My conversation with God and the other person listening to my Fifth Step was indeed a turning point. I became humble and really owned that I could not run the show. It was not just my drinking and using drugs, but I understood that I could not run my life. I could not change myself. I now had real help. Have I developed a humble heart?

Meditations for the Heart

Out of the ashes of selfishness I crawled, and I slowly learned how to sit up. I then learned to stand up. When I put my hand into God's hand, I learned to walk. In the Fifth Step it was as if I could step into a shower and wash off all the ashes of my life. Yesterday was over, and I could not change what had happened. I could only ask my Higher Power to forgive me and honestly and humbly try to follow His will for me. Today is here; and it provides me with a new start, a chance at renewal. I must start each day I am given in this place of a humble heart, and in complete faith and trust in God I will walk forward. I have learned that I cannot yet run, but my steps today are much better than crawling through the ashes of my life. Do I start my day with complete trust and faith that God will lead my way?

Petitions to my Higher Power
God,

Today I pray that I can do Your will and that I will work to make the world a better place to live in. Help me to bring goodness into all that I do, and let me give back what I have been given.
Amen.

* * *

Wisdom for Today   May 9
Transformation seems to be a common occurrence in the program. It is not what I read in a book or even what I heard someone say at a meeting that

135

convinced me that the program works. What really convinced me was seeing what happened in my own life and what I saw happen in the lives of others. I mean, after all, here I was a drunk and a drug addict. I could not stop on my own, but now I was alcohol and drug free. As I saw new people come into the program, I watched the same thing happen to them, if they were willing to go to the necessary lengths.

But it was not just abstinence that convinced me; it was how my life was changed. There was a real level of pathology in my thinking, emotional responses and behaviors. My beliefs were all screwed up. Working my way through the Steps, I became a useful person in society. I saw myself make changes in my thinking, emotional responses and behaviors. I saw myself change my belief system. I saw these things occur in my life and in the lives of others. Transformation does indeed happen in the Twelve Step program. Seeing is believing. Have I seen change in my life and in the lives of those who surround me?

Meditations for the Heart

Am I willing to do the next right thing? It is easy to pay lip service to this question and say "yes," but it is much harder to actually do this day in and day out. Over time I have become convinced that the only way to accomplish this is to have a strong spiritual foundation. This means believing in a divine principle, that God is in charge. I need to be willing to let my Higher Power run the show and trust that He has the knowledge and the love to lead me in the right direction. The other factor involved in this divine principle is the willingness to actually accept and follow this guidance. Most of the time it is easy to know what my Higher Power would want me to do. The hard part is then doing it. Obedience is not always easy; but I have found that when I do follow God's directions, I am less likely to get lost. In the long run this divine principle is the easier, softer way. Do I seek after this divine principle in all that I do?

Petitions to my Higher Power
God,

Sometimes it is not easy to follow Your directions. I find there are things that come up in my life, and I do not want to seek You out for guidance. Yet, time and time again, I see that following You is the easier, softer way in the long run. When I get stubborn or foolish, guide me back to this path. Keep me on the path of truth.
Amen.

* * * *

136

Over time I have watched one newcomer after another walk in through the doors of the program. Many of these individuals have tried desperately to control their use of alcohol or drugs and failed. Many have tried to quit on their own and failed. Still others have been in one treatment program after another and failed. Yet, those that completely give themselves to this simple program find a way to get clean and sober. This fact in and of itself is amazing.

But what really astounds me are the remarkable changes I see these individuals go through. Each of them, just like myself, had severe problems with their personality. There were clearly major problems with my thinking, emotional responses, behavior and beliefs. My disease process had corrupted my personality. Through working the Steps, I have watched myself change, and I have watched one newcomer after another change. If you need proof that the Steps work, just hang around and watch what happens to people in the program who really work the Steps. This evidence not only convinces me that "it works if you work it," but it also shows me that there is a Higher Power at work in our lives. What has happened to others and me is not luck, but it is the grace of God. Am I convinced that a Higher Power can help me change my personality?

Meditations for the Heart

Learning to cooperate with God is not always easy. Sometimes I am convinced that I am my own worst enemy – particularly when it comes to my character defects. It just seems that I really like some of them too much. So how do you give up something that you like? Not an easy task! When I looked closely at my defects of character and personality flaws, I could see how these things were just as destructive as my drinking and using. I knew if I was ever going to change these aspects of who I was and how I behaved, I would need to cooperate with God. This cooperation begins with openly seeking and acknowledging the presence of a Higher Power in our lives. As I became more conscious of the presence of God in my life, it was not hard to find direction for the needed changes. But cooperation means more than just acknowledging God's presence. It also means surrender. Over and over I have surrendered to my Higher Power. The problem is that some of those character defects I take back. I let go, but then I take them back. Over time I have found that I take back these defects less and less often. I just don't need them anymore. Have I become ready to have God remove my defects?

Petitions to my Higher Power

God,

Over time You have convinced me that the program does work. More importantly, You have convinced me that You work for me and for others in

the program. Today I know my faith is stronger because of what You have done for me in my life. Help me to stay on the course and continue to work each of the Steps as I walk through this life. Help me to develop an attitude of cooperation with You.
Amen.

* * * *

Wisdom for Today   May 11

There was no doubt that I could not stop drinking and using drugs on my own. The same was true with my defects of character. My personality flaws were resistant to change. Even when I realized and accepted that these defects were just as destructive to me as my drinking and using, I continued to think, behave and emotionally respond to life in ways that hurt those around me or myself. Even when I tried to change, I continued to come back to my old behavior. My big mistake was thinking that I could change these things on my own.

In Step Six it clearly stated that God was the one who was to remove these defects of character, yet I persisted in trying to do this on my own. I guess that in my stubborn way, I had to learn again that I was powerless. As my attempts to change myself repeatedly failed, I began to see that I could not rid myself of these defects of character. I began to understand my need for God's help. I began to talk with my Higher Power and admit that I was not perfect. In these prayers I began to see that God was my only hope. I began to stop asking for perfection and simply told God that I was ready to get better. Slowly over time, my defects of character have either disappeared or diminished to the point of no longer being destructive. What has surprised me is the fact that my personality strengths have grown. I have learned new ways to cope with life. I don't have to follow the old rules anymore. Do I let the old rules continue to run my life?

Meditations for the Heart

In becoming entirely ready to have God remove these defects, I was reborn of the Spirit. I do not mean that I was literally reborn, but I was given a new chance on how I lived my life. All those old rules that said I had to lie, cheat, be egotistical, fearful, etc. were challenged; and I began to see and live life differently. I began to know a new freedom and was shown new ways to cope and behave differently in my life. I may never fully understand why I behaved the way that I once did, but I don't have to. I can simply accept that this new way of living my life is better than the old way I lived. Making

138

myself ready for change was not an easy or pleasant process, but accepting my own humanity and imperfection opened the door to a new life in and with the Spirit. Do I see the miracle of personality change that is possible in the Spirit?

Petitions to my Higher Power

God,

Today I can thank You for making me uncomfortable with my old ways of thinking, behaving and emotionally responding to life. You have given me a new chance to live life with new rules. Through Your Spirit I have been given new options and a new attitude. I am grateful for the chance to be better. Amen.

* * * *

Wisdom for Today   May 12

Anger and resentment seemed to be constant companions when I first got clean and sober. I don't really know if I understood what I was so angry about. In working my way through the steps, I began to uncover some of the reasons for my anger and resentments. I really hated the fact that I was an alcoholic and an addict. I resented many of the consequences I had experienced and continued to have even though I was clean and sober. I resented some of the people in my life and how I had been treated. I was angry with myself for allowing some of these things to occur.

Step Six showed me that I needed to let go of these resentments. I read in program books about anger and resentment and how they were poison for the alcoholic/addict. But these things were not something that I could just forget or make go away. I needed to be shown how to rid myself of anger and resentment. My sponsor told me to begin to pray for the people who had wronged me. I talked at length with others in the program about how they rid themselves of their resentments. I learned more about forgiveness. These things did not just magically disappear; but over time, the longer I stayed clean and sober, I found that I no longer needed to hold onto these resentments. Do I still harbor resentments?

Meditations for the Heart

I needed to occupy myself with what God wanted me to do. His tasks for me in my recovery became more important than my own agenda. As I did this, I began to find peace of mind. My heart was no longer in an uproar. But if I was going to occupy myself with doing what God wanted me to do, I had to learn to let go of the things that got in the way. I had to stop trying to be both judge and jury and wanting to punish others who had hurt me. I had to stop convicting myself. I needed to let my Higher Power decide if others should experience punishment for their deeds. After all that was His job and not mine. When I began to pray for others and began to practice forgiveness, I found that my resentments slipped away and were replaced with peace of mind. My heart was no longer filled with rage. Am I occupying myself with God's tasks for me?

Petitions to my Higher Power
God,

You know my heart and my mind better than I do myself. Search out my heart and mind, and help me to be rid of resentment. Bless those people who have wronged me. Grant me patience and understanding of others and myself. Grant that I may have a forgiving heart. Let me today be concerned only with Your agenda for me.
Amen.

* * * *

Wisdom for Today   May 13
"Just do it!" was a slogan for a popular athletic shoe company, but I have found it helpful for me in my recovery. You see, recovery is a program that requires action. I had to stop being a couch potato and get up and start doing what I needed to do in recovery. Sometimes things that my sponsor told me or I would hear at a meeting seemed to have little connection to my goals in recovery. For instance, I told my sponsor that I wanted to begin working on my defects of character. I told him that I was having a hard time with grandiosity and arrogance. I asked, "How do I stop acting like a know-it-all when I really don't know anything?"

He responded, "I want you to take a long walk each morning and walk down unfamiliar streets." In my arrogance and confusion I said, "How's that going to help?" He looked at me and said two words, "*Into action.*" (*Alcoholics Anonymous*, Fourth Edition. Page 72) I had no idea what he was talking about. All I knew was I had to just do it. So I did. So each morning I would take a long walk down unfamiliar streets. One morning I got lost and wasn't really sure where I was or even how to retrace my steps. I had been too busy trying to figure out how this was going to help me and what my sponsor was really up to. I wasn't paying attention to where I was going. "Now what" I thought. I stood there for a while not knowing what to do. Eventually, I had to ring a doorbell and ask for help. My trying to figure everything out on my own got me lost. Do I ask for help when I need it?

Meditations for the Heart

Later that week, I talked with my sponsor again. I told him about what had happened, and he said, "And what did you learn?" I had to admit I wasn't sure and jokingly said, "How to get lost." That's when he asked, "And how did that happen?" I sat quietly for a while and began to see that my trying to figure everything out had actually gotten me lost. He said, "That's right, arrogance is blind." Still to this day I recall this discussion. I learned a lot that day. It wasn't up to me to have all the answers, and it wasn't up to me to know all the directions. I am glad I did follow my sponsor's instructions to take a walk, and today I am even glad I got lost. Do I have to have all the answers?

Petitions to my Higher Power

God,

So often in life I get lost, and I am surprised by my unwillingness to ask for help. I just stand there and do nothing. Again and again I have to surrender and admit that I need help. Thank You for letting me ring Your doorbell, and thank You for giving me instruction and direction in life. I will continue to walk the walk, but I know I need You as my guide. Walk with me today.

Amen

* * * *

Wisdom for Today   May 14

One thing that I found important along the way was to remember to thank God. In the selfishness of my addiction I was so far removed from God that I had no relationship with Him at all. As I got clean and sober, I found myself still struggling with selfishness and self-centeredness. Just because I stopped drinking and using didn't mean that I instantly became grateful. I really had to stop and think about what was happening in my life. When I really stopped long enough to realize that nothing that was happening in my life was by my own doing, I finally started to experience gratitude.

It was not just God that I needed to thank; it was also everyone else who had been helping me. I began to seek out those people who would say something at a meeting that I could relate to and express my appreciation. I made a purpose of thanking my sponsor each time we talked. I began to even thank my family members for the support they offered. Most of all, I spent time each morning asking God for help and each evening thanking Him for another day of sobriety. Am I truly grateful for the gifts I receive in recovery?

Meditations for the Heart

In recovery my vision changed. It was not just because my brain came out of the fog; it was because I started to experience a spiritual vision. I could not physically see God, but I could see His actions in my life and in the lives of other addicts and alcoholics. I began to envision myself walking hand-in-hand with my Higher Power on the road to recovery. I envisioned conversations with God along the way. As my spiritual consciousness improved, I began to see life more clearly. I could feel God's presence and His strength. I had been trapped in the prison of addiction; now I could see outside the box. Out there somewhere was my Higher Power, limitless in all of eternity. He was outside of the box, and now I was walking right beside Him. Do I walk with my Higher Power on the path of recovery?

Petitions to my Higher Power

God,

When I stop and think about all the good things that are happening in my life, I know that all this happens only through Your help. For all the gifts that You have given me along the way, I am grateful. Help me this day to keep my spiritual vision and see outside of the box. Let me walk hand-in-hand with You today.

Amen.

* * * *

Wisdom for Today   May 15

In addressing my defects of character, I had to once again submit myself to the will of my Higher Power. Whether it was **D**ishonesty, **E**go, **F**ear, **E**xpectation, **C**arelessness, **T**rustlessness or any other **S**elf-centered behavior, I had to turn it over to God. I became willing to let go of my old ways and find out what my Higher Power's plans for me were. My old ways just didn't work any more. I knew they would simply lead me back to the insanity of addiction.

In turning this over to God, I would be given one lesson after another regarding character. I had to start by learning genuinely to care for others and myself. I had been clean and sober for a while before this concept of really learning to care emerged into my consciousness. I had been going through the motions, trying to "fake it 'til I made it." One night I went to a meeting and a good friend of mine was not there. Something was wrong; he was always at my home group meeting. No one had heard anything from him in days. I learned later that night that he had died of an overdose. Once the shock wore off and I had time to talk with my sponsor, I looked back at all the opportunities I had to show my friend that I cared, but didn't. I know that this could not have prevented what had happened, but I also knew that I could not let these kinds of opportunities pass me by again. Do I show others in the program that I care?

Meditations for the Heart

It was in the darkest of places that God rescued me from my disease. I know now that God would have crossed mountains or deserts to find me. I know He would have crawled through briar patches, broken glass and even the fires of hell to reclaim me. I have learned that nothing can separate me from His love and care. I have learned that I need to join my Higher Power in this quest for those that are lost. In reaching out to others and letting them know I care, I have discovered that I am really helping myself. My carelessness disappears when I reach out to others. This does not mean that I am willing to put myself or my recovery at risk, but it does mean that I need to be willing to carry the message, and I need to be willing to show others I care. Sometimes this means offering someone a ride to a meeting or hanging out with someone after a meeting because they need to talk. Sometimes it means being willing to make a phone call, and at other times it means helping someone laugh out loud. Am I willing to show others that I care?

Petitions to my Higher Power

God,

Today help me not to focus on myself, but on the needs of others. Let me reach out and show someone that I care. Help me not to worry about being self-conscious and trust that You will guide me in my efforts to show others that I do care. I also want to thank You for finding me in that dark place I was and rescuing me from the insanity of my disease.

Amen.

* * * *

Wisdom for Today   May 16

In submitting my character defects to my Higher Power, I developed hope. I began to feel that my life no longer had to be lived by the old rules. This sense of hope was much like I had experienced when I first came into the program. When I first got clean and sober, I saw other people making it. I saw the old timers who had longer-term recovery. When I listened to their stories, I began to feel, "If they can make it, so can I." I began to see that they had managed to let go of the old rules and old behavior. I thought that I had a chance to do this also.

What I found out was letting go of my defects was much like letting go of alcohol and drugs, only harder. This was true probably because many of these attitudes, behaviors and beliefs had been with me much longer, and because some of them I simply enjoyed. But if I wanted to gain a true sense of character, then I would have to stop acting like a defect. I also needed to look for progress and not perfection. My defects of character did not simply disappear because I said a prayer. I had to put into action what my Higher Power wanted for me. Slowly, over time, my defects of character became less and less problematic. My hope that I could be rid of the old rules strengthened. Do I have a strong grasp on hope?

Meditations for the Heart

In God's world there are perfect hope and perfect harmony. Yet in this physical world I have come to realize that I can never have perfect hope or perfect harmony with my Higher Power. Life in recovery is not so much about being better, but about becoming better. Sometimes I have felt that God has let me down. I have seen others in the program and myself want to blame our failures on God. "He let me down." But the truth is that God does not fail. It is because we are not in harmony with our Higher Power that we fail. I have had to accept the fact that sometimes I fail. In these times I need to seek to get back into harmony with God. Back to basics, if I am to become better! I need to work to stay in harmony with my Higher Power. Am I working to stay in harmony with my Higher Power?

Petitions to my Higher Power

God,

Today is a new day, and again You have gifted me with a clean and sober start to my day. Help me this day to strive for harmony with You. Let me take one thing at a time as I walk through this day. Help me to become better in all that I do. Let me this day work at letting go of the old rules and live by Your new rules for my life.

Amen.

* * * *

Wisdom for Today   May 17

One of the slogans you hear early on in the program is, "Easy does it." I needed this slogan a lot in the beginning of my recovery, but I had no idea how important it would become in addressing my character defects. As an addict and alcoholic I was used to doing everything in excess. I drank too much and got high too often. I built up a lot of resentments, worries and confusion. My excesses hurt me physically and mentally. My excesses also had a lot to do with my defects.

Many of my defects were because I had taken things to an extreme. Fear is a healthy reaction when a threat is present. But when fear is taken to an extreme and it controls your every decision, fear becomes unhealthy. My fear became paranoia and controlled much of my life. Self-confidence is a good thing; but when it is exaggerated and becomes grandiosity and arrogance, it also becomes unhealthy. Being carefree can be a good thing until it is taken to the extreme of carelessness. I needed to learn "easy does it" when it came to my defects. I had to work on them one at a time and not try to fix all of them at once. I had to slow down and think before I reacted. I had to stop and ask myself if my actions and behavior were appropriate in every situation. Have I learned to take it easy in addressing my defects?

Meditations for the Heart

I also learned that I had to "be" before I could "do". If I wanted to "be" a person of character, then I had to do the work of becoming honest, humble, trusting and caring if I ever wanted to "do" things that showed I had good character. If I wanted to accomplish much, I had to be much. Who I was affected everything I did in life. If I wanted to "be" a good father, or "be" a good employee, then I had much I needed to change in who I was. Only then would I be able to "do" those things. If I was going to change who I was, I would need help. This is where my Higher Power would come in. In order to do the things that I valued, then I would need my Higher Power's help to "be" what He wanted me to "be." To become a new me was a lot of what needed to happen in my life. Have I asked God for help to "be" what He wants me to be?

Petitions to my Higher Power
God,

Teach me this day to be who You want me to be. Let me take each moment and cherish what You give me. Help me to slow down and live by the guideline, "Easy does it," when I need to. Lead me through this day as I am given opportunity to change who I am.
Amen.

* * * *

Sometimes you hear the same things over and over again at meetings. I often have wondered if I was learning anything new after a while. Then on the "963rd time" I hear something; it clicks! It finally makes sense. It becomes something I can use. These are the moments of spiritual awakening. God seems to work much like this as well. He reveals to me over and over again my defects of character. He shows me myself and helps me see how I turn my life over to dishonesty, ego, fear, expectations, rage, loneliness and many other undesirable powers. I can let these powers take over my life and corrupt my will.

This is why we turn our will and our life over to His care. Left to our own devices, even clean and sober, we can mess it all up. When our defects have been revealed to us enough times and they become painful enough, we ask God to remove them from our lives. We do not need to chase after the answers; God will bring them to us. In the Bible it says, "Be still, and know that I am God." It doesn't say run around like crazy, and you will know God. Defects of character are resistant to change. Yet if we are still, God will bring us the answers. Do I recognize when God brings me an answer?

Meditations for the Heart

Laughter is good medicine. One of the greatest blessings in recovery is the return of genuine laughter. Being able to laugh at the insanity of our disease and ourselves can bring healing to a troubled heart. When I slow down long enough to really think about some of the crazy things I did or that happened to me, I can't help but laugh about them now. At the time some of these things were very painful or even stupid. Yet as I have moved along in my recovery process, I have found that I can now laugh about these same events. One of the promises in the AA Big Book is that *we will not regret the past..."* (*Alcoholics Anonymous,* Fourth Edition. Page 83) It is much nicer to get to a point when we can laugh at ourselves. Has laughter returned to my life?

Petitions to my Higher Power
God,

Today is a day that I know You again will teach me if I only open my mind and listen to Your directions. Help me to do just that and to seek You out in all I do. Create in me a new perspective on life, and help me to again laugh. Let me celebrate this day and all that is in it.
Amen.

* * * *

Wisdom for Today   May 19
Lack of awareness was another one of my shortcomings. The reality was that I had little or no awareness of how my behavior affected other people. I

had been so wrapped up in my own self-centeredness that I just could not see what was happening. It was not just how my behavior affected others that I was missing, but also self-awareness. I had no idea how I really felt. I knew I felt good when people were leaving me alone, and I felt bad when I was being hassled. But as for my emotions, I had no idea what made me happy. I had lost touch with sadness, fear, anger, shame and hurt feelings. Everything was either good or bad.

As I began to come out of the fog, I began to see things for the first time. Anger was probably the first emotion I got in touch with. I was angry I had to go to all those meetings. I was angry that I couldn't do things my way. I was angry I had this disease. As my anger subsided, I got in touch with other emotions – fear, sadness and shame. I began to see how my behavior was affecting others. I began to realize more and more that I had to change if I was ever going to stay in recovery. As I started to put others into the equation of life, my self-centeredness began to slip away. With regular inventory of myself I began to gain better understanding of my emotional responses. I began to see how my thinking, attitudes and behaviors had a lot to do with how I felt. Am I becoming more aware of my actions, my emotions and myself?

Meditations for the Heart

In the program I began to see that those who reached out to me were able to help because they truly understood what I was going through. They had been through many of the same things I was going through. It was one addict or alcoholic helping another. It was their understanding that allowed them to help me. As I hung around the program longer, I began to see that this was also true of my Higher Power. God was able to help me, not just because He was more powerful than I was, but also because He understood. I am not saying that God is an addict or an alcoholic, but He certainly understands pain, fear, sadness, anger and all the other emotions I experience. God also understands joy, serenity and peace of mind. These are things that I had to learn about from God and others. Today awareness is not always easy, but it is real, and I know I can deal with it. Do I reach out to others because I understand them?

Petitions to my Higher Power

God,

Today is a new day, and I do not yet know what this day will bring. Regardless of what cards may be dealt to me this day, I will work to remain aware of my choices. Help me this day to remain aware of my thinking, attitudes and behaviors. Give me courage to deal with my emotions in a healthy way. Let me always be understanding of the needs of others.

Amen.

* * * *

Wisdom for Today   *May 20*

When I was drinking and using drugs, I spent time telling stories about myself. I always was attempting to build myself up as "Mr. Wonderful." I hung out with people who were in worse shape than I was so that I could feel I was better than others. But the reality of my life was that I was not better. In fact, these lies about myself were told because I knew deep down I had not amounted to anything. Many of these lies I told so often that I even started to believe them myself. In my denial I became more and more defensive. I could not admit to myself or anyone else that I actually felt like I was inferior to others.

In early recovery, I continued to have this inferiority complex. I would sit in meetings and plan out what I was going to say when it was my turn to speak. I wanted to sound like I knew what I was doing. This defect in my character was actually getting in the way of my recovery. It fed my dishonesty, and it built a wall between my Higher Power and me. It was keeping me from benefiting from the program. It is hard to swallow our pride and admit that we don't know what we are doing. It is hard to get honest and admit it is all a show. Yet God will reveal this defect again and again until we become ready to genuinely ask for help. Am I still hiding my true self from others?

Meditations for the Heart

God thinks about me all the time. If He were ever to stop thinking about me, I would cease to exist. In recovery I need to train myself to think about God and what His will for me is in all that I do. I know that there is no way that I will ever be able to keep God in my thoughts all the time, but fortunately God will not cease to exist if I stop thinking about Him. He is constant and unchanging. Yet if I am to grow, I need to practice this conscious contact with my Higher Power. Each time I focus on the spiritual aspects of my recovery, I grow. This is now my job description – to focus on the spiritual aspects of my recovery. This is what will bring meaning to my life and who I am. Am I growing in spiritual stature?

Petitions to my Higher Power
God,

You more than anyone know the true me. You know the very workings of my heart. This day help me to be true to myself and true to You. I am convinced that in order to have true meaning in my life, I must continue to focus on You and what it is that You want for me.
Amen.

Wisdom for Today   May 21

Often times I am pleasantly surprised to hear from someone in the fellowship that something I said helped him or her. It is one sign that one of my past character defects has improved. There was a time when my selfishness and self-centeredness would not allow me to even care about others. I was so wrapped up in my disease and myself that I didn't even bother to think of others and what I might do to be charitable.

Being charitable means that I genuinely want to help others. Sometimes I reach out and offer what I can to help other addicts and alcoholics. Frequently I have no idea whether my help was of any benefit or not. This is not important, because even when it looks like I have failed, I know that a seed has been planted. God will determine what happens to that seed. What happens to the seed is not important; what is important is the fact that I have grown in my attempts to help others. I benefit from this. Still it is nice to hear from others once in a while that something I said or did helped them. Am I developing a charitable heart?

Meditations for the Heart

Early in recovery I had a very closed mind. My thinking was rigid, and I always seemed to want to be right. My mind and my thinking were both locked into a box. As I began to open my heart and mind up in the recovery process, I began to wonder what was outside of the box. My ways did not work. I needed to begin to think outside of the box in order to find the answers I needed. This thinking outside of the box helped me to see a Higher Intelligence in the universe. I did not have all the answers. None of the people in the program did either. But each of us in unison and harmony with a Higher Intelligence has found answers we could not have found on our own. Do I think outside of the box?

Petitions to my Higher Power
God,

One day at a time is how You help me to grow spiritually. Help me this day to use the rain you provide in my life for growth. Let me use the sunshine You provide to warm my heart. Help me to be of a charitable mind today. Let me seek Your Higher Intelligence.
Amen.

* * * *

I used to be a real show off, and I acted like a real know-it-all. I really tried to impress people a lot. I would show off and drink one shot after another to impress people. When I was using drugs, I would cut myself a bigger line than everybody else. I also would talk and talk about things I really didn't know much about but somehow would manage to lie my way through each story. I acted like a big shot and would buy other people drinks or turn people on so that they thought I was doing okay financially. I did all these things and more for two reasons. One was to bolster my own denial system; if I pretended hard enough, then even I might start to believe my own games. The other reason was to try and prove to others that I really amounted to something.

The reality was that I wasn't selling this game to anyone, not the people I tried to impress and certainly not myself. I was a loser and didn't fool anyone. Even in recovery I have a tendency to get a big ego. I spent time in early recovery trying to make myself look good to others. But it was still a game. This defect of character can be dangerous because I might get a big head and then even think I am smart enough or cool enough that I can drink or use again. Can I afford to get a swelled ego in recovery?

Meditations for the Heart

Grasping that which is spiritual is not something you can do with your mind. God is beyond all our understanding. We can only grasp pieces of understanding with our mind. We cannot grasp an understanding of God with our hearts. He is beyond our emotional understanding; we can only try to make of Him what we want Him to be. In fact, the only understanding we can truly have comes through faith. It is God who helps us understand Who He is. My Higher Power reveals Himself to me. I do not need to go looking for Him. He comes to me in my prayer and meditation. He comes to me in and through other people. He comes to me through many of the things I read. I don't go looking for a Higher Power; God comes looking for me. All I have to do is let Him find me. Am I still trying to find a Higher Power; or have I decided to let God, as I understand Him, come looking for me?

Petitions to my Higher Power

God,

I see You in the shadows of life and in the brightness of my days. You are all around me and always have been. It was I who was hiding, not You. Walk with me on my journey today. Help me to find and keep humility in my thoughts, words and deeds today. Teach me about Who You are, so that my simple understanding will grow along with my faith.

Amen.

* * * *

Wisdom for Today   May 23

Sometimes it seems that one thing after another goes wrong, even in recovery. It is at times like this when I am most likely to let my character defects come out to play. When things aren't going well and I seem to have lost my spiritual equilibrium, I seem to look to my old behaviors to cope with the situations. What I have learned is there is no problem I have currently that I can't make worse. Early in my recovery it was times like this that I thought about drinking or using. After I figured out how to stay clean and sober, I could screw things up just as bad with my old behaviors.

It is in these times that it becomes especially important for me to rely on my Higher Power. When I rely on my own power, I quickly get into old and unhealthy thinking. I am capable of making poor choices and react to life rather than respond to things in a healthy manner. I have come to accept that I will never get this perfectly right. I just want to make progress. I cannot do this on my own. So when things get rough, I stop and ask for help. My way doesn't work. I know and trust that my Higher Power's way will work better. Do I ask for help when I need to do so?

Meditations for the Heart

Sometimes the road to recovery seems long and hard. I need to rest along the way and know God will give me the rest I need. The problem is that I have a hard time getting back up to continue my journey. I remember hearing someone say at a meeting one time, "If I have one more growth experience, I am going to kill myself." I know just how that person was feeling. Particularly in dealing with character defects, the road seems long. I still think like an addict sometimes and want immediate gratification. Yet I know the easier, quicker way does not provide lasting results. I know I have to get back up and continue on the path that my Higher Power sets before me. When God says it is time to continue the journey, do I want to procrastinate?

Petitions to my Higher Power

God,

I know that recovery is not always easy. In fact, sometimes it seems downright difficult. It is in these times that I need You most. Lead me onward, give me rest when I need it, and inspire me to get back up and continue the journey that You want me to take. Help me to understand that even in the difficult days I sometimes face that You are always with me.

Amen.

* * * *

Wisdom for Today   *May 24*

We are fortunate to live in a day and age when alcoholism and drug addiction is recognized as an illness. It was not always like this. Addicts and alcoholics used to be looked at with ridicule and shamed for having a disease. It probably will never be a perfect world for us; and we still have many battles to fight, so that those who need help can get it. But the alcoholic and addict surely have a much better shot at recovery now than in years gone by.

None of this would have been possible, if it were not for a few individuals who got together and decided to help each other. The genius of the program is that these people actually took the time to write it down and pass it on to others. Because of what these individuals did, I have a shot at recovery. I know that I could not have done it on my own. The founders of the program were not attempting to help to start a movement; they just wanted to find a way out of the insanity. Am I grateful for what these individuals have done for me?

Meditations for the Hear

"It works if you work it." That's right; it takes work! If we are to recover, we must put effort into it. The good news is that God will bless our efforts. This does not always happen in the way in which we would expect it to happen. It also does not always happen as quickly as we might want it to. But I am convinced that it does happen. Recovery is not about sitting back and waiting for a miracle. It takes work. God directs our efforts; sometimes it seems that He directs us against the flow. It seems like we are attempting to paddle upstream. Yet at each stop along our journey, we are given rest; and we are blessed for our efforts. Effort and blessing is an important part of spiritual harmony. They exist together. Am I putting effort into the work of recovery?

Petitions to my Higher Power

God,

I am truly blessed by You. This day I remember in gratitude all the addicts and alcoholics that have gone before me to blaze a trail. Give me strength for this day that I may do the work of recovery. Give me courage so that I may follow Your lead. Help me this day to remember to pray for those who still need to find this program

Amen.

* * * *

I used to say that I was grateful that I found the program. But as my concept and understanding of my Higher Power has changed and grown, I now say that I am glad that the program found me. Yes, I was the one who walked through the doors for the first time, but I have watched others walk through the door only to turn around and not come back. Why is it that I stayed and they left? What was it about the words I heard that kept me coming back?

When you stop and think about it, most alcoholics and addicts never get help. They either end up going crazy, locked-up or dead. Why is it that I was given a chance at recovery? Why is it that my faith in a Higher Power was renewed? Why is it that I have been able to find happiness and contentment and others do not? Many of these questions I will never be able to answer fully. But I have come to believe that my recovery has had more to do with the program finding me than my finding the program? Am I grateful to have been found?

Meditations for the Heart

Sometimes I get so hurried in life that I lose track of what is important. God can work better in me if I just slow down. If I slow down and quietly move from one task to the next taking time to pray in between, I find that I actually get more things done. I know this sounds contradictory, but it is one of the paradoxes of recovery and life itself. If I venture often into the realm of the Spirit, I am given new strength and guidance. I find that I don't complicate things, and I get more done. All work that I do while resting in God's arms is good. Am I finding that I can do many things through my Higher Power?

Petitions to my Higher Power

God,

I am only now beginning to understand Your grace. The song, "Amazing Grace," says, "I once was lost but now am found." These words really do make sense to me now. I am glad and am humbled by what I see happen in my life and the lives of all who are found in the program. Help me this day to slow down and venture often into the realm of Your Spirit. Give me the strength for this new day.

Amen.

* * * *

There is an old song, "I can't get no – satisfaction." I used to feel this way all the time when I was using. I never could get enough. Even in early recovery, when people would ask me what my drug of choice was, I would respond by saying, "MORE!" The truth was that nothing seemed to bring me satisfaction. My drinking and drug use stopped bringing me pleasure long before I stopped using. Even being clean and sober didn't seem like it was enough. Something was definitely missing.

I came to discover, like many people who have stayed clean and sober, that abstinence is not enough. There is a whole lot more to recovery than simply stopping the use. The Twelve Step program teaches us a new way of living. We begin with developing skills to stay out of harm's way. We then find that we need to grow spiritually. We take a good look at ourselves and make changes that are needed in how we perceive the world and how we behave in it. We rebuild our lives and fix what is broken, particularly our relationships with others. We continue to do regular checks on our functioning. We seek to know God, and we carry the message. We become new people. Am I finding satisfaction in my life now?

Meditations for the Heart

The heart is a crazy, mixed up part of who we are. Our emotions, our desires and our will all reside deep within our heart. In addiction the wiring of the heart gets short-circuited and continues to give us grief. The reality is that we cannot go back and rewire our will, our emotions and desires. This is the part of who we are that can get us in the most trouble. In the program there is a slogan that says, "Think, Think, Think." But the question is what are we supposed to think. Only the mind is capable of grasping wisdom. Our mind must seek out wisdom when our hearts are troubling us. A question I have learned to ask myself, "Is it wise?" The words of the Serenity Prayer talk about the wisdom to know the difference. It is wise for me to seek out my Higher Power's will for me. It is wise to do those things that are physically, mentally and spiritually healthy for me. Do I seek out wisdom in all that I do?

Petitions to my Higher Power

God,

It is You that ultimately brings me any satisfaction that I have in my life. Teach me to be wise in all that I do. Let me seek out that which is healthy for me. Help me to recognize when my heart gets out of control, and seek to do Your will and not mine. Guide me on this pathway of recovery, and lead me to the place of true satisfaction in my life.

Amen.

* * * *

One of the most important aspects of using the program effectively is to establish a home group. I found that when I consistently went to the same meeting, I began to form relationships with the members of that group. As these relationships formed, my loyalty to the group and its members grew. I began to feel like if I drank or used, I would not only be letting myself down, but I also would be letting down my group. When I was active in my addiction, I wasn't loyal to anyone. There was no loyalty to my family, my job, my friends and most of all to myself.

In recovery I discovered a group of people that were loyal to each other. They were willing to help each other and were willing to help me. As they got to know me, they were able to provide me with very helpful feedback. They helped me challenge my unrealistic expectations. They were able to help me find new ways to cope with life on life's terms. As I stayed with my home group, I also began to tell others what I thought about what was going on in their lives. I gained not only their loyalty but also their friendship. Am I loyal to my home group?

Meditations for the Heart

It really seemed that I was living in a state of constant agitation when I was drinking and using drugs. I was agitated because I needed to get high or because I was coming off a real bender. Even during the brief periods of time when I was controlling my use, I still was agitated. In recovery I was encouraged to learn the importance of staying calm. If I am calm on the inside, I am not as likely to rush into things. I am more patient. I am more likely to seek out guidance from my Higher Power. I did not know how to be calm on the inside. In fact, the only way I knew how to do this was with alcohol or drugs. Here my home group and sponsor really helped me. They told me the only way to find that inner calmness was to trust in God. Only when I trust God am I able to find the serenity to deal with life in a healthy way. Have I found the inner calmness I need in recovery?

Petitions to my Higher Power
God,

Thank You for the people in my home group that have always remained loyal. They have stood by me when I needed it most. It also feels good to know that they now lean on me. This trust was not something I expected. I value these friendships. I also thank You for the gift of inner calmness that You provide to me. Life suddenly seems less hard and less crazy. Walk with me this day as I continue my journey in recovery.
Amen

Wisdom for Today   May 28

A slogan you will hear at meetings is, "Stick with the winners." Winners are the people you can depend on because they are loyal to the group. You don't have to worry about the winners because they are actively involved, working the steps and serving others. Winners come to meetings regularly and demonstrate through their involvement that they are willing to go to any length. Some are very outgoing, and others are quieter, but regardless of their personality they have a strong spiritual base to their recovery.

Sticking with the winners has been a great help to me in my own recovery. I was encouraged to come to meetings early and was invited out after meetings. It has amazed me how much I learned about recovery in these informal get-togethers. Winners can give you practical advice on dealing with life in recovery. By hanging out with the winners long enough, they teach you to become a winner. Am I becoming a winner in recovery?

Meditations for the Heart

When there is fellowship with the winners in recovery, there is also fellowship with the Divine Spirit. God is always there when addicts and alcoholics gather together to practice the principles of the program. In all human relationships it is God who brings us together and unites us in a way to have an impact on and facilitate change in each other. I have been surprised sometimes at the words that come out of my mouth at a meeting or when I am meeting with others in the program. I know these aren't my words as much as the words of the Divine Spirit coming out of my mouth. The Spirit guides, leads and provides opportunities for change in and through these relationships. No human relationship can be entirely right without the presence of the Divine Spirit of God. It is His gift to us. Can I accept that the Spirit is at work in my life in and through others in the program?

Petitions to my Higher Power
God,

Today let me be a channel of Your Divine Spirit in my interactions with others. Help me to recognize that Your Spirit works in and through others. Help me to use the guidance I receive from these people for good. Lead me to the changes You want me to make, so that I too may be a winner in this program of recovery.
Amen.

* * * *

When I came into the program, I needed more than just a way out of the insanity of addiction. I needed other people. I needed the fellowship. I needed to talk to others about the things that were bugging me and to get help in dealing with the troubles I faced. I needed the strength I found in other people to deal with life. I needed a place to go to help me deal with all my anxiety and excess energy. I needed support and encouragement. I needed help to understand what had happened to me and what I needed to do to change.

There was no way I could give these things to myself. If I had to depend on myself, I know I would have just kept running from life. I needed the people who were making it to help me. What I got was all of this and a whole lot more. At first I needed help from these people every day just to make it from the beginning to end of each day. But over time I was given tools to use to help me stay clean and sober. I didn't choose to become an alcoholic or a drug addict, but I did need to choose to take responsibility for my recovery. Am I grateful for all the help I have received from those in the program?

Meditations for the Heart

One of the most phenomenal changes that occurred in my life of recovery was the removal of doubt. When I look back at my early days in recovery, I was constantly filled with doubt. I doubted that I would be able to stay clean and sober. I doubted that I would ever be able to have fun or enjoy life again. I doubted that the program could work for me. I even doubted that I was worth it. But doubt was replaced with something called faith. This faith started out as a small seed that was planted when at the end of my very first meeting people stood in a circle, prayed and then shouted, "It works, if you work it." Then the gentleman standing next to me turned and looked me right in the eye and said, "It worked for me, and it can work for you." I don't think I believed a word he said, but I soon had several days of clean time under my belt. This became weeks, months and years. That seed was cared for by those people in recovery who were willing to help me until I could begin to help myself. This seed of faith was a gift from my Higher Power, and today has become a strong tree with deep roots. Am I still filled with doubts?

Petitions to my Higher Power

God,

I remember a time when I was filled with doubt and fear. You have given me the precious gift of faith. Through Your help and the help of others in the program my faith has grown. Let me continue to feed this faith by being responsible for my recovery. Today let me be willing to give back to the newcomers and help them find what I have found.

Amen.

* * * *

Wisdom for Today   *May 30*

When I was active in my addiction, I had no self-discipline. Self-control was out of the question. Selfishness and self-centeredness ruled my thinking, behavior and values. In recovery I needed to learn self-discipline. This meant no longer reacting to my emotions, desires or will. It meant that I had to learn to proceed through life, not with my own wisdom, but with the wisdom of others and the wisdom of my Higher Power. Meetings provided me with a place to meet others who certainly knew more about recovery than I did. I needed to seek out their wisdom. It was through the program and the grace of God that I learned the self-discipline of abstinence.

Even later in recovery I discovered that it was important to use self-discipline to give up some of my unhealthy behaviors and character defects. I had a tendency to self-sabotage and ruin what was good in my life. I had to corrupt any real success I had. Again I had to turn to the practice of self-discipline. My will only hurt me. I needed again and again to turn to others in the program and to God to find wisdom to deal with life and receive the encouragement I needed to do the next right thing, or at least do the next thing right. Do I practice self-discipline and seek wisdom from others?

Meditations for the Heart

I needed a guide to help me figure out how to have healthy relationships with other people. Learning how to get along with others and how to be genuine in my relationships was something that I needed to relearn. I knew how to interact with others, but I had no idea how to do this with my mask off. How do I allow myself to be vulnerable and real with others? I was afraid to let people in and afraid to share the real me. What would happen if others could see the blanket of shame I wore on the inside? Continuing to hide behind the mask would not work anymore. I believe this is a part of the reason that sponsorship is encouraged. I found someone whom I could risk letting into my world to see the real me. My sponsor was not only my guide, but he also became my friend. He was a friend who would tell me the truth, a friend who would share his wisdom with me. Am I learning how to have a healthy relationship with others?

Petitions to my Higher Power
God,

My heart is so undisciplined and reactive. My will, my emotions and my desire only seem to get me into trouble. Help me this day to seek out wisdom from others and learn self-discipline. Guide me to others with whom I can have healthy relationships.

Amen.

* * * *

Wisdom for Today *May 31*

"Humbly asked," (*Alcoholics Anonymous,* Fourth Edition. Page 59) are the first two words of Step Seven. This step begins this way because we recognize that we cannot accomplish this task on our own or by our own willpower. Those defects of character that have become so much a part of our personality become ingrained into our behavior. It becomes instinctive to choose these unhealthy options first, particularly when under stress. We ask for help because we cannot change these behaviors on our own. We are humbled by the fact that it is only with the help of our Higher Power that these shortcomings can be removed.

God can and will remove our shortcomings if we are humble and seek to do His will. When we stop long enough to seek His will for us, we no longer react to life instinctively. We respond wisely. We do not seek to find an easier, softer way. We seek to find His way. None of us in recovery is able to do this perfectly, but over time we can see these problems become smaller and smaller in our lives. We find that God gives us new skills for dealing with life's problems. We look back and see that the promises of the program are beginning to come true for us in all that we do. Am I ready to stand humbly before God and ask for His help?

Meditations for the Heart

We can never know all that goes into the making of a personality. We are quite complex creatures. Each of us has our own set of circumstances that molds who and what we are. We all have our own unique set of motivations. Each of us is influenced by such a different set of triumphs and sufferings. No one can know all the things that influence who we are. Because we cannot know everything that goes into making us who we are, or what makes up another individual, we must be cautious in passing judgment on others and ourselves. Too often I have judged others and myself harshly without having any way to understand fully what caused the individual to behave as they did. Only God can truly know who we are, and only He is qualified to judge what He sees. Passing judgment leads one to develop anger, mistrust and resentment. We need to leave it to God to unravel the complexities of who we are. Do I believe that God can teach me to behave differently?

Petitions to my Higher Power

God,

This day I come to You with an understanding that I do not know why I do what I do. Only bits and pieces of my behavior can be understood, and much of what I do makes little sense to me. Help me to seek to do Your will in all that I do this day. Lead me to the changes that You want for me and to become the person that You want. Let me be rid of my old self and find the new me that You want me to be.

Amen.

* * * *

Wisdom for Today   Jun 1

One day I woke up and suddenly realized that I knew how to stay clean and sober. As long as I walked the walk, I knew I could make it. I was no longer worried about whether I could stay that way. But this was only the beginning. As I continued to work the steps, I also found new friends in the program. I wasn't lonely anymore. I had found a new camaraderie and fellowship. I found new relationships with my family – not all of them, but most of my family. The barriers and walls I had built had been torn down. There was a new happiness in my heart.

I also found that many of my troubles and life's problems had either disappeared or diminished to the point that they no longer bothered me. Even my shortcomings were becoming less problematic. They had not vanished into thin air, but I found that I was behaving differently and no longer relied on my defects of character as a means to cope with life. I found that I was dealing with life differently. I found that I was different. God had done a lot to change my life and me. Am I starting to see the benefits of living the program?

Meditations for the Heart

I used to be filled with alcohol and drugs. Now I am filled with my Higher Power. I carry Him on the inside. He is also all around me and walks with me on this journey called recovery. With God on the inside and on the outside, He can see me as no other can. He knows the inner workings of my heart and mind. He sees what I do and how I behave. He is there and reminds me when I still fall short. He is also there to pick me up when I stumble on the path of life. He has given me new goals in life and has shown me the way. Can I see that my Higher Power's way is the best way?

Petitions to my Higher Power
God,

Sometimes I get frustrated when other people don't understand me, but You never frustrate me in this way. You know everything there is to know about me. You know me on the inside and on the outside. You know me even better than I know myself. Help me today to trust Your understanding and to look to You for guidance on this pathway of life. Let me continue to use the program in all that I do today.
Amen.

* * * *

Wisdom for Today   *Jun 2*

There is a real sense of relief when you realize that a Power greater is in charge. When I could finally let go of trying to control everything and let God run the show, I found a new sense of inner peace. It did not take long for me to relax about my ability to stay clean and sober once I truly began to trust and have faith in a Power outside of myself. I knew I couldn't do it on my own. I needed help.

It was only then that I was able to really open myself and take advantage of all the opportunities in recovery. I found that I was not only gaining a feeling of genuine happiness and inner serenity, but I also found that I was becoming useful. Imagine me – useful! I had been the person walking around feeling like a real loser; and now I was being productive, useful and felt like I mattered. I no longer felt like a piece of junk but realized that I was valued. With God in charge I became somebody of worth. Am I enjoying the benefits of letting go and letting God?

Meditations for the Heart

Much of AA had its early roots in many of the principles found in the Bible. There is a passage in the Bible that says, "Seek ye first the Kingdom of God, and all these things will be added unto you." This principle of seeking a strong spiritual foundation first is at the very crux of what makes one successful in recovery. As long as we continue to rely on ourselves or on material things, we do not find that inner peace. Each of us has our own concept and understanding of who or what God is. But it is the reliance on this Power outside us that makes a real difference in our lives. Letting go of my character defects would not have been possible if I had no one to turn them over to. I needed not to just stop behaving the way I did, but I also had to start behaving differently. I could not do this without the help of my Higher Power. Do I have a strong spiritual foundation?

161

Petitions to my Higher Power

God,

I know that for me to experience good things in life is not dependent on what I do. I know that I will never be perfect in my spiritual foundation, but Your grace will provide for me a new life. Help me this day to let go and trust that You are in charge. Teach me the changes I need to make so that I may experience all that You offer.

Amen.

*　*　*　*

Wisdom for Today   Jun 3

I have been at meetings and watched as newcomers enter the room and sit down. The looks on their faces are always the same – quiet desperation. They sit down, often times still smelling from their last binge. Relatively soon one or two good-hearted souls will walk over and welcome this new prospect, offer a cup of coffee and chat with them. What surprises me is the reaction I sometimes see by the other people in the room. There is this avoidance that occurs, little or no eye contact and not even a word to the newcomer. Even after the meeting I see these same people leave without saying a word to this new person.

In the Bible there is a story about the "Good Samaritan." A man lies wounded and robbed on the side of the road. A Levite walks by him quickly and does nothing to help the man. A priest soon follows and does the same thing, leaving the man bleeding and battered. Then a Samaritan walks by, bandages the man's wounds and uses his own money to put him in an inn where he will be cared for and nursed back to health. Too often I believe we forget that we are no different than the wounded and beaten man. My disease completely tore my whole life apart. Too often I think we avoid looking at and reaching out to help the newcomer. Yes, sometimes it is scary for me to look directly into the eyes of addiction, in part because it reminds me of who I am. Yet, am I not responsible to offer help to others, just like I was given help when I walked through the door? Am I willing to be a "Good Samaritan?"

Meditations for the Heart

Reaching out to others is not always easy. I know for myself, I often find that I feel inadequate. Sometimes I let judgment or fear get in the way. However, I have found that in reaching out to others, particularly to newcomers, I am really helping myself. I have also found that I really don't need to worry about being adequate; my Higher Power has a way of taking

162

care of that if I let Him. It is truly wonderful when I see these new prospects returning to meetings day after day, but the real miracle is what happens to me when I act in unselfish ways. For years I felt that I had no real value and was just a worthless person. In reaching out and offering a helping hand, I find that something wonderful happens inside of me. I find that I feel like I have value and that I can be unselfish and giving. This is what makes it all work. Do I help myself by helping others?

Petitions to my Higher Power

God,

As I walk on this path called recovery, I find that I run into others just like myself who need to be bandaged and helped back to life. I know I cannot provide healing, but I do know from experience in my life that You can bring healing to the lives of those in need. Let me not walk away from those who need a helping hand. Give me courage to reach out and carry the message to others when the opportunity arises. Thank You for helping me to feel valuable again.

Amen.

* * * *

Wisdom for Today   Jun 4

Learning to have compassion is important for an alcoholic or an addict who wants to carry the message to others. I needed a compassionate response from others when I first walked through the doors of the program. What is compassion? Well, it means that a person is both sympathetic and patient. It was easy for me to be sympathetic to others new to the program. Their story was just like mine. Yes, the events that had happened in their lives were different than the events in mine, but the struggle with addiction was the same. It was the patience that I really struggled with.

Yet I knew that finding this patience with the newcomer was exactly what they needed, just as I had needed it when I walked through the door. I needed to be willing to let God work in this person just as He worked in me. When I really was honest with myself, I knew that I was probably a real pain to others when I first came to the program. Between the fear, complaining, anger, sadness and just plain stupidity I displayed, I know I must have tried the patience of many who were reaching out to me. Now I was in a place to give back what I had received. Learning to be compassionate was not easy; but it is what I needed to provide the newcomer, just as I had been given this wonderful gift in my early recovery. Am I compassionate with others?

Meditations for the Heart

I hope that I never grow tired of prayer. It seems to me that too often I have wanted to give up praying before I received an answer. Then unexpectedly God provides an answer to the question I have bought before Him. Oftentimes I regret I do not pray more. It is surprising the way many of my prayers are answered. Oftentimes it is not what I expect, but it is always what I need. When I pray for strength, I am given the courage I need. When I pray for an answer, God lets me know in His own way what I should do. As I have prayed, I find that my trust in a Higher Power grows stronger. Prayer is a healthy habit that all addicts and alcoholics should develop. For it is in prayer that I am in communion with God. It is in prayer that I understand His will for me. It is in prayer that my spiritual life is given meaning. Do I come to my Higher Power in prayer?

Petitions to my Higher Power

God,

Teach me to be compassionate to others in need. Help me to reach out and show patience with these individuals. Let me provide this gift to others without passing judgment, just as the gift was given to me. Strengthen me in praying faithfully to You and in seeking Your guidance.

Amen.

* * * *

Wisdom for Today   Jun 5

Humility was never my strong suit. I enjoyed bragging about how much I could drink or use. It made me feel powerful and in control. As my addiction progressed and got worse, I continued to seek after this feeling only to find out I was losing control and my power slipped away. After my disease brought me to my knees, I was left empty and alone.

Eventually I found my way into the Twelve Step program. Here was a place that I could no longer brag. I was faced with the reality of defeat. I also had to acknowledge that I needed to change. I could not do this on my own. I was the problem, and I could not change myself. I had to ask for help. The thought of asking God as I understood Him for help was a difficult one. It was only in this humility that I might begin to find answers and begin to change. Am I willing to seek His help humbly?

Meditations for the Heart

I was willing to put everything on the line to enjoy myself. I was all about having a good time. Soon I began to experience losses. I really didn't understand what I was risking. Many of these risks soon led to even more loses. Until I finally stopped, I did not see any gains. One gain I am glad I have realized is that I now can see the risks. I know just what I might lose if I go back to my old ways. Am I able to see not only the risks associated with relapse but also the losses that I may experience?

Petitions to my Higher Power
God,

Help me to seek Your help. The truth is that I cannot seek Your help on my own. Today I pray that I may seek Your guidance in my life and know what I may lose if I don't turn to You.
Amen.

* * * *

Wisdom for Today   Jun 6
One place I continually fell short in my early recovery was looking at the positive aspects of my life. It was just too easy to get caught up in focusing on the negatives. I would complain and whine about everything in my life and not look at the fact that I through the grace of God had stayed clean and sober one more day. I was a good one for "awful-izing" in recovery. Then my sponsor told me to start a gratitude list. He told me that I needed to identify at least one thing each day for which I was grateful. This assignment did a lot to adjust my attitude about life.

I was beginning to see that just waking up without my head feeling three sizes too big was a good thing. Showing up for work on time and giving an honest day's labor was a good thing. Actually taking time to play with my children was a good thing. Showing my spouse that I valued her support and that I wanted to be a support for her was a big thing. Yes, I continued to make mistakes, and there are times when certain character defects raise their ugly head in my life, but I don't need to focus on just the negative aspects of my life anymore. Do I practice progress, not perfection, in my life?

Meditations for the Heart
A big part of my attitude change was due in large part to an underlying belief that better things would come. I had heard the "promises" read at meetings, and I began to believe that these things could and would happen for me if I stayed clean and sober. I began to see how my Higher Power was looking out for me and that He was working to change my sorrow into joy. I began to genuinely laugh again. I began to look at my whole life differently. I no longer perceived myself as a real loser. I didn't have to walk around covered

165

with shame. I began to see my life and myself differently, but most of all I began to see God differently. I no longer saw God as a punishing judge, but as a friend - a friend who was willing to point out my shortcomings and show me how to overcome them. I could make changes with His help. Do I believe the promises of recovery are available to me?

Petitions to my Higher Power

God,

Too often I take life for granted. Every day You give me breath, and everyday You show me how to remain clean and sober. So much of my life in recovery is filled with good things that I sometimes overlook these events and just focus on the negative aspects of my day. Help me this day to celebrate the good that is so much a part of my life. Help me to remember how it is that these events occur and remain grateful for each gift I receive from You. Amen.

* * * *

Wisdom for Today   Jun 7

Fellowship is such an important part of the program for me. In developing relationships and true friendships with other addicts and alcoholics in recovery, I also was developing a support system. There was a group of people I could fall back on, and they would lift me up. Sometimes I would go for months and even years where everything seemed to go along pretty smoothly. Then some event would occur that seemed to turn my life upside down. Some of these events were consequences of my addiction that did not occur until long after I sobered up. I was still paying the price for my behaviors when using drugs and alcohol even though I had stopped using. Sometimes these events were just a part of life – looking for a new job, a death in the family, illness or other losses.

Regardless of the cause, these events had a way of stealing my serenity. I needed a group of people I could fall back on and trust that they would lift me back up. The fellowship provided that safety net for me. And not just for me! I have seen everyone I know in the program have to deal with complicating factors and life transitions in their recovery process. Those people who had a safety net fared much better. This did not mean that these times were not painful or cause sadness or anger. These events often were scary; but with the help of others willing to pick me up, I could get back on track more quickly. I didn't need to go off the deep end. Do I have a safety net?

Meditations for the Heart

Another Bible story I really like is the story of two men, one who built his house on the sand and another who built his house on the rock. When the storms came the man who had built his house on the sand watched as all his hard work crumbled. The man who had built his house on the rock had his work weather the storm without damage. In working the program, I was asked to search for this rock before I started to build my house. This rock for me has been my Higher Power, my sponsor and my home group. Finding this rock took some time; but looking back, I am really glad that I did not take the "easier, softer way." I have watched those people who built their recovery home on the sand. Eventually, they find out that "*half measures avail them nothing.*" (*Alcoholics Anonymous,* Fourth Edition. Page 59) Is my recovery built on a rock?

Petitions to my Higher Power

God,

Encourage me to build my house on solid rock and develop strong relationships with others in the program. Let me do the maintenance work on my house so that it stands strong against the wind and rain of life. You have the blueprints for this house. Let me follow Your plans so that I rest assured that the house I build in recovery can and will stand even against the most severe storm.

Amen.

* * * *

Wisdom for Today   Jun 8

Sometimes when I was sitting at a meeting, I would hear someone else describe a life struggle, and I would say to myself, "I've been there." Maybe my experience is not exactly the same, but the feeling seemed to be identical. The thinking and beliefs were the same. Then when it was my turn to comment, I stayed with the topic rather than relate my experience. For a long time I did this and I'm not really sure why I did that. Maybe it was because I didn't want to look like a non-conformist. Maybe it was because I was so new in the program and didn't think my life experience was of any value. Maybe it was because I thought that I would sound foolish. I'm not really sure.

But as I grew in my program, I began to reach out to others. I would share my experiences when it was my turn to comment. I would seek people out after the meeting and talk with them further. I began to discover that sharing my life made me feel better. Even if what I had to say didn't help the other person, it helped me. Helping others is one of the best ways to help you stay clean and sober. And when you hear back that sharing your experience actually helped the other person, well, helping someone else has to be one of the greatest of all human experiences. Do I regularly share my experience, strength and hope?

Meditations for the Heart

I can remember times in my recovery where it really felt like I was at war. Dealing with some of my life problems or character defects or matters of self-will, I felt like I was under constant attack from the enemy; and I didn't even really know who the enemy was. Sometimes I felt like I was my own worst enemy. History has been filled with many battles and wars. There have been great leaders, and there have been really sick tyrants. But all these leaders and tyrants pass, wars end, and then someone else tries to dominate. In recovery the real wars we fight are within. Yes, we may want to direct our anger and rage at someone else. We may want to blame others. But the real battles are spiritual battles. It is only in winning these spiritual battles that we experience a victory that leads to joy, peace of mind and an abundant life. I have found that I need to face all my spiritual battles with a heart of courage and one of faith. Do I know that where God is, there is also victory?

Petitions to my Higher Power

God,

Lead me to share my life experience with others in the program, just as others helped me by sharing their life experiences with me. Help me to have a heart filled with courage and faith, so that I may be rewarded with victory in the spiritual battles I face in my life. Let me be a strong warrior in these battles, filled with the confidence that You are on my side.

Amen.

* * * *

Wisdom for Today   Jun 9

Sometimes in my work with addicts and alcoholics, I hear them say they don't get anything out of a meeting. I ask them, "Well, what did you put into it?" One thing the program has taught me is the importance of sharing. When I was drinking and using, I really didn't share much of anything about myself. The reasons for this were many. Often times I didn't share simply because I was so out of touch with what was going on inside of me that I had nothing to share. Other times it was because I was too ashamed to talk about what was happening in my life. Sometimes resentment or judging others got in the way. Probably one of the main reasons I didn't share with others was simply because of my self-centeredness and selfishness. Even though family and my using buddies surrounded me, I was lonely.

When I listen to addicts and alcoholics at meetings, we all have our own way of screaming. As we share, we release many of the frustrations, fears, sadness, pain and other difficulties we face in our lives. We also share what has worked for us. We share what quiets our screaming. What has amazed me about my sharing at meetings is what I get back in return. By telling my story, sharing my experience, strengths and hope, I find that the compulsion to drink or use is removed. I find that I gain new clarity and insight into what I need to change. I find that the problems of my life don't seem so big. I find that I am not alone. I find that I gain an inner peace. It is in giving of myself that I receive these things. Am I sharing in meetings?

Meditations for the Heart

As I shared my story, I found that the road to recovery straightened out. It no longer had as many twists and turns. My character was being developed in this process. God knew that I needed to share. He knew I needed to unload the garbage of my life. Through obedience to His vision and openly sharing, my path was made straight. I still experience some bumps along my journey, but this is always because I loose sight of God's vision and will for me. But even these bumps along the way teach me to return to the basics. I need to go back to meetings and share what is going on. I needed to go back to the steps and once again turn over my will and my life to God's care. I also need to share my life struggles in prayer. In this quiet communion with my Higher Power, I am shown the way to get back on the path and continue my journey of recovery. Do I share my struggles in prayer?

Petitions to my Higher Power

God,

I must stop along the path of recovery today and thank You for all that I receive by sharing my story, my struggles and my hopes. I know that these gifts are from You and that they are not something I earn. They are simply gifts I receive from You because of my participation in the program You have led me to. Help me this day to keep an open mind and to be obedient to Your divine vision. Amen.

* * * *

Wisdom for Today   Jun 10

I remember the incredible honesty of the sharing I heard at meetings when I first started to attend. I was just amazed as one person after another openly described his or her own faults. I was encouraged by the ones I heard share a real sense of hope. It really didn't matter if it was an open meeting, closed meeting, topic or discussion meeting. Even at study meetings when I heard people read from conference-approved literature, their comments were open and honest. I really found it hard to share at first. But as I became more comfortable and less paranoid in meetings, I began to open up as well. It then seemed that the floodgates were opened. All the baggage I had been carrying around had to be unloaded. I found that I felt better when I left the meeting. Something was different.

Even after working through many of the steps and sharing my story of how it was, I have found that I still need to unload sometimes. Life has problems, and I have found that I need meetings as a sounding board. I still need to bounce things off of other people. I still need to do reality testing to check out my thinking and attitudes. Sometimes I still need to talk about the pain that life can bring. Other times I simply need to share the joys that I experience. Do I recognize that sharing is important if I want to stay clean and sober?

Meditations for the Heart

Call on the strengths of God and claim them as your own. I remember walking into the Twelve Step program and feeling like a weakling. The disease had physically, psychologically, morally and spiritually beaten me. I knew that I could not do it on my own; and even if I could muster all the strength I had, it would not be enough. Fortunately the program has taught me not to rely on my strength but on my Higher Power's strength. I know I can also count on the strength of my home group and my sponsor. There is more than enough strength available to me. All I need to do is claim it. When I am facing a struggle or needing to make a decision, I turn to my Higher Power. I ask God for strength and guidance. When I am reasonably sure of the direction that God wants me to go, I claim His strength and move forward with confidence that the strength I have been given will be sufficient to accomplish what I need to do. Each day I am given the strength I need for the journey, and each day I can go back to the renewable source of strength that is God. Do I turn to God daily for the renewable supply of strength I need?

Petitions to my Higher Power
God,

Thank You for the strength I am given for this day. I know I do not need to worry about tomorrow because the source of my strength is You. I can seek renewed strength whenever I need it and can trust that it is always there for me. Help me this day to share all that I need to share. Give me courage not to hold back, because I know that secrets can hurt me.
Amen.

* * * *

One of my biggest struggles in recovery has been to learn patience. My will always wants what it wants, and it wants it right now. Addiction taught me immediate gratification. In recovery I had to learn about delayed gratification. My life did not just turn around because I stopped drinking and using drugs. It has taken time to learn a new way of living. Frequently during this process of change, I have struggled with impatience. Much of this was in part due to unrealistic expectations. It has not been easy to learn to be patient.

I recall going to a meeting one night, and I spent a good deal of time complaining about my day. I was looking for people to agree with me and feel sorry for me because everything that could have gone bad that day did. Several people commented after I had spoken, and then it was passed to an old-timer in the group. I did not receive any pity, nor did he even agree with me and how I felt. He simply looked at me and said that it sounded to him like God had given me many opportunities to practice patience throughout my day. This really angered me, but it also stuck like glue because it was true. If I had been patient throughout the day, my attitude would have been very different when I came to the meeting that night. Soon I began looking at many of life's challenges as opportunities to practice patience. Do I see that the challenges I face must be faced with patience?

Meditations for the Heart

Life is full of challenges. Even in recovery many of these challenges can turn out tragically. When this happens, it is easy to think that somehow I have failed. There is no failure in tragedy; the real failure comes in all the little things I could have done differently before the tragedy occurred. It may not have prevented the tragedy; but if all those little things had been done differently, my ability to cope with the tragedy would be very different. It is often in these little things that I fail. Sometimes it is my impatience. Other times it is my failure to turn it over to my Higher Power. Sometimes it is when I fail to ask for help. There are many reasons. However, when I set my mind to do the next right thing and follow after God's will, I find that tragedy does not seem like a failure to me. I can look back and know that I did everything I could have done. My mind and my heart are better prepared to deal with the tragedy when it does occur. Am I paying attention to the little things?

Petitions to my Higher Power

God,

In addiction I always looked for life in the fast lane. Teach me to slow down and be patient. Help me to stay focused on the little things along the

171

way. Let me practice doing the next right thing. Change how I look at life, and let me see life through Your eyes. Give me direction for this day, and guide my steps.

Amen.

＊　＊　＊　＊

Wisdom for Today   Jun 12

I can remember when I thought I was really unique. I thought I was different and believed that I was not like all "those people" I knew they were "real" alcoholics and addicts. I wasn't like them. I was different. I could control it. I had more willpower. Even when the disease had finally whipped me, I continued to think I was unique. I thought that my problems were worse than others. I thought that no one could possibly understand what I had been through; and even if they could, there was no way they could help me face my unique set of problems. I was suffering with terminal uniqueness.

In recovery I slowly learned that I was not unique. I was no different than every other addict and alcoholic. I struggled with the same disease and the same recovery process. As I began to work through the steps, most of my terminal uniqueness disappeared - with one exception. As an alcoholic and addict I have a unique ability to be useful to others who are in the same boat as I am. I can share my experience, strength and hope with others. This makes me uniquely useful. Twelve Step groups are made up of individuals who are uniquely capable of helping each other. I can take my greatest failures and defeats and use them to help others. Can I see that being someone who has been through active addiction puts me in a unique spot to help others?

Meditations for the Heart

Practice does not make one perfect; it just makes them better. I will never in this life be able to have a perfect relationship with my Higher Power, but practice can make my relationship with God better. Through prayer and meditation I can feel the presence of God. I can experience Him strengthening, protecting and leading me. In every joy I can celebrate His presence and reach out to Him with a grateful heart. In every struggle I can reach out and ask for His help. I can share my fear, frustration, loneliness or anything that is bothering me. I do not need to carry the burden by myself. I try to live life as if God were standing beside me in all that I do. I do not do this perfectly; none of us can. But it is something that can be practiced; and as it is practiced, I find that I get better. Recovery is not about getting well, but it is about getting better. Each year on my anniversary I want to look back and see that I am better than the year before. Do I practice my spiritual relationship with my Higher Power each day?

Petitions to my Higher Power
God,

It is good not to struggle with terminal uniqueness anymore. Help me to use my unique perspectives of life to reach out to others. Let me walk with You by my side today and practice my relationship with You. Keep leading me in each step that I take on this journey of recovery. Help me to show others the way that leads to You.
Amen.

* * * *

Wisdom for Today   Jun 13
One thing I learned relatively quickly in the program was the importance of telling on my disease. Keeping things locked inside did me no good. I had to open up and tell others when my disease was acting out. In the early going, it seemed like this was all the time. My addiction was working overtime to try and convince me to return to the insanity. Sometimes it was cravings or urges to use that I needed to talk about. I had this addictive preoccupation with getting high. I would romance the high, remembering all the good times. I was not thinking about the consequences and pain that my disease had caused. I was glorifying my drinking and my drug use.

Other times it was anger and resentment that was boiling on the inside. Then there were the times that guilt or shame had its way with me. Still other times my denial and dishonesty would play games with me. Regardless of how my addiction was acting out, I needed to share. Keeping secrets only kept me sick. Even now with years into recovery, I find that my disease looks for opportunities to act out. Even though the compulsion to drink or use is no longer present, I can see that my illness will look for any chink in the armor. Recovery at times is a war, and a good friend of mine helped me by telling me to keep my helmet strap tight. He was referring to the armor that any warrior wears. When my disease acts out, do I tell on my disease and keep my helmet strap tight?

Meditations for the Heart
The program gave to me the armor I wear in recovery. I have been provided with the steps and many other tools to protect me from any assault that my disease may bring against me. It is when I remove the armor that I become vulnerable. If I stop going to meetings, stop using the steps or stop

relying on my Higher Power, I put myself at risk. My disease knows this and lies in wait. It sneaks up on me when I least expect it. This is why I need to tell on my disease and share what is going on with me. This is why even years into recovery I still must wear the armor I was provided in the early days of my recovery. When I am under attack, I need to go to more meetings. I need to tell others what is going on with me. If I do this, I know I can be confident that my Higher Power will protect me. Do I wear the armor I have been given?

Petitions to my Higher Power
God,

When I was naked, You clothed me with a fine suit of armor. This armor still protects me today. Even though the battles I fight do not occur as often, I know that I still must wear this suit of armor, for it is only in wearing this armor that I can be confident in battles that I must fight with my disease. You bring victory to me each day that I remain clean and sober. For this I am grateful.

Amen.

* * * *

Wisdom for Today   Jun 14
Recovery is not always easy. When I looked back at all the people I had harmed, there were many with whom I was anxious to make amends. Many of the people I was closest with – my family and friends – the amends began just because I was staying clean and sober. But making amends and repairing the damage done would take me some time and a consistent change in my behavior. The financial amends, although overwhelming, were perhaps the easiest. I simply needed to arrange to pay back what I owed and then be responsible for following through and making the payments.

There were other amends that were much more difficult. Some amends really frightened me, and I would need to find courage – courage that I did not have. Here depending on my sponsor and my Higher Power were essential if the repair work was ever to be completed. There were amends that I simply did not want to make. Anger, resentment and hurt stood in the way. In order to become willing to make these amends, I would need to find a way to forgive these people. No reconciliation would be possible until I could find a way in my heart to forgive the pain caused by these people. Then there were the amends I needed to make with myself. I would need to find a way not only to forgive myself but also accept me for who I was. I would need to become the person I wanted to be. I would need to become the person God wanted me to be. Repairing the damage and changing my behavior was not an easy task. Yet I knew that if I wanted to remain clean and sober, I would need to accomplish this step. Am I ready to begin the process of making amends?

Meditations for the Heart

Sometimes I do really stupid things in recovery. I ask myself, "How could I have been so stupid?" Well, the answer to this question is easy. In almost all of these situations, I reacted to events and did not seek out wisdom before I acted. I have learned through my errors and by my mistakes that simply reacting only to situations can hurt others or me. It is important for me to seek out wisdom before I respond to life on life's terms. I need to talk with my sponsor, other recovering people and to God before choosing a direction for my response to life. In the Serenity Prayer, we pray, "and the wisdom to know the difference." Gaining this wisdom happens only when I am willing to seek it out. Stupidity happens when I don't stop to think. Stupidity happens when I don't talk to others before responding to life. Stupidity happens when I react emotionally to life without thinking about what a wise response would be. The good news is that wisdom is something that can be gained by anyone. Do I seek out wisdom in all that I do?

Petitions to my Higher Power

God,

Somewhere in this day I am likely to have an opportunity to be stupid. Help me not to react without thinking. Let me seek out wisdom in all that I do. Give me the courage to make amends with everyone with whom I need to do this. Let me be wise in doing the repair work that I need to do.
Amen

* * * *

Wisdom for Today   Jun 15

"Made direct amends." (*Alcoholics Anonymous,* Fourth Edition. Page 59) Doing the repair work I needed to do required action on my part. For some of the people I had harmed, I really had no idea even where to begin. Saying I was sorry just would not be enough. I had said that I was sorry a million times. What was required was change. I needed to make a firm commitment not to behave in the ways I had when I was drinking and using drugs. I needed to be different. It was this difference that would potentially repair the damage. I had to be careful though. I could neither assume nor expect that the mending of what I had done would be accepted. Forgiveness and reconciliation are gifts of grace, and there were those whom I had harmed that would not be gracious.

The amends I made were not so much for the other person but for me. I could look at myself and know in my mind and my heart that I had cleaned my side of the street. I could not assume that the other person would be willing to even acknowledge my effort. Fortunately the vast majority of people I knew did accept me again. Forgiveness and reconciliation happened, and new bonds were formed. Perhaps the greatest payoff for me in completing this step was the fact that I no longer was tormented by my past. The Big Book says, "*We will not regret the past, nor will we wish to shut the door on it.*" (*Alcoholics Anonymous,* Fourth Edition. Page 83) I believe this only becomes true in completing this step. Today I can look at the past, but I don't have to stare at it. Can I make amends without expectations?

Meditations for the Heart

It is truly a gift of recovery to be able to reclaim relationships. Through the process of making amends, my relationships with family and friends improved by leaps and bounds. People that I had hurt, lied to, used and manipulated were able to see a new me and risk trusting me again. But I now know this was only possible because God reclaimed me. I had turned away from God and even run from Him in my addiction; but through the process of recovery, brought about by working the steps, I opened the door to a relationship with a Higher Power. As soon as I did this, God reclaimed me. As soon as I made amends to others and they opened the door to me, I could reclaim these relationships. None of this would have been possible without my Higher Power. Do I recognize the gifts that the program brings?

Petitions to my Higher Power

God,

Sometimes I like to take credit for the changes that have occurred in my life. But I know in my heart that none of this would have been possible without You first reclaiming me. Give me the courage to mend the brokenness I caused in my addiction. Let me not be consumed with expectations and simply accept Your gracious gifts.

Amen.

* * * *

Wisdom for Today   Jun 16

I paid my dues for membership in the program through my years of addictive using. But these are the dues only for membership. In recovery I still need to do my part and accept the responsibilities that come with working the program and following its principles. I am part of a much bigger whole, but I am still only one person. The program provides me with the principles I need to discover the life that is hidden inside of me, the life that my Higher Power wants me to live. I still have to walk the walk. I am given privileges in the program as I get more clean time under my belt. It becomes my responsibility to share in the work of the program.

I remember my first responsibility given to me. My sponsor told me to clean up after the meetings. My first reaction was, "Am I the maid?" I did not say this out loud, but complained in my head the whole time. Looking back now, I can see that it was good for me to do this service. I learned about humility. I learned about acceptance. I learned about responsibility. Later I was asked to chair a meeting or give a lead for the topic of discussion. Eventually I was asked to become a general service representative and even asked to plan a presentation for a recovery retreat. Each time I have been asked to serve, I have learned more about myself. I have learned more about what makes the fellowship work. I continue to pay my dues through service. Am I willing to serve and give back what I have been given?

Meditations for the Heart

Gratitude is one of my greatest weapons in the war of addiction. When I find my heart filled with gratitude, I no longer have time for self-pity. There is no room in my heart for deceit when it is filled with gratitude. Gratitude leads me to praise God for all that He has done for me, and it compels me to be of service to others. Gratitude also has a way of creating a strong sense of security in recovery. Gratitude changes my perspective on life, and I begin to see all the little things in life that happen as a part of God's plan for me. Gratitude helps me to discover the life that is inside of me. It leads me to a place of serenity and peace of mind. Gratitude helps me eliminate unrealistic expectations and accept the gifts that are provided to me in abundance. Do I have a grateful heart?

Petitions to my Higher Power

God,

Teach me to be of service to others, so that I might also learn more about me. Help me to see all the gifts that I can receive through a life of service to others. Let me not be obsessed with material things and focus more on the spiritual things that will last. Let me find all the gifts that You provide along this journey and be filled with gratitude.

Amen.

* * * *

177

Not every day in recovery goes smoothly. In fact, I have had a few days that just seemed a little better than a train wreck. When days like this happen, I need to go back to the basics. Don't drink or use, and go to a meeting, say the Serenity Prayer, call my sponsor and anything else I have to do to make it from the beginning of the day till the end of the day. One of the first things I need to do is get out of my heart. My emotions tend to run wild on these kinds of days. It is dangerous for me to get so wrapped up in my emotions. They can add fuel to the fire and make life crazy. My thinking at these times usually isn't much better. That is why it is so important for me to be comfortable and ready to ask for help. To quote the Big Book, "*Without help it is too much for us.*" (*Alcoholics Anonymous,* Fourth Edition. Page 59)

On days when everything is spinning out of control, I really need help to gain a healthy perspective on life. I need other people. It is so easy for me to make everything a catastrophe. My friends in the program are quick to remind me of the principles of the program. They help me see the "big picture." I am reminded that even my worst days clean and sober are better than addiction. I am reminded where my strength comes from. I am reminded to chose God's will for me and to ask for His power to help me through my current troubles. Sometimes my friends can even get me to laugh at myself. It is amazing what friends can do. It is days like this that remind me that, "It works if you work it." Am I willing to go to any length?

Meditations for the Heart

Making it through days like I just described have a profound effect on me. My faith in the program and in my Higher Power is ultimately strengthened. It helps me build character. It helps me see that I really am grateful to have the program and my friends in recovery to fall back on. It is times like these that have really cemented the bond that I have with my sponsor. It also shows me that I can get through the tough times. The principles of surrender, turning it over, checking myself out, admitting my mistakes and renewing my relationship with God all have helped me through the tough times. One of the promises of the program is, "*We will intuitively know how to handle situations that used to baffle us.*" (*Alcoholics Anonymous,* Fourth Edition. Page 84) Getting through the hard times is proof that the promises do come true. Am I grateful for the things I learn in getting through the hard times?

Petitions to my Higher Power
God,

I am not sure why hard times occur, but I am sure that You will help me get through them. I am grateful for the tools that I receive through the program. Most of all, I am grateful for the sense of hope that You provide to me when I need it most. My days are not all bad anymore, and I am sure that You will give me many more good days. Thank You for keeping me clean and sober today!

Amen.

* * * *

Wisdom for Today *Jun 18*

There was a time when this country drafted young men into service of their country. This is not the case with the program. We are not drafted into service, but we volunteer. Service work is a part of what keeps the program strong, and it is a part of what keeps me strong. When I offer to be of service to others in the program, I am volunteering to help myself. Through loyal attendance and generosity of my time, I can find many opportunities to be of service to the program and others. The type of service is not what is important; it is how I go about providing this service.

One thing that I have found true for myself is that when I go about providing service work, if I do this to the best of my ability and am genuinely invested in helping, I leave with a sense of humble thanks for what I get out of doing this work. Whether it is making coffee, chairing a meeting, spending time with a newcomer or sponsoring someone, I am made a better person because of it. I get out of my self-centeredness and become interested in others. I gain a sense of usefulness. I feel like what I am doing is worthwhile. I find many gifts in my life because of the service work I do. Am I willing to give my time and energy back to the program that saved my life?

Meditations for the Heart

Prayer provides answers and strength. It does not matter how we go about praying. Any connection with God is one that brings strength and direction. When I first sobered up, I really had little idea about how to pray. These first prayers in recovery however were some of the most powerful. Simple statements like, "God, help me!" said a lot. I was connected, and I got what I needed from my Higher Power. As I have grown in my relationship with my Higher Power, my prayer life has grown and changed. I still pray for what I need, but I also pray for others and what they need. I pray for guidance in my decision making process. I pray in thanks and gratitude. I pray in new ways, like a simple glace upward and think about what God wants. I pray with tears, and I pray with laughter. I pray with all of me – my mind, my heart, and my very soul. Am I staying plugged into my Higher Power?

Petitions to my Higher Power

God,

Show me this day how I may be of service to others. Let me not be afraid of where this may lead me but trust that You will guide me in all that I do. Thank You for letting me stay plugged into You. Help me this day to reach out to You in all that I do and seek Your direction for my life.

Amen.

* * * *

Wisdom for Today   Jun 19

When I first got clean and sober, I found that there were a lot of times that I continued to glorify my party days. I would "romance the high" in my head. But this only led to trouble. I would get into stinking thinking, and before long came the cravings or urges to drink or get high. When I finally got past that initial obsession and started to settle down in my recovery, I began to realize that there was an awful lot that I didn't miss about my party days. I really didn't miss waking up with my head feeling three sizes too big. I didn't miss all the aches and pains, the stomachaches, or the three-day binges and empty wallet.

I began to enjoy knowing what I did the day before. I really liked that I wasn't constantly chasing after my alibis. I began to like the feeling of fitting in that I found at meetings. I liked being able for a change to look at myself in the mirror. I liked the fact that my hands didn't shake when I was trying to brush my hair, shave or clean my teeth. I started to feel good about my job. I started to feel like I was a part of my family again. In fact, everything seemed to be going better. Do I still miss the party days?

Meditations for the Heart

I believe that each of us is born with a knowledge of God in our heart; a fire that grows in our heart as we become more conscious of Him as we grow spiritually. I all but smothered any awareness of this relationship when I was actively drinking and using. Yet, out of the smoke and ashes of my addiction, God saw to it that a spark remained. And from this spark a new fire could be started within me. This new fire started again with flames of wanting to live the right way. As the fire was fed with new tinder and fuel in the program, it grew into flames that wanted to do things the way my Higher Power would want me to do them. As I grew in my relationship with God, as I understand Him, the fire grew and transformed me from someone who followed my Higher Power into someone who walked with God. The fire grew into a companionship with God. Do I work to keep my spiritual fire burning and growing?

Petitions to my Higher Power

God,

A big part of not missing the past is living in today with You. Help me to keep my spiritual fire burning and increase my desire to be ever closer to Your Divine Spirit. Let me this day begin to increase my willingness to seek You out in all that I do. Constantly remind me that You are with me, and help me to trust that You will always give me the strength I need for the day.

Amen.

* * * *

Wisdom for Today   Jun 20

Because I have learned to put my addiction in God's hands, I am in a unique position to help others do the same thing. When I first came into the program, I really relied on the strength of the group. My home group served as a channel to give the strength that I needed to make it in recovery. It took me a while to understand that what the group did for me was serve as a connection to God's strength. This strength is what I needed, because I was bankrupt of any power of my own. I was powerless. I needed to draw on the strength that my home group, sponsor and ultimately my Higher Power could provide. Today is no different. I still need to draw on that same strength, not so much to stay clean and sober, but to deal with life's problems.

What has changed is that now that the compulsion to drink or use drugs has been removed, I can be a part of the group that serves as a channel to God's strength. Because of His grace, I am now in a unique position to share what I have been given. I can look into a newcomer's eyes and know what they are going through. So with compassion, understanding and patience, I can reach out and offer the strength that is so desperately needed by the newcomer. I can use my own defeat and failures, my experience and my illness to help others. Will I use what I have been given to help others?

Meditations for the Heart

I always used to want my shot glass filled. Now I want my "CUP" filled. Compassion, Understanding and Patience (CUP) are what I need in reaching out to others. I try not to let a day go by without reaching out to someone with this new cup I have been given. Whether it is my children, family, friends or a newcomer that have just walked through the doors of the program, I try to do something to lift up others. Once I was in the pit of despair and discouragement. I was lifted out of this pit. Now it is my turn to reach out to others and raise them to a new place – a place that is filled with hope, courage,

181

faith and health. I can provide strength to others and help them with what burdens them. I can give away what I was so freely given. Am I willing to reach out to others in Compassion, Understanding, and Patience?

Petitions to my Higher Power

God,

I am beginning to understand what the writer of the Psalm meant when he said, "My cup runs over." Truly I am blessed on this path called recovery. I can get what I need from You at anytime I need it. Because of this I am filled and have extra strength to give to others. My shot glass ran dry, but now my cup runs over.

Amen.

* * * *

Wisdom for Today   Jun 21

"Rarely have we seen a person fail who has thoroughly followed our path." (*Alcoholics Anonymous,* Fourth Edition. Page 58) This is the miracle and the stumbling block of the program. I recall feeling like such a failure in my life because of my addiction. I was doing everything that I did not want to do and nothing that I wanted to do. I really did not want to hurt all the people I hurt. I really did not want to experience all the consequences that addiction to alcohol and drugs supplied. I really did not want to get to a point where I would have to use just to feel normal. But this is exactly what happened with my disease, and I was left feeling like a failure.

This sentence provided me with a real sense of hope. The sheer number of people I saw at meetings provided me with hope. I saw the miracle working for others, and this sentence gave me hope that I could get clean and sober as well. All I had to do was thoroughly follow the path. Yet this is where the stumbling block is for so many. I am willing to do everything except . . . This is what made me fall on my face, and I have watched as others fell on their faces as well – all because I was not willing to thoroughly follow the path. Surrender is what finally put me on this pathway to recovery. Am I willing to be thorough today?

Meditations for the Heart

I am not sure when it happened, but somewhere along the line I realized that everything that was happening to me in recovery was a gift. It was not something I earned, but something that was given to me. There are many times when I have strayed away from the path of recovery only to be led back. When I stray, I don't always drink or use. Most of the time it was set by not going to a meeting, not using and working the steps. I acted just like a dumb sheep that wanders away from the flock. Fortunately, my Higher Power is a Good Shepherd that leads me back time and time again. I could never have gotten clean and sober on my own. Recovery is the gift I have been given. My Higher Power keeps me on the path. Do I see the gift that recovery is?

Petitions to my Higher Power
God,

If it were up to me I would have failed over and over again. My way never seems to work. But You have all power, and it is You that keep me on the path. I know I have to walk this path and that no one can walk this path for me, but it is You that keeps me on the path. Thank You for leading me today. Amen.

* * * *

Wisdom for Today   Jun 22

Sometimes the things I hear at meetings confuse me. It seems that some of the things that are said are in direct contradiction to each other. Some that bothered me for a long time were people saying things like, "Get out of your head," and "My best thinking got me drinking." Statements like these are inconsistent with the slogan, "Think, think, think" and the Serenity Prayer's statement, "and the wisdom to know the difference." When things just don't seem to make sense, this is when I need to talk with my sponsor, who always seems to have a way of straightening me out.

He told me that much of the program is filled with paradox, things that don't seem to make sense but work. He explained that there was a big difference between thinking with my emotions and thinking with the wisdom of my Higher Power. For example, when I get into dwelling on events and people that bring up feelings of fear or resentment, I can go for long walks in my head and stray from the path of recovery. However, if I look at the same situation through the eyes of my Higher Power, life looks different. Other paradoxes are more complicated like surrendering to find freedom or quitting in order to win. Yet these paradoxes of recovery indeed work. The good news is I don't have to figure it all out, I just need to trust that it works; and if I am confused, I need to ask for help. Do I have someone to whom I can talk to about my questions?

Meditations for the Heart
The wisdom of the program is something that can be acquired. I know there were times I felt awfully stupid early on. Between my brain just not

working right and my will getting me into trouble, I began to wonder if I would ever get it right. Then I read a statement in the Big Book, *"Are these extravagant promises? We think not. They are happening among us every day."* (*Alcoholics Anonymous,* Fourth Edition. Page 84) The promises of the program tell me that I will intuitively know how to handle situations that baffled me. So I continued to study the program literature, talk with my sponsor, pray and listen at meetings; and I slowly began to learn the wisdom that exists in the program. I could claim it for my use. I could get out of my head and into my Higher Power's head. I memorized key things from my sponsor like, "I will not drink or use no matter how bad life seems." All these things increased my wisdom. But the most important thing I have learned is that I can never stop learning. Am I willing to invest my time and energy into gaining more of the wisdom that the program has to offer?

Petitions to my Higher Power
God,

Get into my head before I do. Help me this day to focus my energy on gaining the wisdom the program has to offer. Let me bring all my thoughts to You and evaluate them in the light of Your will for me. Let me spend my time seeking to improve my contact with You and gain true wisdom for recovery. Amen.

* * * *

Wisdom for Today   Jun 23
"They are naturally incapable of grasping and developing a manner of living that demands rigorous honesty." (*Alcoholics Anonymous,* Fourth Edition. Page 58) This sentence in Chapter 5 of the Big Book really troubled me when I first walked through the doors of the program. It did so in part because I knew that getting honest would not be an easy task. And I was right. In some ways getting honest would be much harder than stopping drinking and using drugs. Every character defect I had stood in the way – pride, fear, shame, grandiosity – all stood in the way of sharing my secrets. Yet deep inside I also wanted a way out of the insanity of my addiction.

I could grasp the concept of being rigorously honesty. I understood that playing games, hiding, covering up would not allow me to attain and keep my sobriety. The real question was, "Am I willing to develop honesty in all I do?" When I looked at getting honest as a developmental process, I began to understand that I could not expect perfection. There was a lot involved in developing the ability to walk. I had to learn to roll over on my stomach, get up on all fours, learn to crawl, pull myself upright with the help of a piece of furniture, take my first steps, fall down, get back up again and eventually walk with confidence. This process did not occur all at once. Developing honesty also did not occur all at once. There are times that I still struggle with total honesty, but I have come a long way from where I began this process. One thing I know – I can never afford to lie to myself about the fact that I am an alcoholic and addict. Where am I on my journey toward honesty?

Meditations for the Heart
As I developed a real relationship with my Higher Power, I discovered this was one place I could not be dishonest. It would do me no good. My understanding of God told me that He was all knowing. He knew the truth even when I didn't. For a while this made it difficult to talk to God, as I understand Him. But this was silly, because He knew my thoughts, motives, brokenness and everything about me. So as I got past my initial fears, I found real comfort in being able to open up and share all my struggles with my Higher Power openly and honestly. I found no rejection, no judgment and no harshness as I had expected, only His grace. I found as I was able to develop my honesty with God, I could talk more openly and honestly with others. This was a new freedom that I had not really known. Am I honest with my Higher Power?

Petitions to my Higher Power
God,
Standing before You this morning, I am comforted to know that Your love and grace welcome me even in my brokenness. I know that You will guide me to grow and develop along spiritual lines. I trust that You will help me to find the honesty I need for this day. Lead me, and I will follow.
Amen.

* * * *

Wisdom for Today   Jun 24
"*Do not be discouraged; no one among us has been able to maintain perfect adherence to these principles.*" (*Alcoholics Anonymous,* Fourth Edition. Page 60) I have heard these words read over and over again at meetings. I have hung onto these words and carry them with me as I walk through my day. They help me keep a realistic perspective on my life. The reality is that there are good days, and there are days that just don't seem to go as well as others. Recovery is a process; it is not a single event. All along the way I need to use the steps and the principles of the program to help me in my life. Sometimes

this seems to come naturally, and other times I seem to just completely forget what I am doing.

When I have those days that I just can't seem to figure out what I am doing wrong, it is important for me to remember these words, "Do not be discouraged." (*Alcoholics Anonymous,* Fourth Edition. Page 60) I have to remember that no one has been able to work the program perfectly. I have to remember that I am human and prone to making mistakes. I also know that I can use my mistakes to learn more about life and learn better ways to cope with my day-to-day life. Over time I have realized that I do not need to be discouraged by life and the setbacks along the way. Am I encouraged by what I am learning through the program?

Meditations for the Heart

There is no way that you can come to trust in a Divine Power and remain self-centered. As I developed my own understanding of who God was for me, I could not stay all wrapped up in myself. In fact, the "self" shrank away; and God became more and more a part of who I was to imitate. Gradually I lost sight of much of my selfishness and learned to love God and my fellow man. At first all of this was only a shadow of what it was to come in my life. I was only a shadow of what God would make me. Today I am excited by what has happened to me and am still curious as to what God's plans are for me in the future. Today I hope that I do reflect an image of what God wants me to be in my life. I have this hope because it is what so many others have done for me in my recovery. They have shown me what it means to walk in the light that God provides. Is my self-centeredness shrinking away and being replaced with what God wants me to be?

Petitions to my Higher Power

God,

There is no way for me to maintain perfect adherence to the principles of the program. Today help me to walk in Your light and remain focused on Your will for me. Teach me along the way to become the person that You want me to be. Take me out of the shadows, and let me become a light for others. Amen.

* * * *

Wisdom for Today   *Jun 25*

"Many of us tried to hold onto our old ideas. The result was nil until we let go absolutely." (*Alcoholics Anonymous,* Fourth Edition. Page 58) Like many addicts and alcoholics, I tried to find an "easier, softer way." I looked for a

186

back door and wanted out of my addiction. In many ways I fought against recovery in the beginning. I wanted to do it my way and on my terms. But my way wasn't working. I kept on getting frustrated because I was trying to do it on my terms. I wanted to get by on just a few meetings. I wanted to still see my old using buddies. But my way just did not work. I guess I tried every game I knew, but the only person I was conning was myself.

I was at a point where I had to make a decision. I either had to go back to the insanity of my addiction and lose more than I already had, or I had to let go and follow the program. Funny thing is that when you are at the end of your rope, it is hard to let go! I had no way of knowing what was going to happen. This letting go meant that I had to trust the program blindly. I knew I could not keep holding onto my addiction. That would only lead to a path of destruction. I had to let go absolutely. It was the only sane option I had left. Have I let go absolutely?

Meditations for the Heart

Love is the power that transformed my life. It was God's love for me that saved me from the pit of absolute despair, destruction and death. I crawled out of the depression left by my disease only with God's help. Love also changed everything else in my life. When I started to reach out to my family, to others in the program and friends with love, things definitely began to change. When I began to reach out to my Higher Power with genuine gratitude and love, more good things started to happen for me. This love for God, as I understand Him, was rooted in the acknowledgment that He had blessed me with a chance at recovery. He continues to bless me by showing me the path that I need to take each day. I am not sure when it happened exactly, but somewhere along the way I also learned to love myself again. Do I continue to thank God for His many blessings?

Petitions to my Higher Power
God,

Looking back, I really don't understand why it was so hard to let go. I just know that it was hard. I am so grateful for the miracles You have brought about in my life. Forgive me when I lose sight of what got me to where I am now. Help me again this day to keep letting go and trusting You to be in charge of my life.
Amen.

* * * *

Sometimes when I stop and think about it, I realize just how fortunate I am. What would I have done if there were no Twelve Step program around? I think about what it must have been like in the days when alcoholics and addicts ended up in the asylum and were declared hopeless by the doctors that treated them. I know I would have ended up dead. But I was fortunate enough to get good treatment and get introduced to the Twelve Step program. When I read about the history of the beginnings of AA and think about what it must have been like for these people, sometimes waiting a month or more to get to a meeting, I am amazed they even made it. Guess it just shows that working the steps, trusting in a Higher Power and taking it one day at a time really works.

The program has taken my life from a pile of rubble and transformed it into something wonderful. This is not to say that I don't still have my share of problems; I do. But my life has been rebuilt through the process of working the steps and using the tools I have been given. The program has taken my personality, beliefs and attitudes and reshaped them and molded me into something that I really like. I am grateful for this new way of living and for the wealth of resources that are available to me. Have I found a better way to live my life through the program?

Meditations for the Heart

When I have a million things going on in my life, it becomes especially hard to listen to God. It seems that my attention is torn in many different directions at once, and none of these directions leads to a place of communion with my Higher Power. In these busy times it is very important to start my day with the same routine, reading my program literature and talking to God in prayer. It is important for me to start off my day centered with God. If I don't do this, I find that I hurry into my day and get off center very quickly. Just this simple act in the morning can keep me centered throughout my day. On those days that I seem to be loosing touch and drifting off center, my morning routine reminds me that I need to stop long enough to get back in touch with my Higher Power and get centered again. Do I have a routine for starting my day off right?

Petitions to my Higher Power

God,

In quietness I come to You to listen to You talk to me through my thoughts and feelings. I come to You to be filled with the strength I need for the day. I come to You to help me focus on what is important and how to accomplish the tasks I have. Thank You for the wonderful people You have placed in my life – this fellowship of brothers and sisters that can listen to me scream and can listen to me laugh. I am truly grateful for the program and for my relationship with You.

Amen.

* * * *

Wisdom for Today *Jun 27*

If the program has taught me anything, it has taught me patience. I never was willing to wait for anything, and I had little tolerance for things not going my way or in my time. I always wanted it my way now. I couldn't wait to get something to drink. I couldn't wait to get high. I couldn't wait for my problems to go away. Unfortunately, I was waiting for magic that never came. I was no different when I walked into the program. I wanted it now. I struggled at first to accept that recovery takes time. I remember my sponsor asking me how long it took me to become addicted and how long I spent drinking and drugging. He was implying that my recovery would take at least as long. I was not happy about this question.

I prayed simply asking God, "How long?" and "When?" My impatience seemed to get me nowhere. It really wasn't until I stopped being so concerned about time and more concerned about my willingness to change that things started to improve. When I stopped focusing on timeframes and expectations and finally started to focus on being open to God's plan and His timeframe, things suddenly seemed different. Life was better, and I was no longer in such a hurry. I have opportunities every day to practice patience. Some times I do pretty well with this, and other times I do less well. Can I look back and see that I am more patient and tolerant than I used to be?

Meditations for the Heart

Soul sickness is a big part of what happens in addiction. It is a big part of what needs to heal in recovery. I had reached a point in my life when I couldn't even recognize that I even had a soul, let alone care if I did. Recovery has helped me to care again for my soul, the part of me that gives true meaning to life. Life seemed so meaningless in active addiction, but in recovery I have found new meaning for my life. I have learned to care for my soul by connecting to a Divine Spirit who leads, guides and shows me the way. I find deeper and deeper meaning in my life the longer I stay clean and sober and the longer I keep using the steps and principles of the program. Today my soul can shout out, "If God is with me, then who can be against me." I no longer have to fear if my soul is being cared for. Do I care for myself, body and soul?

189

Petitions to my Higher Power

God,

Help me this day to focus on living life in Your timeframes. Guide me, lead me and show me the way to tolerance and patience. Teach me to care for myself in all that I do. Let me find continued healing by continuing my recovery work today. Let me not hurry through my day, but slow down enough to see the bigger picture of life.

Amen.

* * * *

Wisdom for Today   Jun 28

In looking at myself and my actions throughout the day, I have a tendency to jump quickly through my list and not really look at the problems I experience very closely. I think this is true for all of us. No one likes to look at his or her problems. I have natural defenses that pop up and try to block me from honestly evaluating what has happened. Yet I know that if I really want to grow in my recovery, I need to take a close look at my problems. I need to take inventory.

It typically is not that I am unwilling; it is just that I am in a hurry, or I want to make light of my problems. I do have a choice however. I can chose to slow down and not make excuses and look closely at my behavior and my motives. I can choose to learn from my experiences in life, or I can keep doing things the same way. When I am willing to look at my role in the problems I experience and at what I was hoping to accomplish, when I look at why I behaved the way I did and the choices I made, then I open the door to growth. Growth is a choice. It is not always easy, but it always is of benefit to me. Am I willing to keep growing in my recovery?

Meditations for the Heart

I think that there are times when each of us in recovery gets stuck. I find there are times when I just stagnate or get lazy or simply avoid the work needed to keep growing. Generally these stuck points do not threaten my recovery if I am willing to get back on track and do what I need to do. I know, however, that these stuck points in my recovery if ignored can really get me in trouble. They are no different than my addiction to alcohol and drugs – short-term gain and long-term pain. In these times when I get stuck in my recovery and can't seem to move forward, it becomes especially important for me to turn to my Higher Power. I need to ask for help again to get unstuck, whatever the problem. Whether it is fear, sadness, shame and anger or hurt that blocks

190

me, I need to turn this over to God and open the door to growing past my stuck point. Early in my recovery seeds of hope were planted in my life, took root and started to grow. I have a choice. I can wait for someone to bring me flowers, which never happens; or I can grow my own with God's help. Do I continue to work in my garden to grow the flowers of my life?

Petitions to my Higher Power
God,

You know everything about me. You have examined my heart and know my inmost motives. Teach me to recognize the motives I have and help me to choose healthy motives for my behavior. Let me follow after You today in all that I do. Should I get stuck along the way, help me to find the courage I need to move onward and continue to grow in my recovery, a recovery that is a gift from You.
Amen.

* * * *

Wisdom for Today   Jun 29
I have to admit that I used alcohol and drugs to escape even if it was only temporarily. I wanted a way out of my boredom. I wanted a way out of my troubles. I wanted to relieve my stress and anxiety. What I got was a quick fix and long-term pain. Substance use was not the answer I was looking for. Instead I ended up in more trouble and in more stress. My boredom was replaced by fear.

In the program I have found a healthy escape. I am not bored, and I have found true relief. Many of my problems have improved over time. I no longer walk in anxiety and fear. When I was drinking, I looked for self-importance. I looked for friends I could buy or manipulate. In the program I am not interested in self-importance. I have learned about things like self-respect and honesty and humility. Today these are of much more value to me than that inflated shell of a person I was. I find a true satisfaction in knowing myself, both the strengths and the weaknesses. Have I found a healthier way to live in recovery?

Meditations for the Heart
I believe that God's power and my faith can accomplish anything. Even the difficulties I face in life now can be handled in a way that brings me to a place of peace. I can accomplish much with the help of my Higher Power. Walls that stand in my way can be made to crumble because of the strength, courage and hope I am given daily in recovery. Yes, it is easy to slide back

into "old" behaviors and beliefs when I get wrapped up in my problems or myself. But when I stay focused on God's will for me, I am given the power to carry out the task. No matter how big or how small, I know I have help. Am I willing to ask for help when I need it? Do I do this daily?

Petitions to my Higher Power

God,

Today give me faith, and help me to know that You are with me in all that I do. Teach me to walk with humility along this path. This path is not one that I know. Guide me to a willingness to ask for help along the way.

Amen.

* * * *

Wisdom for Today   Jun 30

In facing our weaknesses, we find strength. I know this has been true for me, and it is true of life. Much like a diamond when it is first taken from the earth, I was dirty and rough; and there was no sparkle in my life. But just like a diamond when it is cleaned up, the rough edges removed and it is polished, I found sparkle in my life. In my drinking and drugging, I was a very stubborn person; but I used my stubbornness in very unhealthy ways. When I cleaned up, I began to become stubborn about my recovery; nothing was going to keep me from my primary purpose.

Many of my personality characteristics that I saw as liabilities actually became assets in recovery. Rock climbers seek out small imperfections, crags, and rough places to get a grip to climb to their goal. I, too, was able to use many of my destructive characteristics in healthy ways once I got clean and sober. Today I can look back at all my years of active addiction and can say I am grateful for this experience. My drinking and drugging was a necessary part of my life existence to bring me to the place I am today. In my weakness I discovered strength through the program. I discovered a new way of living. I found ways to have my liabilities become assets. But just like the rock climber, I had to grab on and face the climb to reach this goal. Am I finding ways to turn my weakness into strength?

Meditations for the Heart

"Be still, and know that I am God." This quote from the Bible speaks of our relationship with God. This statement does not say run around like a crazed maniac and know that I am. When I can stop and sit quietly, I can think about this Higher Power. I can begin to think outside the box of space and time and imagine a Power that exceeds this. I can begin to see the limitlessness of this Power. I can see the necessity of a Power Greater that watches over this universe and beyond. When I think of God, as I understand Him, in these terms, I am left standing in awe. Who can this be? Who is so limitless, so powerful? Awe is a place that I think all recovering addicts and alcoholics get to in their relationship with a Higher Power. Who is this that has taken me out of my brokenness and restored me? Who is this, that Power that I experience in my recovery everyday? I cannot get my mind around this. It is too big for me to understand fully, but I understand more and more each day what this Power has done for me. Yes, in a quiet place, a still place, I can know God. Is my understanding of God changing in and through recovery?

Petitions to my Higher Power
God,

You have taken my weakness and shown me how to use this and find strength. You have opened me up to seeing myself differently, and You have opened me up to seeing You differently. I pray that I may continue my journey along spiritual lines and more will be revealed to me. I pray that Your Spirit will not be removed from my life.

Amen.

* * * *

Wisdom for Today   Jul 1
My motivations for behaving the ways I did were not always healthy and often times got me into more trouble. When I look back at my active addiction to alcohol and drugs, it is clear that one driving motivation I had was fear. I lied to cover up the mistakes I made. I hid my drinking and using from other people so as not to be discovered. I didn't want anyone to know how much or how often I was getting wasted. I let fear make many of my decisions for me. I would avoid doing things because I was afraid. I would pretend I was okay even when I wasn't, because I was afraid to admit to myself how sick I was becoming..

Fear began to take over my whole life. It prevented me from being close with anyone. It made me run from a relationship with God. Fear would drive me to work harder to prove to myself I was okay. In the program I learned I could let go of my fears. I could turn them over, and I could let my Higher Power do for me what I could not do for myself. I learned I could ask others for help. I learned to trust people again and actually begin to make friends. Fear no longer had to control my life. Fear no longer had to motivate me to behave in self-destructive patterns. Fear could be replaced with faith in a Power greater than myself. Is fear still a motivating factor in my decisions, behaviors and beliefs?

Meditations for the Heart

God molds and shapes in our recovery. He cuts away the pieces of our lives that are unhealthy. He shapes and sculpts us into His new creation. This new shape becomes a vessel for our spiritual life. It allows us to experience ourselves as a complete person. I no longer have to walk around feeling like I am incomplete. I know that I am still a work in progress, but I also know that I am as complete as God wants me to be today. As I walk though my days of recovery, the vessel that God is creating becomes easier for me to see. I can begin to understand what He is doing and where I am being led. I can see that what He is doing is making me a better person. He is allowing me to learn a new way to live life to its fullest. Do I stand in the way of God shaping and molding me?

Petitions to my Higher Power

God,

You know me on the inside and on the outside. You know how I can let fear get in the way of Your work in my life. Help me this day to be open to changes that You have in mind for me. Let me be open to becoming the person that You want me to be.

Amen.

* * * *

Wisdom for Today   Jul 2

One of my motivations for drinking and using drugs was to get away from it all. I told myself I was drinking and using to escape. I wanted to get away from the stress of life. I wanted to get away from what caused me pain. I wanted to get away from the arguments, the responsibilities and the guilt. I wanted to get away from the loneliness and sadness. But this was not the real reason I was drinking and using drugs. This is not what I was trying to escape from.

The real reason I was trying to escape was to try and get away from myself. I could not stand the person I was. I wanted to blame everything and everyone else. But the real reason was I couldn't stand me. I didn't like me. I didn't like being in my own skin. I didn't like how I behaved, the choices I made. I didn't like what I was becoming. I violated my own value system. I hurt those I cared for. I hurt myself. I had an underlying motive to destroy and punish myself.

194

Recovery has changed all that. I no longer need to run from the person staring back at me in the mirror. Do I still try to run from myself?

Meditations for the Heart

God knows what it is that I need. I just need to go to Him and ask for what I need. I do not need to go to my Higher Power in the same way that others turn to Him. I need to go to God for my needs. When I am weak, I go to God for strength. When I am strong, I go to Him for humility. When I want to fight, I go to God for leadership. When I am afraid, I go to Him for reassurance and safety. When I need help, I go to my Higher Power for direction. God will supply my needs if I go to Him in an unselfish way and ask for what I need. When I am lonely, He is my friend. He does not always supply my needs in the way that I would expect, but He always sees to it that my needs are cared for. This is why I turn my will and my life over to His care. He fulfills my needs better than I ever could. Do I ask my Higher Power to fulfill my needs?

Petitions to my Higher Power

God,

So often I get things all turned around because I do not examine my motives, the real reasons I behave the way that I do. Help me this day to examine my motives and make choices that are healthy for me. Let me not overlook my motives, but instead turn to You to fulfill my needs. Even when I am not sure of what I need or am not clear about my motives, help me to do the next right thing.

Amen.

* * * *

Wisdom for Today   Jul 3

When I would go to the bar and the bartender would ask me what I wanted, I would respond, "Top shelf!" When I talked with my dealer and He would ask what I wanted, I would say, "More!" These responses were really a sign of a much deeper problem. I always wanted more. I always wanted it all, the best and a little bit of everything. I wanted to have money. I wanted happiness. I wanted to be a good husband and father. I wanted the best job. I wanted to be important. I wanted, and I wanted.

When it came right down to the heart of it, I was just plain greedy. Greed was a huge motivator for me. I envied others who had more than I did. I hated those people who found success when I could not find it. I was jealous of my friends when they had something I did not have. I wanted it all. My addiction to alcohol and drugs took away most of what I did have. My self-worth was diminished to a pile of rubble, and I still wanted it all. Greed motivated me to do things that I am not proud of: stealing, manipulating and using others for my gain. In recovery I admitted defeat and no longer was greedy for anything. I just wanted to live. In recovery I have experienced grace and received much. Everything I have is as a result of God doing for me what I could not do for myself. I regained my family, got out of debt, no longer worry about police officers coming to get me and have found satisfaction and gratitude. Does greed still motivate my thinking, actions and decision-making?

Meditations for the Heart

At the end of many of the Twelve Step meetings I attend, they close with a prayer from the Bible – the "Our Father." This is a prayer that I had prayed many times as a child, yet had little understanding about it. In my drunkenness and active addiction to drugs, I rebelled against God. In recovery I was left with no choice but to turn back to God as I understand Him. Calling my Higher Power, "Father" was something that bothered me a lot at first. Maybe it was because of my own shame, or because of the issues I had with my own father, or maybe it was just because I had been such a poor father myself; but I struggled with the whole concept of calling my Higher Power, "Father." I am not really sure of all the reasons. However, in recovery, as I got more and more honest with myself, it became easier to see how childish I had behaved in my addiction. I was a child who needed a father. I guess that is how I always behaved. My Higher Power is there for me and loves me like the Heavenly Father He is, and today I can love Him back like a child. Do I see that I really need a Spiritual Father?

Petitions to my Higher Power
God,

You are indeed my Spiritual Father; and You reach out to me and care for me. Give me direction, and love me simply because I am Your child. Forgive me for all my childish behaviors. Help me this day to rid myself of greed and to seek instead to be of service. Teach me to know Your will for me.
Amen.

* * *

Wisdom for Today   Jul 4
Understanding that with freedom also comes responsibility is central to the process of recovery. If we are to celebrate our independence from drugs and alcohol, our freedom from active addiction, then we must accept the

responsibility for our recovery. We are not going to have a truly effective program if we are attempting to stay clean and sober for someone else. It is only when we take responsibility for our thinking, impulses and actions and do this for ourselves that we can hope to find the freedom that exists in the program.

This freedom by no means indicates that we have been cured. Only when we are responsible and do what our Higher Power wants us to do can we expect to know freedom from the insanity of the disease. We are able to gain a sense of security in this freedom, and we begin to comprehend peace of mind. This freedom by no means is a reflection of a trouble free life. It does mean that we will have the tools and courage to live life on life's terms. Am I willing to be responsible with my recovery to gain this freedom?

Meditations for the Heart

Taking responsibility for our recovery becomes easier over time. As we grow accustomed to the discipline of the program and accepting our doing His will rather than trying to run the show our way, we begin to enjoy the responsibility of working a program. However, just because it gets easier over time does not mean that our responsibility lessens. Each and every day I must take responsibility for my life. Each and every day I need to seek greater understanding of God's will for me. Each and every day I need to continue to use the steps. Each and every day I need to do something for my recovery. The requirements of this responsibility change over time, and I need to continue to grow and adapt to the changing needs I have in recovery. This responsibility defines what it is to be willing. This responsibility defines what it is that I need to do to maintain my freedom. The freedom we all have is a gift, but it is our responsibility to care for this gift we have been given. Do I value the freedom I have been given?

Petitions to my Higher Power
God,

In gratitude I acknowledge the gift of freedom I have been given. Grant me a willing heart that I may be responsible for this gift. Help me this day to seek out and accomplish all that I need to be responsible for in my recovery. Let me be diligent in this search and give me the courage, strength and wisdom I need for this day.
Amen.

* * * *

Wisdom for Today   Jul 5
There are really two reasons that we attend meetings. The first is obvious; we do it to stay clean and sober. Many people have tried to stay sober on their

own only to fail. In fact, when I relapsed early in my recovery, I had stopped going to meetings. And just about everyone who relapses stops attending meetings prior to their relapse. We just can't do it on our own. I have found that I need to be around other recovering people in order to stay clean and sober myself. There have been times that I did not go that often, and invariably my thinking gets screwed up.

The other reason that we go to meetings is to help other people. It is in helping others that we learn more about ourselves. I'm not sure if this is God's way of keeping us awake. But on more than one occasion, as I was listening to another addict or alcoholic, I would hear them say things that directly applied to my life. Over time I have learned that one addict or alcoholic is not smarter than another; they are just individuals that have more life experience. Often times the most important lessons I have learned in recovery have come from newcomers. Even when it comes to my character defects, these newcomers can often teach me a thing or two. Yes, I still seek the advice of the old-timers because of their life experience, but even the newcomer has much to offer me. Have I recognized that I cannot stay clean and sober without the help of others?

Meditations for the Heart

Sometimes I find that I really need a change in my perspective. I know something is not right, but I'm not really sure what. I just know that I am not functioning the way I need to. I have found that one of the best ways for me to change my perspective is to stop looking at what is going on in my life and start looking to my Higher Power through eyes of faith. When I stop looking through my eyes and start looking through the eyes of faith, my whole perspective on life changes. When I look through the eyes of faith, things like despair, worry, fear and weakness disappear. When I look through the eyes of faith, I find peace of mind, reassurance, strength and vital power to move forward in my life. It is through these eyes of faith that God grants serenity. It is with these eyes that I can receive His gifts. Will I look at life through eyes of faith today?

Petitions to my Higher Power

God,

More and more each day I see the miracle You have created in my life. My heart does not feel so heavy, and my thoughts no longer race. You have given me the tools I need for this day. You have surrounded me with others who can teach me along the way. Help me to look to You though eyes of faith, and grant me serenity in my day.

Amen.

* * * *

Wisdom for Today *Jul 6*

One important word I heard from my sponsor over and over again was the word, "Yet." During the early days of my recovery, I spent a good deal of time comparing myself to others and looking for how I was different and unique. Repeatedly my sponsor reminded me that every difference I could come up with had not happened to me yet. He understood the progressive nature of the disease of addiction to alcohol and drugs. He helped me learn about the progression of this illness. The truth was that I was looking for excuses. I was looking for a way out of having to work a recovery program. I was looking for ways to reinforce my denial.

But that word, "yet," is a powerful word. It was a word I definitely needed to hear. I needed to understand that my addiction indeed could and would get worse if I let it. Before the program I really didn't have a choice. I simply obeyed the voice of addiction. Once I got clean and sober, I did have a choice to continue to listen to the voice of addiction, or to listen to the words of wisdom that my sponsor provided. I had to accept the reality that addiction was cunning, baffling and powerful. I had to accept that it was patient and would wait for me. Do I understand that "YET" can happen to me?

Meditations for the Heart

Reaching out to others has helped me a great deal in my recovery. But reaching out for things of the Spirit is what has kept me focused. When I reach out for things like beauty, love, honesty and unselfishness, I have been able to enjoy fully an abundant life in my recovery. It is reaching out for things of the Spirit that has changed my inmost being. In the program we learn of the promises that recovery has to offer. This too is an important "yet." The promises can and do come true for those that work the program and accept the gifts that the Spirit brings. Do I take time each day to reach out for things of the Spirit?

Petitions to my Higher Power

God,

Thank You for the people You have placed in my life to teach me the importance of the word "yet." Let me this day be focused on things of the Spirit. Let me reach out for the gifts of the program, so that I may claim the gifts and promises that You have to offer. Let me walk through this day seeking only to do Your will.

Amen.

* * * *

Wisdom for Today *Jul 7*

A part of my trouble in recovery has been always to want to put things off. "Procrastination" should have been my middle name. When I was actively using alcohol and drugs, I was always trying to delay the inevitable. But this only kept me sick. I was very good at saying to myself, "I'll quit tomorrow." But tomorrow never came, and I would continue to get wasted. Stopping my insanity was not the only thing about which I procrastinated. I would put off paying bills and any other responsibility I could just so I would have more time to drink and use drugs.

In recovery I soon discovered that this character defect was still very active in my life. My sponsor would ask me to do something; and I would put it off as long as I could, always providing lots of excuses. I still did not want to put any energy into my recovery. I kept looking for an easier, softer way. Delay tactics and avoidance abounded in my life. It wasn't until I honestly admitted to others and myself that procrastination is what my will wanted to do that a door was finally opened. I began to understand that if I was going to surrender completely, I needed to turn over my will to my Higher Power. I began asking God, as I understand Him, what He wanted me to do and began to do those things. Whether it was as simple as going to work or completing step work for my sponsor, I was able to begin to accomplish things. I still do not do this perfectly, but I keep getting better at it. I am making progress. How much is procrastination a part of my life?

Meditations for the Heart

Many people have asked the question, "What is the purpose of life?" I am not a philosopher or someone that pretends to know everything, but I believe for the alcoholic and addict the answer to this question lies within the program. *"Having had a spiritual awakening as the result of these steps, we ..."* (*Alcoholics Anonymous,* Fourth Edition. Page 60) Our purpose is to achieve this spiritual awakening. We work through each of the steps and are training the soul for this awakening. In each of the steps we learn spiritual principles, acceptance, hope, turning it over, surrender, confession, etc. As a result of honestly working these steps, we achieve this awakening. Our character is molded and shaped by our experience in working these steps. A revolution takes place in our soul, and we are awakened to a newness of life. We gain a new understanding of the meaning and purpose for our lives. Am I training my soul through working the steps?

Petitions to my Higher Power
God,

Each day I need to remind myself to do Your will and not my will. Help me this day to accept the tasks that You set before me and to continue to do the next right thing. Help me to let You decide when I need to rest and when I need to work. Let me actively engage myself in training my soul for Your Divine Purpose.

Amen.

*   *   *   *

Wisdom for Today   ***Jul 8***

Today is a wonderful day, for I have no reason to fear. There was a time when this was not the case. I can remember always looking in the rearview mirror and expecting to see the police. I recall always being concerned about what my boss was thinking and wondering if he was on to me. I recall being wrapped up and controlled by fear. It made many of my decisions for me. I no longer need to be afraid because of what the program has done and continues to do for me.

Facing addiction to alcohol and drugs is not something I need to do alone. I have a support system of other addicts and alcoholics in my corner. I have a strong relationship with my Higher Power. I have a sponsor and many friends I can rely on to see me through the struggles I have in my life. Not having to face life alone and having confidence that my support system will not let me down has helped me rid my life of constant fear. Knowing that I can go to my Higher Power for strength and courage helps me to stay on track and deal with problems I may face rather than looking for a way out. Yes, today is a wonderful day. Am I facing life with courage?

Meditations for the Heart

One thing I learned in my addiction was that drinking and drugging were not as reliable as I first thought they were. In recovery I am really beginning to understand that God, as I understand Him, is very reliable. He is always there for me. All I need to do is turn to Him and let Him know what is going on and ask for direction. In His own way He reaches out to me and lets me know what I need to do. Sometimes I hear His words in what others say at meetings. Sometimes I hear His words in my morning readings and meditations. Sometimes I hear Him in the quiet places of my soul. But He is always there and always reliable. This is more than I can say for alcohol and drugs. They left me hanging in the lurch all the time. I never knew where to turn. I didn't know which way was up. In recovery I have learned to look up for my answers. Do I have faith in the reliability of my Higher Power?

Petitions to my Higher Power

God,

Let me rejoice in this day because it is a day that I no longer have to fear. I know that this gift is from You, my Divine Spirit. Let me always turn to You in my time of need. Let me always listen for Your voice for the answers I am seeking. Help me this day to walk the walk that You want me to walk. Keep me on the right path.

Amen.

* * * *

Wisdom for Today   Jul 9

Sometimes I grow restless in my recovery. I have an itch that something is not right with my life. I grow impatient, and I want my life to change. This restlessness of the spirit is something that all addicts and alcoholics experience from time to time in the recovery process. We can try to ignore the itch, but this does not work. The restlessness continues. When I grow restless, I have discovered that it is often because I have left something undone. I have unfinished work to do. It may be because I have more work to do on one of the steps. It may be because I have become lazy in my spiritual life and not attended to taking care of myself spiritually. It may be because I have become stubborn about not making changes that I need to make. It may be that I have let my meeting attendance or service work slip.

Regardless of the reason, my restlessness is a sign to which I need to pay attention. This restlessness of my spirit tells me that something is amiss in my life. Ignoring this, restlessness only can lead to trouble. All of us know what happens when we ignore a health problem and try to be our own physician. The problem becomes worse until we finally seek help. Unfortunately, sometimes people wait when they become restless until it is too late, and the consequences can be severe or even deadly. When my spirit becomes restless, I know I must not try to be my own physician. I need to reach out to others in the program and talk about what is going on until I discover what the cause of my restlessness is. Once I discover what this restlessness is about, I continue to use others in recovery to help me bring the restlessness to an end. Do I pay attention to my spirit when it becomes restless?

Meditations for the Heart

To know peace is to receive a gift from God. In the midst of a world that often surrounds me with noise and confusion, I can know peace. I can know a peace that passes all human understanding. I can know a peace that is a gift from God, with whom I have a relationship. I can have a serenity that allows me not to be bothered by all the noise and confusion. I can walk through my day without being troubled by worry. I truly wish I were capable of hanging onto this peace in all that I do, but the reality is that I can get caught up in all the distractions that the noise and confusion can bring. In recovery I give thanks for the time I can hold onto this peace. I get better at holding onto it for longer periods of time the longer I stay clean and sober. Still I find too often I want to get back in charge and end up ruining the peace I have. At times when this happens, I go back to the beginning and honestly admit that I am lost again. I ask my Higher Power to lead me back to the path that leads to His peace. I surrender, and I find the peace again, or more accurately I should say His peace finds me. Am I open to accepting His peace?

Petitions to my Higher Power
God,

You know how I can get off track and know how easy it is for me to be distracted. Help me this day to stay focused and open to receive Your gift of peace. Should I become restless today, help me to take action to correct whatever is out of whack. Help me to use the tools and the people You have put in my life. Let me not ignore restlessness in my spirit.
Amen.

* * * *

Wisdom for Today   Jul 10
There are many things that determine if someone is going to be successful in staying clean and sober. But it starts in one place for all of us, a capacity to be honest. Each of us regardless of how far down we have gone must start recovery with an honest admission that we are licked. I had to admit that living my life my way just didn't work. Like many addicts and alcoholics I continued to play games and tried to make bargains with recovery, but it just didn't work. Eventually I had to honestly admit defeat. Addiction had won; it was stronger than I was.

At the point of my admission that I was defeated came the beginning of victory. In desperation I reached out, and I looked deep within. I drew on the last bits of decency inside of me and on the finite possibility that there might be another way. I was fortunate to have had some spiritual training as a child. I could draw on these memories and reach out to a God that I really didn't yet understand and honestly ask for help. I was able to draw on the last pieces of morality that existed inside. I have had to do an awful lot since that day to stay clean and sober, but I know that this honest admission is where recovery started for me. This honest admission that I was desperate and needed help was the beginning. Have I had this spiritual experience?

Meditations for the Heart

Today I have learned much about what it is that I need to do to stay clean and sober. I have learned much about how to live my life. I do not do this perfectly, but I am always making progress. I have had to deal with many traumatic events in my life in recovery just like many of my peers. Just because we stop drinking and using does not mean that we don't have any more problems. But those that handle these problems with help from others and do it without relapse all have something in common. Each of us has worked hard to make countless small deposits into out spiritual bank. Each time I am filled with gratitude and praise for the grace I have been given, I make a deposit. Each moment I spend in prayer and meditation I make a deposit. Each time I rely on God's will for me rather than my own, I make a deposit. Each time I seek to improve my conscious contact with God, as I understand Him, I make a deposit. Steadily over time these deposits grow. Then when tragedy comes – and in this life it does happen, I am able to make withdrawals from my spiritual bank. My Higher Power, who manages this account, always sees to it that I have enough reserves. He never gives me more than I can handle. He makes sure that I have what I need to cope with any crisis, struggle or setback. Am I faithfully making deposits in my spiritual bank?

Petitions to my Higher Power

God,

You indeed have shown me Your love. I have done nothing to deserve Your care and concern, yet You have graciously reached out to me in moments of defeat and lifted me up. You make sure that I have what I need each day. Let me walk with You hand-in- hand today on this journey of recovery.
Amen.

* * * *

Wisdom for Today   *Jul 11*

"Once an alcoholic or addict – always one!" If we keep drinking and using, we only get worse. The only questions are how quickly and how bad. There is no cure for this disease. It can only be arrested. We are granted a daily reprieve and must make choices one day at a time how we are going to live. It does not matter how long I have been clean and sober. I know if I were to go back, it would not take long, and I would be as bad as or worse off than I was when I was first granted this daily reprieve. In looking at the history of the program, this point has been proven over and over. No one has been able to go back and recapture the "good old times."

Finally, I came to my bottom. For each of us this bottom is relative. Many of us lose jobs or family. Many are financially devastated and left broke. Some end up in jails and prisons, and others in hospitals or institutions. Regardless of how far down we have traveled, all of us have a profound soul sickness. We become spiritually bankrupt. We hate what we have become and our way of living. I did not think life was worth living anymore. I was left with no choice except to die or do something about it. Am I glad that I have chosen to do something about my addiction? Am I making good choices just for today?

Meditations for the Heart

Faith is not a matter of my heart or mind seeing; it is simply a matter of trusting. I was not sure that I could even make it in recovery. I came into the program and saw others making it. I was close-minded. I had no vision for the future. Fortunately I did not need this vision. God is not in a box. He is not contained in space or time. He is timeless and not limited in space. His vision for my life was all that I needed. I came to believe that God's vision for me was better than my vision. I was trapped inside this box that addiction created. God was not trapped by this box and could see for me things that I could not see for myself. He knew where I needed to go and what I needed to do. All I needed to do was find faith to believe that God could and would lead me out of the box. Today I recognize that even this faith that I received is a gift of His grace. I did not come to believe on my own. I came to believe because He helped me believe. Have I gotten a vision of faith since coming into the program?

Petitions to my Higher Power

God,

Today I want to walk in harmony with You. Help me this day to follow You with eyes of faith. Strengthen my belief that You are in my life to help me out of the box of addiction. Grant that I may find healing for my soul sickness. Lead me on the path that leads to serenity.

Amen.

* * * *

Wisdom for Today   Jul 12

I can remember sitting in a dark room, holding a bottle, my mind spinning and thinking, "I must be crazy; only a crazy person would act the way I do." Even during times when my mind wasn't clouded with drugs or alcohol, I can remember wondering if I was just plain evil. I recall feeling as if I had no moral character whatsoever. I could not understand why I was so weak and could not say "No" to drugs or alcohol. Even when I wanted to say "No," I could not. There had to be something terribly wrong with me. I had to be mentally ill or just a bad person or something.

Then I walked into the program and was given a new vision of whom I was. I was told that I had an illness. I was told that my drinking and drugging had a name, a name called "Addiction." I listened to people share their history and knew that my experiences were very similar to what they were talking about. This was a tremendous discovery – to find out that I was not alone. Other people had been through the same thing I had been through. They had found a way to stop drinking and using. They had found a way to stop the insanity. They had found a new freedom. They found something that I wanted. Am I willing to go to any length to get what the program offers?

Meditations for the Heart

I recall very early in my recovery walking on the shore of a large lake wondering if I was going to make it. I remember screaming at God that night wondering where He was. I recall being filled with anger and feeling like too much was being asked of me. I was so wrapped up in my own world that I didn't even notice the storm that was approaching behind me. Suddenly there was a bright flash of lightning and a crack of thunder. A moment later the skies opened up and a drenching rain came down, and the wind howled. I ran back to my vehicle and climbed inside. Then I drove to the clubhouse to go to a meeting. When I walked in someone looked at me and said, "I see you survived the storm." The program indeed helps us survive the storms of life if we build our recovery on a solid foundation. God is that rock for me. Obedience to His will is what has kept my recovery going even through the storms of life. Have I discovered that God still loves me and cares for me even when I am angry with Him?

Petitions to my Higher Power

God,

Today I am grateful for all the people who have gone before me to show me the way. I am grateful for their stories and have learned much from them to help point me in the right direction. Sometimes I still get frustrated and even angry along this journey. Thank You for being my rock, a rock that remains solid even in my anger and wayward ways. Thank You for loving me always. Amen.

* * * *

Wisdom for Today

Wisdom for Today *Jul 13*

In recovery I have had to learn to change my thinking. I needed to rehab my mind and begin to use wisdom as a guide. I had to learn to think, think, think. I could no longer think of drinking or drugging in the same way. I had to look beyond the short-term gain and focus on the long-term pain. I cannot afford the short view. It tells me that somehow this time will be different. It tells me that drinking or drugging will somehow cure my problems and that it will help me cope. It tells me that no one will know; but, of course, I will know. This short-term view will only lead to more pain.

The long-term view forces me to look past the bottle. It forces me to see beyond the night of partying to the morning after. It forces me to see that no matter how good alcohol or drugs look right now, the picture will look very different the next day. Recovery forces me to take a long-term view of alcohol and drugs. It has taught me to reeducate my mind and seek after God's will for me. Even on the days that recovery requires me to do things I don't want to do, I have learned that I need to listen to that still, small voice of my Higher Power and remain obedient to His plans for me. Have I learned to change my thinking and see the long-term pain that addiction always brings?

Meditations for the Heart

If I am honestly working to live the way that my Higher Power wants me to live, I can seek and find His guidance through quiet meditation. When I focus my mind on His will for me, I am given answers to decisions I must make. I am given direction for my path in life. I am given encouragement and strength for my day. The words of the Lord's Prayer, "Thy will be done," take on a whole new meaning. Recovery is not about my will, but it is about listening to and obeying His will for me. If I act on the clear guidance I receive when I meditate on His will for me, I am much more likely to look back at the end of my day and have no regret. The problems I have today are because I again slip into a life of self-will. However, the serenity and peace of mind I have are directly proportionate to my willingness to use God's wisdom as my guiding principle. Am I seeking His guidance through quiet meditation? Am I willing to obey the guidance I receive?

Petitions to my Higher Power

God,

Today let me seek after Your wisdom through quiet meditation. Give me courage to act on and obey the wisdom I receive from You. Help me to change my thinking and adopt a long-term view of addiction. Let me see the insanity of a short-term view.

Amen

* * * *

Wisdom for Today
Jul 14

Fellowship without the steps is empty. Fellowship in and of itself is wonderful at first. It is what attracts many of us to the program. We find a place where we feel like we fit in. We don't feel so alone. But the wonder of the fellowship soon dims, and we find that we can become disillusioned by it all. We may find that we get caught up in the gossip and talk about others rather than talk about ourselves. We may find that we get bored and lose interest in even going to meetings anymore. We may even find that we lose sight of our goal to remain clean and sober. Some may even begin to see the fellowship as a place to take advantage of others. We find that fellowship with others is not the answer we thought it was.

Many of these things rang too true for me as I got further into my sobriety. A more accurate statement would be that without the steps I was dry and miserable. Something was definitely missing. Many things were being suggested to me, but I was not following through and doing them. I was not calling my sponsor as often. I wasn't reading the books that were suggested. And I wasn't really working the steps. When I look back now, I see just how close to relapse I was. I had to go back and retrace my steps and start at the beginning again. This time I had to really work the steps. When I did, things started to happen. I got refocused on what was important. I began to pray again. I talked honestly about what was really going on. I used the tools, and I again found a healthy sense of true fellowship in the program. I stopped trying to run the show, and I was able to pray with honesty again – "Thy will be done." Do I recognize when I am working the program with only half measures?

Meditations for the Heart

I don't recall what movie it was that I saw; but I remember a line that the lead character said, "There is wonder in knowing you are being watched over." With God in charge I am not only watched over, but I am also led. When I stop to really think about this wonder, I begin to only scratch the surface of God's bounty and goodness. God has a plan for me, and it is my job to follow where He will lead. His way is filled with wonder, and His way is filled with ceaseless knowledge. The more I focus my inner being on this fact, the more I will grow in my recovery. As I improve my conscious contact with my Higher Power, the more I can realize His vision for me. I do not know where His plan will take me, but I do know and trust that His way will bring me peace. Nothing I have is more valuable than this relationship. No material possession can even come close to the value found in His care for me. Do I know and trust that I am being watched over?

Petitions to my Higher Power

God,

I call You Father because I know that You do truly watch over me. You guide my steps, and You lead me on the right path. I also call You Father because I know I am Your child. I guess that is how I act sometimes. I am grateful that You are always there and reach out to me when I act childish or wander off and get lost. I know that Your arms are always open for me. Let me follow where You will lead me today.

Amen.

*   *   *   *

Wisdom for Today   Jul 15

There was a time that I thought that alcohol and drugs were my friends. When I was down and out, they would lift me up. There were rewards attached to their use. They did what I wanted and were reliable. I could trust that they would be there for me if I needed them, but that all changed. I really can't pinpoint when the change occurred, but somewhere along the way alcohol and drugs became my enemy. It really doesn't matter when this change happened; what is important is that I recognize that what had been friendly was now clearly my enemy.

Alcohol and drugs no longer provided me with the lift I was looking for. I began using in an attempt just to feel normal, but that didn't even work anymore. Rather than rewards, I began to experience one consequence after another. I could no longer predict what would happen once I started drinking or using drugs. They were no longer reliable. I could no longer trust alcohol or drugs. Worse yet, I could no longer trust myself. Now I find it helpful to go to a First Step meeting just to remind me who I am. It takes me back to look at the enemy within. Is staying clean and sober still my main focus?

Meditations for the Heart

I tried changing circumstances, and I tried changing my surroundings. I tried limiting myself, and I tried to control my use. I tried dozens and dozens of ways to make alcohol and drugs friendly again. It was hard to admit that my friend had turned on me like it did. It was harder yet to admit that I had changed and that alcohol and drugs had defeated me. However, in defeat I also found victory. I had to get to a place of absolute defeat to recognize the possibility of a new way of living. Through the steps I learned a new way of living. I underwent tremendous change. God was doing for me what I could not do for myself. Today I look to my Higher Power for direction in my life. I cannot afford not to follow this direction and need to take advantage of every opportunity for growth that God provides. Do I trust that God is working in my life for good?

Petitions to my Higher Power
God,

I know that I am a work in progress and that You are not done with me. I will trust You to lead me this day. Show me what Your will for me is this day, and give me the wisdom and courage I need to accomplish the tasks that You set before me. Let me not put off till tomorrow what You wish me to do today. Guide my steps in this journey today.
Amen.

* * * *

Wisdom for Today   Jul 16
There were times early in my recovery process where I simply "white knuckled" it. The fear of relapse was very real. This was a time that I had to draw on faith that my Higher Power would not let me down. There were days when I simply had to take it a few hours at a time. There were still other days when I had to take it one hour, or even a few minutes at a time. I used my Higher Power a lot in these times. But as I look back, it was not just faith that I used to get me through these tough times. I used the fellowship. I used my sponsor. I used the steps. I used the literature from the program. I used whatever worked.

One thing I found that helped me over and over again was talking to the newcomer. The pain of their addiction was so fresh and vivid; it reminded me where I came from. Mind you, I did not talk to these newcomers alone. My sponsor always led me to these people after a meeting and encouraged me to reach out and help them. Guess my sponsor knew what he was doing, because talking with these individuals always bought me back to the pain of my addiction. It reminded me that I did not want to go back and drink or use. Faith was needed to get me through these times, but so were all of the other components of my recovery. I needed lots of support, and I got it at meetings. I got support in reaching out to others. I got support though the wisdom of my sponsor. I got it in many ways. My Higher Power knew I needed more than just faith in these situations. I needed to put it all into action. Do I use all the tools available to me?

Meditations for the Heart
One thing the program has taught me is to seek out God each morning before my day becomes busy with the events of life. I have learned that I need to do this each day so that I may ask for the strength and guidance I need. I cannot afford to wait until life's problems come up and then seek God. I need to do this on an ongoing basis. If I wait until I am "white knuckling" it, I cannot trust myself to seek God first. By starting my day this way everyday, I plan to seek God first in all that I do. I can really tell a difference when I don't do this. My day doesn't start out right, and I am quick to mess it up further. Seeking God first becomes a way of life with enough practice. Then should life throw me a curve ball, I can stand ready, knowing that God is standing there with me. In making a decision to turn my will and life over to the care of God, as I understand Him, do I put Him first in my day?

Petitions to my Higher Power
God,
Let me always remember to start my day with You. Help me to prepare myself for the day and to stand in faith with You in all that I do. Lead me this day along the path that I walk. Help me put into action what I have learned. Help me to keep my past present in my day so that I do not forget who I am and my ongoing need for You.
Amen.

* * * *

Wisdom for Today   *Jul 17*
One privilege I earned by coming into the program was the possibility of living two lives. When you stop and think about it, most people do not get such a chance. I had the opportunity to live one life as a drug addict and an alcoholic. I lived through the failures, the deceit, the insanity, the defeat of addiction. My life of addiction is not one that I am proud of, yet it is also not something that I regret. Much of my life as an addict and an alcoholic has gone into making me what I am today.

Then I was given a new chance at life. When I walked through the doors of the program, I was simply hoping that I could stop the insanity so that I would not die. Yet here it was, a chance to start all over again and a chance to live a whole new life. Those of us that have taken advantage of this opportunity have the privilege of being a walking miracle. What could be more wonderful than this – to start all over again and become something new? God has given us this privilege, and He has shown us how to be rid of the loneliness, insanity, hopelessness and despair. Today I can see that the time I have each day is part of the gift of recovery. By all rights I should be dead, but God has blessed me with the privilege of a new start. What will I do with this new start I have been given?

Meditations for the Heart

I try to think often of God as my Higher Power. I think of the love He must have for me as an alcoholic and addict to give me this second chance at life. I also try to think of Him as my protector. He guards me from all evil and rescues me from the bondage of self-will. God is my lifeline to the future. He gives me the time I have this day and each day to come. I can choose to ignore this gift, or I can use it for good. I can choose to ignore this gift, or I can choose to grow along spiritual lines. In growing spiritually, I open myself to God's will for me. He gives me the strength I need to overcome all temptation, and He will give me help to quiet my fears. He is always there for me to ask for help. He grants me courage and gives me wisdom to grow beyond my faults. He gives me purpose, and He directs my path. Can I ignore the miracle that is my life?

Petitions to my Higher Power
God,

Help me to keep You at the forefront of my thoughts. Let me seek You out in all that I do. Let me not waste the opportunity You have given me for a new life. Let me take this privilege seriously. Today help me when I need it, and guide the steps that I take on this journey called recovery. Help me to seek Your vision for my life. In gratitude I pray.
Amen.

* * * *

Wisdom for Today   Jul 18
At meetings you hear the program described as a "simple program." (*Alcoholics Anonymous,* Fourth Edition. Page 58) This statement is true; the concepts and principles of the program are simple. But recovery is not easy; in fact, I believe recovery is the hardest thing anyone of us can do. The fact is that we have met the enemy, and the enemy is in us. Our own self-will constantly works to lead us astray. This does not mean that recovery is not worth it. Each of us is worth the effort it takes to get clean and sober and stay that way.

212

The adventure of recovery is also exciting. It is this adventure of living a new life that is worthwhile. Recovery is so much better than our old way of living. There is no comparison with the joy, peace of mind and happiness we are seeking to find. Without the program and a Higher Power, we have no chance of finding this happiness. It is only with the program and the grace of God that we can begin this adventure, and it is only through working the steps and the fellowship that we make progress toward our goal. In this adventure, we find that we can have reasonably good lives. Our lives are not trouble free, but we learn how to deal with adversity and struggles within and without because of the program. God knows that we are worth the battle; and He knows that we will have what we need to fight the battle, because He has given us the tools to use through the program. Am I fighting the battle for recovery?

Meditations for the Heart

A strong spiritual foundation is made up of two distinct parts. The first part is lived out in prayer and meditation. It is here that we maintain communion with our Higher Power. It is here that we seek knowledge of His will for us. It is here that we establish gratitude, and it is here that we seek to meet our needs in recovery. Each day I need to spend time in prayer and meditation to keep the foundation of my recovery strong. The other part of a strong spiritual life is found in service to others. Every time I reach out to others and offer a word of encouragement, or share my experience or act in unselfish service, I also strengthen the foundation of my recovery. When I can describe a victory I have had in the battle of recovery and share this with others, I am giving away what I have received. This service and others just like it take me out of my self-centeredness and allow me to show others that the battle over self-will can indeed be won. When I share these victories with others, I become aware that this victory occurred, not because of my will, but because I followed God's will for me. Do I work to strengthen my foundation?

Petitions to my Higher Power

God,

You have given me this adventure called recovery, and I am grateful for all the possibilities it brings. It is not always easy; in fact, sometimes it is quite hard. Still, I know it is better than what life would be in active addiction. Today I seek You out to strengthen me for this adventure, and I pray that I may give away what I have learned in this adventure.

Amen.

* * * *

213

Anger and resentment have slipped away. Those things that used to drive me up a wall and leave me hot under the collar have been lost. The thought of seeking revenge or a way to get even have not been a part of my thinking in my recovery. This did not happen right away, but this poison is not something I wish to drink any longer. There was a time when all I did was plot and scheme on ways to act on my hidden anger and rage against the world, my friends and my family. Why did they have to judge me? Who gave them the right? How would I pay them back? These questions and others just like them tore my insides apart in the past, but they are needed no longer.

Hanging on to resentments only hurt me. I was never foolish enough to really act out my rage. Instead I turned this anger inward on my self. I found ways in recovery to let go and found that as I turned things over to God, I no longer needed to carry these burdens. Hate was not something I needed anymore; it only served to provide another excuse to drink or use. In its place I was able to look at my part in the problem. I could look at what I needed to change. In its place I discovered things like forgiveness, tolerance, and understanding. As the rage departed and the resentments hushed, I found something called peace. Yes, losing the burden of anger and resentment has turned out to be a good thing. Do I continue to carry the burden of anger and resentment?

Meditations for the Heart

How I react to and treat others has changed dramatically over time. This was not so much up to me as it was up to His grace. Yes, I have done much of the footwork by working the steps, but the changes that occurred as a result of this really happened not because of what I had done, but because of my Higher Power's interventions. He has changed the way I think. He has changed the way I view life. He has changed the way I interact with others. I still am called to interact with others daily. I am still called to do the next right thing. I am still called to do His will. These choices I make, but as for the outcome of these choices, I leave that all up to God. He helps me to perceive the world in a new and different light. He helps me to think before I speak. He helps me to find new ways to solve old and difficult conflicts. His grace makes this happen in my life. Am I doing the footwork and leaving the outcome up to God?

Petitions to my Higher Power

God,

In Your wisdom You show me what is needed. When I need to look in the mirror, You provide me with someone who will reflect what they see back

to me. When I need to see beyond my own thinking, You provide me with another opinion. When I need to look straight ahead, You give me a straight and narrow path. When I need to struggle with something, You provide me with a wide berth and allow me to look at things for as long as I need to. Continue this day to show me the way.
Amen.

* * * *

Wisdom for Today   Jul 20

Sometimes it is just important to laugh at ourselves. When I look back at all the games I played and all the ways I tried to make bargains with myself, deny my problems, or just lie to myself, it is amazing that I am still here to talk about it. There is a story that dates back to the beginnings of the program that tells of a man who was meeting with the founders of the Twelve Step program. In this story the man is asked if he wants to stop drinking. He responds, "Yes, I need to stop for at least six to eight months." The men meeting with him in the hospital at the time smile and laugh at his response. They laugh, not at him, but at themselves for they also played this game.

I needed people who would laugh at my insanity – people who would listen to the schemes, games and denial I presented and would laugh at me and with me. They were entitled to laugh because they had done the same crazy things. These individuals taught me to laugh at myself. They taught me to consider new options. They taught me to laugh at my own games. They taught me to laugh at my disease. Addiction to alcohol and drugs is no laughing matter. It is a matter of life and death. But learning to laugh at the insanity of my disease, the games, bargains, denial and dishonesty helped me to understand that my way would not work. Have I learned to laugh at my disease and myself?

Meditations for the Heart

Laughing at my disease and myself also had a spiritual benefit. Laughing at the insanity of my behavior taught me to be humble. Only a man who is not filled with egocentric pride can laugh at himself. Only a man who is not filled with arrogance and self-centeredness can laugh at himself, and humility is something that I lacked early in my recovery. Humility meant that I could admit my brokenness and that I could admit recovery was not possible without outside intervention. I love listening to others tell of their experiences. Invariably I hear them recount stories of crazy, stupid and useless attempts to control their behavior. I laugh sometimes out loud and sometimes on the

215

inside because I realize how senseless my same attempts were. I laugh because of the humility I am given in recognizing my own powerlessness. Sometimes I even imagine that God, as I understand Him, must laugh, too. Does my laughter bring humility in the face of despair?

Petitions to my Higher Power
God,

Teach me to laugh at myself. Teach me to laugh at all the desperate ways I used to play games with myself. Teach me to use this laughter to see myself in a new light. Teach me to use this laughter to understand the cunning and baffling ways my disease talks to me. Teach me to laugh at my disease. Teach me humility.
Amen.

* * * *

Wisdom for Today   Jul 21
There was a time when I really didn't want to do many of the things that were suggested to me in recovery. The reasons for this were many. Sometimes it was because I was just lazy and didn't want to do the work. Other times it was fear that held me motionless. Sometimes depression got in the way, and still other times it was pride or arrogance. I look back now and am surprised at the progress I have made despite all the reasons I didn't want to do what was necessary for my recovery.

The reality was that something kept pushing me, urging me, guiding me each step of the way. These things did not happen because of what I was doing. There was a Power outside of me that kept me moving in the right direction. Sanity returned to my life even when I was doing things to get in the way. Hope returned to my life. Over time, one day at a time, my life has come back together. I have changed not because of what I do, but because of what is being done for me. Belief that miracles happen only requires that you open yourself to growth along spiritual lines. Miracles surround me at meetings. Miracles exist in my life. Yes, when I look back at all the struggles I had and what has happened in my life, belief is simple. Do I see that all that I have is a gift given to me in recovery?

Meditations for the Heart
Recovery has a way of growing on you. The longer you stay clean and sober, the more likely you are to open yourself to this growth. What I am talking about is how "maybes" begin to appear in your life in recovery. I have had one maybe after another come into my life. Maybe there is a way

out. Maybe there is a chance that I can make it. Maybe I need to grow in my understanding of God. Maybe I need to repair the damage done. Maybe I am an okay person. Maybe I can help others. Maybe I can ask for help. Each and every maybe that has come into my life has opened the door to spiritual growth. Sometimes the maybes have come quickly, and at other times the maybes seem to be slow in coming. But the maybes are there and are revealed over and over again. God knows when I am ready for the maybes in my life. He sees to it that each of these maybes happens when I need them. Each of these maybes opens me to new possibilities. Do I stop long enough to recognize the maybes in my life?

Petitions to my Higher Power
God,

Where will You lead me today? What new maybes will You reveal to me? How do You want me to grow today? I do not yet know the answers to these questions, but I am open to the maybes that You will present to me in Your time. Increase in me the willingness needed to follow where I am led. Thank You for the growth I have received. Most of all thank You for the miracle of new life You have given me.

Amen.

✳ ✳ ✳ ✳

Wisdom for Today   *Jul 22*

Sometimes I think we all get stuck along the path of recovery. I know there have been several times when I reached a point that I just didn't know what to do or simply wanted to quit working the program. It is not so much that I wanted to go back to drinking or using. It is just that the issue or problem I faced seems to be too big. These stuck points are a normal part of the recovery process. Getting stuck is not how I get myself into trouble. It is what I do or don't do when I am stuck that can cause real problems. This is when it is most important for me to remember the first word of the First Step – "We."

Getting stuck means that what I am doing or not doing is not working. It means that I can't handle it on my own. I need others to help me. I need to ask for help. I need a fresh perspective or a new viewpoint regarding my situation. I need new ideas and redirection. I need others to tell me what to do. I need to gain insight, understanding and wisdom. I need encouragement to get back into action. I need help finding what I have missed. I need to be shown what to do. I need not to avoid, ignore or run away from the issue. I need new hope and guidance. I need to be reminded, and I need to go back to the basics. I need to keep it simple. When I go back to the concept of living as "We" rather than "I," life seems to get unstuck. I get back on track and find new energy. Do I do what I need to when I get stuck?

Meditations for the Heart

"Thy rod and thy staff comfort me." These words in the Psalms describe a shepherd caring for his sheep. A few summers ago I had the opportunity to spend some time on a sheep ranch. Sheep are not the brightest creatures on the planet. Sometimes they wander from the flock and can become lost or get into trouble. A shepherd searches them out and leads them back to where they belong. He uses a rod and staff to guide the sheep. A sheep that gets lost or in trouble becomes anxious and scared. The rod and staff comfort the sheep because it realizes it is being cared for and guided to where it belongs. I am not so different. When I get lost in recovery or stuck in some dangerous spots, I also need a rod and staff to comfort me. When I use God as my shepherd, He will use the program and the fellowship to guide me back to safety. He uses the voices of wisdom and the understanding of those that have been there to lead me back. Do I trust my Higher Power as a sheep trusts its shepherd?

Petitions to my Higher Power

God,

Sometimes along the path of recovery I get lost or into trouble. I am so grateful that You are there to find me and lead me back. Give me the courage to ask for help when I need it. Lead me with Your rod and staff back to a place of safety. Comfort my fears when they arise in my spirit.

Amen.

* * * *

Wisdom for Today   Jul 23

Every so often in my recovery process I am pleasantly surprised. It's like something happens that has it all make sense. It's like a light goes on, and the struggle that I have been facing looks different. For a long time I just wanted to believe these experiences were just a coincidence, but my viewpoint on these events has changed. As I look back on all of these events in my life, I can now see that each of these events in my life was a part of my spiritual awakening.

How did the fear and hopelessness change into confidence and hope? How did loneliness change into friendship? How did confusion change into insight? How did mistrust turn into faith? How did resentment and anger turn into forgiveness? How did insecurity turn into peace of mind? How did isolation turn into relationship? How did manipulation and deceit turn into honesty? How did shame turn into self-acceptance? How did all these things and more happen when I had little to do with making them happen? How did my spirit, which was dead, rise and wake? These events are all a part of my awakening, an awakening that has occurred because of the program, the steps and my Higher Power. Has my spirit been awakened?

Meditations for the Heart

In my addiction to alcohol and drugs I always looked for a way out. I would run to my alcohol and drugs to escape, to hide and to avoid dealing with life. Just because I stopped drinking and using did not mean that I automatically stopped running. I continued to look for a way out. I looked for an easier, softer way. I hid from reality, and I still wanted to escape. I even ran from God because I did not understand how He could help me. Even after I had some time under my belt, I would still turn to this old behavior whenever I faced pain, struggles, fear or loss. My way did not work. Running got me nowhere. I just spun around in circles, remaining miserable. However, when I stopped doing the same old thing expecting different results, my life changed. When I stopped running and started to deal with life on life's terms and I started to look for God in the middle of my pain, my life changed. When I stopped running, I was able to find light in the middle of my darkness. Have I stopped running?

Petitions to my Higher Power

God,

I am so grateful to be in this place. To stand in Your presence and know that You are my God and that You will always care for me. I am so grateful for each and every light switch You have shown me along this journey. I am grateful for the light that I have in my life and to be reawakened.
Amen.

* * * *

Wisdom for Today   Jul 24

All of us face failure at different times in the recovery process. For some of us this leads to relapse. For others it leads to getting stuck and being "dry." For others it comes in the form of taking the "easier, softer way," only to find out it doesn't work. Failure comes in many forms. I have experienced the tremendous sense of failure, falling flat on my face on more than one occasion. But recovery has taught me that failure is not a bad thing. It is what we do with failure that determines whether or not it becomes devastating or not. When I have run into failure in my recovery, it is easy to want to just give up. It is easy to want to run away or hide. It takes courage to stand up and learn from failure.

Much can be learned from failure, if we open ourselves up to finding out what went wrong. When I have opened myself up to this learning, the lessons have become some of the most important I have gained in my recovery process. I have learned not to face failure alone. I need to ask for help to sort through what went wrong. If I don't, I am too quick to look for something or someone to blame, including myself. Blame doesn't change the problem. I have to become willing to do the work necessary to find the answers. I must learn the lesson so that I don't repeat the failure. Failure can be a good teacher. Am I willing to open myself to learning even in my failures?

Meditations for the Heart

Each of us needs to find our own way to develop a relationship with a Higher Power. It is a process, not a single event. It is a process of growth. For me one of the biggest struggles was simply learning how to quiet myself to become open to hearing God. I spent time yelling at God, as I understood Him. When I was yelling in my frustration and anger, I could not hear His voice. I spent time in quiet prayer, but my head was still spinning with the events of the day, and I could not hear Him. I spent time in silence hoping He would speak and still could not hear Him. It was difficult to hear my Higher Power with all the noise in my head. Then one day I tried whispering to God, as I understood Him, and waited for Him to whisper back. What I discovered for me is that God was not a booming voice, nor was He silent. God whispers in a still, small voice. It requires a good ear. Sometimes He speaks to me through other people. Sometimes He whispers to my conscience. Other times I hear Him in my heart. It takes practice, but you can learn to listen to God. Am I willing to open myself up to hear His voice?

Petitions to my Higher Power
God,

You have and will continue to help me face failure in my life. Open me to learning from these failures. Let me walk through this day with my head up. Help me not to give up and hide myself in shame when I face failure. Give me courage to listen for Your voice today.
Amen.

* * * *

Sometimes even in recovery I still feel like I am riding a roller coaster. It is usually a roller coaster of emotions related to events going on in my life. The difference now is – I can get off the roller coaster. With addiction I had no choice. I simply continued the ride until I crashed and burned. In recovery the emotional roller coaster I get on can spin me around and around if I let it. Or I can use tools that I have learned in recovery to slow down and stop safely. Perhaps the most important tool I have is something called "intelligent faith." What is this tool you might ask? Well, let me explain.

Intelligent faith has two components. The first is the wisdom to know the difference, just as it is said in the Serenity Prayer. I need to sort out all my emotions and decide what it is that I am really feeling. Then I can make intelligent choices about whether or not it is something I can change or not. I can make intelligent and wise choices about how I respond to my emotions. The second component is to trust my Higher Power and have faith that He will walk through the emotions with me. I can turn over the fear, sadness, anger, guilt or any other distressing emotion and ask God to help me. But asking for help is only part of the puzzle. I have to have faith that He indeed will help me. Yes, intelligent faith has stopped the crazy ride in recovery more than once. Do I use intelligent faith when I need to?

Meditations for the Heart

If I am to be a spiritual person, it is proper for me to seek out spiritual things. One thing that I am always looking for is serenity and peace of mind. When my world gets turned on end and life is filled with surprises, I find that intelligent faith is the only way I can again reclaim serenity and peace of mind. When everything is spinning around and around, I know that if I use wisdom and I turn things over to my Higher Power, I am more likely to calm down. I am more likely to breathe a sigh of relief, and I am more likely to let go and let God do for me what I cannot do without Him. When I calm down and can breathe in His peace, I begin to see a broader picture. Life seems fuller. I realize that what is going on in the moment will pass, and God is with me. Manageability returns, and I find decision making to be easier and definitely wiser. When things get really crazy, as they sometimes will, I seek harder to find these spiritual things. Do I know that God will give me both wisdom and faith if I ask for them?

Petitions to my Higher Power

God,

Today is a new day, and I ask You to walk with me as I face the day. Help me to use the tools I am given for the greater good. Help me to seek

out both wisdom and faith in You as I walk through this day. Let me not be overwhelmed with emotional responses to life's events. Instead help me to remain calm and serene.
Amen.

∗ ∗ ∗ ∗

Wisdom for Today   *Jul 26*

As we go through recovery, each of us will be called upon to carry the message. I believe each of us needs to be ready and willing to carry the message of recovery when called upon to do so. I know for myself, I came up with lots of excuses at first. I felt like I wasn't qualified or that I didn't know what to say. But the truth was all I needed. All I had to do was simply tell others about my experience and what I did to find a way out of the insanity of addiction. My experiences in addiction qualified me to carry this message, and my experience in using the steps gave me the truth of my experience.

Each day I try to live for a greater purpose. Each day I look to my Higher Power and ask that He lead me. I have come to realize that God indeed will give me opportunity to carry the message to the alcoholic or addict that still suffers. I have an obligation to repay the program for what it has done for me, to give back what I have received freely. Yes, there are times when it would be easier to just let Twelve Step work slide or let someone else do it, but I also need to recognize that God cannot do His work in and through me unless I make myself available to Him and to others. It is important for each of us to have a greater purpose than just to be selfish. Carrying the message to others in whatever way we can do this serves that greater purpose. Am I willing to answer the call to serve?

Meditations for the Heart

In my addiction I was blinded by the insanity and denial of my addiction. In recovery my eyes become opened. As the layers and layers of self-deception are removed, I can begin to see life in a new way. Yet it is not until I become willing to see with eyes of faith that my life can take on new meaning. In addiction the only meaning I had in my life was to serve my self-centeredness. With eyes of faith I can serve my Higher Power. I can seek after His will for me, and I can see the things that He wants me to do with my life. It is only when I begin to see things with eyes of faith that His miracles can happen in my personality. When I think of the miracles in my life, I know that each of them has happened in my personality. It was faith that bought me to a place where I could surrender my will. It was faith that bought about changes in

222

my character. It was faith that bought me to a place where I became willing to do the repair work in my life and in the lives of those affected by my addiction. It was faith that bought me to a place where I could establish a personal relationship with my Higher Power. Am I looking at life through the eyes of faith?

Petitions to my Higher Power

God,

Today is a new day, and You have given me an opportunity to increase my willingness to serve You and others. Help me to take advantage of this opportunity and to begin to look at life differently. Open my eyes so that I may see through eyes of faith. Grant that I may find new meaning in my life by following Your will for me this day.

Amen.

* * * *

Wisdom for Today   Jul 27

There was a time for me when life was filled with doubts, but recovery changed much of that. There is something really wonderful about sitting down with old-timers who share how doubt was removed when he or she decided to turn their life over to the care of God, as they understand Him. But there is one thing that will bring doubt back quickly, and that is self-centered fear. This is the fear that says we are not getting what we want or what we deserve. This is the self-centered fear that will lead us into resentment. It is the fear that opens the door to let doubt back into our lives.

I know that when I open this door even a crack, I open the door to dozens and dozens of opportunities for my disease to play with my emotions and mess with my thinking. When I open this door to self-centered fear, I begin to want what I want; and I want it all right now. This type of thinking can get me into more trouble than anything else. When I allow myself to feel dissatisfied and cheated by life, I am quick to want to give up. I am quick to build resentment, and I am quick to get back into stinking thinking. However, when I make a conscious decision to turn my will and life over to God each morning, I leave no room for doubt and open the door only to faith. Do I close the door to self-centered fear each morning?

Meditations for the Heart

Each of us in recovery draws on images to strengthen our resolve to stay clean and sober. One image that has been very helpful for me is to think of the Red Sea. When I begin to feel surrounded by the troubles of life, I imagine

223

myself standing by the Red Sea with the hordes of evil about to pounce upon me and then having the sea parted by God's power. I gain a sense of renewed strength and renewed hope. I am provided with a new path where I can cross safely to the other side. Yes, I have an active imagination; but the reality is that this is what happens in recovery. When I am surrounded by the noise and confusion of life if I call on God for help and talk to others in the program, new options for dealing with my problems open up to me. I am given new choices and I am guided safely to another place, a place where life does not seem so difficult. Do I have an image of God's power and strength to draw on?

Petitions to my Higher Power

God,

In gratitude I can look out on my day without doubt, because I know You are always near. Should I become surrounded by the noise and confusion of life today, quiet me and let me see Your power working in my life to lead me safely to a new place. Help me to accept the tasks that I have in this day, and increase in me the strength and faith that only You can provide.

Amen.

* * * *

Wisdom for Today   Jul 28

When I first got clean and sober, I felt very weak, like I didn't have the strength needed for the task of not using. But I began to create linkage between others and myself in the program. I developed a reliance on a Power outside of myself because I could not rely on my own power. Soon all the links in this chain felt strong, and I began to feel like I could actually stay clean and sober one day at a time. But there was one thing I forgot: A chain is only as strong as its weakest link.

Despite having several strong links in my chain of recovery, I found that when I was at my weakest moments, my program began to break; and I faced failure. This is why it was so important for me to build my faith in a Higher Power. During these times of weakness, I needed to pray, sometimes every five minutes. In these prayers I began to discover what my weak links were. I was able to begin to guard against some of these weak links. I began to see how my emotions could throw me off track. I saw how my unwillingness to call someone and ask for help was a real problem. I learned the wisdom of the program through some very difficult lessons. I think that each of us needs to learn these lessons and how to use intelligent faith to strengthen each and every weak link. Do I know what my weak links are and how to guard against them?

Meditations for the Heart

I have to keep my batteries well charged to keep my spirit alive and well. Each day I find that I need to make conscious contact with the Divine Spirit to get my batteries charged. Through quiet time and through prayer and meditation, I find that I can indeed recharge my batteries. I also get recharged at meetings and by talking with others in the program. As I make these connections, my very spirit is filled; and His Spirit flows into me and recharges me. When I grow weary, it is even more important to stop and rest with my Higher Power. Here I can gain strength and power to continue my journey. Here I can get recharged so that I am ready for whatever comes my way. In these quiet times I can rest until every worry, every fear and every concern is relieved. When my batteries are recharged, I feel a sense of serenity and inner peace. I know His love, and I know joy in that moment. It fills me with whatever I need. Do I keep my batteries well charged?

Petitions to my Higher Power

God,

Today let me seek out any weak links in my chain and learn to guard against these weak links. Help me to find Your strength and use it to renew and recharge my batteries. Let me stay plugged into You in all that I do this day. Grant that I may seek after Your will for me today; and give me the courage, power and strength I need to accomplish Your will for me today. Amen.

* * * *

Wisdom for Today   Jul 29

In my addiction to alcohol and drugs I simply was not comfortable being me. I did everything I could to avoid myself. I deceived myself. I spent time living in tomorrow or yesterday. I focused on other people and found ways to blame them for my problems. I spent time sleeping when I should have been awake, just to avoid myself. It was too painful being "me." I didn't like who I had become. I didn't like how I behaved and how I hurt others. Most of all, I would run to the alcohol and drugs just to escape reality and escape myself. I didn't like me, and I didn't like thinking about my life.

Then recovery came along, and I was able to barely look at myself in the mirror. There was so much shame. I was disgusted with myself, and now I didn't have the drugs and booze to run to. I got into the steps and began to find my way out of the fog. I began to spend time in the fellowship and even began laughing occasionally. Over time my whole outlook changed, and I even began to like this "new me." I was able to forgive myself and accept who I was. I got comfortable living in my own skin. For this I am grateful. Am I getting comfortable living in my own skin?

Meditations for the Heart

Sometimes I wonder what God sees when He looks at me. Is He happy with me today? Is He happy with the choices I am making in my life? I know that often times I don't measure up. I am not perfect, but I have to believe that God likes what He sees since I have cleaned up my act. I guess I want to do things that are pleasing to God now. Before all I ever wanted to do was please myself. I was so wrapped up in my self-centeredness I could not see God. I am glad He continued to watch over me in my insanity. When I think about how God sees me through His eyes, I know He sees a much bigger picture of me than I will ever see. This makes it much easier to trust that He is leading me to where He wants me to be. God's vision is clear, and He sees me in a whole different light that I do. Am I open to God's vision for me?

Petitions to my Higher Power

God,

Each day I stay clean and sober is a gift from You. Thank You for this gift, and thank You for helping me to become comfortable in my own skin. Help me this day to follow after Your vision for me. Teach me to live the program. Grant me this day new light and a new vision of myself.

Amen.

* * * *

Wisdom for Today   Jul 30

One of my biggest personal weaknesses was deep inside. I struggled with all the unstable emotions I carried. Alcohol and drugs helped to keep me anesthetized so I simply did not have to feel. As my disease progressed, I had increasing mental conflicts; and my emotions became more and more unstable. I began looking for ways to escape by drowning my troubles in alcohol and drugs. I looked for anything to help me push away the reality of my life. I would experience short-term gain only to suffer long-term pain.

Eventually I became so numb and so out of touch with reality that I had no idea what I was truly feeling anymore. I was just a balled up mess of confusion, rage, shame, fear and sadness. I guess this is why the steps are numbered. I needed to learn how to stay clean and sober before I even began to untangle the weakness deep inside. I needed to begin to unpeel the layers and layers of emotional mess to find an inner calm. I did not do this alone. I needed the fellowship and my sponsor to help me sort through the mess. Eventually I was able to deal with my emotions as they came up and learned healthy ways to cope with all my feelings without alcohol and drugs. Nothing about this was easy, but the inner calm I now have has been worth it. Am I ready to untangle the unstable emotional wreckage of my life?

Meditations for the Heart

Probably the biggest struggle I had was not letting my resentments get the best of me. Often times they would get in the way and prevent me from doing the next right thing. I would get resentful, and my behavior would soon be misdirected and get me off track. I would find excuses for my actions and even look to blame others. But this simply kept me sick. I needed to find a way to let go of these resentments. I searched my heart for ways to accept the other person. I was told to pray for them. When I could accept that the people I was so angry and resentful toward were human and that their behavior had been their way of trying to deal with my insanity, I began to find room in my heart for forgiveness. I found that I could do this to help me in my life. It was not so much to make them feel better, but it was so that I could feel better by letting go. Even the ones that I could not find a way to accept or forgive, I found a way to let go and let God do for me what I could not do for myself. Do I still harbor resentments against others?

Petitions to my Higher Power

God,

Another new day, God, and I am clean and sober! I grow each day You grant me reprieve from my addiction. Sometimes I am purposeful in my growth, and other times I am surprised by how You help me grow. Help me this day to seek and find an inner peace. Help me to deal with life on life's terms and not be controlled by unstable emotions. Take from me the roadblocks that I have that get in the way of doing the next right thing. Amen.

* * * *

Wisdom for Today   Jul 31

I did not choose to become an alcoholic or an addict. No one came to my school when I was growing up and said, "Who in here wants to be an alcoholic or an addict when they grow up?" I didn't raise my hand, and I didn't volunteer to have this affliction. No one chooses to become addicted. I started out just wanting to have a good time just like everyone else. I do not know what caused me to get this disease – genetics, my psychological make-up, social pressure or some combination of a lot of things. It does not matter. I have this disease.

I may not have chosen to become addicted to alcohol and drugs; but once I found out that I did have this problem, once my denial was broken, I became responsible for the choices I made regarding my recovery. I made the choice to continue going to meetings. I made the choice to work the steps. I made the choice to use my sponsor and the fellowship to help me along the way. Perhaps the only choice I did not make was God, as I understand Him. He chose me. Each day I have to make choices regarding my program. Each day I have to decide what I will value. Each day I have to make choices to do the next right thing. Each day I must walk the walk. For this I am responsible. Am I taking responsibility for my recovery?

Meditations for the Heart

"There is a time for every season under heaven." In fact, there is a proper time for everything. This is why the steps are numbered. This is why we must learn patience. I cannot hurry recovery. I must learn that I have to do things in a certain order. If I hurry things, I may do things at the wrong time leading to the wrong results. Timing is important, and this is why I had a sponsor to advise me when to do things in my recovery. This is why I listened to others at meetings to learn when to do things and in what order. If I tried to make amends before examining my character defects and my motives, I would have likely fallen on my face; or I would have hurt others further. I had to learn balance before I could risk stepping away from the chair holding me up. In the same way I had to learn balance in my recovery before I could even begin to trust my decisions. This is why I need to stop along the path and rest when it is needed. This is why I must ask for help and guidance when it is needed. Do I pause to consider timing along my journey?

Petitions to my Higher Power

God,

Taking responsibility is something I seldom did. Teach me responsibility in my recovery. Help me to listen for Your will for me, and provide me with the power I need to carry out Your desire. Help me to judge the timing of my behavior, and teach me to wait in patience when I need to. Let me seek out wisdom through others in the program who will show me the way.
Amen.

* * * *

Wisdom for Today *Aug 1*

I remember one time when I asked my sponsor, "What is your secret? I mean how do you stay happy?" He just laughed as he often did when I asked him a question. Then he looked at me seriously, and he said, "Take it as it comes." I wasn't really sure what he meant, but over the next years I began to understand what he said more and more. What he was referring to was taking life as it comes. Deal with your troubles as they arise; maintain a sense of inner calm in the middle of your problems, knowing that God is near; and rise above the problems of life, keeping yourself spiritually healthy. This was the secret that was at first hidden to me in my sponsor's statement, "Take it as it comes."

In my recovery I like many others have had to face many different problems. Often times I have felt weighted down by the inescapable events of life and the pain that sometimes comes with these events. Loss in particular has been hard, whether it is the death of a loved one, or loss of a job due to economic pressures and downsizing or loss of health. Any loss can be difficult, but I have learned in recovery to take it as it comes. I can face problems as they arise. I can maintain an inner calm in the storms of life. I can rise above and stay spiritually healthy. Do I "Take it as it comes?"

Meditations for the Heart

The other important part of my sponsor's message was the fact that I also had to learn to take the blessings I received as they came. It became important for me to learn to recognize each blessing I got along the journey of recovery. It became important for me to carry these blessings with me. It also became important for me to give these blessings away to others in the program. My sponsor told me that I would receive blessings along the way in recovery, but I had no idea that so many good things could happen to me. Every time a window was closed, God has opened a door somewhere else for me. Each time I felt weak, I have been given strength. Each time I give away these things to others in the program, I am blessed again. Because each time I give it away, I am allowed to keep what I have. Do I bring blessings to others along my journey?

Petitions to my Higher Power

God,

One day at a time I have learned to walk with You on this road of recovery. You have placed people in my life that have shared their wisdom and courage and strength with me. Show me now how to be a blessing to others in my life that they may reap the blessings of recovery just as I have.

Amen.

* * * *

229

Wisdom for Today   Aug 2

It seemed like I was always bored when I was using. Nothing really interested me anymore. I drank and used to escape this boredom, or I would work to create a crisis in my life to find a way out of the boredom. Sure there were times when I had fun, but most of the time I was just bored. Sometimes I would make up stories and lie just to make myself look good. Yes, I enjoyed the scamming and the tall tales; but every night I would go home to the same old thing. I really didn't have any friends, just people with whom I passed the time.

Early in recovery I thought that AA was boring. I thought that staying clean and sober was a terrible way to have to exist. I was wrong. Why was it that so many people decided to stay after the meeting? What was it that kept them interested? I began to hang out after the meetings and soon learned that recovery had many faces, none of which are boring. Here I learned of truth. Here I learned how to value friendship. Here I learned about trust. No longer did I need to scam. These people were genuine and real. They talked honestly and openly. I found a new sense of energy and no longer was bored. Have I found new meaning and something exciting about life in recovery?

Meditations for the Heart

Hope can accomplish many things in recovery. I have watched as one obstacle after another fell or disappeared from my life simply because I was willing to hold onto hope – hope that God could and would if He were sought, hope that the promises could be true even for me. Hope comes through working these steps. It comes to us as a gift of His grace. Hope comes to us in surrender, and it grows in our hearts with each new day. Sometimes it seems elusive, and at other times hope can seem very distant. Yet if we search, there is always hope. Have I found hope in the Twelve Steps?

Petitions to my Higher Power

God,

You have helped me find new meaning in my life. You have planted a seed of hope deep within my heart. Help me this day to cultivate and nourish this hope. Let it ever grow to strengthen me. Guide me always back to the roots of this hope for a new life in the program.

Amen.

* * *

Wisdom for Today   Aug 3

For a long period of time recovery seemed to be a long series of tasks that I didn't want to do but needed to do and then waited to find out why. And in many ways this is exactly what recovery is meant to be. The Twelve Step program is a process of seeking continually to improve our lives and who we are. It is more about being on the path to our goal, rather than achieving it. It is tempting to begin and measure how long we have been clean and sober in years, but the truth is that none of us ever fully reaches our goals or is fully cured. Many of the steps seem to be difficult, and often times I wanted to avoid or skip over some of the steps. But I kept remembering the statement from the Big Book, "*Half measures availed us nothing.*" (*Alcoholics Anonymous,* Fourth Edition. Page 59)

It became more important to stick with the program and work through the steps than risk relapse. Over time I began to see the effects of the program in my life. The promises started to come true in my life. I was changing, and life was getting better. It then became easier to want to sit back and rest. Then I discovered there could be no long rest stops. I needed to keep working the steps in all situations that I faced in my life. My addiction was only held in check by continuing to work my program one day at a time. Am I continuing to work on improving my life in recovery?

Meditations for the Heart

Most projects in life require some preparation before actually doing the work. This is certainly the case in recovery. Each of us in the program did the preparation work necessary to become members of the program. Our addiction earned us a place at meetings. Each step in the program prepares us for the next. Each meeting I attend prepares me for the events of my life. For a long time I heard people at meetings say, "Take what works and leave the rest." I know in part this statement refers to maintaining confidentiality and anonymity, but it didn't tell me how to use what I had heard. Then one day I heard someone say this statement differently. He said, "Take what works and store the rest." I liked this concept. It meant that everything I heard at meetings could be saved and used when it was needed. Today I see meetings as a way to stay prepared for whatever cards I am dealt in life. Am I storing the knowledge I hear at meetings?

Petitions to my Higher Power
God,

Thank You for welcoming me into a new day. Let me take this day and use it to accomplish any task that You set before me. Help me to increase my willingness and to find courage to move ahead when I am called on to do so. Let me seize every opportunity to make progress that is given me.
Amen.

* * * *

"Just for today!" – Three small words with a lot of meaning! Today was a very hard place to live in my addiction. Most of the time I lived in the past and was filled with regret and remorse, or I lived in the future and experienced life with a sense of morbid fear. What was going to be the next bad thing to happen in my life? Could it get any worse? Learning to live in today is a skill that I had to learn. I understood the words but had little understanding of how to put them into action. In early recovery it seemed I spent a lot of time dreaming about the past. It seemed that I couldn't stop thinking about getting wasted. If I wasn't thinking about the past, I worried about the future. Would recovery be worth it? Would I ever be happy again? I just didn't know.

It seemed like I didn't have the slightest clue of how to live in today. I worried about staying clean and sober for the rest of my life. I thought about all the bad things I had done. I just couldn't seem to get in today. Then one night at a meeting it all seemed to click. I was making myself miserable. Nobody else was doing this to me; I was doing it to myself. If I put even half the energy into staying in today as I did the future or the past, maybe, just maybe, I could be happier. I am not sure what happened at that meeting or even what was said to get me thinking this way, but it worked. I started focusing on just staying in today. Life didn't seem so complicated. Life got better - just for today! Do I live in today?

Meditations for Today

I like getting up in the morning. This was not always the case. I used to worry about what I did the night before, but today things are different. I can wake up and start my day in a good way. I can start my day with my best friend. This is how I came to know my Higher Power. My Higher Power became my best friend, and I can start my day each day with Him. Some days I do better with this than others, but I know He is there for me each and every morning. Spending time with my best friend is a great way to start my day. It keeps me centered. It keeps me focused. It keeps me happy. It gives me someone to bring my problems to. I find answers to the questions I have. I find new questions to ask. I gain strength, hope; and occasionally I even get some wisdom. Yes, getting up in the morning is not hard to do at all anymore. Do I start my days differently now?

Petitions to my Higher Power

God,

Each day You give me new breath. What I do with that breath is up to me. Help me to do what You want me to do today. Let me stay consciously aware of this day and Your plans for me in it. Thanks for being my friend and for all You do for me!

Amen.

∗   ∗   ∗   ∗

Wisdom for Today   Aug 5

The program has taught me how to live life. I am not really sure how or even when this happened, but life started to make sense, and using the Twelve Steps in my life started to make sense. Today I can see what to do when problems come up in my life. I don't have to sweat it out like I did in my days of active use of alcohol and drugs. I know I have a support system behind me that will help me through any problem I have. No, they won't do my taxes for me; but they will help me have the right attitude when I do them. They won't help me in my parenting, but they will teach me how to change the things I can and accept what I can't change.

Recovery is about learning to live again. And there are many lessons to learn; but it is nice to know that I do not face life alone, no matter what. I can count on the program. I can count on my Higher Power. I can count on the steps. I can use the tools, and it works. Yes, the program has taught me how to live; but it has also given me many gifts. I never thought the promises would come true for me. But they continue to happen in my life. I can trust the program to be there for me no matter what is going on in my life. Have I learned to count on the program?

Meditations for the Heart

Life also teaches me. Sometimes the lessons are difficult and other times the lessons are quite pleasant, but either way life is a good teacher. As I am on this journey called recovery, it is important for me to stop from time to time and look at the big picture. It is easy to get caught up in all the day-to-day details of life and forget about the bigger picture. Simple questions help me do this. How is my life going? How is my recovery work going? Am I getting to the place my higher Power wants me to be? Am I happy? Are the promises of the program coming true for me? Is there anything I need to change in my life? What are the roadblocks that seem to be getting in the way? These types of questions help me to focus on the bigger picture. Do I take time out to look at the bigger picture?

Petitions to my Higher Power

God,

Today is another gift from You. Teach me Your plans for me today, and give me courage for the road ahead. Help me to take my blinders off and to

233

see the bigger picture of life. Help me to keep going in the direction I need to go to keep growing.

Amen.

* * * *

Wisdom for Today   Aug 6

One temptation we all seem to face at one time or another is over-confidence. For me it happens when everything seems to be going along smoothly. It becomes easy to forget the gift that recovery is and begin to take it all for granted. Then I seem somehow to switch my thinking and no longer see His grace in my life. I no longer accept that I was given such a precious opportunity as recovery, and I begin to assume that somehow I have done something that has caused me no longer to need the program. I begin to become self-confident and assume I can deal with my disease on my own. I don't need help. Humility exits stage right, and I am left holding the bag. Denial creeps back into my life, and I am suddenly vulnerable to the voice of addiction.

This voice begins to whisper in my ear, and I begin to think I can handle things on my own. Addiction keeps on talking; and soon it has me in its clutches, trying to convince me that "one won't hurt," or "No one will know." Yes, self-confidence is a very dangerous road to travel. It most certainly can lead to relapse. But even if I resist this voice, I still find myself isolated and miserable. The only way out is to go back to the beginning. Go back to the steps. I have to admit I am powerless and out of control. I need to realize that there is hope, and as the Big Book says, "*There is one who has all power; may you find Him now.*" (*Alcoholics Anonymous,* Fourth Edition. Page 59) Do I allow myself to become over-confident?

Meditations for the Heart

Recovery is not a stagnant process. We are either moving ahead, stuck and immobilized or backsliding. Each of us experiences each of these states in our recovery to a different extent. The important thing is that we see when we are getting into trouble and then do something about it. We need to put the program into action to stay on the right path. We need to walk in humility and be willing to ask for help along the way. Recovery is a program of action, and I need to be willing to take the steps necessary to stay on track. I need to be willing to go to any length to achieve and maintain sobriety. I need to listen to only one voice and that is the voice of God, as I understand Him. I cannot afford to risk listening to the voice of addiction. It is cunning, baffling and powerful. Do I watch to make sure I am staying on the right path?

234

Petitions to my Higher Power
God,

Help me this day to walk in humility and to value the gift I have been given in recovery. Let me not take anything for granted and stay focused on Your will for me. Give me this day the strength and courage I need to walk the path You lay before me. Keep me from becoming prideful, and help me in all that I do today.
Amen.

* * * *

Wisdom for Today Aug 7

One of the promises of the program states, "*We will intuitively know how to handle problems which used to baffle us.*" (*Alcoholics Anonymous,* Fourth Edition. Page 84) Well, I am not sure how intuitive I am; but I do know that the Twelve Step program has indeed taught me a better way to understand my problems and my role in them. I have learned many new habits in the program. I know that I have choices today that I did not have before. I can ask for help. I can get feedback from others in the program. I do not need to overreact or under react to the problems that come up in my life. I can deal with each new issue or concern as it arises. I can turn things over to my Higher Power.

One thing is for sure; as each new twenty-four hours pass, I gain new insights and new ideas. I find that I do not need to run from my problems. I do not need to isolate. I do not need to use alcohol or drugs to escape. I can stand firm and know that with the help of the program, I will be able to deal with problems that come up in my life. I no longer need to let fear, sorrow, anger and frustration, or loss lead me into trouble. I do not need to try so hard anymore, because I have come to trust that the program works. Am I finding it easier to deal with problems now?

Meditations for the Heart

Daily we learn lessons in recovery. God provides us with many opportunities to learn new insights, new behaviors, new habits and new ways of thinking. Recovery helps to change our faulty belief systems. Perhaps one of the more difficult lessons I have had to learn is to remain calm in the middle of life's storms. Yet regardless of the events that take place in our lives, God's command and promise are the same. "Fear not, for I am with you always." Learning to trust in His power is a task that we all face. When I am stressed out by life, I need to remember to stay calm. When troubles come into my day, I need to remember to stay calm. I need to remember that He is with me every step of the way. I need to trust in His Power. I need to trust in His wisdom. I need to trust in His understanding and in His grace. Do I remain calm in the storm?

Petitions to my Higher Power
God,

I do not know what this day has in store for me. But I do know that whatever life brings my way, I can trust that You are with me. Help me to remain calm in the difficulties I may face. Let me reach out to others and ask for their guidance and help. Let me also be of service in the things I do this day. Let me follow after You, because You know where best to lead.
Amen.

* * * *

Wisdom for Today   Aug 8
We owe a lot to the founders of the AA program. Although these same people would say that what they did was simply borrowed from others, they indeed put the pieces together to develop a program of recovery that works. It all started with two men desperate to find a way out of the insanity of alcoholism. They met and shared their stories with each other. They were not looking to help the other person, but looking for a way to help themselves. From these original two individuals, a group was formed. Then other groups formed following the same principles. Today there are hundreds and hundreds of groups worldwide. There are thousands upon thousands of people who have used the Twelve Steps to find recovery.

Each and every day new people join these groups. In each person's case, the beginning starts with admitting powerlessness and in turning it over to the care of a Power greater than themselves. This Higher Power surely has done great things in and among the individuals of these groups. Yes, it all started with two people who found strength in and with each other and through a Higher Power. I can look back now and know that I owe a great deal to this program. It saved my life. Am I doing what I can to help the program grow and flourish?

Meditations to my Higher Power
Many of the original principles of the program were adapted from the Bible and its teachings. One verse often cited by our founders was, "Blessed are they that hunger and thirst after righteousness, for they will be filled." I know I could never be filled when I was drinking and using drugs. I always

was left empty and spiritually bankrupt. I knew once I got into the program that I was hungry for something, but I really didn't know what. I just knew I had to stop, and I didn't know how. It did not take long though for me to hear and learn the steps. I began to realize that I would need to hunger and thirst after something other than drugs and alcohol. I would need to hunger and thirst after the will of a Power outside of myself. My way just did not work. Today I find that I still hunger and thirst; but now it is for the courage to do the will of God, as I understand Him. Do I know that I will be filled if I do God's will for me?

Petitions to my Higher Power
God,

Each day I wake up hungry for Your guidance. I thirst after Your strength and power in my life. Give me courage to become a servant in the groups I attend. Let me be willing to do any service work I am requested to do. Let me always remain grateful for the gift of this program and what it has done for me.
Amen.

* * * *

Wisdom for Today   Aug 9
I was one who always wanted to understand things. Sometimes this was very helpful, and at other times this knowledge seeking seemed to get in the way. For a long time I tried to understand the word humility as it is used in program literature. I spent hours paging through dictionaries, references, reading and re-reading but just couldn't seem to gain understanding. Finally in frustration I asked for help at a meeting. The very thing that I was looking for was the thing that was stopping me from getting an answer. A lack of humility kept me from asking for help until I was so frustrated that I was miserable.

An old-timer on the other side of the room spoke up, "Sometimes you just have to be stupid." I had known this individual for quite some time and knew he had only a third grade education. He could hardly read or write. But he was absolutely right. I had let my own ego and pride get in the way of asking for help. He went on to say, "I spent years trying to be something I wasn't. I didn't want to be me. Now I am spending time learning how to be the best me I can." He talked about hiding behind his mask of alcoholism and addiction. He talked about walking out of the cloud of denial and walking into the light of truth. He talked of learning to accept himself – the good, the bad and the ugly. He said, "Today there is a whole lot less bad and ugly and a whole lot more good. People in the program showed me how to do that." Am I finding a humble self-acceptance?

Meditations for the Heart

Learning can happen in a variety of different ways, but perhaps the most powerful learning I do is from my mistakes. When I fall on my face, stumble or miss the boat figuratively, I can use these experiences to learn. I can talk with others in the program and seek out different ways to handle similar situations in the future. I don't have to keep making the same mistakes. In fact, today I believe the only mistakes that exist are the ones I do not learn from. In this life no one can achieve perfection in all that they do. We all miss the boat, fall on our face and stumble as we walk through life. When this happens, we have an opportunity to learn, take corrective action and change our behavior. My addiction was no mistake. I have learned much from this experience. I have learned a whole new way of living, thanks to the program and the wonderful fellowship of friends I have. Am I willing to learn from my mistakes?

Petitions to my Higher Power

God,

Each new day I am given new challenges and have Your assurance that You will walk with me. Help me this day to remain humble and open to asking for help. Let me learn how to truly accept who and what I am. Give me eyes to see my strengths and eyes to see my weaknesses. Keep me realistic in my opinion of myself.

Amen.

* * * *

Wisdom for Today   Aug 10

When I was drinking and using drugs, I could find every excuse imaginable to justify my getting drunk or high and explain my behavior. This in part helped to support my denial system. As long as I could blame, excuse or explain everything to others and myself, I was okay. But it did not take long, and my excuses no longer worked. My own rationalizations and reasons didn't hold water, let alone a drink. The games I played with myself were complex and filled with self-deceit. Eventually I began to realize that what I was doing was not normal. It wasn't even close.

I faced my addiction to alcohol and drugs and realized I had to find a way to stop. But even here, my excuses continued. My disease was not about to give up without a struggle. Even when I finally did give up and got clean and sober, I still worked hard to find excuses. Then I heard a comment at a meeting that stuck with me. Someone I had never met before and never saw again at a meeting, probably a visitor in the area stated, "Being alcoholic does not give me permission to act alcoholically." This statement remains with me today. It has become one of the treasures I received in the program. Am I done with my excuses?

Meditations for the Heart

God, as I understand Him, has grown in my life in recovery. My concept and my openness to Him have changed remarkably in my recovery process. What I once perceived as Judge now has become my Friend. What I once perceived as distant has now become close. What I once perceived as unreachable has now become reachable. This change is certainly most welcome in my life. Having a relationship with this Holy Power that is active, close and reachable has opened many doors that I thought were closed. Even more importantly, when doors were closed, a window was opened for me. I no longer have to walk blindly along the path and now have a most experienced Guide. As my excuses, which prevented a relationship with a Higher Power, disappeared, I found security, hope, strength and humility. Do I have roadblocks standing in the way of my relationship with God?

Petitions to my Higher Power

God,

Help me this day to be honest in all that I do. Let me not seek to hide behind excuses and games. Instead let me find ways to be genuine and real. Let me seek to improve my conscious contact with You and seek to do Your will in the tasks that I face this day. Hold me close in Your protective arms. Amen.

* * * *

Wisdom for Today   Aug 11

Sometimes even in recovery I just get in a bad mood. I don't even need a reason for this to happen. It just seems like I got out of bed on the wrong side that morning. Even my morning meditation doesn't seem to get me back on track. Then I rush off, headlong into my day with my bad mood. These are the times when I am most likely to feel like it just isn't working. I get frustrated easily. I get crabby and irritable. Someone can look at me the wrong way or say the wrong thing to me, and I am off to the races. I can take it personally and become judgmental or even lash out in a manner that does not show any respect for the other person.

Sometimes by mid-morning or early afternoon I realize that I am having a bad day. At the end of my day I look back and regret how I behaved, and I don't like what I see. This is where Step Ten becomes so important for my recovery. I look back over my day and can honestly see that most if not all of my difficulty has to do with my attitude and my behavior. I need to look back and admit my mistakes, I may even have some amends to make the next time I talk with the people with whom I have interacted throughout my day. I also need to look back and see what went wrong. If I am unwilling to learn from these days, I will likely repeat them. Here I have found that talking to my sponsor or someone else in the program is important. I need to bounce things off of someone else and do some reality testing. Do I take inventory at the end of my day?

Meditations for the Heart

Often times when my day is screwed up, I need to look at where I am in my spirituality. Have I behaved in a way that my Higher Power would want me to? Invariably the answer to this question is "No." I may have gone through the motions of a morning meditation, but I never really made conscious contact with God, as I understand Him. Just going through the motions doesn't work for me. My day started off badly because I took things for granted. I took my Higher Power for granted. I just did not want to really take the time to ask for help or direction. I just mouthed the words. But God has a sense of humor. He looks at me and laughs at the mess I get myself into and says, "He'll be back." Then God waits silently for me to come back; and when I do, He laughs and says, "Did it again, huh? Tried walking through the forest with a blindfold on, and you fell on your face. When are you going to learn?" Do I know where to turn when I get off track?

Petitions to my Higher Power

God,

This morning let me not move too quickly and just take things for granted. Slow me down and encourage me to open my ears to Your voice. Let me remember that You are my friend, and I need to treat my relationship with You as one who is my best friend. Be my guide this day, and grant me a willing heart to follow.

Amen.

* * * *

Wisdom for Today   Aug 12

There were literally thousands of reasons I drank and used drugs. I used because it was a good day, and I used because it was a bad day. I drank and used because I was happy, and I drank and used because I was miserable. I spent hour after hour trying to figure out why I could not drink or use like other people. Many of us seek help and advice from a variety of professionals. Some of us spend time in hospitals or in jails only to find out they offer only a temporary reprieve. Even when I thought I found out why I drank and used the way I did, it did not stop me from continuing my obsession.

Eventually I had to realize I had gone too far. I was over the edge and falling fast. I was drinking like an alcoholic. I was using drugs like an addict. Even this did not stop me. It gave me more reasons to use. I was destroying my life, and I couldn't stop. I wasn't trying to destroy myself, but I couldn't stop it either. My will to stop the insanity was defeated. In utter powerlessness I had to admit to myself that my way did not work. Figuring out the answers did not work. Understanding the reasons did not work. If I ever was going to stop, I had to find an answer that was not my answer. Have I stopped the obsession with trying my way?

Meditations for the Heart

Where would I find this answer if it was not going to be mine? To whom could I turn? "Ask, and you shall receive." This line was where I found the answers to my obsession. I knew I could not stop the insanity on my own. What I didn't know until I came into the program was that I could do almost anything if I asked for God's help. Early in recovery I kept trying to convince myself that I was a useless person who could never do anything right. The program changed all that. I found that I could indeed accomplish much with the help of God, as I understood Him. If I called on His strength and wisdom, it was there waiting for me. All I had to do was accept this gift. All I had to do was follow, and I would be led to a new place. I would lose the obsession. I would learn a new way of living my life. Have I accepted the gift of His grace?

Petitions to my Higher Power

God,

Today I pray for acceptance of the wonderful gift of Your grace in my life. Let me willingly follow You where I am being led. Help me to let go of my old ways of thinking and behaving and learn a new way of living my life. Help me to be rid of my obsession completely.

Amen.

∗   ∗   ∗   ∗

There are those times when anger just seems to bubble up in life. It really doesn't matter what the cause of the anger is, what is important is how we react to the anger. Anger can be a very strong emotion that can play havoc in our lives. It is perhaps the emotion that we are most likely to lose control of, as if we really had any control to begin with. Each of us has our own unique set of clues that we are angry. Perhaps it is when you clench your jaw tighter or when your breathing becomes deeper. We know that anger is lurking in our lives when these clues tell us it is close by.

Anger can jump up out of nowhere, and it can silently sneak up on us. Still, when this happens, we have choices. We have a choice not to run to the bottle. We have a choice not to run to drugs. We have a choice about how we behave when anger occurs. The program gives us these choices and many more. When anger comes up for me, I know that my thinking gets screwed up quickly; and so I know I must use the steps and ask my Higher Power for help. I need to stay aware of my character defects coming into play. I need to take slow breaths and seek shelter from the storm. I call my sponsor and discuss the matter. I pray. I use the steps, and I find healthier ways to respond to life. Do I know what I need to do when I become angry?

Meditations for the Heart

Painful as early recovery can be, one day each of us finds out the reasons for this pain. It is important for me to be open to learning in my pain, because I know these can indeed be valuable life lessons. Pain is not just about being tested or about loss; it can also be a time of instruction and also preparation for the rest of our journey in recovery. When I am in the middle of a painful situation, I don't like it. It is uncomfortable, and it hurts. Today I have learned much from my painful times. It brings me into much closer contact with my Higher Power. It can teach faith in the struggle. It can bring new insights into how our own behavior is at least in part responsible for the pain. Pain also can strengthen and toughen the spirit. Pain also can be a strong way of telling us that what we are seeking is not good for us. Pain can be a very good teacher. Am I open to learning the lessons that pain can teach? Do I know that all pain eventually subsides and goes away?

Petitions to my Higher Power

God,

Today I pray that if I am tested, I also will be willing to grow through the process. Help me to remain focused on my responsibilities when I am angry or in pain. Lift me up so that I might know that You are with me. Let me trust You with the outcome.

Amen.

* * * *

Wisdom for Today   *Aug 14*

Most of us can look back and see that long before we finally quit drinking and using, we were out of control. I know for myself, I clearly went through a period of time where I refused to admit I had a problem, even though I knew the evidence was there to say I did. I hung onto my denial as long as I could. But my denial did not stop the consequences from happening. My disease was following the only course it knew. Addiction's job is to progress and cause pain, and that is exactly what happened in my case.

Like most addicts, it took a lot to finally convince me that I had a problem. After enough pain and the denial falling apart, I had no other choice but to finally admit that I was sick and could not control it. This was an important turning point and an important lesson. I was defeated by alcohol and drugs. I learned that alcohol and drugs have no equal at handing out pain. I also knew I had no choice but to give up and stop trying to hold on to my old ideas. My way just did not work; and as long I kept trying, my disease would continue to take me down. Am I firmly convinced I am beaten?

Meditations for the Heart

"*There is one who has all power, may you find Him now.*" (*Alcoholics Anonymous,* Fourth Edition. Page 59) For me this One who has all power is a force for good in my life. God always is about good. As long as I seek after His plans for me, I know that He will bring about good in my life. This doesn't mean I never will have problems in my life, but it does mean that my Higher Power will give me what I need to deal with these struggles. It does mean that if I follow His will, I will find good in my life. I also know that He has a purpose for me in this life I lead. God wants me to have my desires to become aligned with His desires. If I am able to do this, I can be assured that everything will be all right. I will be on God's side. Do I seek to align my will with that of God, as I understand Him?

Petitions to my Higher Power

God,

Each day I am reminded that I need to seek after Your will for me. I do this because I choose not to fall back into the insanity of my life. I do this to grow. Teach me, mold me, and shape me into what You want me to be. Let me understand Your purpose for me in this day. Let me trust that where You lead me will be a good place.

Amen.

* * * *

Today we live in a time of much confusion and delusion regarding our basic beliefs about who we are as spiritual beings. In fact, many of us have thrown out our old ideas completely and have not looked for answers outside of ourselves. This narrow view that we are the center of the universe leads people to rely only on themselves. Many addicts and alcoholics experience this same confusion and delusion. "I am the center of the universe, and I can rely on no one except myself," is the mindset by which many addicts live. This narrow view in part leads to a terrible sense of anxiety. "What if I don't do it right? What if I can't make it? What if . . . ?"

Yet the program directs us not to look at ourselves, but to look for a Higher Power outside of ourselves. In fact, the program even names this Higher Power - God, as we understand Him. I know that when I walked into the doors of the program, I walked in filled with a strong sense of anxiety and failure. I was spiritually bankrupt. I needed to find hope somewhere, and this is exactly what I found. I found this hope not by looking in myself, but by looking outside of self. This is the hope that relieved my anxiety. Have I ceased relying only on myself?

Meditations for the Heart

Fence sitting is exactly what many addicts and alcoholics do. We do not want to make any decisions. Doubt keeps us captive on the fence. We just do not know which way to turn. I remember many times using the words, "I don't know." I would say these words to my family, and I would say them at meetings and to my sponsor. These words kept me from taking any action. I just couldn't get off the fence. There were many issues that I sat on the fence about. What recovery has taught me is to say, "Yes!" to the will of my Higher Power. Saying "Yes" leads me down the paths to a better place in my recovery. "Yes" brings me to a place to find strength and power. "Yes" brings me to a place to find courage and willingness. "Yes" brings me to a place where I am filled with His wisdom. Do I still let doubt and fence sitting keep me stuck?

Petitions to my Higher Power

God,

You have helped me remove the veil of confusion and doubt. My heart has been calmed, and I no longer live in an anxious state. I am grateful that I no longer have to live a life run by self-centered thinking. I am learning that the ways of the program do work, and I am willing to get off the fence and get into action. Lead me this new day.

Amen.

* * *

This program is not a religious one, but a spiritual one. People in the program do not claim to be theologians. Instead we simply talk about the process of learning to live a spiritual life. We talk about matters like faith and hope. We describe how turning things over to a Higher Power has benefited our life. I can't graph out the spiritual process, nor can I draw you a roadmap on how to get there. But I can share how living a spiritual life of faith has led me out of loneliness. I can tell you how the hope I received in the program has calmed my anxiety and relieved my fears. I can tell you of many events that have happened in my life that have bought me happiness, inner peace and serenity. I can tell you that by living a spiritual life I have learned how to get along with other people.

Learning to live spiritually is accomplished through the steps, and it is learned from watching others in the program and following their example. Over time things such as depression, sorrow and pain are removed. Even the desire to drink or use drugs is removed. This does not mean that I am cured. It just is a benefit of living the program and having faith. It comes through obedience to the will of a Higher Power. It is His care to which we turn, and He will not let us down. Life is not always easy, and there are still bumps in the road. I still have problems, but these problems are by far much better than the ones I used to have. I still take five steps ahead and two steps back. Yet over time, living a Spirit-filled life leads to progress. Am I learning to live a Spirit-filled life?

Meditations for the Heart

A question that has popped into my head in the past was, "Is it okay to expect a miracle?" Well, the answer is a resounding – YES! Take a look around when you are at your next meeting, and you will see a room full of them. Ask any old-timer in the program if they ever experienced a miracle, and they undoubtedly will tell you of many in their recovery process. Miracles happen every day in recovery. You just have to look for them. Some people are a little reluctant to call them miracles and instead call these things change. But if you press them into how these changes occurred, you will hear them say it happened by walking the walk and by trusting in a Higher Power to do things they could not do for themselves. I would call that a miracle. Many things have happened in my recovery that I can't explain any other way. Do you expect a miracle? Are you willing to wait for the miracle to occur?

Petitions to my Higher Power
    God,
I start my day with a quiet time with You. In this conversation with You I both listen and talk to You. Help me this day to carry Your words and guidance with me. Teach me to live in the light of Your Spirit. Help me to stay on the path of spiritual living. Let me continue to experience Your miracles in my life. Walk with me this day.
Amen.

$$* \quad * \quad * \quad *$$

Wisdom for Today   *Aug 17*
    Today is a gift. Each and every day I stay clean and sober is a gift from the program and from my Higher Power. I have choices in how I enter this day and in how I use this time I am given. Most of us, when we receive a gift, do not immediately jump up and down on it and break it. We value the gift we have received. And so it is with this day we have been given. When I see each day as a gift and value it, my approach to my day is different. I can start my day with a true sense of gratitude and thank God for all that He has done for me. I can eagerly ask for His help and guidance throughout my day. I can end my day and look back and realize that the gift I received was valued and that I did all I could to use my time wisely.
    Each day unfolds differently. None of us can foresee the events that are about to occur. However, no matter what happens in my day, I have come to believe that when I walk through it with my Higher Power, I will be kept safe. Having this security is truly a wonder. No matter what problems arise, I know that I can be assured I will be given all the strength and courage I need for the day. I know that I can make constructive choices and follow the narrow path upon which God leads me. All I need do is listen for the heartbeat of His Spirit and follow it. Do I truly value the gift of another day?

Meditations for the Heart
    "God is not finished with me yet." This realization brings a whole new perspective for me. When I think about how God rescued me from drowning in a raging flood of addiction, I can be confident that He did not do this only to throw me back again. Yes, I can choose to jump back in, or I can walk too closely to the edge and slide back into the torrents, but this is not His plan for me. An Emergency Medical Technician does not administer CPR only to turn around and suffocate you once you have been revived. I do not know where God's plan for me will lead, but I am confident that His plan is better than mine. His will is to lead me to the promises of the program; I simply

need follow. I need to do the footwork. I need to be open and willing to follow His lead. Am I honestly working to follow His will for me?

Petitions to my Higher Power
God,

Today give me a heart that is willing to rely on You and Your plan for me. Help me to find true security in Your loving arms. Guide me through the steps of this day. I trust You to keep me in the way and give me the strength to not let go.

Amen.

* * * *

Wisdom for Today

Each and every day I am faced with a choice. A choice to continue on the path of recovery or a choice to do an about face and return to the insanity. One choice leads to life, and the other choice leads to death. None of us knows for sure, certainly not I, where my next drunken high might lead. But one thing is certain. Making the choice gets easier if I really value my recovery. If I truly value my own life, if I truly value my relationship with a Higher Power, if I truly value honesty and if I truly value what recovery has given me, then making the choice is not so hard.

So the question each addict and alcoholic faces is this - What do I truly value? It is easy to say the words that I value my recovery, but it is entirely something different to look at where I spend my time. My sponsor once told me that all I had to do to determine what I really valued was to look at how I was spending my time. If I truly valued the program, I would spend time at meetings and working the steps. If I truly valued a relationship with my Higher Power, I would spend time with Him in prayer and meditation. If I truly valued honesty and the things that recovery had gifted me with, then this is where I would spend my time. What do I really value today?

Meditations for the Heart
The real work of the program is to grow spiritually. It is too easy to grow complacent and lazy about my spiritual life. It takes real commitment to develop good spiritual habits. Each day I have a routine to build my relationship with God. But a strong spiritual life exists far beyond the morning and evening routine. It is about seeking after good in all that I do. It is about becoming willing to be obedient to His will for me. It is about seeking His treasure for me that exists here in this life. Only when I am diligent about this search in all that I do can I hope to find the hidden treasure. And what

is this treasure? Well, the program speaks of the promises of recovery. It talks of things like peace of mind and serenity. It speaks of a new way of living, being no longer baffled by life. Are these things too high a goal? I think not. I have seen these things in my own life, and I have seen these things in the lives of many other recovering people. It takes work, but the goal is worth it. Am I working to grow spiritually?

Petitions to my Higher Power
God,

You know the inner workings of my soul. You know my true desire and what I really value. Help me this day to seek after what You want in my life. Lead me to a place of willingness and teach me to become obedient. Let me this day grow along spiritual lines and learn to value the gift of recovery I have been given.

Amen.

* * * *

Wisdom for Today   Aug 19
Probably one of the biggest changes I have experienced in recovery has been achieving serenity and peace of mind. I do not have this all the time, but more often than not I can go through my day and not live in a state of constant anxiety. When I was actively drinking and using, some of the anxiety I felt was physical. I would wake up in the morning and feel sick. My body felt like a truck had hit it. My body ached; and I was agitated, shaky and nervous. But that was a small part of what was going on inside of me. It was much more the mental anguish.

I lived in a state of fear. I suffered in quiet desperation. I always felt different; and I was lonely and isolated from everyone, even myself. I didn't know myself anymore. I lived with a growing sense of inferiority, guilt and shame. There was no inner peace. I had no serenity. The program and working the steps changed all of that. I am not really sure when I first began to gain the sense of inner calmness; but as my behavior, beliefs and thinking all began to change through my being clean and sober, something changed on the inside. I began to know peace, and I began to know serenity. Am I changing on the inside? Do I know more peace of mind in recovery?

Meditations for the Heart
As an addict and alcoholic I know I need to look for guidance from my Higher Power. But one place more than any other has this been true – my daily interaction with other people. I have learned just how easy it is

for me to get off track with my thinking, my emotions and my self-image if I don't turn to my Higher Power and ask for direction in my interactions with other people. God can and will lead me if I turn to Him. He will care for me in all my relationships with other people. He will keep me from temptation and failure if I follow where He leads. He will protect me in all my interpersonal interactions with others. I am led to places where I can grow in my relationships with others. I am shown how to develop trust and rebuild my interpersonal life with others. I find ways to live properly and treat others as I would want to be treated. My loneliness disappears. Am I finding that my Higher Power teaches me to have healthy relationships?

Petitions to my Higher Power
God,

I am grateful for the sense of inner peace You have given me. The inner serenity I experience, even in the middle of life's storms, is a gift from You. Thank You for showing me the way to get to this place in my life. Help me to continue to grow in my relationships with others. Lead me, teach me and show me what I need to do in this day.
Amen.

* * * *

Wisdom for Today   Aug 20
It took me a while to really understand what this thing called serenity or peace of mind was all about. I kept waiting for someone or something to flip the switch – I would have a spiritual awakening, and then I would have and understand this thing called serenity and peace of mind. But this is not what happened. I had to work at the steps, and I had to learn how to live the program. Slowly and without someone flipping a switch, I began to become comfortable living in my own skin. My anxiety about life decreased. I began to develop relationships with people I met in the program. I began to open myself up to the concept of a Higher Power.

This was not a new concept, as I had been raised in a religious family, which helped. But having contact with God, having a personal relationship with Him was a very new concept. As time went by, I gradually began to understand that inner peace was already happening to me. I found that even when the little things in life that normally would upset me happened, I still was okay. Even when big problems emerged in my life, I had trust that I would make it through these problems okay. This is when I finally knew I had this thing called serenity. Deep down inside I knew that no matter what was happening in my life, eventually things would work out for the best. Being clean and sober allowed me the opportunity to grow in a way that I could find serenity. Am I willing to grow to find inner peace?

Meditations for the Heart

Each of us at one time or another climbs up a ladder. When we do this, if we are wise, we always make sure that the ladder is on good footing. Recovery is much the same. We climb this ladder one step at a time. God is there to hold the ladder steady and to make sure it does not slide out from under us. Think about it, do you really think that God would place this ladder on uneven ground? Do you think He would let go and let the ladder fall with us on it? The answers are obviously no. God cares for us and guides us up each of these steps. He is there to help us each step of the way. Each time God asks us to take the next step, we can be confident that God knows we are ready to move on. All God asks is that we have faith that the ladder is secure and His guidance is sure. Do I know that He will give me all the power and courage I need to climb this ladder?

Petitions to my Higher Power

God,

I begin this new day and am willing to trust Your guidance. Let me take this time to listen to Your voice and know that You will answer. Help me to accept the answers I receive this day and trust that You are with me always. Let me find inner peace in knowing You care for me.
Amen.

* * * *

Wisdom for Today   Aug 21

Did you ever have one of those days that was just good all the way around? Recovery has blessed me with many of these kinds of days. I don't think I can say that about my days when I was active in my addiction. Sure, there were good times, times when I wasn't in trouble; and those days were marked by luck when I was still getting high. Drinking became more and more a part of my life. Using drugs never seemed to slow down. But I really don't think I could ever say that I had a really good day – a day when I was at peace with the world and with myself. Using just seemed to take any real joy out of the day.

One thing that has really helped me to have those good days in recovery has been to learn to sing the song, "Don't bring me down." What I mean is this. There is nothing in this life that is so heavy or that can upset me so much that it gets me down. I have learned to have a deep abiding faith that my Higher Power walks with me in all that I do. He is always there to take care of me. Yes, things still go wrong in my life; and I have problems but nothing that will bring me down to the depths that my addiction once did. I am climbing out of those depths only to reach new heights. It is a part of His plan for my life in recovery. Do I know that I will never go back to the depths as long as I keep my Higher Power by my side?

Meditations for the Heart

There was a time when I walked through the desert of life. The burning sun sapped the life out of me. Then I came to the program and like a big rock in the middle of that desert, it provided shade for me. It was a shelter from that which certainly would have brought me death. It provided shade for me from the searing heat. At first, this safe place was wonderful. Then early in recovery I began to wonder if I could ever leave the safety that this rock represented. I began to think that I was stuck out in the middle of the desert and would never be able to leave the safety of the shade that the program offered. It was purely an act of faith to leave this spot in hopes of finding green valleys which I heard so many talk of in the program. I was surprised to find out that the rock followed me. This is what God does. He lifts the rock and carries it so that we always have a safe place to go to. God is our refuge and our strength. Am I finding the faith to continue my journey in recovery?

Petitions to my Higher Power

God,

I do not know yet what this day will bring, but I am confident in You. I have watched You provide a safe place for me day after day in my journey. It is Your strength that I rely on. This is not something I could do without Your help and guidance. Let me have a strong faith in Your everlasting help. Help me to know that every day in recovery is a good day.

Amen.

* * * *

Wisdom for Today   Aug 22

Every one of us in the program has clay feet. However, we do not all have the same weaknesses. This is why we depend on the group as a whole. We do not want to rely on any one person alone, even our sponsor. While sponsors are individuals who have a good deal of clean time under their belt, they too have clay feet. This is why the fellowship and the group are so important to us. We need other people to bounce ideas off of. We need to be able to talk to others when we are not finding the help we are seeking. The program teaches us "not to put all our eggs in one basket." Sponsors are not perfect, and neither is anyone else in the program.

I feel sorry for those that do not develop a number of relationships in the program. They are choosing to walk on thin ice. What happens if the person they are depending on most relapses? What happens if the person they are depending on most moves away? Each of us needs to find a sponsor that helps us find our way in recovery, but we should all take caution in relying only on this person. There is only one that we can rely on always and that one is our Higher Power. God is always there for us, but we still need others we can talk to and who will give us feedback. Putting someone on a pedestal and relying on just that one person can lead to big trouble for us in our recovery. Have I developed a network of individuals for the ongoing support I need?

Meditations for the Heart

There is a peace that cannot be taken from us. That peace is an inner peace that passes all understanding. It is an inner peace that is a gift from God. No one person has the power to disrupt this inner peace. They can't take it from us. Only we can disrupt this peace by refusing to work the program and falling on our faces. We must guard this peace with a real sense of purpose. We must guard it, as if it is the most valuable possession we have. We must be careful not to let the world's insanity and problems into this inner peace. If we do, it is too easy for us to be distracted by these problems and lose the gift of our inner peace. This does not mean that we ignore problems when they arise; it just means that we must always have a safe place to go when we start to get overwhelmed by the problems around us. This inner peace provides us with solitude to think, to meditate, to ask for help, to receive strength and courage. Yes, we must keep on our guard to value this gift. Do I protect my inner peace and value the gift I have received?

Petitions to my Higher Power

God,

I am so grateful for the gift of inner peace that I have received. Help me to do what is necessary to protect this inner peace by not letting the insanity and problems of life get to me on the inside. Help me this day to expand my network of friends in recovery and in the world. Give me courage to ask for help when I need it. Teach me to rely on this group of friends.

Amen.

* * * *

At almost every meeting I attend, I hear words of wisdom. Sometimes this wisdom comes from an old-timer in the program, and at other times it may come from someone who is brand new to the program. Sometimes I even surprise myself and hear the words coming out of my mouth. These words of wisdom may be a quick one liner, or they may come from someone who speaks for several minutes. I never really know where I will hear these words of wisdom. I just know that it is my job to listen for them.

It may be that I hear an old idea restated in a different way that sheds light on my current issues. It may be that I am hearing something for the first time, or it may simply be that it is the first time that what was said makes sense. Over time I have learned that I need to listen for these words because I never know when I might need them. It may be the same day, or it may be months from now that I will be able to use these words in my own life. One thing I do know is that without these words of wisdom, I still might be stuck at Step One. These words of wisdom have taught me how to live the program. These words of wisdom have helped me time after time deal with difficult situations in my life. These words have helped to save my life. Do I put the words I hear into action?

Meditations for the Heart

Sometimes I still behave in ways that I later regret. I say things to someone else that I wish I hadn't, or I behave in ways I wish never happened. Each of us in recovery has these experiences. What is important about these experiences is that we learn from them. What could I have done differently? What amends might I need to make? What is the real issue underneath my behavior? What character defect emerged in this situation? What was my part in what happened? It has been important for me to ask myself questions like this in my recovery. It has also been important for me to talk with others about situations like this, so that I can gain insight and perspective. Sometimes, in fact frequently, I discover that I simply did not have a good answer to my issue. This is why talking to others has helped me in my recovery. Other times I find new solutions to old problems. Do I remain open to growing in my recovery?

Petitions to my Higher Power

God,

Life is sometimes hard, and I am not sure how to handle it. I screw up and I make mistakes. I am so grateful that You put people in my life to help me sort through these difficulties. Grant me this day an open mind and good ears to listen for words of wisdom that may help me along my journey. Grant me humility to admit my mistakes and learn from them.

Amen.

* * * *

Wisdom for Today   Aug 24

I used to spend a lot of time wondering about the future. I had these images of what it meant to be successful. I dreamed of having a high power job and making lots of money. I dreamed of having a wonderful family. I dreamed of one day sitting on my front porch and drinking a beer and enjoying all the fruits of my labors. Addiction changed all those dreams into nightmares. I couldn't find a decent job. I didn't finish school. My family life became dysfunctional, and all those dreams and hopes melted away.

In recovery I see things differently. I have learned that I do not have to wonder about my tomorrows as long as I take care of today. I can rest assured that tomorrow will take care of itself as long as I am doing what I need to do today. Many of those dreams I had are indeed coming true for me now. I managed to go back to school and finish what I had started. Although my family life has not turned out as I had once imagined, I am thrilled with the family life I do have. I even found a job that I love doing. I no longer wonder about tomorrow. I simply wonder about what my Higher Power has planned for me today; the rest will take care of itself. Am I living life to its fullest today?

Meditations for the Heart

I do love opening presents and finding out what is inside of the beautifully wrapped boxes. Sometimes I find the things I need, and at other times I find a real surprise. I think all of us enjoy this experience. For me recovery has been much the same. It is like opening a whole bunch of wonderful presents. Many of the gifts I receive in recovery are very much the things I really need and others are a pleasant surprise. Sometimes the gifts of recovery are an encouraging word from a friend. Sometimes it is a new insight or maybe being accepted and forgiven. Still other times are a complete surprise. God turns the pages of my life in a whole new direction. I did not always recognize the gifts I received early in recovery, but today I look for these gifts and work to cherish the gifts that I receive, as they are more valuable to me than any earthly possession. Do I recognize and cherish the gifts that recovery brings?

Petitions to my Higher Power

God,

So many good things have happened to me in recovery, and I now know these are all gifts. By all rights, my addiction should have taken all these

254

things from me; but You rescued me from this fate. Help me this day to acknowledge and cherish the gifts of recovery. Teach me to live in today with wisdom, courage and faith.

Amen.

* * * *

Wisdom for Today *Aug 25*

One of my favorite aspects of attending meetings is the incredible diversity of the people who attend. We all come into the program from different walks of life. There can be everything from a homeless street addict to a top CEO from business and industry. You will see doctors, lawyers and Indian chiefs, housewives, blue-collar workers and teenagers, old-timers and people of every color. Addiction to alcohol and drugs shows no partiality. This very diversity of the program is one of its greatest assets. Each of us brings our own unique perspectives on life in recovery. We are able to teach each other by sharing our experience, strength and hopes with one another. What is one person's character defect, shortcoming or weakness may in some instances be someone else's strength.

Each of us in the program has something to offer another. What is my weakness may be your strength. And my strength may be exactly what you are looking for. These strengths and weakness that exist within the program help to balance out the whole. Finding balance is something we all need, and the program helps us to achieve just this. We may all have the same problem, but it is this very diversity within the program that helps us learn how to live life again. It is important for each of us to recognize that we have something to offer. It is just as important for each of us to see that we have something to learn. Do I see that balance and learning to live can be achieved through the members of the program?

Meditations for the Heart

"Stay connected" – these are the words my sponsor gave me over and over again. He wasn't just talking about our relationship, although he expected me to call him everyday in the beginning. He was talking about staying connected to my home group. He was talking about staying connected to the program and the steps. He was talking about staying connected to my Higher Power. At first staying connected meant being glued to my support system. As I got further along in recovery, it meant staying plugged in. This connection to all the support has kept me from going back to relying only on myself, and I know that would be nothing but trouble. I have seen people with years of recovery under their belt get unplugged from their support system only to see them eventually get unplugged from recovery. Because of this I know better. Do I stay connected?

Petitions to my Higher Power
God,

You have created the world as a place of marked diversity, a place in Your own image. This very diversity is what helps me become a better person and teaches me how to live with balance. Balance helps me maintain a true sense of humility. This day help me to stay connected to the support that is always available to me. Teach me not to fear asking for help. Let me also be willing to give help when I am asked.
Amen.

* * * *

Wisdom for Today   Aug 26
When I was active in my addiction, it took every ounce of energy I had just to hold on. It didn't seem to matter how tightly I held on; things continued to slip away. First, it was my relationships with my parents and siblings. Then my relationship with God fell by the wayside. Soon my friends started to disappear, and then my job started to get away from me. In every way possible my life was slipping away, and I knew it was just a matter of time before I lost my life as well. All meaning in life just seemed to fade away. I was living with only limited time left.

The program and the grace of God gave life back to me. Today I understand that this time I have been given is borrowed. I owe the program and my Higher Power for saving my life. My whole attitude about my life has changed since coming into the program. I now understand that the life I hold onto today is a gift. I realize that I need to hold this life in trust for the program and for God. This is why I try to give back in some small measure what I have been given. I feel a sense of responsibility to help others in any way that I can accept the gift that is freely given by God and by the program. Do I hold my life in trust for God and the program?

Meditations for the Heart
Think deeply about the gift of recovery that has been given to you. When I really stop and think about what could have been and where I am at in my life today, I sit in awe. A miracle has happened. Not only do I have life, but also I have found happiness and inner peace. Then when I think about what it means to have this gift and to hold it in trust, it becomes easy to do the things

I need to do in recovery. When I realize what has happened to me in recovery, I become convinced that anything is possible. I only need to practice these principles in all that I do. I believe that more miracles will occur in my life if I hold my life in trust for God. When I do what He wants me to do, good things happen. I simply need to follow His lead and leave the results up to Him. I know everything will be good. Even in my struggles, I have learned that good can come from these trials. Am I making good on the trust I have been given?

Petitions to my Higher Power
God,

This is a day to celebrate the miracle of my life. In humble gratitude I know I have been entrusted to live my life as You would want me to. Let me not forget all that has been done for me by the people in the program and by Your mighty hand. Today I know I can celebrate because of the gift of a new day. Let me use this gift wisely.
Amen.

* * * *

Wisdom for Today   Aug 27
The real question we all must face is, "Can I learn from my experience and grow and help others?" Tough question! – Because in each of us there is the tendency to live in extremes. On the one hand, there is the side of us that plays the role of the rebel. We grow tired of all the structure which recovery demands of us. We resist doing what we know we should. We refuse to follow the lead of our Higher Power. The role of the rebel does not lead to growth. On the other extreme there is the tendency to assume perfection. Perfection simply is not attainable and always leads us to a place where we feel defeated and worthless.

In order to grow in our experiences, we need to find something in the middle of these two extremes. What we find here is something called humility. Here we learn to accept who and what we are. Here is where we learn what we can become. Here is where we can share our experience to help others. It has only been in a place of humble acceptance that I have learned from my experiences. I have learned the impediment to growth that both perfectionism and rebellion cause. The course of relative humility is the only place I really learn anything. The progress is not always quick, but the lessons are essential for my recovery. Have I stopped trying to live in extremes?

Meditations for the Heart
One of the greatest joys I have experienced in recovery is to watch a room full of addicts and alcoholics suddenly burst into laughter. Usually it is

because of a story being shared to which we all can relate. We see the humor in our stupidity. We learn to laugh at the insanity of the illness. It is as if everyone in the room suddenly has had a light of self-acceptance turned on, and we can all laugh about our crazy behavior at the same time. It is not so much the laughter that heals, but the genuine self-acceptance we experience in this moment. When these moments happen, I like to file them away, so that in times of beating myself up or in times when I get too self-reliant I can think back to this genuine self-acceptance. These moments act as a good mirror for me and allow me to look at myself in a true reflection of who I am. Have I found a genuine self-acceptance?

Petitions to my Higher Power
God,

Teach me to walk a humble path this day, for it is on this path that I learn the lessons of recovery. Keep me open to Your vision for my life. Help me find a good mirror so that I can see myself in Your light. Grant me this day what I need for the journey.

Amen.

* * * *

Wisdom for Today   Aug 28

Desire is one aspect of addiction that can really get out of hand. All human beings are born with abundant natural desires. But add alcohol and drugs to these natural desires, and it isn't strange that we often far exceed their intended purpose. We all desire liquid to quiet our thirst. But when our desire is for a "cold one," then we have a tendency to let our desire run wild. When desire drives us blindly or we willfully demand more than what is possible, then we head down a road of self-destruction. For many of us it was not just the alcohol or drugs that we desired. But desire took us looking for money, power, sex and even revenge. Addiction and desire became warped and took us to our bottom.

If we ask, God will certainly forgive our insatiable thirst for satisfaction of our warped desires. But He does not leave us without desires. Even in recovery, desire can be our friend or our foe. If we desire a life - clean and sober, then desire can be our friend. When we desire to follow the path of the steps, then we find happiness. However, if we continue to let desire lead us in an unhealthy direction, then we will reap the consequences this brings. If we desire to run the show our way, it is certain to bring us back to our knees. In recovery we learn that we must desire to do His will if we want to find freedom. Where are my desires taking me?

Meditations for the Heart

One temptation I face is to pray for specific outcomes for others I care about. I admit that the prayers I pray are often well intended, because I seek to have God help someone I care about. But when I ask God to remove their pain, to relieve their struggle, I am also at risk for assuming that I know what God's will for an individual is. These prayers are said as well-intended requests of God. Yet, these very same prayers can get me into trouble. It is all too easy for me to begin to suppose to know the will of God. It is as if I ask these things assuming that this is His will. This type of presumption and conceit can lead me into a very bad place. It took me a while to understand this temptation - to see that I was acting as if I knew what God's plan was. In the program I have learned that I ought to pray for God's will to be done for others as well as for myself. Do I pray with the presumption of my knowing God's will?

Petitions to my Higher Power

God,

Your wisdom is far beyond my understanding. Your plan is beyond my knowledge. Help me this day to trust Your wisdom and Your plan not just for me, but also for others. Teach me not to presume knowledge of Your will and simply to follow where You lead. Free me from unhealthy desires and to long only Your will for me and the power to carry this out.
Amen.

* * * *

Wisdom for Today   Aug 29

One hard lesson we all had to learn is that we will never be the same again. Once we got the program given to us, this gift changed us forever. Some of us have tried to go back out there and found out the hard way that drinking and using drugs just wasn't what we thought it would be. Relapse is a hard lesson; and once we have tried it, we soon find out that the fantasy of normal drinking or social use was just that, a fantasy. We think to ourselves, "They were right after all. I am not able to control it. It controls me."

Relapse frequently ends up with feelings of extreme guilt, shame and loneliness. The consequences are often profound. This is why it is so important for us to get back to the program and stay there. We learn the hard way, but the important thing is that we learn. I finally had to ask myself, "How far do I want to dig this hole I have gotten into?" I had to go back and walk through the doors again and start over. I had to learn what I didn't learn when I first walked through the doors of the program. Today I know that I can't go back.

I don't even want to. The program has given me so much that I do not want to even risk losing it again. I'm glad I will never be the same again. Have I stopped digging the hole deeper?

Meditations for the Heart

I have been in meetings with individuals whose religious training was far superior to mine. I have watched them struggle with the reality that all their convictions and beliefs had not stopped the insanity of addiction. I have watched as these same individuals questioned why their faith had failed and others have succeeded. "Why didn't all my religious training save me from this insanity?" they ask. It is not that their training did not save them; rather it is the best example that faith alone does not work. If we sit on the sideline faithfully waiting for God to fix us, nothing happens. Yet when we attend every practice session and work hard to develop our skills, God sees that we have been faithful in our effort and rewards us by sending us into the game of life. We have to walk the walk, not just talk the talk. We cannot simply hope our way into recovery. For me recovery comes not so much because I have faith; instead it comes because I am faithful in following where I am led. Am I willing to be faithful?

Petitions to my Higher Power

God,

Am I ever grateful that I have learned that I no longer need to keep digging the hole of addiction! More so, I am glad that I have been taught to do the repair work needed to keep my recovery going strong. Today I will be faithful to Your calling and Your direction. Lead me on this path to where You wish me to be.

Amen.

* * * *

Wisdom for Today   Aug 30

When at last we reach the end of our days, how will we look back on our life on this earth? We can be sure that nothing we have gained here in the way of material possessions will we take with us. No earthly possession will be ours to take; it all must be left behind. But what of the Spirit will be ours for the taking? None of us really know the answer, for this is entirely in God's hands. I like to think that the things we may take with us are the things we gave away. If we have given our love and care to another, perhaps we take this love with us. If we have given of our time to help another in need, perhaps we take this spirit of generosity with us. No one knows for sure. But one thing is for sure. When we reach the end of our time here on earth, we can look back and be pleased; or we can look back and be empty.

This question is what is important for each of us. Am I doing that on which I can look back and be proud? Am I treating my fellow man as I would want him to treat me? Am I generous with my time for those that need it? Am I creating the kind of human relationships that are lasting and truthful? Each of these questions can only be answered one day at a time; but I know that if I work the steps and practice the principles of the program in all that I do, one day I will look back and will feel good about what has been accomplished in my life. So I seek to fill my heart with spiritual things and walk the path that is laid before me. Am I seeking what's good in all that I do?

Meditations for the Heart

Can I call upon the name of God to help me in all that I do? The answer to this question is most certainly, "Yes!" Yet it is such an easy thing to forget. God's Spirit is among us at all times, and He stands ready to help us. All we need do is ask. His Spirit is here to help make us better people. His Spirit is here to guide us on our journey. His Spirit is here to help us when we need it – not just when we need it most, but in all that we do. Sometimes I seem to forget this and hurry into my day without asking for help. I get headstrong, or I get distracted, and I just do not ask for that which I need. I can really tell the difference in my day when I don't ask for help in what I do. I get more easily frustrated. I get off track. I accomplish less. Sometimes I miss the boat completely. The good news is that I can always start again. I can stop and ask for help anytime and know that it will come. Do I ask for help often enough?

Petitions to my Higher Power

God,

Let me begin this day by turning to You and asking for Your help in all that I do. Give me courage and wisdom to continue to ask for Your help throughout my day. Let me take steps today that add to my spiritual life. Let me seek to help others and to treat all those that I come into contact with as I would want to be treated. Let me seize every opportunity to do good for others in this day.

Amen.

$$* \quad * \quad * \quad *$$

Wisdom for Today   Aug 31

Addiction is not a great teacher. Day after day it reveals more pain and suffering. Still, in spite of the lessons we are given, we have difficulty letting go of this way of life. We see the physical, emotional and social pain. We experience the spiritual emptiness, and yet we hang on. We continue to hope the next time will be different. We think we will somehow regain the ability to control our use. Most of us continue on this path until we finally experience a crisis that gives us a brief wake up call. We are given an opportunity to break out of the insanity.

Fortunately the Twelve Step program is a good teacher. Not only does it teach us how to stop drinking and drugging, but it also teaches us a new way of living. Through the process of going to meetings, working the steps and living the principles, we are transformed. The program teaches us the wisdom of keeping things simple. It teaches us the way to find freedom and happiness. It opens our eyes to the insanity of our ways and enlightens us with hope. We learn to fear that first drink, pill or fix. Do I have any doubt about the power of addiction?

Meditations for the Heart

Walk humbly in the presence of God. This has become a statement that guides the way I try to live. At first my understanding of turning it over was very naive. I simply didn't drink or use drugs, went to meetings and worked the steps. But over time I have grown in my understanding of this principle. Today I work to recognize that I walk through this life in the presence of God. He is always around. There is no place that I can hide from Him. Certainly the bottle and the drugs did not hide me from His presence. I was simply too wasted to know that He was near, but this did not mean that He was not watching out for me. As I approach any situation in my life, I try to remember His presence. I attempt to live life in a way that He would want me to live. His presence has become a guiding principle for me. Do I know that God walks with me?

Petitions to my Higher Power

God,

Today I understand what a friend You have been in my life. Keep me focused on Your presence in my life, and help me to make decisions about my life based on this knowledge. Give me courage for this day; and grant me patience, understanding and wisdom in all that I do. Let me live this day knowing You are always near.

Amen.

* * * *

In admitting our addiction, we acknowledge that we are powerless over alcohol and drugs. Yet in making this admission, we are also saying that we recognize that as long as alcohol and drugs are in our life, we will remain unmanageable and out of control. In Step Two we gain a sense of hope that we can be restored to sanity in our lives. By placing our lives in God's hands and becoming obedient to His will, we surrender our disease, our lives and our will. It is here that we learn that we have a choice not to let addiction have power in our lives. This freedom is to be desired more than alcohol and drugs.

We can never fully understand our addiction, its causes or be rid of our secret faults. Yet the steps warn us this is the only way we can find freedom from the bondage of addiction. We are also told that if we are willing to take these steps, we will know great reward. Yes, recovery promises great rewards if we are willing to go to any length to gain what the program offers. If we work the steps, addiction loses its power and dominion over us. We learn to live right, and we find the freedom to walk through life without the insanity of the disease. Have I made the choice not to let addiction have power in my life today?

Meditations for the Heart

As a child I recall playing a game of tag where, if I was about to be tagged, I could yell out, "Force Field" and know that I was safe. This force field was imaginary, but it prevented the person who was "It" from tagging me. In recovery we have a force field that is real. God can and will shield us from harm's way. None of life's daggers can cut into our lives and truly harm us when we let God become our force field. This does not mean that life will be problem free. It does mean that any problem, any scorn from others or any shame can be kept outside of this force field if we put our trust in our Higher Power. This trust acts as a shield we can attain. It will build an inner peace that will allow us to deal effectively with life's problems. We learn that resentment has no place in our lives. We find a healthy path to walk on. Do I allow God to be a force in my life?

Petitions to my Higher Power

God,

You have given me the choice not to let addiction have power in my life today. You have shown me a healthy path to walk on. Today I will put my trust in You. I will walk the path set before me with confidence of inner peace. Let me draw on Your strength as I live this day. Guide me to the knowledge of freedom. Let me not become out of sorts with events that happen around me.

Amen.

* * * *

Wisdom for Today   *Sep 2*

Sometimes the unexpected happens, things that we just don't count on. Life can take sudden turns, and it is easy to let these sudden changes knock us off track. Change is a part of life. Sometimes these changes occur slowly, and it is easy to adjust; other times it is as if life has thrown us a real curve ball. When things start to get out of whack because of sudden changes in life, I need something I can fall back on. This is why ongoing involvement in the program has become so important to me. The fellowship provides me with two things that I need in these times of sudden change and unpredictability. First, there is consistency. If I have a sponsor, a home group, the program, the steps and a relationship with a Higher Power, these things do not change even when change is happening all around me. The second thing I am provided is accountability. My recovery support system helps me stay on track even when everything else in my life seems to have derailed.

To be sure, I have yet to encounter anything that has completely overwhelmed me when I was connected to the program in this way. But when I got away from this consistency and accountability and tried to handle things on my own, I ended up in real trouble. None of us would stand inside a burning building without the tools to put the fire out. In the same way, a solid recovery support system can help to put the flames of change out. Do I use my support system to prevent fires in my life?

Meditations for my Heart

Change is difficult because of the unpredictability that comes with it. This unpredictability can bring up feelings of anxiety and fear. In some cases change can bring feelings of anger. Not all change is bad. In fact, many of the changes we experience end up being for the better. Still the process of change can be uncomfortable, even when the outcome is good. Change also brings us to a point where we often have to simply have faith that God will see us through. Faith is important that He will be there for us when we need Him. Faith that we will be given the strength, courage and wisdom that we need to deal with change is needed. Faith is essential that these things will indeed be provided for us if we ask. Do I have faith that He walks with me always?

Petitions to my Higher Power

God,

Life is not always easy and sometimes seems unfair. It can be difficult. Increase in me the faith I need to have in these times of change. Give me patience and inner peace that I may walk through times of change knowing

that You are by my side. Let me also be willing to provide consistency and accountability to my fellow addicts and alcoholics when they need it. Let me give freely what has been given to me.
Amen.

∗   ∗   ∗   ∗

Wisdom for Today   *Sep 3*

There are two days each week that we should not worry about. Two days that we don't need to fear! Two days that we don't have any control over! One of these days is yesterday. Yesterday is already gone. Everything that happened yesterday cannot be undone. It is beyond our control. The mistakes that we made yesterday, any cares that we had, any aches and pains are already over. There is not anything that we can do to go back and change them. Money cannot buy back our yesterday. Prayers cannot undo what has already happened. We cannot take back the words that we said yesterday. We cannot undo a single activity that we have already completed. Yesterday is gone.

The other day that we should not worry about is tomorrow. Tomorrow brings with it all of its possible adversities, all of its promises and all of its potential burdens. Tomorrow is also beyond our immediate control. We do not know what tomorrow may bring, but we can be certain that tomorrow the sun will rise and set just like any other day. We will not know until tomorrow whether or not we had mistakes in the day to come at all. It does us no good to worry about yesterday or tomorrow. We only have today. We have all of the choices that lay only before us this day. We can only try today to do what is right. Have I stopped worrying about yesterday and tomorrow?

Meditations for the Heart

As for today, worry does us no good either. God has promised that He will only give us what we can handle for this day. He has promised us that He will give us the strength that we need. He will give us courage to fight fears. He will provide inner peace to keep us centered in our day. He does not say that we will never experience temptation; He only has promised us that He will give us the strength, courage and wisdom to deal with temptation. We only need to put our faith and our trust in Him. With these helps we can face anything that happens today. With His help we can make good choices. Today we live life on life's terms. Today we look to make progress in our recovery and in our lives. Am I making good choices for today?

Petitions to my Higher Power
God,

I pray that I may face every situation that I face in this day with courage and wisdom. I pray that I may let go of yesterday and not fear tomorrow and live in this day with Your guidance and help. Show me the path that I am to take today. Guide each step that I take. Let me place my faith and my trust only in You.

Amen.

* * * *

Wisdom for Today   Sep 4
Alcoholics Anonymous is not a new program with new ideas. The founders of the program tell us that all the ideas of the program are borrowed. These ideas were borrowed from medicine, psychiatry and religion. The people that started the program took the ideas that seemed best. This is the same advice that you hear in meetings today. "Take what works, and leave the rest." It is this very principle that makes the program so adaptable for so many people. In the program we are able to find the things that work for us.

The results speak for themselves. Using the Twelve Steps has helped thousands and thousands of alcoholics and addicts. In the program we find the things that help us to become better people. We do not go to the program to try and make it better. Instead we use the things that we find there that will work for us. This program has everything that we need. In it we find the tools that we're looking for to help us stay clean and sober. What works for each of us is different. For some of us it is finding out that we suffer from the disease of addiction. For others of us it is finding out how our thinking and emotions are all mixed up. For others it is the spiritual aspects of the program that are most important. For some of us we need all of these aspects. Regardless of what we need, we can find it in the program. It is this very taking of what works and leaving the rest that makes this program so powerful for each of us. Do I try and follow the program just as it is?

Meditations for the Heart
It is important for each of us to find meaning and purpose in our life. In the program we are taught to strive for union between our purpose and the purpose of a Higher Power. In finding union between our purpose and purpose of our Higher Power, we find the direction that we all seek. We can find no bond here on this earth as strong as the bond that exists between a human soul and that of God. It is this union that makes recovery possible.

266

When we take our will and our thinking and align them with that of God, we find the happiness that we seek. When our purpose is one with God, we're able to accomplish the task of staying clean and sober. But more than this, we find that we're able to live life fully. We find that we're able to experience the promises of the program. We find freedom from addiction, not a cure, but freedom. Is my purpose one with God's?

Petitions to my Higher Power
God,

As I sit in meetings and talk with other recovering people, I am given pearls of wisdom, clear direction and hope. I am able to find purpose in my life. I am also able to find Your purpose for my life. Help me this day to align my purpose with Yours. Give me strength to accomplish Your purpose in my life. Help me to continue to find the things that I need in the program. Help me to find a new way of living.
Amen.

* * * *

Wisdom for Today   Sep 5
We in the program have discovered a common solution. We do not need to go looking for something unique and different. The common solution is what works for us all. This is not to say that we do not have unique needs. Some of us indeed need medical help, and others do not. Some of us need psychological help, and others of us do not. Some are spiritually bankrupt, and others still have an inner faith. All of us need the common solution found in working the steps.

It is through working these steps that we find the freedom we are looking for. We find the freedom from self-will run riot. We find the freedom from the insanity of addiction. We find a new hope and a new way of living. We find a spiritual connectedness to our Higher Power. This common solution is what works. We do not need to improve on this common solution. It has already been shown to work. If it works, don't fix it. Am I willing to accept this common solution?

Meditations for the Heart
"Praying only for knowledge of His will for us and the power to carry that out." (*Alcoholics Anonymous,* Fourth Edition. Page 59) In seeking out knowledge of His will, I have found no simple answer. Sometimes it is easy. It is simply a matter of what is right and wrong. At other times it has been much more difficult to discern His will. Here I must prayerfully seek and keep on seeking

until I know in my heart that I am heading in the right direction. Sometimes I can only proceed on faith that I will be shown as I move forward. One thing that has helped me is to think about what the addict and alcoholic in me would do, and then do the exact opposite. Sometimes I find knowledge of His will for me only through effort, and at other times I find it only in rest. Meditation and prayer are the only answer we are given in the steps. For each one of us this is different, but it comes to us in a common solution. Do I seek His will every day?

Petitions to my Higher Power
God,

Today I turn to You for guidance and for strength. Help me to follow willingly the path You lay before me. Let me seek Your way and not my own. Let me humbly walk with You this day.
Amen.

* * * *

Wisdom for Today   Sep 6
The most important job we have in recovery is to remain completely abstinent from all mood-altering chemicals. Without abstinence all of our hard work is for nothing. Once we go back to drinking or using, a terrible cycle is set in motion. The truth is that for those of us who have relapsed, we really have no idea why we did it. We may come up with reasons or excuses, but the truth is that when we look deep into our heart, we really have no idea what took us back to drinking and using. Those reasons or excuses may satisfy us for brief period of time, but in the long run why we went back to the insanity makes no sense of all.

At some point in time we all crossed the line. We no longer are normal drinkers or normal users. We have to come to grips with the fact that we have no power to stop our desire. We have no control. When it comes right down to it, we're powerless. We drink or drug simply because we're addicted. Abstinence is our first goal, but it is not the only one. We soon find out that we have to change our way of living. We discover that we need to change and need to learn to live life differently. We find out that if we want to be happy, we can never go back. There is no problem that we have that drinking or using drugs won't make worse. Am I convinced that I have crossed the line?

Meditations for the Heart
When you stop to think about the beauty that was brought out of the chaos of the beginning to this world and the Power that made all this happen,

268

it is truly amazing. It is this Power that can bring beauty out of the chaos of our addiction. It is this Power that tells the rose when it is time to bloom. It is the same Power that tells us when it is time to grow and blossom in our recovery. It is this Power that paints the palettes of our seasons. This same Power paints the palettes of our lives. Out of the darkest winters of addiction, He leads us into the light of the new spring. Out of the darkness of our lives, He brings new order and inner peace. This is the gift that is given to us all through His grace. We do nothing to deserve this grace, yet it is given to us freely. Sometimes I ask myself what I should do with this wonderful gift. The only answer for this question is to do what my Higher Power wants me to do with this gift. I need to cherish this gift called recovery and value it more than any other gift I have. Do I value this gift called recovery?

Petitions to my Higher Power
God,

Today I ask that You help me out of any chaos that remains in my life. Help me to find the gift of inner peace. Teach me to grow in the ways that only You know. Help me to grow a wonderful garden in my life. Teach me to share the flowers that bloom in my garden with others. Let me walk through this day being fully convinced that I have crossed the line and can never go back.

Amen.

$$* \quad * \quad * \quad *$$

Wisdom for Today   Sep 7
A recovery program must be built, and to build a program that works we all need tools. Most of the tools we need to construct our recovery we do not own when we first walk through the doors of the program. These tools must be borrowed from others, and we need others to show us how to use them. But using these tools revolutionizes our whole way of living. Our spiritual attitude towards life changes in remarkable ways. No longer do we attempt to hide, but learn to open up to others. We no longer run, but we learn to face reality and take responsibility for our lives. We no longer scheme and manipulate, but we learn to stand in truth. We realize that we are not the center of the universe; instead we humbly accept our place in the universe.

We find that we are not capable of operating every tool we need in order to construct a solid recovery program. Instead we learn that we must rely on a Higher Power to help us in the things we cannot do for ourselves. Soon we discover that this Power dwells within us, and that He is doing for us what we could not do for ourselves. One day after months or even years of using these tools, our construction project is finished; and we can call our program home. But even when our construction is complete, we find that there is ongoing maintenance needed. We must care for our new home. Am I letting God help me with the construction and maintenance of this new home?

Meditations for the Heart

The very moment that we see that something is wrong or in need of repair, our obligation to fix the problem begins. If we notice a small leak in the plumbing or a drain not working properly and we ignore this problem, bigger problems can emerge. If a plug is not working properly, it is a signal that something is wrong. Ongoing maintenance of our recovery program is essential. We have been given this home called recovery, and we have an obligation to care for it. If we do not, over time the home becomes dilapidated. It can even become unlivable, if we let things go completely. Our responsibility is to take care of the gift we have received. We must value this new home. If indeed we do value it and care for it, we will be protected from the storms that life may bring. We will rest secure in the knowledge that our new home will bring us years and years of happiness. Do I take care of problems and needed repair work right away?

Petitions to my Higher Power

God,

Help me this day to be a fellow worker with You in the construction of this new home called recovery. Let me stay alert for problems and needed repair work that may need to be done. Let me not postpone needed work and initiate action as soon as I am aware that work is needed. Teach me to use the tools necessary to do the job right, and let me rely on You to do the work that I cannot do on my own.

Amen.

* * * *

Wisdom for Today   Sep 8

With addiction there are but two choices. The first is to go on to addiction's bitter end. To do this we must blot out all of the painful memories and reality of our current existence. We also dare not look at the future. If we choose the path of staying with our addiction, we cannot live in the past; we cannot live in today and we cannot live in tomorrow. We can only live in the world filled with self-delusion. With addiction we must continue to try to live in the lie.

The existence of living in addiction is intolerable unless we continue to stay completely numb to our own existence.

The other choice is to accept spiritual help. This perhaps is one of the hardest things for an alcoholic or an addict to do. We have lived a life of self-will run riot. In recovery we must learn that we can no longer rely on our will and learn to follow a Divine will. We need to become willing to maintain a simple attitude toward life. A Higher Power exists and is here to help us. This is a simple principle; yet is often easier said than done. It is so easy for us to go back to our old ways. We struggle with continually going back to running the show our way. It is not until we were ready to let go absolutely and turn our will and our life over to the care of God, as we understand Him, that we truly began to make progress. We must learn that our way doesn't work, and surrendering to His will is the only thing that does. It is in this surrender that we find freedom. Am I making the right choice today?

Meditations for the Heart

Each day we need look in the mirror and examine ourselves. This needs to become a daily ritual for us all. We must examine our character. We must look at our behavior, our thinking and our intentions. We must look at all of these things in relationship to our daily lives, to those we love and in relationship to our Higher Power. This daily examination of ourselves should lead us to recognition of our shortcomings, as well as help us to identify where we have been wrong. Part of our task each day will need to be cleaning up our side of the street. We need to admit our wrongs and then seek to right them. We must examine our lives and make decisions about where we need to grow. Most importantly, we need to determine if we are indeed following God's will. We must seek to understand the ways in which He wants us to change. We must ask for His help and guidance in making these changes. Recovery is a process of always growing. Am I willing to look in the mirror each day?

Petitions to my Higher Power

God,

Help me this day to examine my life. Help me this day to seize every opportunity for growth. Give me the courage and strength to make progress toward a better life. Help me never to be satisfied with who I am; instead help me to seek who it is You want me to be. Let me live my life today as you would want me to live.

Amen.

* * * *

None of us likes to think we are different. We all want to believe that we are just like everyone else. We fight desperately to hang on to our belief that we can drink or use just like everyone else. But the truth is that we are different. We are different because we react to alcohol and drugs differently than others do. Our bodies, our brain chemistry and our mental responses are different. This is what happens with addiction. As long as we hang on to our delusion that we are the same as others, we continue to try and prove it not only to them but also to ourselves. This delusion is characterized by countless vain attempts to show we are like others. We continue to fall face first into failure. This delusion leads us down a road of self-destruction. It also destroys those things we value most – our families, our self-worth, our hope for the future and all meaning in life.

This delusion must be smashed and destroyed. It has been shown over and over again that an alcoholic or addict cannot ever regain control. We cannot even be cured. We can only arrest the disease and learn how to live normally once again in recovery. Addiction is predictable. It will wait. It is patient. Should we fall back into the delusion of relapse, we can only expect things to get worse, never better. We can never return to being normal drinkers or drug users. However, we can return to being normal in our life. I never thought I would say that I wanted to be normal, but I am glad that I have been given the chance in recovery. Today I will value the normal things of life. Have I given up my delusion of being a normal drinker or user?

Meditations for the Heart

I was grateful to get the chance at a normal life again, but to my surprise what I have is a chance at a truly abundant life. Recovery has bought me so much, and it can bring me even more if I continue on the right path. Life in recovery can be spiritually, mentally, physically and emotionally rewarding. Life can be filled with joy. Life can be exciting. All we need to do is accept the gift of abundance in our lives from God. It is free for all who wish to claim it. This was hard for me at first, because I somehow felt that I did not deserve it. The truth is that I don't deserve it, but in His gracious love God grants wonderful things to those who will simply stretch out their hands and accept the gifts He has to offer. These gifts do not always come in the way that we would expect. Often times they come in very simple packages and are simple gifts, but their value is priceless. Some turn their heads and shun the gifts that are offered. Do not let this be true of you. Am I willing to accept these simple gifts?

Petitions to my Higher Power

God,

Do not let me turn my head or shun the gifts that You so freely offer to me in recovery. Grant that I may value these gifts and use them wisely. Let me always value what You have to offer me. Keep me from falling back into the delusion of my being in control. Help me always to trust in Your guidance. Amen.

*   *   *   *

Wisdom for Today   Sep 10

Fantasies, doubts and reservations are something I can ill afford with regard to my disease. I cannot afford to have any lurking notion that someday I will be able to go back and safely drink or use. I have no hidden immunity to this disease. Learning more about it will not prepare me to go back. Staying sober and drying out for a period of time does not make me immune. Attending lots of meetings or reading all the program literature cannot prepare me to drink or use successfully. There is no cure. No magic pill will make it go away. I can have no reservations about this. I must know and accept the fact that once an addict, I will always be addicted.

Many of us, if we search, find that we carry still an insane excuse that would make it okay to go back to drinking or drugging. These excuses, no matter how trivial they seem, can lead us back down the path of destruction. We must rid ourselves of all excuses to pick up the bottle or the drugs. Within a short period of time we are back as bad as we were, if not worse. There is no room in our minds or our hearts for these excuses. A man does not walk into a shed full of dynamite with a lit match and a blowtorch because it is not windy inside. We cannot risk any excuse. Do I still have any reservations about the reality that I can never go back?

Meditations for the Heart

None of us can fight this disease alone. In the Twelve Steps, the very first word in Step One is "We." God says that where two or more of us gather, He will be there with us. When we gather at meetings or with our sponsor, or even on the phone and we seek to do His will, God will be with us. He will reveal His plans for us. He will give us guidance. This is the place where the miracles of recovery occur. In union with one another we find strength, wisdom and courage. In fellowship with each other we find answers, truth and joy. It is in union with each other that we can be one. "WE" become one unified group, with one purpose and of one mind with God. This is the power of common purpose and group unity. This is what we all should strive for. For it is in doing this that all our excuses are destroyed. All our fantasies and illusions of returning to our old ways are eliminated. Honesty is born in our heart. Am I trying to fight alone?

Petitions to my Higher Power
God,

Shed light on any excuse I may still carry, and give me wisdom and courage to destroy my excuses before they may come back to destroy me. Let me risk unity with my fellow man in the program so that I may find truth and power. Let me experience the miracles of recovery that the program offers. Help me this day to walk in Your light. Take not Your Spirit from me, but fill me with all that is good.
Amen.

* * * *

Wisdom for Today   Sep 11
Without question addiction is a very strange disease. One would think that we could stop the insanity on our own, but we cannot. Willpower has proven ineffective. No matter how strong our determination, there is nothing we can do about our desire to drink or use drugs simply by putting our mind to it. Self-knowledge will do us no good either. Even if it were possible to figure out why we do what we do, we still are not able to stop the insanity of the disease. All the knowledge and all the desire have proven to fall short time after time. It is as if there is some strange mental blank spot that keeps us from knowing what to do. It is as if there is some inner flaw that we cannot detect that keeps us trapped.

Yet through simple steps we are set free. We cannot hang on to that last flicker of conviction that somehow, someway we will get it right. We must let go of such things as determination, conviction, knowledge or desire being a way out. We must grab onto spiritual principles and recognize that this and this alone can solve our problem. We are completely helpless apart from Divine help. We cannot ask for a cure, as one does not exist. We can only ask for a strong defense. This comes to us from a Power Greater than ourselves. Here and here alone can we find hope, strength, courage and wisdom. Our faith in these spiritual forces is our defense. We must put into action the steps necessary to find freedom. Have I accepted the spiritual answer of action through the steps?

274

Meditations for the Heart

This program of recovery is a program of action. Yet all the action we must take requires energy and will fatigue us if we do not also rest and recharge. Each of us needs to find ways to rest along the way in our journey. It is only when we rest that healthy and willing work can follow. It is only when we are recharged that our energy for this work is renewed. So where do we find this rest? Where do we go to be recharged? God says, "Come to Me and I will give you rest." So this is where I turn when I grow tired in the journey. In prayer we can turn to our Higher Power and seek rest. In allowing others to help us along the way, we become recharged. We give our energy to the work of recovery, and we rest. We receive energy from God and others when we ask for help. God's Spirit is always available to us to strengthen a tired mind or body. We can rest in His arms, and we can find strength. We gain energy for the new day in communion with others. This is why we go to these meetings. Have I found it safe to rest in His arms? Am I recharged for the journey by attending meetings and talking with others?

Petitions to my Higher Power

God,

I pray that this energy I receive will make me effective in the work You want me to do. Grant me strength for the journey before me today. Let me use the spiritual tools I am given. Grant me needed rest as I walk this path and encourage me to move back into action when I need to. Let me be free of self-will and seek only to follow Your direction for me this day.

Amen.

* * * *

Wisdom for Today   Sep 12

When you look at the reality of our position in life, we really are not in a bad place at all. I watch people struggle all the time with problems that come up in life. They are the same kinds of problems that we have to deal with, but they do not have a program to help them deal with these problems. We, on the other hand, have steps and a fellowship of people to fall back on. I can be dealing with the exact same kinds of problems as others who are not in recovery, and my perspective on these problems can be very different. They may become overwhelmed by the problems, and I know that I can only deal with life one day at a time. This gives me a very different perspective on life.

I know I can only accomplish so much in any given day. Each day I can do my best with the tasks before me; and I know that if I do this, my problems will eventually be taken care of. Even some of the problems that I have had to face that seemed huge at the time got smaller and smaller as time went on. I have learned also to rely on my friends in the program to help me gain proper perspective on life and the problems that come with it. When I get wrapped up in the emotions of my day, I can count on my friends in the program to help me sort things out. I have learned how to use the steps and the principles of the program. The slogans, the prayers, the words of wisdom I hear are all available to me and help me each day. I have learned to be grateful for life, even the problems, as each experience I face clean and sober teaches me a lesson. Am I practicing the principles in all my affairs?

Meditations for the Heart

In recovery we learn how to deal with life on life's terms. We learn that we do not need to live any longer in the extremes. We find that we do not need to face any situation alone. Life continues onward. There is nothing we can do to stop life from occurring, but we find that we can change how we react to life. We can seek solitude with our Higher Power and seek His wisdom and strength to walk through our days. We learn about, "Easy does it." We do not need to work harder at life, just smarter. The advantages that this brings us are indeed phenomenal. It simply works. I do not know if I ever will be able to fully understand what has happened to me because of the program, but I do not have to. I just need to keep doing the next right thing. I know that the answers I need will be there for me when I need them. I know that God will be there for me always. I can always count on the program and the fellowship to help me; all I need do is ask. Do I trust what works?

Petitions to my Higher Power

God,

Help me this day to keep a good perspective on life. Help me to use the tools I have been given. Let me seek out help whenever I need it. Let me seek wise counsel from those in recovery that can help me. Let me seek You out in prayer as I walk through life and use Your strength and guidance in all that I do.

Amen.

* * * *

Wisdom for Today   Sep 13

For the atheist or agnostic, the program can be a hard pill to swallow. All the talk of God, a Power Greater and spirituality can make involvement with a Twelve Step program very difficult. But the reality is that all addicts and alcoholics must find a Power outside of ourselves if we want to recover. Our own power does not work. We have tried and tried our way, and it does not work. We lack the power needed to overcome our compulsion to drink and use. To continue on a path of self-reliance means certain disaster. This dilemma of choosing between self-reliance and a Power Greater is difficult but not impossible.

The simple fact is this: All of us have already turned our will and our life over to a power outside of our self. We all have turned our lives over to alcohol or drugs. Each of us has had the experience of doing things against our own wishes when we were drinking or using drugs. For some of us we have turned our life over to a Judge and jury. Some of us have turned our lives over to a hospital or institution. These powers did not stop us from drinking or using. They may have been a temporary fix, but soon we were right back at it. We must find the Power Greater that works. It is a tough choice for many, but it is a choice that leads us out of the insanity of addiction. This choice gives us a Power by which we can live. Have I found a Power Greater, by which I can live my life in recovery?

Meditations for the Heart

God's grace is like sunshine for the soul. We all have walked through the storms of addiction. We searched for shelter from the ravages of this storm and found none. It was not until we found this grace that the sun shone in our lives again. Now we learn to walk in this new light, a light that was hidden from us behind the storm clouds. Although it was hidden, it was there all the time. We simply ask that this light be revealed to us. Only this Power outside of us can reveal this new light to us. It is not something that we can do for ourselves. It is only when we allow ourselves to be enveloped in this Divine sunshine that we can see beyond the darkness of addiction. Faith is the breathing in of this sunshine and holding it deep within. This sunshine does wonders for the soul. It brings healing to our brokenness. It shines brightly on the path that we must take in order to stay clean and sober. Have I found this sunshine in my life?

Petitions to my Higher Power

God,

None of us can truly come to You on our own. All I can do is ask that Your grace shine brightly in my life. I am ever grateful that You have given me new light in my life. Help those that struggle with finding You in the darkness that they may walk in this sunshine also. Let me begin my day in this new sunrise and walk the path that You have chosen for me.

Amen.

* * * *

There is wide variation in the way that we approach this concept of a spiritual life. Each one of us has our own concept of a Higher Power and how He works for us in recovery. We do not need to agree with what everyone else's concepts are. We only need to formulate our own understanding. This is not to say that we cannot learn from others what works for them and incorporate this into what works for us. Whether or not we agree with others' concepts is of little importance for us as individuals. What does matter is that we put aside any prejudice or judgment and simply open ourselves to growing along spiritual lines. To be sure, there are questions that each of us need to answer in our spiritual search. It is doubtful that we will suddenly see a bright light and have all the answers we need. Growth is a process that occurs over time.

One thing is for sure: Those of us who have opened the door to the concept of a Power Greater have seen miraculous things happen. We find that we are able to do things that before used to baffle us. We see things happen in our life in recovery that we cannot fully explain. To say that these things are mere coincidence falls way short of the mark. We experience a miraculous change in our thinking and our way of living, and it works. If this were mere coincidence, why then does it happen for all addicts and alcoholics who completely give themselves to this simple program? Am I seeing miraculous changes in my life?

Meditations for the Heart

Rumination can be the ruin of the soul. When we spend time dwelling on every mistake, every fault and every failure of the past, it is far too easy then to proceed into shame, guilt, remorse and contempt for self. These things indeed can be very destructive for our soul, and they also can be huge reasons to relapse. We need to make conscious decisions not to dwell on these issues. This does not mean ignore them, but it does mean that we must use the steps to bring healing to our past. We can learn to rely on our Higher Power's help to rebuild our damaged self-esteem and lost self-respect. We need to open our minds and our hearts to His care for our brokenness. He can and will bring power, love and healing to our soul. We simply need to open ourselves to this Divine Presence in our lives. In recovery we learn to respect ourselves again; and in doing so, we gain the respect of others as well. We cannot worry about the places where we fall down. We simply must arise again, brush the dirt off and continue our journey. Am I keeping my eye on the goal?

278

God,

Life is good when I stay focused on Your will for me today. Do not let me dwell in the past and give me courage to get back up again when I fall. Stay with me throughout this day, and keep me conscious of the goal.
Amen.

* * * *

Wisdom for Today   *Sep 15*

Life has emergencies that come up. For those of us in recovery, we need to be especially cautious during these times. First of all, the program teaches us that we are responsible for our recovery. What this means is that we should be prepared for these difficult times. What will I do should an emergency occur? To whom will I turn? Where do I go for safety in these difficult times? All these questions and more need to be thought through and decisions made regarding our action plans should an emergency occur. If we wait until we are in a crisis and have no plans in place, we put ourselves at risk. If we are prepared and know what to do, we will find we are able to get through life's difficult times.

Just as important is to stay focused after the crisis has passed. It is in this time that we are more likely to let our guard down and falter in our responsible self-care. We handle the crisis and breathe a sigh of relief. Then our addicted mind takes over and tells us to reward ourselves for a job well done. These tests in recovery are not always easy. We can become frustrated, confused and even frightened. It is easy to get wrapped up in the crisis or emergency and forget to take care of ourselves. Here especially we must hold on to the gift of our recovery and turn it over to the care of our Higher Power. He has promised that no matter how big the crisis He will stand by us. Do I have good plans in place should everything suddenly get thrown out of whack?

Meditations for the Heart

My sponsor used to look at me and say, "This too shall pass." He wanted me to know and trust that no crisis or emergency lasts forever. This was important information for me to have. However, it was his next line that always stuck with me. "It is what you do with it that will determine whether or not it gets complicated." He talked to me at length about how my thinking, emotional responses and behavior would significantly impact how I made it through these tough times. He would go on to say, "It can pass like a breeze in the night or it can pass like a kidney stone. This in large part depends on you and what you do." He taught me how important it was to be in regular prayer with my Higher Power in these struggles. "Listen for His wisdom," he would say. "Use the tools and stay close to the program." Use the slogans, the steps, whatever you need to get through the tough times; and you will be made stronger because of it. I am grateful for these words. Do I have good advice and suggestions to which I listen?

Petitions to my Higher Power
God,

Sometimes life takes strange turns. Some of these seem unfair and others seem to overwhelm me. I am grateful to know that no matter what the emergencies in my life might be, You are always there for me to call on. Help me to make plans for these rough times in my life so that I am not caught off guard. Walk with me this day, and let me walk with You.
Amen.

* * * *

Wisdom for Today   Sep 16
It took a while but I finally got used to the fact that I no longer live in crisis. For quite a while, I found recovery and working a program boring. I had become so used to living in crisis that I found living a normal life boring. Addiction to alcohol and drugs always had a way of creating a crisis in my life. If it wasn't one thing, it was another. Even in early recovery I seemed to need to create a crisis in my life. It was as if I craved the uncertainty and excitement. Over time I began to realize that recovery meant a whole lot more than simply stopping drinking and using drugs. It was about changing lifestyle.

I began to recognize how my character defects continued to get me into trouble. I began to see how I continued to stir the pot and walk on the edge. As I settled into recovery and really began to work the steps, I began to experience less and less turmoil in my life. Things quieted down, and I began to experience less chaos in my life. I grew restless and bored. This was a dangerous time for me because I struggled with life going well. There was something about my personality that seemed to need to be in crisis. Yet in spite of myself and only through the grace of God did I adjust and begin to enjoy life. The predictability and security of recovery and the program became a stable force in my life. Today I can walk through my day and not need to disrupt my Higher Power's plans for me. Do I still need to create crises in my life?

Meditations for the Heart
We tried to carry the message to those who still suffered, and we practiced these principles in all our affairs. For each of us in recovery there will come

a time when we will have the opportunity to share our experience, strength and hope with others. And this is what the program asks of us. We do not turn from this responsibility but instead welcome the opportunity. We tell our story and share what has worked for us, what didn't and where we hope to be by continuing our journey. By giving away what we have learned, we are able to keep it. However, we must be cautious not to attempt to carry the addict or alcoholic, only the message. It is then up to God to use our message to help the other person. Perhaps one of the best ways we do this is through our example. Step Twelve asks us to become living examples of the program, to live the program in all that we do. When someone new to the program sees someone as a living example of the promises come true, it provides hope. We carry the message of hope to the newcomer. Am I willing to live as an example?

Petitions to my Higher Power
God,

Thank You for helping me to find out that I no longer need to live in crisis. Help me this day to live as an example of the program really working. Let me continue to practice the principles of the program in all that I do. I have not yet achieved the goal, but I am on the way that leads to it. Let me be a messenger of hope to others.
Amen.

* * * *

Wisdom for Today   Sep 17
Pride goes before the fall. This statement certainly can be true for the alcoholic or addict. When we allow ourselves to become filled with pride about our recovery, it is too easy then to begin to take credit for it. Certainly all of us in recovery put work into it, and it is only natural to feel good about the efforts we have made. But when we begin to take the credit and flaunt it, we forget how this thing called recovery really happened. It was not we who alone conquered this problem. The truth is that we never will be able to conquer it. We are only able to recover with the help of the program and our Higher Power. Yes, we all have met those individuals who say they quit on their own. This may be true, but it is also true either that they never were addicted in the first place, or they have only become dry. Often times these individuals are not happy at all about being dry. They are an example of why we choose to use the steps, all twelve of them.

Yes, we certainly can feel positive about what we have done in recovery and the progress we have made. But we also need to remain humble and give thanks for the miracle that has occurred in our lives. Yes, we put effort into this miracle; but none of us can honestly say we did this on our own. Staying humble also brings us inner peace because we know that there is a Power Greater working in our lives. Staying humble also teaches us to look outside of ourselves for strength and courage. Do I continue to recognize the gift I have received?

Meditations for the Heart

With the program continuing to grow and the ever changing and expanding world of communication, it is now easier than ever to make connections with others who can help us. We forget how hard it was in the beginning for the founders of the program, who often times went days and weeks without talking to a fellow member of the program. Many could not afford the price of a phone call. Many had to travel long distances to get to a meeting. Perhaps the miracle of recovery was more evident then. I don't know, but what is certain is that we today have no excuse for not being able to make these vital connections with others in the program. We indeed are very fortunate to be able to meet with or talk with others so freely. We can get all the support we need; all we have to do is ask. Still I know that asking for help is not always an easy thing to do. It goes against the very nature of addiction. It is a lesson we all must learn. Do I take advantage of the resources available to me for help?

Petitions to my Higher Power

God,

Surround me with Your love and Your strength as I walk though this day. Grant me wisdom in the decisions I face in this day. Continue to provide me with courage as I need it, and let me remain willing always to reach out and ask for help. Remove from me any pride that would compromise my recovery, and let me walk humbly before You in all that I do.

Amen.

* * * *

Wisdom for Today   Sep 18

In life there are heroes, and the program is no exception. We meet them at every meeting we attend. Every time someone introduces himself or herself at a meeting, we are looking into the eyes of a hero. Some may question this, but I believe it to be true. Heroes are people who act in the face of fear to help others. When a newcomer walks though the door for the first time, they are greeted by others in the program. Inside the newcomer trembles with fear. Yet these individuals stare fear in the face and reach out to offer a helping hand. Each of us learns to be a hero in the program. When we are willing to offer forgiveness to others even when it raises fear in us, we act as heroes. When we say, "Yes!" to telling our story, even though the thought of speaking before a group terrifies us, we learn to be heroes.

When we carry the message to anyone who still suffers, we become heroes. In life when someone rushes into a burning building to help someone inside, they are considered a hero. Yet after the event most heroes do not go around bragging about what they have done. They speak humbly about the event. The same must be true for each of us. We do not brag about the Twelve Step call we just made. We do not look down on others because they did not go. We feel a sense of inner goodness in these acts of helping others, but we do not speak of this in an arrogant manner. Carrying the message is an act of heroism, but we do not claim superiority for doing this. We do this in humility and out of genuine concern for others. Am I willing to carry the message to others when given the opportunity to do so?

Meditations for the Heart

Responsibility is our goal in recovery. First, we take responsibility for working the steps and doing what is needed to stay clean and sober. Next we take responsibility to clean up our lives and repair the damage done in our active addiction. We become responsible for reaching out to others in the program to offer them what was so freely given to us. We continue to practice these responsibilities in all that we do. Through acting responsibly we make gains in our lives – physically, mentally, socially and spiritually. We become better people through this process and are rewarded with seeing the promises of the program come true in our lives. These gifts come to us only through working the program, and responsibility is a very big part of working this program. Am I working on personal responsibility?

Petitions to my Higher Power
God,

Each and every day I face choices and need to be responsible with what I choose to do. Grant me wisdom in making the choices I need to make today. Let me look for each opportunity to carry the message to others and to do this with humility. Give me the courage I will need in the face of any fear that might arise. Let me find the gifts that are so freely given by You along this pathway.

Amen.

* * * *

In life we are called on to interact with other people every day. This is no different in recovery. We interact with our family, coworkers, friends and people we just run into in the course of the day. Why is this important? Well, the truth is: What we do and how we choose to do so in our interactions with others have a lot to do with recovery. Active addiction tore relationships apart. In recovery we are taught to make amends and taught to forgive others. We are taught about reconciliation with God, as we understand Him; and we are taught about reconciliation with others.

The choices we have in recovery are many. With our interactions with other people we must begin with honesty and with willingness. We work to become willing to make amends. We work to become willing to forgive others and to ask for forgiveness. We work to build bridges and attempt to rebuild what has been broken. We do a regular inventory, and we look to see if we have wronged anyone. Yes, the choices are many; and sometimes the work is hard. But if we want what the program offers to us, then we will do the work. Am I working to rebuild my relationships with others?

Meditations for the Heart

When we were drinking and using, our heart was often empty because of the brokenness of our relationships with others and with God. As we work the steps and begin to rebuild our lives, we soon find that this emptiness is being filled again. We learn to do the next right thing in all our relationships with others. We learn to walk through our days without regret. Happiness again comes to our heart as we regain trust from others in our lives. We do run into those people that no matter what we do, they will not come close to us again. We have no control over their behavior or their choices. We are only responsible for attempting to repair the damage and rebuild the relationship. We remain open to the possibility that someday they may again open their hearts to us, and we pray for them. Am I finding joy in renewed relationships with people in my life?

Petitions to my Higher Power

God,

You are the giver of all good things. Certainly it is You who has again filled my heart with the joy known only in healthy and honest relationships. Give me an open mind with regard to the doors that may still be closed by others. Help them to see that judgment and resentment are not the answer. Help me to forgive those who have hurt me, and help me to rebuild wherever I can.

Amen.

* * * *

Wisdom for Today   Sep 20

Doubt can be a real stumbling block for those in recovery. Doubt for me was the absence of faith in a Power Greater and even in myself. I did not trust my own decisions, and I had plenty of reason not to trust myself. Doubting that "*God could and would if He were sought,*" (*Alcoholics Anonymous,* Fourth Edition. Page 60) was another matter entirely. I had grown up in a very religious family and had even had some spiritual experiences as a teenager before my addiction got out of hand, but as an adult I really had no true belief that a Power Greater than I would indeed help me. Why would God want to help me after all that I had done? Certainly I was not worth His time or energy. Even if He wanted to help me, I was not certain that He could. This doubt kept me frozen in my recovery.

But God, being more powerful than I can even begin to describe, thought differently than I did. He brought sunshine into my life and thawed the frozen wasteland of my life. I listened to others talk in meetings over and over again about how the program had changed them. I could tell from their stories that they were not just saying this but really meant it. I began to develop a feeble sense of hope that maybe, just maybe, God could work for me. Over time that feeble hope has grown, and now I have no doubt in my mind or my heart that God has done things for me that I could not do for myself. Over time I had heard hundreds and hundreds of stories like mine. When this many people all say that reliance on a Power outside of them works, it is hard to doubt the presence of a spiritual and loving God working in our lives. What am I relying on today?

Meditations for the Heart

"Behold, I make all things new." These are words found in the Bible. Regardless of your religious background, these words do describe what God can and will do for each and every one of us, if we only believe. Breaking down all the barriers to believing in a Power Greater, a Divine Presence, a Spiritual Guide or whatever you wish to call Him can be difficult to do with a closed mind. In recovery we are asked to open our minds and our hearts to this possibility. I can be made new. We are not asked to believe that we can make ourselves new, as we have all tried and failed in our attempts to do this. We learn that recovery is a gift that we can receive only if we ask for His help. What has surprised me is that I continue to be made new again and again through working the steps in my life. I guess that by now this shouldn't surprise me, but it still does. Recovery is about becoming new in all that we do. Do I use these principles of faith and ask for help each day?

Petitions to my Higher Power
God,

You ask nothing of me other than faith and obedience. These are the steps I am to follow to be made new. Yet to trust and obey, I need Your presence and help. Help me always to rely on You for direction and give me a willing heart to accomplish what You desire of me. Help me this day to continue to grow in my faith, and lead me to a path of newness of life.
Amen.

* * * *

Wisdom for Today   *Sep 21*
Who am I to say there is no God? This is the question that all who struggle with the concept of a Higher Power or Divine Principle exists must ask. All addicts and alcoholics know that we have lost our ability to control our use of alcohol and drugs. We know that our way is not working. Still there are many who come to the spiritual aspects of working the program and throw up walls and are unwilling to open their minds and their hearts to the possibility that this spiritual principle is the only thing that will work. Often it is the realization that we are indeed defeated that finally opens the door to another possibility.

Can any of us deny that we are social animals? We all want relationship with our fellow man. Is it so hard to dig down inside and recognize that man seeks relationships and then opens the door to the possibility to a relationship with a Power Greater than ourselves? Each of us seeks to have faith in something more than our self. We looked to the bottle or drugs and had faith that one or both would take away our problems. This did not work. Is it so hard to have faith in a Greater Spirit as this answer? We see it working for so many; there must be some truth in this concept. It is only when we completely give ourselves to this simple concept that we can find that this spiritual principle can work for us. Am I continuing to fight against what works for so many?

Meditations for the Heart
Why do we all resist the truth of recovery and how it works? For some of us it is the arrogance that we are different, or we know better or that we still believe we can learn control. For others the resistance lies in some deep-seated prejudice, or denial or even doubt. Many of us keep fighting simply because we enjoy the challenge or because we are afraid to stop. But when push comes to shove, it does not really even matter why we fight or resist. All

286

that really matters for us is that we need to stop fighting and open ourselves to new possibilities. The moment we stop fighting and resisting, we discover that life can be different. The only one holding us hostage in our addictive thinking is our own self. When we open the door to new possibilities, we can be set free, free to explore a new reality and a new way of thinking. We are set free to challenge our own beliefs and open to examine new beliefs. We are set free to find new answers and find new behavior. Am I still fighting or resisting the truth of recovery?

Petitions to my Higher Power

God,

I really can't even begin to fully understand who or what You are. I simply know that my way does not work; and if I continue to fight or resist the truth of recovery, I will never find the freedom I seek. Open my mind and my heart that I may grow along spiritual lines. Release me from the bondage of self, the chains of close-mindedness and the roadblocks that stand in my way. Help me to see the truth.

Amen.

* * * *

Wisdom for Today   Sep 22

"*Those who do not recover are people who are constitutionally incapable of being honest with themselves …* " (*Alcoholics Anonymous,* Fourth Edition. Page 58) When I first read these words, I became very frightened. I knew I was a liar when I was drinking and using, but what really scared me was that I was unsure if I was capable of being honest with myself. Fortunately, I discovered that I was capable of being honest. I could admit that my drinking and drug use was out of control. I knew my life was unmanageable. I could be honest about all the dishonesty I had in my life. I could let go of my denial and find the truth of my life.

I also learned that I could be honest with other people. It was not easy at first because I still wanted to hide the truth because of the incredible guilt and shame I had. Over time as I became more comfortable at meetings and with my sponsor, I learned to open up about my crazy thinking. I let down my wall of defenses and could face the reality of whom and what I was. I learned I had a disease from which I could recover through working the steps. I also learned that I had to keep working on honesty, because dishonesty has a way of creeping back into my life. I also have seen what has happened over and over again to those who refuse to get honest or are incapable of being honest with themselves. The AA Big Book says it plainly; "*There are such unfortunates …*"

(*Alcoholics Anonymous,* Fourth Edition. Page 58) Am I developing a manner of living that demands rigorous honesty?

Meditations for the Heart

Sometimes I look back at how far I have come in this program. I am amazed at the progress that has happened in my life. When I came into the program I just wanted a way out of the insanity. I did not expect to find happiness, peace of mind and all the other promises that recovery offers. It is good to do this every so often. Looking back and seeing the progress made helps to instill a true sense of gratitude. It also helps us with humility. We realize that what has happened to us in the process of recovery did not all happen because of what we have done. We see, perhaps more clearly, the miracle that recovery is. Yes, each of us must do the work; but the changes that happen are not just a result of that work. It is a result of something more powerful. Looking back helps me accept the spiritual changes that have occurred through Divine intervention. Looking back helps me see that I was saved from the ravages of addiction. Looking back helps me to see that I have grown in ways I did not expect. Looking back helps me to see that I did not do this all on my own. Do I truly appreciate what has happened to me in recovery?

Petitions to my Higher Power

God,

Your mercy, wisdom and grace have brought me this far. Today let me live my life with gratitude for all that has happened. Let me live this day in hope for what will be as long as I walk this path with You. Let me search my heart and mind this day for any self-deceit that may remain in my life and confront any dishonesty that may remain. Strengthen me for this day.

Amen.

* * * *

Wisdom for Today   Sep 23

In recovery, we all come to a point when we realize that we must do more than simply stay clean and sober. If we are going to stay clean and sober, we must also do a thorough personal housecleaning. Each of us carries things within ourselves that act as a block to growth. We find layer upon layer of garbage in our house that must be cleaned up. It is not enough to walk around abstinent and live in a house filled with garbage. It is also not enough just to sweep it all into a corner. We find that we must pick up the garbage and get rid of it. We must then go in and thoroughly clean the house in which we live.

We must be honest in doing this housecleaning. We take stock of what is messed up and what can be salvaged from the mess. We find strengths, and we find weaknesses. We look honestly at the causes of this mess. We see that we are the number one reason. We find that our thinking, emotions and behaviors have led us into this mess, and we are the ones who must take responsibility to clean it up. Some want to avoid this step and find that to do this leads to chronic unhappiness. It is no fun to live in this mess. It is difficult to clean up, but we discover that we are worth the effort. We find freedom from resentment and anger, hopelessness, fear and many other pieces of garbage that we do not need to live with. Have I taken steps to clean up the garbage in my life?

Meditations for the Heart

In running any race, it is important to keep your focus on the goal. It is no different in recovery. We stay focused on the goal in life that we hope to attain. We cannot be distracted by events in our life and loose sight of the goal. These distractions can seduce us into not finishing the race. As addicts and alcoholics we cannot afford not to finish the race. We take this race one step at a time and one day at a time. Our purpose is to finish this race. As we complete each step and as we live each day, we see that we are closer to the goal. Each step brings us new insights. Each step brings us new freedom. Each step brings us closer and closer to our goal. Sometimes we grow weary, and we face obstacles and distractions. In these times especially, we must look beyond and forward to our goal. Am I staying focused on what I need to do today to reach my goal?

Petitions to my Higher Power
God,

Help me to see that accomplishing each step is not the goal. Let me complete each step with the knowledge that what I seek is what is promised. Let me rely on You today to keep me on track. Let me not be distracted or loose sight of my goal.
Amen.

* * * *

Wisdom for Today   Sep 24

How big a part of my life is the program? Am I only involved on the fringes, or am I actively involved? Are meetings something I do occasionally and sometimes not at all, or do I attend meetings regularly? Do I structure time into my schedule to work on the steps, or do I simply ignore the steps?

Do I have and utilize a sponsor, or do I just run my own recovery without input from someone who can lead and guide me? Do I take time to think about what I have heard in meetings or simply assume that I have heard it all before? Do I offer to let others know about the program that may need it, or do I look the other way and assume they will eventually find what they need? These are questions we all need to ask ourselves throughout our time in recovery?

Keeping the program and all that goes with it central in our lives is important. Ask an old-timer how they keep what the program offers, and they will tell you that they carry the program with them in all that they do? Many will say that the program has become the solid foundation for all their life. Still others will talk about how it is important to give it away in order to keep it. Regardless of how they say it, all are working to keep the program central in their lives. I am not sure when the program switched from just a way to stay clean and sober to a way of life, but I am glad that it has. I used to think that having this disease was a curse. Now I see it as a blessing, for it teaches me how to live life abundantly. Am I keeping the program central in my life?

Meditations for the Heart

There is so much that can bring us down. Each of these things, whether they are failures, shortcomings or mistakes, we bring to our Higher Power and lay them before Him. We learn not to dwell on these things but to look for ways not to repeat them. We leave these things that bring us down in His caring hands. We rely on the Spirit to be our mediator with God. We allow this Divine Spirit to say what needs to be said and fix what needs to be fixed. This Spirit can and will help us to be reconciled. It is never too late for this to happen. It is when we learn to let go and rely on this Spirit to do for us what we cannot do for ourselves that we become right with our Higher Power. It is in this act of letting go that God smiles on us. In letting go we are brought closer to Him. Am I willing to let go of what I cannot change and focus on what I can change?

Petitions to my Higher Power

God,

In order to keep the program central in my life, I know I must start with You. Let me not become lazy or arrogant or cavalier with my program. Help me to practice the principles in all that I do. Let me also rely on Your Spirit to bring me into reconciliation with You, so that I might walk closely with You and in Your Light. Give me wisdom and courage to change the things I can today.

Amen.

* * * *

Wisdom for Today   *Sep 25*

The most valuable lessons we learn in the program come from practical experience, and one way in which we can receive this kind of experience is through working with others. I can't count the number of times I have been talking with someone else in the program and words will come out of my mouth to which I need to listen. There I am talking with a newcomer about his anger and resentment and listen to these words about self-centered fear come out of my mouth. Yes, it becomes obvious to me that the real reason he is unhappy and angry or resentful is because he is not getting what he wants. This thinking is coming from self-centered fear. Then as I talk about how this was true for me, I begin to realize that the same type of thinking causes some current frustration in my life.

The words coming from my mouth are meant as much for me as the newcomer. Over time I have really come to appreciate these experiences and see the true value in helping others. When I reach out to others, I am really helping myself. I have come to believe that there is nothing else that can so much insure our sobriety than helping others. But there are steps to doing this properly. First and foremost, I believe that whenever we work with others, we should first reach out to our Higher Power and ask for His direction of our thoughts. We also ask that He remove any selfish desire in our effort. Then we trust Him to lead our words and actions. When we do this, we find that we gain credibility with our peers. We find that they are open to listening to the words we share. We find too that God often times works through us not only to help the newcomer but also ourselves. In each of these interchanges we gain practical experience. Do I use my Higher Power as a guide when I reach out to help others?

Meditations for the Heart

Breathe in the Spirit, and you will be filled with goodness and truth. For if we are but willing, then the Spirit will fill our every need. In breathing in this Spirit, we find selfishness and hate are exhaled and replaced with generosity and love. But we must accept these gifts; for in breathing in the Spirit, we also breathe in the power of choice. We are given the option to accept or reject these gifts. We can choose to close our hearts, or we can graciously open them up to our Higher Power. In opening our hearts, we do not know with what God may choose to fill us; but we trust that in Him all things are good. He did not make us like robots that only follow orders; instead He granted us free will. Even though the Spirit is willing to fill us up with His good gifts, we still have the power to reject what He offers. Am I willing to accept the good gifts from my Higher Power?

Petitions to my Higher Power

God,

In this day let me be filled with your Spirit and accept whatever gifts I am granted. Help me to be open to seeing the gifts I am offered each and every day. Let me also be open to sharing these gifts with others as the opportunity may arise. Grant me wisdom to learn from these practical experiences each day. Amen.

* * * *

Wisdom for Today   Sep 26

My first Twelve Step call was quite a learning experience. I got a call from my sponsor, who asked me if I was up for a road trip. Knowing that my sponsor always was looking for ways to help me get better, I said sure. Minutes latter I was in his car and on my way to talk with someone who probably needed the program. My sponsor had gotten the call from a family friend. We arrived at the home and rang the doorbell. A woman answered the door and showed us to the bedroom. Inside was a man who was crying and swearing. It was clear that he was unhappy. His wife introduced my sponsor, and he in turn introduced me. We sat on the floor near the bed, and my sponsor began to speak. He talked for about a half hour of his trials with alcohol. Then he looked at me and without saying a word I knew he wanted me to tell my story. Before I even had the first word out of my mouth, the man said, "What am I supposed to do?"

My sponsor again looked at me. Here I was, and I had no idea what I was to say. I began by talking about what had worked for me. I talked of the struggles I had and the triumph I had experienced in the program. Somehow I knew I was not to label this man an alcoholic; he would need to decide this on his own. I saw the beads of sweat on his forehead and the trembling of his hands, but this was a question he would need to ask himself. His tears continued, and he said, "I'll do anything." Moments later we were in the car on the way to the hospital. My sponsor and I visited him every day while he was in Detox. Weeks later when he was done with rehab, we picked him up and drove him home. He still comes to meetings today. My sponsor and I talked about this experience several times. I learned that we carried a message, but it was up to this man to accept what had been said. This experience still is strong in my memory and so is the help that I received in taking part in this process. Am I willing to carry the message without passing judgment?

Meditations for the Heart

It would be so easy to criticize, judge or even blame when talking with others; but we cannot give any credence to these thoughts. Instead we must control these thoughts and in their place trust our Higher Power to give us the words that are needed. Having a firm foundation spiritually is what is needed when staring addiction in the face. Remembering who we are and what has happened to us is important, but we also cannot forget that our experiences in recovery are all a gift. It did not happen because we regained self-control. We listen to the person, but we do not allow ourselves to get wrapped up in his or her denial. We do not let ourselves get wrapped up in our own emotions. Instead we simply let God work through us to carry the message of recovery. In this way we carry a message of hope. Do I know that my Higher Power will be with me on any Twelve Step call I make?

Petitions to my Higher Power

God,

You choose me to carry the message; let me choose You when I go to deliver hope. Help me to let go of my own issues and only provide Your message given me in this program. Today I do not know whether or not this opportunity will present itself; but should the opportunity arise, let me accept this willingly. Walk with me this day, and provide guidance for each step I take.

Amen.

* * * *

Wisdom for Today   Sep 27

It is important not to give a newcomer the brand of "alcoholic" or "addict." We must let them draw their own conclusions. It does not matter what we think; what matters is the decision they make. What we can do is talk to them about the hopelessness of addiction. We can talk of our own experience and how we found strength through the grace of God and the program. We can share how we found hope. In sharing our experience, it is important to talk of how addiction to alcohol or drugs affected our lives and the consequences we have experienced. We talk of how drinking and drugging influenced our thinking and our behavior. We describe the sense of desperation we felt. We describe the insanity of trying over and over again to control our use, only to fail and jump right back into the same traps. We share our own denial and how it kept us trapped.

293

We share openly the spiritual aspects of recovery. We talk of the fellowship and the friends we have made and the support we have gained. Tell the newcomer that he or she does not need to accept our ideas exactly as we present them, but describe the reality of success that thousands and thousands of us have found in working the steps and in finding answers that none of us found previously on our own. Use language that the newcomer will understand and make sense to him or her. The important thing is that we let them decide if they want what we have. We share that they too can learn to live without alcohol and drugs if they are simply willing to live by these spiritual principles found in the steps. Am I willing to share openly the spiritual principles that helped me find recovery?

Meditations for the Heart

God is a constant in our life. He is unchanging, and He never leaves our side. He is untiring, and He is love. This is the very love to which we turn our will and our life over. His constancy is what we rely on. No matter how big or how small our need is, He is there for us. He knows the proper path for us to follow, and He will always lead us. All we need do is ask and obey, and we will be given the keys to a new and wonderful life. However, this simple concept is not always easy to do. In each of us there is a rebel that still wants to run the show our way. God will not stand in the way of our arrogance, pride or foolishness. He grants us the freedom to make such a choice. What this means is that I must make a choice each and every day – a choice to do it my way or a choice to do it His way. Yes, we are often tempted to get back in charge, but this never proves to be a wise choice. What choice will I make for myself today?

Petitions to my Higher Power

God,

In Your loving kindness, You have reached out to me and offered to show me the way to freedom. You know every step I take even before I do. Grant me willingness to follow and obey You this day. Let me follow You in all that I do this day. Remove from me any arrogance, pride or foolishness that may tempt me and lead me astray. Give me courage to share the spiritual message of recovery through the steps.

Amen.

* * * *

Wisdom for Today   Sep 28

"...and practice these principles in all our affairs." (Alcoholics Anonymous, Fourth Edition. Page 60) The Twelfth Step reminds us to practice what we do in all areas of our lives, with practice being the operative word. I recall as I was growing up, my parents always saying, "Practice makes perfect." But this has not been my experience; in fact, in recovery I think a better statement would be practice makes progress. Practice never made anything I did perfect, but I know it made me better in sports. It made me better at many of the things I do. This is certainly the case with recovery. Over time I have had my eyes opened as to how I could utilize the principles of the program throughout my life.

I have come to realize that there is very little in my life that I can control. I have learned to ask for help in many of the things I do, my work, my relationships, my faith and my goals. I have learned to look really hard at myself and my role in what I do, my decisions and my mistakes. I can use the program to help me in fixing or at least improving many of the situations I face each and every day. I have learned that I need to right my wrongs whenever I can, or at least do what I can in avoiding making the same mistakes over and over again. I have come to realize how important it is to be healthy in all that I do. Still I must practice, practice and practice. This is how I will make progress in all areas of my life. Am I willing to apply and practice the principles of recovery in all that I do?

Meditations for the Heart

Life is sometimes funny. We can look at something over and over again and not see what is really there. This is certainly true for many of us in recovery. The reasons for this are many – denial, self-delusion, dishonesty, lack of awareness and even our belief system. To be sure, this is not a complete list; but certainly they are major reasons that addicts and alcoholics walk through life with blinders on or with rose-colored glasses. When we finally have our eyes opened and can see the reality of our lives, we are given an opportunity for change. This is not always an easy choice to make. Sometimes it seems easier to fall right back into our old ways. This is not just true about our addiction, but also true about all of our life. The program tells us to deal with life on life's terms. It also teaches us the value of honesty. It really is uncanny how we can fool ourselves; but I have come to believe that God reveals to us the errors in our perceptions, beliefs and thinking. Do I see that my Higher Power presents me with opportunities for change throughout my life?

Petitions to my Higher Power

God,

Today I know that You will give me many opportunities for progress. Give me sight and strength to seize these opportunities. Let me practice what I know in all that I do. Let me take today and use it as an opportunity to learn new ways to live in a healthier way. Let me make the changes that You want from me. Help me to seek out Your direction for me in all that I do. Amen.

* * * *

Wisdom for Today   Sep 29

When working with a newcomer, it is important to describe what addiction was like, what happened and what life is like now. Tell him or her about the insanity of repeatedly attempting to solve a problem with no answers other than recovery. Explain how you found acceptance and surrender to a Power Greater than yourself. Describe how you took an honest look at yourself, how you worked to straighten out your past and what you are doing to stay that way. It is important to share why you are attempting to help them now. Let them know how helping others has become a vital part of your own recovery.

In sharing all these things, the newcomer will likely be more open to accepting what is said. They will see that there is no hidden agenda and that you are sincere in your effort. Should the newcomer show genuine interest, offer to share more – perhaps a phone number or let them borrow your Big Book. Suggest meetings that you have found helpful, and offer to take them or meet them there. In doing this, the newcomer is more likely to accept the suggestions you offer. Do not be afraid to offer this help, for you can be assured that God will work through your effort. Seeds will be planted; and you will find that even if they do not take with the newcomer, they will take and grow in you. Can I share the message of hope that the program offers?

Meditations for the Heart

Making Twelve Step calls and helping the newcomer is not so much about what you do as it is about how God works through you. Step out of the way, and let God do the work, and remember that you are only an instrument in His hand. Your Higher Power knows far better the needs of the newcomer than you do. He can see in them just as He could see in you when you first walked through the door. He knows what is needed and when it is needed. We only need to trust in His wisdom and in His strength. God only desires us to be obedient to this new way of living our life. Let Him choose how to use you. Be sure that God will offer you opportunity after opportunity to carry the message. Let Him decide when the time is right. Do not turn down the opportunities He presents, for you will be rewarded in the ways that He chooses. Accept every opportunity you are given to tell your story whether this is at a meeting or in the home of a new prospect. This willingness provides reward after reward. Am I willing to be His messenger when the opportunity presents itself?

Petitions to my Higher Power
God,

Let me be Your messenger in all that I do. Let me be Your representative in my actions, words and thoughts. Grant me a willing heart and a courageous spirit. Today I pray that I do not act as an obstacle to Your plan but as an active participant in it. Let me keep You central and in charge of my actions. Amen.

* * * *

Wisdom for Today   Sep 30
Working with a newcomer can be frustrating at times. It is important to understand that what we get frustrated with is the disease and not the person. Newcomers will act the way the disease of addiction still influences them to act. If the disease wants a newcomer to present us with one excuse after another, this is exactly what the newcomer will do. If the disease wants the newcomer to present us with a wall of denial or dishonesty, this is exactly what the newcomer will do. We must realize that they will continue to act this way until they stop turning their power over to addiction and begin to turn their will over to the care of God, as One who understands Him.

It is not unusual for a newcomer to place all kinds of conditions on their recovery. "I won't be able to stay clean and sober until I get my family back." "I can't do this unless I get a job." Regardless of the excuses, denial or dishonesty, we must remember that we deal with a disease that is cunning, baffling and powerful. This is not who the person is anymore than we were truly ourselves when we first walked through the doors of the program. Recovery is not an event, but it is a process for each of us, and we must stay conscious of the fact that the newcomer is just beginning this process. We should offer to do whatever is within our power to help the newcomer, just as others helped us learn the way. We confront the games, excuses, dishonesty and denial and point out that these do not work. We share honestly with the newcomer how these same things kept us from doing what we needed to do early in our recovery. Do I recognize all the games, excuses, denial and dishonesty of the newcomer as the way addiction is expressing itself in that person's life?

Meditations for the Heart
To believe in the Unseen is necessary in the recovery process. None of us question the presence of air, which is unseen, until we are deprived of it. No

one questions the presence of electricity in the wiring of a home. This too is unseen, but we do not shove a piece of metal into the outlet because we believe in this unseen. Our Higher Power too is unseen, but His actions in our lives and in the lives of other addicts and alcoholics cannot be doubted. Much like we can see the light when we turn on the light switch, we can see the light of our Higher Power shining brightly all around us. God's light is there all the time, and He will relieve us of our burdens. He will make light our load. His light will bring us new vision for the day. It will warm our hearts with His peace and His security. No, we cannot doubt the Unseen in our recovery and in our life. He is all around us and always present. We cannot doubt this anymore than we doubt the presence of air. Each day we look for the Unseen is a day when we will see more of the Unseen. Am I willing to have faith in the Unseen?

Petitions to my Higher Power
God,

I cannot see You, but I can feel Your presence much like I cannot see air but can feel its presence when a breeze blows. Help me today in Your Unseen ways. Guide me with Your unseen Spirit. Grant me wisdom and courage when I work with a newcomer. Let me see them as a person and not as their disease. Grant me this day Your love.
Amen.

* * * *

Wisdom for Today   Oct 1
It is important for all of us to remember who we are. It is equally important to remember who other people are. There is one group of people we know that continues to use alcohol and even drugs, but do not seem to have the sort of problems that we encountered in our own life. These individuals seem to drink normally and even their drug use does not appear to violate their values. We must be careful not to grow intolerant of these people or hate them. This has never proven to be helpful for any addict or alcoholic. We may need to avoid contact with them particularly in drinking or using situations in order to protect our recovery, but to grow resentful toward them because they can still drink or use will not help. The program teaches us that we have no business in drinking or using situations unless we are there for a legitimate reason, such as a family wedding or other celebration. Even then we should only attend if we are in a solid place spiritually.

The other group of people we know are those who clearly have problems with their alcohol and drug use. We have no business being around these people at all unless they call wanting to know more about how we got clean and sober. These Twelve Step calls are best done with someone else in the program, so that we avoid the emotional traps of old friendships. We do not belong in slippery places. We hear at meetings to avoid old people, places and things. This is good advice as we have seen many who have tried to hang out in old haunts that have failed to stay clean and sober as a result. We are people who tend to live life in extremes. In recovery we cannot afford to do this anymore. We cannot live in the extreme of hating all who still use, and we cannot live in the extreme of living life on the edge of certain relapse. Have I learned to tolerate those who drink or use in a socially responsible manner? Have I accepted that I must avoid old playgrounds?

Meditations for the Heart

We must learn to live life in a way that petty annoyances do not weigh us down. We can make healthy choices not to react to emotional unrest in others with emotional unrest of our own. We can hold onto the inner peace that God gives us even in the most difficult of situations. We can learn to allow this inner calmness to be our guide in our interactions with others. We no longer need to pick fights with others, and we no longer need to accept invitations to argue with others. This does not mean that we avoid problems; rather we seek solutions to the problems that may arise in and around us. Here we learn that we cannot always rely on our own strength, but we can always draw on His strength. When we lose our inner peace and react to these situations with anger or malice, we are closing the door on God's Spirit. Am I working to keep the door open to His Spirit?

Petitions to my Higher Power

God,

Help me to find healthy balance in my life, my attitudes and my behavior. Let me always seek tolerance, wisdom and find that which is healthy for me in all I do. Remove from me any judgment of others, and let me not find room in my heart for resentment. Grant me inner peace as I walk through this day. Amen.

* * * *

Wisdom for Today   Oct 2

I cannot forget that addiction is my number one problem. This disease has ways of continually trying to sneak up on me in my life, even when I am strong and active in my program. It is especially cunning, baffling and powerful when other problems are occurring in my life. This is why it is so important for me to keep, "First things first." I must always remember

I have this disease and not put other problems I may have in front of my recovery. The reality is that I have only two problems. One is staying clean and sober, and two is all the rest. I will not ever be able to deal with all the rest effectively if I do not deal with my number one problem first. I need to continue to work my program and stay in a good place spiritually if I am to find solutions for my other problems whatever they may be. I cannot put family problems, occupational problems, legal problems and financial problems ahead of my recovery.

I also must be cautious of becoming too relaxed in my recovery. Success has a way of making me feel too comfortable in my sobriety. Here is where my disease can seize an opportunity to catch me when I am not looking. I cannot let success blind me from the fact that this disease continues to live in me even with years of success under my belt. Overconfidence has been the downfall of many leading them back to relapse. Any problem can be dangerous for us, but none more than the disease of addiction. Do I keep "First things first?"

Meditations for the Heart

Progress is what we seek. Each day we can find new opportunity for growth. We can build on the gains made yesterday. We can find that new strength, new wisdom and new courage can be ours today if we only seek to do God's will for us. We need to open our eyes to the opportunities He affords us. We can learn from each mistake, and we can learn from each success. When I stay grounded in the truth of progress and not perfection, I find that I stay willing to keep growing in my recovery and in my spirituality. Some days the progress comes in the form of not repeating past errors in judgment. Other days I find that my faith is strengthened. Other days I may find that my relationships with others are improved. Wherever the progress occurs in my life, I must be grateful to have been led to the opportunity for growth. Each of these opportunities is one that I would not have had if I did not find this program. Today I can even be sure that the truth is that the program found me. Do I seek to make progress every day in my recovery?

Petitions to my Higher Power

God,

Help me always to seek to make progress. To do this I know I must keep first things first. This means that I must always keep You first, for without You I know recovery does not happen. Grant me keen eyes, so that I may see every opportunity that is provided me for growth. Help me to trust that You will provide for me what is needed for the task of this growth.

Amen.

* * * *

Recovery is not always easy. In fact there are times when it is down right hard. In these difficult times we must be careful not to act impulsively. This is where the AA motto, "Think, Think, Think!" comes in. First, we must think the drink or drug through till the end. What this means is that we must think past the drinking or drugging to the consequences that wait for us on the other side. And they do wait; and because we are alcoholics and addicts, we cannot know how bad these consequences may be. Secondly, we must think about what the program tells us to do in these situations. How can we use the steps to help us get through these difficult times? What would my sponsor say to me? What principles of the program can I rely on to help me choose to do the next right thing?

Finally, I must think about what my Higher Power would want me to do in this situation. How can I use God to help me with my current situation? What does my Higher Power want me to do? Each of these statements summarizes a plan to help me deal with life on life's terms. So when things get difficult as they sometimes do, I must train myself to use this motto in my life as a plan of action. This motto will help me make healthy decisions. It will guide me step-by-step back to a place of stability in my recovery. I can even use this motto when life is not so difficult. It will keep me on track, and I will be less likely to end up in difficult situations. Do I use, "Think, think, think!" in my daily life?

Meditations for the Heart

As we grow closer and closer to our God, as we understand Him, we become less and less entangled in the frustrations of humanity and its limitations. Man is filled with shortcomings and cannot satisfy all our desires. But God can indeed fill our every need. Whenever we need His help, He is there. Whenever we need His encouragement, He is there. Whenever we need His guidance, He is there. And whenever we need His wisdom, He is there. This is where we all need to look to have our needs fulfilled. Should we turn only to our fellow man to satisfy our needs, we will surely be let down sooner or later. But God always satisfies our needs. This does not always happen in the ways which we might expect, but it will happen in the way God wants it to. Do I go to God and lay my needs before Him?

Petitions to my Higher Power

God,

Sometimes life gets frustrating, and I know I need to turn to You for help. Let me learn to use the program as a guide for my life, and let me always slow down and look to You for whatever I need. Give me answers for this day, and help me to think before I act. Let me use Your wisdom in the difficult times I may face.

Amen.

* * * *

Wisdom for Today   Oct 4

As addicts and alcoholics, we are a people of excess. Much of how we have lived our lives has been in excess. I can remember jokingly telling others that my drug of choice was, "MORE." Recovery has a way of changing this kind of thinking. One of my favorite mottos in the program is, "Easy does it." This tells us to do the best we can with what we have and not to get too bent out of shape over things that happen both within the program and outside of it. For many of us we drank or used drugs to help us cope with a myriad of emotions. It did not take much to push our buttons, and we would go on an emotional tear. It did not matter if it was anger, guilt, sadness or fear; each of these emotions and others we would experience in the extreme. This was not because the situation warranted it, but it was because we lived life in the extreme. Our personalities and character would multiply our emotions until we had to find a way to escape.

"Easy does it," tells me that I need to learn patience, tolerance, understanding, delayed gratification and wisdom. It teaches me to learn moderation in my response to life's twists and turns. It teaches me to relax and to wait. It shows me the importance of slowing down enough to check things out with my Higher Power. It lets me know that I am not running the world and do not have to be responsible for more than God asks me to do. It teaches me that if I am going to live in a normal world as a normal person, I need to make adjustments in how I live and experience the world. Have I learned to take life on life's terms and not let things go to extremes?

Meditations for the Heart

God is our refuge and our strength. Both of these qualities of God are important for addicts and alcoholics. Each of us needs a place of refuge. Many of us used to hide in the bottle or hide in the fog of drug abuse. But in recovery we find we do not so much need a place to hide as much as we need security. Addiction provides no safety, but the arms of our Higher Power wait to hold us in a place of deep security and safety. Here we can find a place to rest, reflect and meditate on His will for us. Here we also find His strength and are provided with His power – the power we all need to carry out His will for us. No bottle, pill or fix ever provided this for us. But God grants this to us all freely. All we need do is accept the gift. To feel secure and strong was something I could not imagine when I was active in my addiction. In recovery I cannot imagine being without security and strength. Have I found refuge in my Higher Power's arms?

Petitions to my Higher Power
God,

Remind me to take a deep breath and slow down when I get caught up in the fast pace I am so easily attracted to. Teach me to take life in an easy manner and to seek refuge in Your arms whenever I need to. Help me this day to live life fully and abundantly, but not in extreme. Let me feel the security and strength that You so freely provide.
Amen.

* * * *

Wisdom for Today   Oct 5
Somewhere in the recovery process, as we truly begin to develop our spiritual lives, we come to realize that we did not achieve sobriety on our own. A genuine sense of recognition comes that recovery was achieved, "But for the grace of God." This program motto reminds us not to take too much credit for our sobriety. Yes, we have to walk the walk; but none of us would have even found the path, let alone stayed on it without His grace. As we walk through the process of recovery, all of us will see those who choose not to accept His grace. These individuals end up back in the sauce. We also will run into those who need the program, but are not yet ready. Here we look at these individuals and say, "But for the grace of God, there go I."

This statement helps to remind us of who we are. It reminds us that we still have this disease. Yes, we may be strong in our recovery today, but this is only true because we have accepted His gracious gift. This statement also reminds us to be grateful for what we have been given. And we are certainly given much in the recovery process. Each of the promises of the program only happens through our willingness to put into action suggestions given us and through the grace that our Higher Power gives us each and every day. These enable us to remain clean and sober. Humbly we stand before our Higher Power, and we see the majesty of what He has done and continues to do for us. Have I accepted the gift of recovery through His grace?

Meditations for the Heart
I am not sure that I can look back and say with any certainty when I knew in my heart that God loved me. In my brokenness and shame, I stood in the door of a clubhouse wanting desperately to find a way out of the insanity. I had

no idea what awaited me and could not even begin to imagine where the path of recovery would lead. I do know that once I really knew in my heart that God loved me, my whole life changed. Gratitude was a constant companion, especially when I walked through difficult times. Cares and worries seemed to just disappear as I began to realize that I was being helped and could see that much of the goodness I experienced in life came about, not because of what I was doing, but because of what He was doing. I began to see that not only was I cared for, but I also began to see that I had a friend. Am I grateful for this love that is given me so freely?

Petitions to my Higher Power
God,

It is You who have walked with me each and every step of this path. I am truly grateful for the guidance and direction I receive. The outpouring of love and care I receive from You humbles me. I do not understand this grace, but I am glad in my heart for this gift. Help those that still suffer, and open their hearts to accept this wonderful gift of recovery.
Amen.

* * * *

Wisdom for Today   Oct 6
Boredom can be a real enemy of an addict or alcoholic early in recovery. Idle time can bring on a busy mind. I know I struggled with this issue a lot in my early days. I had grown so attached to the excitement and rush of the nightlife that going to another meeting just didn't seem to take the place of chasing the dream of being high or wasted again. Now that I was clean and sober didn't mean that I was out of the woods yet. I had time on my hands and didn't know what to do with it. My mind frequently would be preoccupied with romancing the high again. It wasn't that I was bored; it was the fact that I was grieving the loss of my previous lifestyle. I didn't miss the insanity, but I did miss the fun. I missed the camaraderie of my using and drinking buddies.

But I told myself I was bored. In truth, I was depressed and lonely and sad. I would even get into playing games with myself and trying to convince myself I didn't need to go to a meeting. Then one night I heard someone say, "When I think I don't need a meeting that is when I need to go the most." This didn't make any sense to me at the time, but I am glad I listened to this suggestion. Months later when I really began to settle into recovery and my brain started to become clearer, I could really see how I was setting myself up. I could see the addictive preoccupation I had. I do not know how I made it through this time without using or drinking; I just know that going to meetings saved me from returning to the insanity. Do I accept that I will always need meetings?

Meditations for the Heart

In the program camaraderie with drinking buddies and using friends is replaced with fellowship. This fellowship often happens before meetings and again after meetings. It occurs in time spent with sponsors and in time spent at conventions, workshops and program social events. It also occurs in relationship with a Higher Power. Today I know how important this fellowship is with others in the program. Much of what I have learned along the way has occurred outside of the meetings themselves. The reality is that many of my toughest battles in recovery have been fought with the help of others who were willing to spend time with me before or after a meeting. Service work also has helped me gain a deeper appreciation of all that goes on behind the scenes. It has also helped me grow in many ways. Do not underestimate the importance of this fellowship with others; for many of us this is where real change occurs. Do I take advantage of opportunities to build fellowship with others?

Petitions to my Higher Power

God,

This day is not unlike others. I stand here before You as an alcoholic and addict. Help me this day to do the next right thing. Encourage me to be in fellowship with others. Grant me this day ears to listen to every suggestion that is offered. Give me wisdom to use these suggestions in ways that help me grow in my recovery.

Amen.

* * * *

Wisdom for Today   Oct 7

As addicts and alcoholics we often spent time looking for a magic bullet. We wanted something that would make all the pain go away. We looked to alcohol and drugs to be our magic bullet only to find out that this bullet exploded in our face. Addiction did not solve our problems and only made them worse. As I got clean and sober, my search for the magic bullet did not end. At first I thought the program would be that magic bullet, but it is not. It took quite a while finally to understand that there is no magic bullet. Recovery is not like that. It is a process and not a single event.

What I have discovered is that recovery is more like opening doors and finding pieces to a puzzle. Sometimes I find pieces of the puzzle through working the steps. Other pieces are found in the fellowship, and still others are found through prayer and meditation. Regardless of where we find the pieces to the puzzle, we still need to find a way to put the pieces together. The problem here is that none of us are very good at putting the pieces of the puzzle together. This is where grace comes in. I could not figure out the puzzle on my own, but slowly over time piece after piece was put together. I know today I did not do this, but it was done for me. Through God's grace the pieces fit together, and the picture is beautiful. Am I willing to have faith that His grace will put the pieces of my life back together again?

Meditations for the Heart

Shame seemed to be a huge roadblock in my recovery process. I was absolutely convinced that there was something wrong with what I was. Somehow I had become damaged, broken and worthless. Here especially I found piece after piece of brokenness and certainly felt that there was little I could do to put these pieces of my life back together. I wasn't even sure if I had all the pieces necessary to make the picture complete. Through a lot of work on self-acceptance and finding out how to forgive myself, the pieces slowly came together. But it did not all come together. In fact, the harder I tried the more frustrated I got. This is when the program came through for me again. I learned that I needed to collect all the pieces I could find and then turn them over to a Power Greater than myself. It was only in turning it over and letting go that I could hope for an answer. Here God surprised me. Not only did He put the pieces together, but He filled in the blank spots. The missing pieces and brokenness came together in and through this Higher Power. Am I willing to let go of the brokenness and have faith that God can and will put the puzzle together for me?

Petitions to my Higher Power

God,

Today let me turn to You in faith. Let me trust in Your wisdom and strength to put the pieces of my life back together again. Help me to feel whole, complete and beautiful again. Lead me this day to the doors where I will find the puzzle pieces. Guide me in this search. Let me bring these pieces to You, so that You may create in me the picture of oneness in You.

Amen.

* * * *

Sometimes I would find myself feeling like just giving up. Life would just get too hard. It seemed that it was too hard to keep fighting the good fight, to stay on track. Even keeping the sense of hope alive seemed difficult. This is when the words of my sponsor seemed to be the only thing left to hang onto. What he would say to me in times like this was, "Don't give up before the miracle happens." I can remember sputtering under my breath, "What miracle?" But each time I looked into my sponsor's eyes, I knew he believed it would. Somehow that kept me hanging on. I would just keep putting one foot in front of the other. I would make one meeting after another. One day after another I kept on going. Before long my life seemed easier. The load I was carrying seemed lighter. Just doing the next right thing seemed to be working.

Perhaps this is the miracle. Each day I stay clean and sober is a miracle. Each day I accept God's grace in my life is a miracle. And as far as not giving up, sometimes it is real work. But most of all it is about keeping the faith that the miracle will happen, gaining real trust that God will make miracles happen for me if I simply do what He wants me to do. Each day I need to work at hanging in there. Some days it is by a long rope and other days it is by a shorter one. Regardless the length of the rope, I know the miracle will happen. Do I have faith that the miracle will happen?

Meditations for the Heart

Hope is a seed that is planted when we first make the decision to stop drinking or using. But this seed will quickly die if it has no water and no sun. Where do we get this water and sun? In Step Two we learn that we only need come to believe. It is a matter of faith that we trust the sun will rise tomorrow. We also trust that the rain will fall. In recovery we certainly find that we have sunny days and rainy ones. This is what produces growth. Before long the seed breaks through the soil and reaches higher and higher for the sun. Over time new leaves form and branches begin to grow. Life begins to take on new meaning, and we begin to blossom in this new life. This is what recovery brings. Each day we find new life in recovery. We find new meaning. We learn to open our lives to the newness of creation. We learn to open our lives to the goodness that is all around us. We learn to open ourselves to His love, His light and His truth. Do I feel the seed of hope growing in me?

Petitions to my Higher Power

God,

Today let me trust in Your wisdom and Your direction. Fill me with encouragement and strengthen my faith in the miracle of life in recovery. Let me weather both the sunny days as well as the rainy days. Give me courage and confidence in what You want for me.

Amen.

* * * *

Wisdom for Today   Oct 9

In recovery we also have good days. These days begin to happen more and more often the longer we stay clean and sober. But there is a catch. This only happens as long as we continue to work the steps and use the principles of the program. In my own life when I get lazy and don't use the tools I have been given, things seemed to fall apart. As soon as I got back on track, things started to go well again. This is not just my experience, but also the experience of others. I have heard this story time and time again from others. When I stop working the program, the program stops working for me.

What this means is that if I want to stay on track and string together more good days than bad ones, I have to keep doing my part. To keep the serenity going, I need to keep going. This by itself has convinced me that I still have this disease. I still think like an addict and an alcoholic. For me not to begin to behave like one, working the program on an ongoing basis is important. Today I will choose to use the tools and work the steps. I do this because I want more good days. I want everything that recovery offers me. Am I willing to use the tools each and every day?

Meditations for the Heart

Sometimes I get so busy and seem to run from one task to another without stopping. These are the times when I am most likely to get myself tired. When I get tired, I know that I do not think very clearly. I also tend to over react to situations. This is when "HALT" becomes very important for me. "Halt" tells me to slow down and get my rest. "Halt" tells me to take care of myself and my recovery. Rest is important in keeping a sense of balance in my life. If I get out of balance, my whole world seems out of kilter. When this happens, I find it is important to go back to the basics. I take my morning meditations more seriously. I work at eating right. I get to my meetings, and I stick to a reasonable schedule. As I do these things, my life seems to come back into focus; and I regain balance. Slowing down and getting back to the basics works. Do I use "HALT" when I need to?

Petitions to my Higher Power

God,

Life is not always fair, but I know that You are. Help me to listen for Your cues that I need to slow down and get back to the basics. Let me use the tools I have been given to keep myself on track. Should I lose my balance, let me seek You out first; for nothing helps me more than being in a good place spiritually.

Amen.

＊ ＊ ＊ ＊

Wisdom for Today *Oct 10*

Back when I was drinking and using, I would fantasize about the future. I had dreams and aspirations of a fine life with a happy family, a good job and many other good things. In recovery I have found many of these good things because of what the program has taught me. Sometimes I now fantasize about what my life would have been like if I never found the program. It is not a pretty picture. Yet this ugly picture is something I carry with me as a reminder – a reminder of what will happen should I choose to go back to the insanity of addiction.

Whatever the ways we find to convince ourselves that addiction is wrong for us, we all need to face the truth of addiction. Addiction to alcohol or drugs only gets worse over time. There is no cure for this disease; it can be arrested but not cured. In the end without recovery, it will destroy all that is precious to us. I hold this truth close to me so that I cannot forget the finality of the disease process – death, insanity or institutions. I hold this close also so that I may be grateful for all the good things I have been given in recovery. Have I found a way to hold the truth of addiction close so that I will not forget its finality?

Meditations for the Heart

Fantasy and imagination can serve us well in recovery. This was not my original thinking, but over time it has changed much like many other things in recovery. In Step Eleven we are asked to seek through prayer and meditation to improve our conscious contact with God. At first I thought meditation was for people in another culture or for people who were just plain weird. I was wrong about this, just like I was wrong about many other things. Using meditation to fantasize or imagine what God wants me to do in my life has turned out to be a good thing. When I think deeply about what God wants and consider the wisdom that He wants me to have, only good can come of this. When I imagine myself securely in His arms, my fears slip away. When I imagine myself being given courage for the day, my strength is increased. The Psalm says it best, "Surely goodness and mercy shall follow me all the days of my life." Do I take time to meditate regularly?

Petitions to my Higher Power
God,

Be with me this day and walk with me in all that I do. Let me guard closely the truth of addiction and what it can do to me. Let me hold Your truth in front of me as my shield this day. Let me take time to spend in dialog with You. Let me think deeply about Your will for me this day.
Amen.

* * * *

Wisdom for Today   Oct 11
Recovery is a spiritual journey. For each of us this journey is different. We all use the same steps, but the process is different and unique for each of us even though we travel the same path. Each of us must find our own understanding of personal acceptance and surrender. Each of us must find our own personal relationship with a Power outside of ourselves. Each of us must look deeply and honestly at ourselves. Each of us must make the changes necessary to live life in recovery. Each of us has our own repair work to do to restore the brokenness of our lives. And each of us must find a way to maintain our ongoing growth.

Yet in all that we need do, there is one constant: None of what we must do can be done alone. All of what we must do to walk this walk is done in the spirit of "We." This 'We' may be the relationships we build in and through the fellowship. It may be the relationship we build with a Greater Spirit, or it may be the unity we all share in the journey called recovery. All of what is described here is spiritual. It becomes a part of who we are, and this spiritual experience leads us along this journey. This common spiritual experience is what makes recovery work for each of us. Do I see the common spiritual experience working for me in my recovery?

Meditations for the Heart
Recovery brings us a sense of freedom and happiness we have never known before. We can perhaps for the first time in our lives experience joy. Our problems seem to disappear as we work the steps and use the principles of this program to guide us. Those problems we still have do not trouble us, for we know that we have been given the tools we need to address whatever may come our way. One day after another passes, and we see the promises happen in our lives. From time to time we look back and see just how far we have come, but we also know that the journey is not over. Each day we will be given new tasks to which we need pay attention. Each day we are given opportunity for growth.

Each day we gain new insights and new understanding of who we are and who our Higher Power is. Do I see each day as an opportunity for growth?

Petitions to my Higher Power
God,

Deepen my understanding of who You are and how important You are for my recovery. Deepen my gratitude for the mystery of all that is spiritual. Expand my vision and open my ears to see and hear Your presence in my life. Let me continue on my personal spiritual journey this day wherever You may lead me.
Amen.

* * * *

Wisdom for Today   Oct 12
Learning to share what is really going on in our lives is not always easy. Sometimes it is difficult for us to even know what is going on with us. We have kept ourselves and our lives hidden from others. Opening our thinking, feelings and beliefs about how we see the world can be threatening for many of us. Yet it is in the risk of revealing ourselves to others that we find healing. To discuss our resentment, fears, grief and loss, guilt and shame with others helps us to sort through the layers of pain we all carry inside. In opening up, we find that we are not alone. We find healthier ways to let go of the burdens that have weighed us down for so long.

Is this an easy process? – NO! But it is simple; we simply need to open our mouth and begin to discuss with another in the program what is troubling us. Sometimes even when we do not know what is bugging us, as we begin to talk with another, we soon sort through whatever it is and gain clarity. In recovery we learn that we need to tell on our disease and on ourselves. In the honesty of sharing what troubles us, we find that the load we carry is no longer heavy. We find that new answers are gained. Over time it is this act of sharing that brings us out of isolation and into a new light of community with others. This is how we move from living a life of self-centered fear to a life of "WE." Am "I" moving from isolation to a sense of fellowship?

Meditations for the Heart
I can remember thinking that I was such a loser, that I was no good and worthless. As I began to open up and share my experiences with addiction, I began to see just how silly I sounded. Friends in the program would help me open new doors and turn on new lights so that I could see just how unfairly I was judging myself. No one was harder on me than I was on myself. I began to see that others perceived me very differently than I perceived myself. Simple

311

questions like, "Did you stay clean and sober today?" began to challenge my thinking and beliefs and feelings in such a way as to help me see that at least for today I was not a loser. Friends would point out to me the good that they saw in me. I began to regain a sense of self-esteem. I began to separate the things I did from who I was. I soon realized just how much addiction had controlled my actions and behavior, as well as, my beliefs, thinking and emotions. I could see that what I had done was not what I would have done had I not been in the bondage that addiction creates. Am I gaining a better understanding of who I am?

Petitions to my Higher Power
God,

This program acts like a mirror for me and helps me to see myself more clearly. Thank You for all the people You have placed in my life to listen to me as I sort through all the misperceptions, dishonesty and insanity that addiction has brought into my life. Give me courage to speak openly as I sort through all the layers of garbage I have accumulated along the way.
Amen.

* * * *

Wisdom for Today   Oct 13
When active in my addiction I found lots of reasons to keep on drinking and using. Many of these reasons were just excuses, but I was also using to help fulfill many of the needs I had. I needed to feel like I fit in. I needed to feel strong and confident. I needed to find relief. I needed to have a sense of security. Simply returning to the bottle or my drugs over and over again filled many different needs. I entered the program and soon realized that it was not just the alcohol and drugs I was giving up, but I was also giving up a way to meet those needs. I began to wonder if I was now simply to go through life depressed, lonely, bored and stupid. Even worse was I to end up like many of those self-righteous people I had met?

I knew I needed to stay clean and sober, but the real question was how. I also had no idea how to meet the many other needs I had. Fortunately, the program offered the answers I was looking for. Not only did the program teach me how to stay clean and sober, but it also helped me to meet my needs in a new and healthier way. I gained a sense of belonging and felt like I fit in. I also began to feel less fearful and gained strength. The steps and the fellowship not only provided a sense of relief, but also a sense of real security. I no longer worry so much about how to meet my needs. I have found a healthier way to meet my needs. Have I found a good substitute for alcohol and drugs?

Meditations for the Heart

I always walked around feeling like a total failure until I found the program. Today I know I do not need to rely on my strength, ability or wisdom. I can rely on the strength, ability and wisdom of the program and my Higher Power. In God there can be no failure. My sponsor would ask me over and over again, "Do you want to make the best life you can for yourself?" I think this is a question to which each of us would say "Yes!" He would go on to say, "Then live close to God." This simple suggestion has become a guide for my life. Living close to my Higher Power and following His will does provide me with all the strength, ability and wisdom I need. I do not need to have fear of failure any more than I need to fear success. If living close to God is sure, I can know that as long as I walk the path with Him I will succeed. This may or may not happen in the way that I expect it to, but I am confident it can and will happen. Do I continue to feel like a failure?

Petitions to my Higher Power

God,

I walk the path that I am given and hold close to You. Let me not become overconfident and rely on myself. Give me knowledge that my real security comes from You. Let me bring every need that I have to You confident that You will show me the way to fulfill these needs.

Amen.

* * * *

Wisdom for Today   *Oct 14*

What is it that draws us into the fellowship? For each of us the answer is both unique and common. We hear the stories, and we sense the hope that others have gained in living the program. We share common experiences, and we find that we are not alone. We share our struggles and our victories. Our eyes are opened to new possibilities. Growth becomes an option for each of us through the steps. Each of these things and many more draw us into the fellowship. Many are drawn by the powerful stories shared. Many are drawn by the simple structure and truth that abounds. Many enter the doors for these reasons.

But for each of us there are also things that are unique to our personal experience that draw us in and hold us within the fellowship. For some it is the laughter that can be found. For others it is the mirror that the program and fellowship provides that allows us to see ourselves in a new and healthy way. Each of us will find our own unique reasons for being drawn into the fellowship. Perhaps it will be the indescribable look that a sponsor can provide. Perhaps it is the warmth found burning in your heart. These are but a few of the unique and individual reasons we are drawn in and held in the arms of the program. Regardless of what has attracted us, all of it – both common and unique – is a part of the spiritual experience. Can I see the Spirit at work in my life helping me to find a new home?

Meditations for the Heart

Recovery is about being of single purpose. Our vision of this single purpose grows and expands as we move through recovery. At first our single purpose is to stay clean and sober. As we grow, our vision of this purpose grows into a desire to do His will. It is when we work to maintain this focus on a single purpose that balance is achieved. Much like the acrobat who walks along a tightrope, if we place one foot in front of the other and maintain our focus, we will not fall. It is this single purpose that leads us in our journey. Unfortunately, all of us struggle at times to keep our focus. In these times we begin to lose balance. It is only possible for us to regain this balance by again focusing on our single purpose. What does my Higher Power want me to do today?

Petitions to my Higher Power

God,

You know my needs better than I know my needs. Let me follow You this day with a willing heart, trusting Your direction, knowing that You will provide for my needs along the way. Give me the vision of single purpose knowing that Your will for me can only lead me to a good place. Guide my feet with each step I take.

Amen.

* * * *

Wisdom for Today   Oct 15

When I first walked through the doors of the program, I realized that I knew nothing about how to stay clean and sober. Over time God and the people in the program have constantly shown more and more to me about the ways to establish and maintain recovery. I ask each day for more to be revealed. Each day I ask how and what I can do to help those who still suffer. I ask for willingness to share freely the things that have been given me. Each of these revelations and increased knowledge of recovery is a part of the miracle of recovery.

Sharing this information with others is a part of the small way I participate in the miracle happening for others. In sharing with others, I am also helping myself. It is important to share freely what has been learned in the process of recovery. It is equally important to say, "I do not have the answer." We can only give away what we know. This is in part why it is so important to keep learning and making a life-long study of the program. Do I continue to study the principles of the program?

Meditations for the Heart

In the study of the program, we gain confidence in what works. We learn to have faith in these spiritual principles that underlie the entire program. We find strength in the quiet meditation and quietness. We learn from others, and we share what we know. Study, however, does require effort. We must discipline ourselves to spend time reading and in discussion with others to gain this understanding and knowledge. We will not gain anything without effort. We ask for willingness to give this effort. We schedule time in our day to learn. We learn to build our understanding of what works. We learn to understand the history of the program. We learn from the wisdom of those who have walked the path before us. We find new answers, and we implement them in our lives. Do I spend time in study of the program?

Petitions to my Higher Power

God,

This day I ask You to teach me. Provide me with opportunity to learn what You want for me to learn today. Give me openness to expand my knowledge and to share what I know with others. Open my mind to see what You want me to see this day. Open my ears so that I might hear what You want me to hear today.

Amen.

* * * *

Wisdom for Today   Oct 16

What are the principles on which the program was founded? All it takes is a short review of the steps themselves to understand the principles. Step One deals with meeting the requirement for membership. In our admission that we are alcoholics and addicts, we are also claiming membership. We also acknowledge our inability to recover on our own. The spiritual principle is introduced to us in Steps Two, Three, and Eleven. Next we are introduced to the principle of personal inventory. Then in Steps Four, Five, Six, Seven and Ten we are taught to look at ourselves and to let God change who we are. In

Steps Eight and Nine we are told to make restitution and repair the damage done by our addiction. Finally, in the Twelfth Step we are shown the need to pass on to others what has first been given to us.

These five principles of the program we are to carry with us daily. Each day we are to claim membership in the program. Each day we turn our lives over and let the spiritual principles guide us. Each day we are to look for personal change. Each day we are to repair any damage we find, and finally we are to carry the message. These principles are the guides to living life in recovery. They are the guides to happiness and serenity. All we need do is contained in these principles. Do I integrate these principles into my life daily?

Meditations for the Heart

Life with God is like a river that flows throughout all we experience. Just like a river brings nourishment to the trees, flowers and grasses along its banks, our Higher Power brings nourishment to our life. The flowers of our life bloom and bring color into our lives. The trees shoot forth new leaves to shade us from the heat of anger, resentment and fear. The grasses grow thick to cushion our walk. Through the dry parts of our life, God brings forth new life. Even when the skies open and the rains fall and the river swells, God will guide us to the high ground where it is safe. It is because of this river that we grow in our spiritual life and become willing to serve. It is because of this river that we live, for without it we would be stranded in a desert wasteland. Do I sense this river flowing through all I experience?

Petitions to my Higher Power

God,

Help me this day to integrate the principles of the program into all I do. Let me experience Your nourishment in my day so that I may bring forth new growth. Shade me from the heat of anger and resentment. Guard me from fear. Strengthen me and guide each step I take. Help those who still suffer; and lead them also to the door of the program, just as You have led me in my journey of recovery.

Amen.

* * * *

Wisdom for Today   Oct 17

In looking at the membership requirement of the program, we must admit our powerlessness and that our lives are unmanageable. For most of us this is either the hardest step to take or the easiest. For many, like myself, we enter the program not yet ready to become members. Denial and dishonesty keep us from accepting the reality of our illness. But there is something about sitting in those meetings and hearing other people's stories that breaks down the wall of denial, and dishonesty crumbles away, letting the reality of addiction come to light. Here is where membership in gained.

For others the consequences of their disease screams so loudly that it cannot be denied. Membership is not only accepted, but it is wanted. In desperation the alcoholic or addict embraces the program and its membership. Regardless of how we enter the program or what road we take to its doors, membership must be accepted and claimed for the program to work. It has only one requirement, a desire to stop the insanity of addiction. For those of us that have claimed this membership, we know that we have but started our journey. Each day we claim anew to be a member of this fellowship. Each day we claim the need for the program in our lives. Have I accepted membership in this program of recovery?

Meditations for the Heart

"I once was lost, but now I'm found." This line in the song, *Amazing Grace*, says it all. We walk through the door lost, but in the program we become found. In this program we are provided with a roadmap to recovery. We are given the principles and the steps that lead us on a journey of recovery. The path we must travel is not always easy, particularly in the early going. Over time the path widens, and it is no longer steep and winding. This is not to say that there are no twists or turns, just that as we become more and more familiar with using the roadmap, our journey becomes more predictable and more secure. In recovery we have many guides who will lead us from one point to another. These are but trusted servants who know the way better than we do. We simply need to follow the suggestions we are given, and these servants will lead us to a new horizon in our journey. Do I use the suggestions I am given?

Petitions to my Higher Power

God,

Thank You for leading me to the doorway of recovery. Here my eyes have been opened, and I can now claim membership in this program. Remind me each day to claim this membership again and again. This principle will keep me in a place to continue my journey. Thank You also for the trusted servants that so freely share what works and how to travel this path. Without them and Your guidance I would surely become lost again.

Amen.

* * * *

The spiritual aspects of the program form the second principle of the program. In the Second, Third and Eleventh steps of the program we find hope, help and relationship from our Higher Power. In these steps we find the possibility of restoration, the need for surrender, and the need for conversation with God to gain understanding and willingness. In conjunction with acceptance of our membership requirements, the spiritual aspects of the program form a solid foundation on which our house of recovery stands. Without this foundation our struggle will continue.

Here we turn our powerlessness into strength and our unmanageability into obedience to His will for us. We begin to understand the need for relying on a Power outside of ourselves. Here we learn the necessity of letting go of the need to control, manipulate and deceive. We are relieved of the insanity of our compulsion to use. Here we find our faith is tested and unshaken. Here we find the answers to the questions our heart and soul ask. Here we find freedom from the bondage with which we have lived. Are the spiritual principles a part of my daily living?

Meditations for the Heart

When we turn our thoughts and words to God, He listens. God turns His ear to those who speak to Him, and He listens to what we say. He listens to the words of our heart and mind. He listens to our needs, and He leads us to a place where these needs can be met. No matter how we talk with God, He will turn His ear to hear us. Even when we turn to Him in anger, He will not shut the door on us. He will show how to quiet the rage and resentments we have. We can bring anything to God, and He will not turn from us. Every hurt and pain we carry, He will listen to. He will bring healing into our hearts. Every fear that we imagine, He will stand ready to calm. We can carry our shame and self-hatred to Him only to have God reflect back a very different image of ourselves. He will take our sadness and loss and teach us how to live with this until we have a sense of joy and completeness. Do I trust that my Higher Power listens to me?

Petitions to my Higher Power

God,

Living with You in my life has changed my heart and my mind. Each day I am assured again that You will care for me. Even in the most difficult times of my life, You hang in there with me. You are willing to support and carry me when I need this. You bring encouragement to me and needed strength in whatever I face. You teach me not to fear. Stay with me this day, and lead me. Amen.

* * *

Wisdom for Today   *Oct 19*

Moving on to the principle of personal inventory: Looking at ourselves honestly is an absolute must in recovery. Steps Four, Five, Six, Seven and Ten point us in this direction. The truth is that for many of us that we have spent years running from the truth – not just about our addiction, but also the truth of who we are. Facing the reality of our defects, our wrongs, our secrets and our own selves is vital to maintaining recovery. We need to turn over every rock and find out if there is dirt under it. This is not easy, but if we refuse to be searching in this process, we are simply setting ourselves up to drink or use again.

It is not enough to simply locate the dirt in our lives. We must also do what we can to clean up our act. We need to work at correcting our faults. We look for where we have been dishonest, self-centered and fearful. We look at how our attitudes, behavior and beliefs have set us on a path of destruction; and we do what is necessary to change our direction. We do not do this only once, but we do this every day. Each day we fall short in some way, and we look at what we must do to live the program. These steps are more that just identifying our shortcomings, but looking at and making the changes we need to make to live happily in recovery. Am I dealing with reality in my inventory?

Meditations for the Heart

The changes we all must face in ourselves are not something we need to do alone. Each of us has help through a Power outside of ourselves. This Power is accessed through faith. All of us must come to believe that this help is available to us. Not one of us has been successful in changing our faults on our own. These defects resist change. Unless we turn our will over and humbly ask for the help that is available to us all, our chance for successfully making changes in our lives and who we are is nil. All we need do is look around at the countless faces of those who have completed these steps, and we have ample evidence that this Power lives among us. He is the One who will author our change. It is in His light that we are shown the path of needed change. The proof is in millions of changed lives. Do I have faith that God can and will show me how to change what I need to change?

Petitions to my Higher Power

God,

Looking at myself in the mirror of honesty is not always easy. I do not always like what I see. But You reflect not only who I am but also who I can be. Let me not fear change, for I know that any change You encourage me to make will be for my own good. Let me embrace these changes of personal growth as an opportunity to become the person You want me to be. Amen.

* * * *

Wisdom for Today   Oct 20
Making restitution is the next principle of the program. This is something that is not always easy, and many of us want to avoid. We must swallow our pride and go to the people we have harmed and attempt to undo the damage and repair what we can. Here again we do inventory, not of ourselves, but of how our attitude, behavior and beliefs have affected others. We make a list and then set about to rectify the problems we have caused. We pay back what we have taken, and we let others know how we have wronged them. We make a genuine attempt to rebuild the bridges we have burned.

As difficult as this process may be, the rewards we gain are even greater. Even when the apology is not accepted, it is important that we extend the effort. All of these efforts are made not just to repair the damage done, but also to relieve us from the burdens or guilt and shame we carry. Often times we find that this process if genuine and done in humility can change years of anger, frustration and even hate by others we have harmed into friendship and reconciliation. Here we often find forgiveness. Here we find love reborn. Here mending broken fences makes good neighbors. But most of all we find our conscience is cleared. Have I done my best at making restitution to those I have wronged?

Meditations for the Heart
Living a spiritual life brings joy and peace of mind. If these are not present in your life, there is still spiritual growth to be done. Here we must stretch our faith and learn to grow along spiritual lines. This growth may come slowly or happen quite rapidly. We look to remove any roadblocks that stand in the way of expanding our spiritual growth. We remove self-reliance and replace it with reliance on a Higher Power. We remove doubt and replace it with trust. We remove grandiosity and replace it with humility. We remove fear and replace it with the security of knowing that we have a strong foundation in the program. Over time as we work the steps and live the program, we experience a spiritual awakening. The sleep of addiction is replaced by a brilliant awareness of a new light in our life. Have I found joy and peace of mind?

Petitions to my Higher Power
God,

Give me the courage this day that I might need to do the repair work still needed in my life. Help me to find a genuine desire to fix the brokenness of the lives I have harmed along the road of destruction that addiction is. Let me become willing to make any restitution I may need to make. Give me strength in this part of my journey.

Amen

* * * *

Wisdom for Today   *Oct 21*

There is nothing more powerful than one drunk or user helping another. This is the last principle of the program. When I stop and reflect back on all the things that have helped me along the journey of recovery, certainly what I have heard from those around the tables and from my sponsor leads the way. At my first meeting someone got up and shared his story. It was like they had followed me around and now were relaying what had happened in my life. Sometimes it is a catchy one-liner, and at other times it has been through hours of discussion that the light finally gets turned on inside my head and the pieces of the puzzle come together. Regardless of how I have learned what I needed to learn, most of it came from the mouth of someone else that had been there.

I still look for answers in this way, but I also find that I get answers by sharing my own story. Sometimes telling my story again helps me to see things from a different perspective. Sometimes it is the questions I am asked by others that makes me dig deeper into the mysteries and miracle of recovery. I also find that it is important for me to share not just my successes, but my failures, struggles and what has not worked. In sharing these things, I find I am reminded of what does work. I know today that I need to carry the message to others in the program. This helps me stay clean and sober. Am I responsible, and do I reach out to carry the message to others?

Meditations for the Heart

Recovery for me is like turning on lights. It is important for me to shine the lights of the program on all that I do. In this way I can see clearly any dirt that I need to clean up in my life. With the lights of recovery shining brightly, I can see the path that I am to take. It is easier to see what God's will for me is with the lights on. This is the exact opposite of what I did in my addiction. Then I wanted nothing but darkness – darkness that would hide the shame and guilt I carried with me – darkness that would hide the fear and darkness that would keep me going in circles with my disease. The light of the program is found in the principles of recovery. It brightens my spirit; and it shines on the mirror of the Twelve Steps, which in turn reflects back to me what I need to do next. Have I been drawn to the light of recovery?

Petitions to my Higher Power

God,

This day shine brightly in my life. Continue to guide my steps, and give me willingness to give back to the program. Guide me when I speak, and grant me words to help others on this path. Let me always seek out others with any need that I may have. Help me to listen to the suggestions I receive. Let me take these suggestions as a roadmap to the freedom that recovery brings. Amen.

* * * *

Wisdom for Today   Oct 22

Each of us in the program has problems within our personality. These character defects are the core of our problems. Even though we stop drinking and using, these problems can continue in recovery. We can make concerted efforts to rid ourselves of these personality flaws, and they continue to exist deep within our being. They will continue to thrive within us until we honestly work the steps and have a spiritual experience. In the Big Book of Alcoholics Anonymous the term "spiritual experience" is defined as something that brings about personality change.

It comes through the process of surrendering our lives to God, as we understand Him. In this surrender we turn our will over. We ask Him humbly to remove our shortcomings. Then it is through obedience to His will for us and through faith that this spiritual experience will happen for us that we indeed are changed. This does not necessarily happen in one fell swoop, but is more likely to occur over time as we continue to use the steps and work the program. It does not require a vast faith or extreme God-consciousness. It simply requires that we continue to do the next right thing. In most cases the changes are gradual but continuous. It becomes clear to us that we are not the same as we were the week before or the month before. Over time the change in our personality does occur. Do I see the gradual change in what I am, my thinking, my behavior and my beliefs?

Meditations for the Heart

"Lord, to whom shall I go?" These words from the Bible remind us that we can only turn to God. Only He has the answers to the questions we have inside. Only God can relieve us of the compulsion to drink or use. Only God will bring about the changes needed in what we are and how we behave. We can find God in every place we are willing to see Him, for He is always with us. In our moments of despair, He is there. In our moments of fear, He stands ready to comfort us. In our anger, He will quench the fire that burns within. In our sadness, He will dry our tears. And in our joy, He celebrates with us. All we need do is look, and we can find Him in our midst. His Spirit is always by our side. His wisdom is always available to us. His strength is within our hearts, and He will provide us with courage. Where do I go with the burdens I still carry?

Petitions to my Higher Power
God,

You have the words that I need to hear. You share these words through others with whom I share my burdens. You share Your words deep within my conscience. Your strength is always available to me. Give me this day the openness to see You at work in my life. Let me hear the words that my heart and mind need for this day. Walk with me always.
Amen.

* * * *

Wisdom for Today   Oct 23
For most of us the spiritual experience we talk about is not from a brilliant flash of light that causes a profound change in our personality; rather it comes to us through a process of education. This was certainly the case for me. As I walked the path of recovery, I began learning about my disease and how it affected my thinking, my emotions, my perceptions of the world, my beliefs, and most of all my behavior. I learned about this through listening to countless people at meetings as they shared their stories. I learned about this through listening to my sponsor. I learned through reading program literature. I learned in ways that I cannot even fully describe.

I would recount things that happened to me in my recovery journey, and my sponsor would always ask me, "How do you think that happened?" He continually pointed out examples of how a Higher Power was working in my life and in the lives of others I met at meetings. Others at meetings began to point out how I had changed even before I could see the changes in myself. Over and over again I was inundated with new information and provided with example after example of how God was doing for me what I could not do for myself. Eventually I could begin to see the differences in how I viewed the world. I could feel the differences in my emotional responses to life. I could see that I was indeed thinking differently. Am I beginning to see the difference in my life because of this spiritual experience?

Meditations for the Heart

There is gladness in your heart when you are in God's service. As addicts and alcoholics, none of us can consider any job beneath us. For any job that is in service to God is a good one. Everyday we interact with other people. It is important for us to see all people as an opportunity for service. We never really know whom our Higher Power may bring into our life. He may bring them into our lives so that we can be of service to them. Who are we to turn down this opportunity? He may bring these people into our life to teach us more about life or more about recovery. We should be open to learning from each of these experiences. We do not know what God's plan for us may be. All we know is that if we do what our Higher Power wants, then we will be rewarded with gladness in our heart. Am I willing to serve others?

Petitions to my Higher Power

God,

Today let me be open to learning the lessons You want me to learn. Help me to continue to grow along spiritual lines. Let me stand ready to serve in any way that I am asked. Let me find a humble, courageous and glad heart. Amen.

*   *   *   *

Wisdom for Today   Oct 24

As we grow in our recovery, we begin to realize that there is much to change about ourselves. Most of us will go through the struggle of attempting to change who we are and how we behave through a process of self-discipline. We may even find that in part we are successful at this. But if we are honest with ourselves, we will soon admit that there are parts of who we are that just don't want to change, even with our best efforts. This can often be very frustrating and can make us even begin to question our own resolve. We go back again and again to the steps trying in vain to change these parts of ourselves.

Here again we find some success, but some pieces of our personality are just too stubborn. The only way to create permanent change is through a spiritual experience. Talk with those that have had this experience, and they will all say that they have found a Power greater that has brought about change in their lives. This is central to the process of change. We ask His help in making the changes that we so need to make. We work to become willing to follow the path laid before us. We honestly surrender and follow His lead. What often occurs is that we find that change has been waiting for us all along. What takes only a matter of a short time could not have been accomplished through years of self-discipline. Have I asked God to help me in the changes I need to make?

Meditations for the Heart

God's ability to help us is infinite. However, our willingness to accept His help is directly proportional to our understanding and acceptance of His grace. When we go about trying to run the show our way, we accomplish little. When we open our hearts and minds to His love and simply accept that He can indeed accomplish for us what we could not do for ourselves, we begin to understand His grace. God is indeed willing to help us always, but we too often return to our bull-headed ways of attempting to do it our way. It is up to us to get out of the way and let God, as we understand Him, do for us as He wishes to do. In getting out of the way, we accept His power as greater than our own. It is an act of faith. Here is often our biggest stumbling block. Do I have faith in His grace?

Petitions to my Higher Power

God,

I begin this new day in Your presence. Give me willingness this day to get out of the way and let You lead me to a new place. Help me to make the changes I still need to make in my life. Let me rely on Your Power this day and not my own. Give me the courage to trust You more today than I did in the past. Let this faith continue to grow in me daily.

Amen.

* * * *

Wisdom for Today *Oct 25*

Throughout our recovery process it is important continually to make the program a part of us. We do this through attending meetings, talking with our sponsors and by reading and studying program literature. In each of these ways we improve our knowledge of the program. We can never have too much knowledge of the program. The more we understand, the better our chances. However, this knowledge is only of value to us if we put it into action. We must take this knowledge and live it. Listening to others and reading does help us prepare to think the program. It helps us to know what to do next. It helps us discern the truth.

Working the program becomes second nature to us only when we make the program a part of us. It needs to become a natural instinct and a habit if we are to *"intuitively know how to handle situations which used to baffle us."* (*Alcoholics Anonymous,* Fourth Edition. Page 84) This only happens with study and practice. Therefore, we can never learn enough. We read and reread passages in the Big Book. We study our meditation books, and we study the Twelve Steps. We attend program workshops to increase our knowledge. It may be that we do not truly understand what we read or hear until the fourth, seventh, or even twentieth time we study it. Am I continually working to improve my understanding and living of the program?

Meditations for the Heart

In order to share fully the experience of recovery, we must immerse ourselves in it. We work to accept the discipline of the structure that the program offers. It is in this structure that we find the answers to the questions we ask. We learn to practice what we know to be true. In this practice of the program, we find that the program takes on new meaning. As the meaning of the program changes for us, we also change. We gain a deeper understanding and appreciation of what the program really means for us. As we rely more and more on the principles of the program, our faith is increased. As our faith increases, we find that our fears are relieved. We find that we begin to hope for more than simple sobriety, but we hope to find a way of living life with an inner sense of security and peace. Am I willing to immerse myself in the program?

Petitions to my Higher Power

God,

Today let the sunlight of the program shine on me. Let me carry this sunshine into all that I do. Let me take time today to study further this program and deepen my understanding of it. Open new doors for me, and let me not fear walking through them. Let me never close the doors that lead to a greater knowledge of the program.

Amen.

* * * *

Wisdom for Today

Oct 26

As we become more established in the program and integrate the program into our lives, we discover the necessity to maintain balance. We find that we need to remain focused on our goal of recovery, but we also need to spend time paying attention to everything else in our lives. There is a temptation for many of us to just invest our time and energy into the program and ignore all the rest. This happens for many reasons. For some of us, we unconsciously use the program to hide from our other responsibilities. For some of us, we do this simply because we are still afraid of dealing with life on life's terms. For others, we find the camaraderie of the fellowship so inviting that we see it as a way to get all of our intimacy needs met. None of these reasons is healthy for our recovery.

Recovery is about more than simple abstinence. It is about learning to live again, and we cannot do this if we are avoiding life. Our number one priority is to remain clean and sober, but we should not use this to avoid our other responsibilities. Each of us has other responsibilities in our life. We have family, occupational, financial, health and personal responsibilities that exist outside of the meetings. We need to carry the program into each of these areas of our life and apply the principles of the program to all that we do. Here is where we practice the principles. We crawled out of the mire of addiction, and we now must learn to walk through life. Walking requires that we learn balance. Have I learned to balance program and life's responsibilities?

Meditations for the Heart

Where do I find the strength I require to find balance and accept the responsibilities I have? It is easy to become overwhelmed if we rely only on our strength. To find the strength necessary for the tasks at hand, we learn to rely on our Higher Power as the resource of our strength. We turn to God daily and ask for His ceaseless supply of strength to be added to our own. We tap into this supply of strength each day and go about doing what God wants us to do in each area of our life. As long as we rely on His strength, we find that we are able to accomplish much. When we run low, we simply return to our Higher Power and ask that our energy be renewed. God will indeed refuel our engines. Here we find the strength we seek and are filled with newness of spirit. Do I seek out His strength each day?

Petitions to my Higher Power

God,

Sometimes I feel like I am juggling too much. Help me this day to set my priorities in the way that You would want me to. Help me to remain balanced in my walk through life. Give me the strength and energy I need for this day. Let me not use the program as a place to hide from my responsibilities, rather let me use the program as a guide to be more responsible with the activities of my life. Amen.

* * * *

The program depends on us as much as we depend on the program. It works on the principle of service. Everything within the program itself happens through the service of others. Whether it is the individual who arrives early to setup and make coffee, the meeting chairperson, volunteering to serve on a committee, speaking at a meeting or workshop or doing Twelve Step work, the program depends on volunteers to keep going and growing. It is through the willingness to volunteer service that the program works.

As we walk through the recovery process, each of us will be given opportunities to serve. The program depends on our willingness to say yes to these opportunities. This willingness on our part is what makes the program effective. This service work is equally important for us, as we find that in saying yes to the program, we are also helping ourselves. In volunteering we help to carry the program, and the program in turn helps to carry us. Do I do my part to carry the load? Am I willing to do something concrete to help the program? Will I volunteer to give service to others? These are all questions we need to ask ourselves. By doing our part, we help to keep the program healthy; and in turn the program keeps us healthy. Am I doing my part to grow in and with the program?

Meditations for the Heart

It is in our times of weakness and pain that we perhaps need to find God more than any other. It is in these times that He is most available to us. In these troubling times, we reach out in quiet desperation; and we find His quiet strength – a strength that passes our understanding. It is in these tough times that we struggle most with our daily routine, structure and responsibilities. Yet it is in these times that we rely on His quiet strength to lead us and guide us. This quiet strength will renew our courage for the day. This quiet strength will feed us in compassion and will provide us with the energy that we need. It will quiet our unrest and bring us inner peace. This quiet strength is always available to us; all we need do is accept it into our lives. This supply of quiet strength is ceaseless and will never run out. In it we can be filled with whatever we need for the tasks of the day. Do I seek His quiet strength in all that I do?

Petitions to my Higher Power

God,

You do not scream from some mountaintop, but instead You come to me in quiet strength. Help me to be aware of this quiet strength in my day today. Open my eyes this day to the opportunities to give back to the program; for this service will strengthen the program, and it will strengthen me. Help me to have a mindset to say yes to these opportunities and to carry my share of the load.

Amen.

*   *   *   *

Wisdom for Today   Oct 28

Early in my recovery process, I was overly self-conscious. I feared what others might think if I spoke. I worried about making the right impression. I was fearful about what might happen if I shared my story. I was so worried about what others might think, say or do that I simply chose to say nothing. I kept my comments inside. What was really going on was a form of self-centered pride. I was putting my image first. What would happen if people really knew me? What would happen if others could see my inner brokenness? This pride kept me closed in and made it impossible for me to make real connections with others in the program.

I would sit in meetings and rehearse in my mind my comments, trying to look good to others. There was little that was genuine or real in what I shared. This certainly was not helping me and was of no benefit to others. I was holding back because I was afraid I would not make the right impression. Night after night I would go to a meeting. I listened to others who shared from their hearts. What they shared was real and filled with truth. Eventually I began to share what was really going on inside – my thoughts, my feelings, and my beliefs. As I got more honest and let go of my self-centered pride, I began to hear others say they could really relate to what I shared. I began to gain new insights and a healthier perspective on life. Taking the risk of honest self-disclosure rather than giving a rehearsed speech began to set me free. Am I still attempting to manage other people's impressions of me?

Meditations for the Heart

"Seek ye first the kingdom of God." This is most important for the addict or alcoholic. When I seek to build my own kingdom, rather than seek to belong to His kingdom, my life gets turned upside down. When I put my will before God's will, I get all out of sorts. My irritability increases, as things don't go my way. I become more and more cynical. My frustration increases the more that my kingdom does not turn out as I wish. In seeking His kingdom, I find an inner peace and serenity. I feel comforted to know that in His kingdom for me all is good. When I follow His will, I can trust that I will stay securely on the path of recovery. My thinking and will can lead me off this path, so I seek His wisdom and direction. Even when I am struggling with life's problems, when I keep His kingdom in my heart, I know that I will end up where I need to be. Do I seek His kingdom for my life?

Petitions to my Higher Power
God,

Free me from the bondage of self-centered pride. Help me to let go of the fear and need to control others' impressions. Grant that I may embrace Your kingdom in my heart and walk closely with You as I walk through this day. Let me find freedom in Your truth.
Amen.

* * * *

Wisdom for Today   Oct 29
I remember the first time I was asked to share my story at a meeting. I was absolutely terrified. I recalled all those speech classes in high school and how nervous I was. When my sponsor asked me to speak at an open meeting, I really wanted to say no; but the word "sure" came out of my mouth. In the day and a half before I was to speak, I sat and thought about what I would say. I really didn't think I had much to offer and was sure that I would make a fool of myself. I was sick to my stomach hours before the meeting. I called my sponsor and was going to beg out of the responsibility. My sponsor listened to me for a moment and then cut me off. "Talk to your HP, and I will see you at the meeting," he said.

So I did talk to God, and I asked for the words I needed to say. I asked for the strength and the courage I needed to make it through the next few hours. The meeting began in its usual way, and then I was introduced. My mouth was dry, and I could not swallow. I could feel beads of sweat on my forehead. I introduced myself, and my mind went blank. All the thoughts I had for my talk left my mind. I don't recall much of the rest that I said that night, but I stood there for nearly forty-five minutes sharing. After the meeting many friends in the program and even some I did not recognize came up to me and made statements about how genuine my talk was and how it had been from my heart. Some shared how much it had helped them. No, I don't remember what I shared, but I learned a lot about how God would help me and that sharing honestly from the heart was all I needed to do. When I speak at meetings are my comments from the heart?

Meditations for the Heart
In the Lord's Prayer there is a line that goes, "Thy will be done." This is a most important line in this prayer for an alcoholic or an addict. My

understanding of this line in this prayer has changed dramatically over time. At first, these were words that I simply said but really did not pay much attention to them. Over time I began to pay more attention to these words. The steps really forced me to look at them closer. There were times that I really appreciated these words, and there have been times that I have rebelled against these same words. In those times of rebellion, I simply wanted to be back in charge; I wanted to run the show again. Other times when I really appreciated these words, it became clear to me that I had no idea what I was doing and I needed help. As I have grown in recovery I have repeated these words often. Over time I have worked hard to grow in the acceptance of these words. When I have honestly tried to do His will and humbly accepted the results, I have found myself to be happier, at peace and secure in my recovery. Do I seek to do God's will in all that I do?

Petitions to my Higher Power
God,

This day is just beginning, and I know that I must start this day with Your will being first on my list. Give me the courage and the strength I need this day to follow where You lead me. Let me seek this day to be honest, open and willing to move forward in the direction You lead me. Let me seek to follow You in all areas of my life this day.
Amen.

* * * *

Wisdom for Today   Oct 30
When I am sitting in a meeting, I look around at the myriad of faces. I see people from all walks of life. There are professionals, blue-collar workers, housewives, those that are wealthy and those that are penniless. This disease surely shows no bias in whom it attacks. But the real question is how I view these people sitting in the room with me. Do I pass judgment on them because of how they look or what they say? Do I sit and think that they don't have a chance because they do not think the right way or do not appear genuine in their efforts to get clean and sober? Do I listen intently to their every word trying to determine if they are being honest? Am I skeptical of others at meetings?

If I feel I can judge another and his or her attempt to get clean and sober, then I am hurting that person. And in hurting that person I am also hurting myself. Before I could ever point a finger at others, I must first point the finger at myself. I need to ask myself these same questions about myself. Certainly if I am busy judging others, then I am being arrogant; for I am no different and fully capable of any self-delusion that others might be capable of. Anyone sitting in the meeting will be able to hear my criticism of others and will see that I am not being genuine in my attempt to help others. In judging others, I also am not being genuine in an attempt to help myself. I must check this attitude of criticism and judgment at the door. I can ill afford to isolate others or myself from the program. Do I work to accept all people as my equal in meetings?

Meditations for the Heart

None of us is capable of coming to God by our own free will. In order to come to a relationship with a Higher Power, we all must be Spirit led. We can only open our hearts and minds to this Spirit and trust that He will lead us to this relationship with God. Looking back at my own life, I know I did not open the doors to this relationship by myself. For that matter, I would not have even known where to look for the doors. I started this journey in childhood, and addiction quickly led me down a different path. I lost all contact with a Power greater than myself. This disease beat me, and I finally gave up in defeat. I got back on track by simply bringing my body to meetings. In doing this and by working the steps, I came to believe again. Throughout the recovery process, the Spirit will lead us to new doors and help us to expand our understanding, our faith and our relationship with this Power Greater. Do I open my heart and mind to this spiritual journey?

Petitions to my Higher Power

God,

Let me stand beside my brothers and sisters in this program of recovery as an equal. Do not let me give rise to personal judgment or criticism of others. Instead let me speak to them words from my heart and about my experiences. Let me share what has worked, as well as those things that did not. Let me not fear opening myself to them, and give me an accepting heart. Let me follow the light of Your Spirit today.

Amen.

* * * *

Wisdom for Today   Oct 31

Each of us has separate and unique gifts for service in the program. It is the combination of all of these gifts among the membership that makes the program work. All of these gifts for service work are needed within the fellowship, and all are important. For some the gift is the willingness to come in early, make coffee and greet others. For others it is the gift of running a meeting with purpose. For still others the gift is being able to reach out to the newcomer and offer encouragement and direction. Still others find that they are good at sponsoring others. And there are those that take on the role of GSR or other leadership roles within the program. It does not matter if all you do is offer to sweep the floor after the meeting; every job for which you volunteer is equally important. It is all needed.

Each of us has been blessed with a special gift to serve. All we need do is discover what it is and then go about providing this service. Some of us do not want to look for these gifts or offer our time to serve for the better good of the program. Yet if we are working a good program, the steps will point us in the direction of service work. We cannot allow laziness, arrogance or any other character defects to stand in the way of our willingness to serve. Instead each of us needs to seek out these opportunities and trust that the Spirit will guide us to use our gifts. We may be surprised by what we learn through these experiences. We may find out things about ourselves we had no idea were there. Remember that your willingness and the Spirit are all that is needed. Am I willing to give of my time?

Meditations for the Heart

"He shall preserve your coming in and your going out from this day forth..." All that we do in this life is guided by His hand. God will lead us as we move through our days. As we reach out to others for help, He is there with us. As we share our gifts in the program, He is with us. As we share our experience, strength and hope with someone who is suffering, He is there to guide our words. In our own struggles He is with us each hour. In our rebellion and unwillingness He stands with us, and He opens His arms to welcome us back time and time again. Regardless of where the path of recovery leads us, He is with us each step of the way. His constancy is forever. His love for us is always. He will shine brightly in our darkest times, and He will laugh with us in our joy. Do I know this Spirit guides my every movement?

Petitions to my Higher Power

God,

Sometimes I wonder what it is You want me to do next. Grant me a heart and mind that will trust that the path You lay before me is where You want me to be. Recovery has had its ups and downs; but when I look back, I can see that You were always there for me. Increase my awareness of this in my day today. Open me to the gifts of service, and lead me with Your wisdom, strength and love.

Amen.

* * * *

As I got further into my recovery and had made my first trip through the steps, I found that I had amassed a significant amount of knowledge about recovery and what worked and what didn't. But I still had more lessons to learn. I had been chairing meetings and giving leads for quite a while. I began to feel important in the program. This self-importance was made up of arrogance and pride. I began to feel like my opinion was more important than others. I began to make assumptions about what others needed from me. I began to get all wrapped up in the limelight of success. These attitudes began to get in the way of what was really important, and fortunately my sponsor could see me when I could not see myself.

One night after a meeting where I had taken a dominant role, my sponsor asked me to go for a walk. This request was unusual, but I agreed. We walked for quite a ways, and my sponsor was quiet the whole time. I began to get annoyed and wondered why he had asked me to walk with him. Finally, I couldn't stand his silence anymore and blurted out, "What is this all about?" He turned to me and gave me a look that stopped me in my tracks. "Do you know that AA will get along just fine without you?" he said. I couldn't believe what I was hearing, but I knew my sponsor well enough to know he was up to something. He went on to point out my self-important attitudes. He explained that my pride was actually hurting the group, as I was not allowing newer members the opportunity to grow because I was hogging the limelight. I didn't like what I heard that night, but I knew my sponsor was right. Months later he told me that his sponsor had given him the same speech. Do I know that the program is more essential than one individual?

Mediations for the Heart

Humility in the program is so very important. We all have things to offer, but I had to learn that I did not need to be the only one offering wisdom to others. I still had wisdom to learn. Wisdom is something that is grown over time and through experience. In this situation I still had more growing to do. Today I hope that I never stop growing and that I always remain open to learning from others. Humility however is not something that is grown. It is a gift that is given to us by the Spirit. This gift along with all the other gifts and promises of the program provide us not only with gratitude, but also a sense of humility. It is in recognizing this gift that we also recognize that we are not God. We recognize that the gift comes from the Spirit and that through this gift of humility, we can fully accept ourselves for whom and what we are. It is in this sense of humility that we realize that we are His children, and we find His peace. Do I let anything get in the way of accepting the gift of humility?

Petitions to my Higher Power
God,

Help me to check my arrogance, pride and self-importance each day. Let me not place roadblocks in the way of accepting Your gift of a humble heart. Let me share my experience, strength and hope with others in equal proportion to my willingness to learn from others' experience, strength and hope. Guide me in my steps along the path of recovery today, for You alone know where I am to be this day.

Amen.

* * * *

Wisdom for Today   *Nov 2*

When I look back at my days of active addiction to alcohol and drugs, it is clear that the primary thing that motivated my thinking, behavior and choices was selfishness. I got high because I wanted to, and I got drunk because I wanted to. It was all about me. I really didn't stop to think about others; my drinking and drugging always came first. It didn't matter that it was important to others that I be responsible for my actions and choices. It didn't matter what consequences I might experience because of my choices or behavior. It didn't matter whom I hurt, including myself. What did matter was satisfying my compulsion to drink and get high.

Even when I was hitting bottom, I still thought about my desire to get high before I thought about others or myself. I really didn't care anymore about anything except my own selfish needs. In recovery I have learned a new way of living my life. Learning this new way of living was not something I could have done on my own. It has happened only because my Higher Power has done something for me that I could not do for myself. He has freed me from the selfishness that controlled my life. I am not bothered by the compulsion that drove me to an insane way of living. I can now get outside of my own selfish desires and seek to follow the path that the program has set before me. I can use each of the steps and the principles of the program to deal with any situation that happens in my life. I do not do this perfectly, but I am making progress. I have not yet reached the goal, but I am on the way that leads to it. Do I let selfishness come back into my life?

Meditations for the Heart

One step at a time, putting one foot in front of the other, I have followed the lead of my Higher Power to a new place. This new place is about change, and change is not always easy. In fact, I am often my own worst enemy. It does

335

not matter if things are going well or things in my life are going badly. There is no situation in my life I can't make worse. In success I can get arrogant and over-confidant. In failure I can get self-destructive and want to just give up. Change is a part of life. I have a choice to accept that God will walk with me through all changes I face, or I can go back to dealing with life on my own terms. The longer I am in recovery the more natural it feels to let go and let God. It becomes second nature to seek after His will for me and ask for the power I need to carry out His will. If I turn to my Higher Power in all that I face, both the good times as well as the bad, I can be confident that He will lead me to where it is that I am supposed to be. Have I made a decision to turn my life over?

Petitions to my Higher Power
God,

Keep me on the path of recovery today. Help me to seek You out in all that I do. Let me be of service to Your will as I walk through this day. Let me not even consider my own selfish ways, but instead help me to use the principles of the program to serve as my guide today. Help not only me but also all addicts and alcoholics who turn to You today for help and guidance. Amen.

* * * *

Wisdom for Today   Nov 3

Perhaps one of the most difficult lessons I had to learn in recovery "was not to put all my eggs in one basket." Relatively early in the recovery process, my sponsor was talking with me and said, "I am not the one to put your faith in." I assumed that he meant that I was to put my faith only in my Higher Power, but this is not what he was referring to. He went on to tell me about his relationship with his first sponsor. I had never even asked him about his relationship with his sponsor, I guess I was still too wrapped up in my own world, so that I never thought to inquire. My sponsor went on to tell me that when his first sponsor relapsed, he also relapsed. I had not known that my sponsor ever had relapsed until that night. He talked at length about how his first sponsor got drunk and was killed in a car accident. Needless to say, I was blown away by this story.

I thought about it for many hours after our talk. It was clear that my sponsor was teaching me again. He was sharing his experience and how he had relied so much on his sponsor to keep him clean and sober, that when the worst happened, he fell down himself. My sponsor had twenty years under his belt when he shared this story with me. I couldn't believe he was telling me not to have faith in him. This really shook me, but I also knew that my sponsor was right. If I relied on him alone and his recovery fell apart, what would happen to me? We had several more discussions about this topic, and he continued to share why it was so important to rely on the group, the program and on God and not just one person. I continued to rely extensively on my sponsor until he died. Fortunately, he taught me to rely on more than just on him. Can I afford to set myself up to fall down because I put all my eggs in one basket?

Meditations for the Heart

Each of us in the program has our own set of "clay feet." We all have our weaknesses and vulnerabilities. But the Big Book clearly states, "There is One who has all power; may you find Him now." (*Alcoholics Anonymous, Fourth Edition*, Page 59) We are indeed weak, but He is strong. We can always turn to God. He hears us in our times of need. He will provide us with His strength when we are weak. All we need do is ask for His help. God will stand beside us in our times of struggle, sorrow and failure. He will lead us beyond these times to a place of joy and victory. None of us needs to feel bad about our weaknesses. It is in our weakness that we are perhaps most open to His help and intervention. We learn from our weaknesses, just as we learn from our strengths. We learn that God will strengthen our clay feet and help us to walk the path of recovery. Do I put my trust in the One who has all power?

Petitions to my Higher Power
God,

In my weakness, I come before You this morning. Strengthen me for this day. Help me to follow the path on which You lead me. Give me the wisdom to rely not only on You, but also on the program and the fellowship. For it is through the steps and through these fellow members of the program that I am taught the lessons of recovery. Give me willingness to reach out to others when I am weak.
Amen.

* * * *

Wisdom for Today   Nov 4
The program is growing all the time. New groups get started every day. But what happens when members of a group split off and begin a new group. What is my attitude when members of a group that I attend leave to start a new meeting? Do I wish them well and encourage them as they head out the door to start a new group? Or am I angry that they have disrupted the group

that I attend? Do I get frustrated when the group I am in shrinks in size? Do I have hard feelings towards the members that leave the group, or do I support them? This is the reality of the program: we all experience changing schedules and changing needs. As this occurs, it is not uncommon for factions of a group to split off and begin a new meeting.

My attitude regarding change is essential to how well I will accept, support and encourage this change. If I perceive this change as something unwanted and not positive, I will likely complain, judge and possibly even work to undermine the change. If, however, I perceive this change as something good for the growth of the program and support other members seeking to meet their needs, I am more likely to give my blessing and support. I am more likely to visit this new group and support it through my involvement. This is how the program grows. This is what makes meetings more available to others in need. Do I support the growth of the program? Do I see this as positive?

Meditations for the Heart

Prayer is our way of communicating with our Higher Power. In prayer we both reach out, and we become receptive. Prayer is something we need to do often. We need to pray and pray until we find serenity in a relationship with God, as we understand Him. It is in this manner of communication that we find many needed things. In prayer we can find wisdom and knowledge of His will for our lives. It is in prayer that we can find hope and strength. In this relationship we find courage for each day – the courage to stay clean and sober, the courage for change and the courage to be honest. In prayer we are able to unload our burdens, and we are able to find rest. It is in prayer that we can find healing of our brokenness. Our resentments and fears can be quieted. Most of all, we find that we are not alone. Here we find communion with His Spirit, and we find acceptance. Do I pray often?

Petitions to my Higher Power

God,

Today I need only You to be present in my life. I need Your presence to guide me on the pathway of recovery. Give me this day an open mind, an accepting heart and Your peace. Let me remember to support the program, its growth and its changes, just as the program supports me and helps me to grow and change. Amen.

* * * *

Wisdom for Today   Nov 5

How willing am I to sit in a meeting and listen to the same things over and over again? All of us who have stuck with the program have been to hundreds of meetings on each of the steps. We have heard story after story, some of which are long winded and others that seem to go into great detail regarding the history of addiction. We have heard comment after comment on what works and what does not. We have sat through meetings also and felt bored. If it is simply repetition and boredom that rings out in meetings, why do we keep coming back?

Well, each of us in the program needs to remember that we are not the most important person at a meeting. We all need to find patience and tolerance for others. We need to let go of our judgmental attitudes. We need to realize that when others are sharing, they are doing this for their own good. To spill out our personal history and share our ideas and discuss our views is something we all need to do. All persons at a meeting are there for themselves and their recovery. They are not there only to be of help to me. When they share their stories, ideas and concepts, we need to realize that in some way God is encouraging them. Perhaps sharing is helping them in some way. Perhaps sharing is helping someone else in the room. Meetings are not always comfortable to sit through; yet the one thing we all need to remember is that the program is more important than we are. Am I willing to be tolerant and patient in meetings? Do I put the strength of the program before my own personal needs?

Meditations for the Heart

God is the picture of unity in this life. He works to draw us all closer to Himself. He wants to be in healthy relationships with mankind in general. He also wants us to be in relationship with each other. In the program we talk of the need for the unity of the group being central to a group's success. We talk about the need for groups to be in unity with each other. This unity is of utmost importance to the survival of the program, which in turn is vital to our own survival. This unity would not be possible without the guidance of the Spirit. It also would not be possible without our personal effort. Each of us must work to insure this unity. We do this by welcoming each newcomer into the group. We do this through practicing patience and tolerance. We accomplish this unity by willingness to help each other and a willingness to put the group needs before our own needs. Do I work to support the unity of the group?

Petitions to my Higher Power

God,

I do not know where the path I am on will lead me today, but I do know that Your guidance is necessary. Let me seek to remain in unity with You and with the program. Teach me this day to be tolerant and patient with others

339

in the program. Help me to understand that my well-being is dependent on the program's well-being.
Amen.

* * * *

Wisdom for Today   *Nov 6*

In the program we hear others talk and say things like, "You can't keep it, unless you give it away." This statement in a nutshell outlines our obligation to the program itself. The program certainly gives us much – our sobriety, our life, our sanity and much more are returned to us in the program. If we hope to hold on to these things and gain the other rewards from the program, then we need to give back to it. Some seem to think they are only involved in the program to get what they can and leave. Because they do not give back to the program, they never find the real gifts that come with working the steps and giving back to the program. Some find it difficult to hang on to the basics that happen in recovery, and others end up losing everything altogether.

It is only when we develop a deep debt of gratitude to the program and the fellowship that we begin to take our obligation to give back seriously. In giving back, we share our experience, strength and hope. We share, and we gain a healthy sense of pride to be a part of something so wonderful. In being a part of the fellowship and giving back what we have learned, we experience what it means to be a part of the miracle. The marvelous things that we experience as we see others making the program a part of their lives in some small way because of what we share are a true blessing. Something wonderful happens inside of us when we are a part of the great work of this program. Do I feel a strong sense of obligation to give back what I have been given?

Meditations for the Heart

When I was actively drinking and using drugs, it was not just the emptiness inside that was so painful. It was also the fact that I knew I was not right on the inside. My heart and my mind were not in the right place, and as a result I was not right. In the program we have the opportunity to get right on the inside again. For some of us it gives us the opportunity to get right on the inside for the first time in our lives. The changes I needed to make had to begin on the inside. I had to get in my right mind, and I had to get my heart in the right place if I ever was to be right with the world. Regardless of what we may know when we walk into the program, we all have needed to make changes on the inside. Some of the wrongs we have committed in our addiction, we may never be able to right. However, we can always look to the inside and find and correct what is broken there. We can learn not only to do the next right thing, but also we can learn to be right on the inside. Am I working on being right on the inside?

Petitions to my Higher Power
God,

Today help me to seek opportunities to fulfill my obligations to the program. Lead me in the way of a grateful heart. Help me to seek Your will in all that I do. Let me start on the inside and work to expand my gratitude to giving to others and the program. Let me listen to Your voice as I walk through this day
Amen.

* * * *

Wisdom for Today   *Nov 7*
In fulfilling our obligation to give back to the program, we also receive many benefits. Sharing my experience, strength and hope have really forced me to learn more and more about the program. As I share with others in the program, I am continually confronted with new questions – questions for which I do not immediately have answers. This in turn motivates me to find these answers, not just because I want to help others, but because it also helps me when I find these answers. Someday I may need these answers for myself. Frequently when asked a question, I need to go back to the AA Big Book or the Twelve and Twelve and reread sections to remind myself what the program teaches. It has had me go back to my sponsor to have long discussions on certain topics. It has increased my desire to learn more. It has increased my willingness to change the things I can.

When I don't have the answers and then discover them through researching program literature or talking with others, I find I am stronger. I go back to the person who originally asked me the question and share what I have learned and how I came to know what I have learned. They are always grateful, and we may talk at length about this information. New connections are formed, and my circle of recovery grows larger and stronger. I learn more from hearing others' viewpoints, frustrations and triumphs. It is these types of interactions that are really at the heart of the program – one alcoholic or addict sharing with another. I am helped and so is the other person. I am glad that I don't know everything about the program. These types of interactions keep me growing. Am I willing to learn the answers I do not know?

Meditations for the Heart
For a long time, I did not understand why I needed to keep going to meetings and reading program materials. I thought that eventually I would know enough to get through life without having to continue my connections in the program. Fortunately, God in His wisdom knows that I will always

341

need to keep learning and growing in my recovery. He sees to it that I face new and different situations in my life that keep bringing me back to the tables of the program. Even when I have a good understanding of the principles of the program, I am faced with new situations in my life that cause me to apply these principles in new and different ways. The word "powerless" for me has had to be applied to many different events and situations in my life. I have had to learn to use the steps, not just with my addiction, but also with life. Being able to share these experiences with others has been good for me because I in turn have my beliefs strengthened and my program broadened. Do I know I need to keep growing?

Petitions to my Higher Power
God,

Let me begin this day as an open book where You write the words. Let me read the words You inscribe and learn from them how to live my life. Let me always be open to new growth. Help me to expand my knowledge of the program and teach me to use what I have learned. Keep me open to sharing from my experience, so that others may benefit, and I in turn learn more. Amen.

* * * *

Wisdom for Today   Nov 8
In sharing with others, I have discovered much about myself. I have been able to uncover many of the things that make me tick. I have been able to discover much of what motivates me, and I have seen how many of my character defects work. This knowledge of myself has been very valuable for me in my daily interactions with others. Knowing myself and what is going on with me helps me to make better decisions in my life. Knowing myself helps me take better care of myself – physically, emotionally, mentally and spiritually. Sharing with others is like standing before a mirror that provides a true reflection of myself.

I begin to really understand how this disease of addiction has rooted itself in my life. I can see how it has the potential to affect all areas of my life. Some of the pointed questions I am asked by others force me to re-evaluate my own life and how I am working the program. In working with others, I gain a greater appreciation of my oneness with everyone else in the program. I no longer feel alone but a part of something. This helps me to have a stronger sense of belonging, and I lose my sense of uniqueness. Do I appreciate the benefits of working with others?

Meditations for the Heart

I used to be very paranoid about someone knocking on my door. I was never sure if it was the police, a debt collector or someone that I had harmed in my addiction. Recovery has changed all that, and I no longer have to live in fear. However, this does not mean that no one knocks on my door anymore. I have many friends who now knock on my door, but more important is the fact that this is the knock that occurs on my spiritual door. I could not hear this knock when I was active in my addiction, but I am now convinced it was there. Each and every day my Higher Power knocks on this door; all I need do is answer this door. He is constantly seeking me out; and when I open the door to my Higher Power, He greets me and invites me to follow Him. All I need do is listen for His knock and open the door to Him spiritually and my life is changed. Am I willing to listen for the knock on my spiritual door each day? Am I willing to follow where He will lead me?

Petitions to my Higher Power

God,

Each time I work with others, more is revealed to me about myself. Thank You for bringing me into this program and giving me the opportunity to learn more about myself. Let me listen for Your knock at my door and be open to follow You today. Help me to not only listen for Your knock, but to be a good listener in all that I do.

Amen.

* * * *

Wisdom for Today   Nov 9

Another benefit in doing service work and sharing my story has been the fact that I have become fully resigned to the need to remain totally abstinent from mood-altering chemicals. I no longer need even to entertain ideas that I can drink or use again. In my own way and through the struggles of early recovery, I have found surrender. With this comes an inner acceptance and trust that the program and God, as I understand Him, will provide me with whatever I need to face any situation in my life. No traumatic event can give me reason to return to the insanity of addiction.

No mind games are needed or accepted. I know that even if I were totally isolated from all mankind and given the opportunity to drink or use drugs, I would not need to or want to. I know that even in such isolation I still have a Higher Power, who will watch over me. Having this kind of inner peace and sharing this message with those who have not yet traveled far on the path of recovery imparts a great message of hope. When I think back to those that shared this message with me, I remember thinking that there really must be something in the steps that actually works. This has proven to be true not just for me but also for thousands and thousands of others in the program. Doing this service work and sharing my experience, strength and hope cements His hope in my life. Have I reached the point where I know that drinking or using drugs is not only not needed, but no longer desired or even an option?

Meditations for the Heart

This faith and trust that comes from honestly working the steps and using the principles is built one day at a time. I used to think that if I did the steps just right, I would have this profound experience, the light would come on, and I would be filled with the inner peace I sought. This may happen for some, but for most of us the process is more gradual. Based on one experience after another in the program and making it through one struggle after another, trust is built up. Assurance that the program works if you work it grows. Faith that the light in my life will grow brighter and brighter is attained as one gift after another is accepted from the Father of Creation. Sharing my experience only serves to reinforce this faith and trust. Inner confidence is gained, not in myself, but in the program, the fellowship and my Higher Power. Do I see my faith and trust increasing each day that I remain clean and sober?

Petitions to my Higher Power

God,

Your light has been what has shown me the way thus far. In gratitude I continue to follow this light. I am truly humbled by the events and life changes I have seen in my life and the lives of those who work these steps. Let me share this hope with those who still seek what is offered through Your grace.

Amen.

* * * *

Wisdom for Today   Nov 10

One of the other gains I have received from working with others and sharing my story has been developing the capacity to be honest. I found that when I talked with other addicts and alcoholics that I did not feel the need to hide the truth. I could be totally honest with them and did not need to worry about my self-image, nor did I have to fear reprisal. Sharing openly and honestly about my addiction as well as my struggles and victories in recovery helped me come to terms with myself. I found that I no longer needed to hide. What has been even more rewarding has been the fact that I have been able to take the new honesty into other areas of my life and into other relationships.

I cannot say that I have been able completely to rid myself of the character defect of dishonesty, as I occasionally still catch myself falling back into old behaviors; but I can say that the standard of perfection is no longer my goal. I have learned that I only need to seek progress. Through the service work I have done and continue to do, I have developed a manner of living life honestly. When I do catch myself falling back into old behaviors, I quickly go back and honestly share what I have done and get myself back on track. Even this has become easy now. None of this would have been possible without my working with others. There is just something about looking into the eyes of someone else who has crawled through the minefield of addiction that promotes the growth of honesty. Am I willing to share honestly with other addicts and alcoholics?

Meditations for the Heart

I remember when I was a little boy and my parents would leave to go out. Even though I was well cared for by whoever was watching after me, I would watch and wait for my parents to come home. When I would see the car drive up or hear the door open and see they were back, I would feel a real sense of relief. As I got older, the roles would reverse. My parents would wait up for me and breathe a sigh of relief when I came home safe. Now I sometimes imagine that this is very much what my Higher Power must have been through with me. He sat waiting and waiting, always watching for me to return. He would pray earnestly on my behalf that someday I would come back to Him. I imagine what a joyous celebration He must have had when I finally returned home. Today I celebrate also, because I know that in the program I am home. In the program I live with Him in my life everyday. Nothing could be better than being home. Have I found a home in the program?

Petitions to my Higher Power
God,

You never cease to amaze me. When I am tired, You find a way to revive and refresh my spirit. When I am angry, You find a way to calm my sprit and bring me peace. When I am sad, You find a way to make me smile again and offer me new hope. Thank You for all that You do for me in my life. Give me courage for this new day, and lead me on the pathway of honesty.
Amen.

* * * *

A great benefit that occurs as a direct result of sharing with others is the realization that we are only one among many. In my addiction I became very wrapped up in my own self-centered world. I was the king that ruled my own little universe of pain. I had no relationship with a Higher Power because I believed I was my own power. This self-deception crumbled with doing service work and helping others. The world did not revolve around me any more, and I was not the most important person in my universe. In reaching out to others, I began to gain greater understanding that I was only one of God's children. I began to understand more about the true power of this One I called God.

I began to see more and more why it was so important for all addicts and alcoholics to depend on God. I could not fix these newcomers any more than I could fix myself. I began to rely more on God and His wisdom because of my interactions with other fellow members of the program. I began to appreciate His strength, wisdom and grace more because of what I saw happening in my own life and the lives of others. Working with others and sharing my story has helped me see that I am on the way to where God is leading me. It helps me to see that we are all in His hands. Do I know that I am not the center of the universe?

Meditations for the Heart

"But for the grace of God" - This statement is repeated over and over again at meetings; but just what does this grace mean? I think for each of us it has different meanings, but what this grace is combines all of these meanings and more. This grace means that we can walk in His security and do not need to depend on anything other than His grace. This grace means protection against all that is evil for us if we simply choose to accept this gift. The world cannot hurt us if we are wrapped in this grace. Sure, each of us will have struggles that we will face and even great pains at times, but we can ultimately not be harmed by this if we walk in His grace. It is this grace that enables us to find new life. It is this grace that provides for our needs. These words are not empty for the alcoholic or addict. His grace is all. Do I meditate on His grace in my life?

Petitions to my Higher Power

God,

Without Your grace I would not be where I am in my life today. Let me be an example of Your grace to others. Give me words to help others know the security, protection, new life and freedom that Your grace brings. Let me encourage all whom I meet in the program to accept the gift that You offer. Amen.

* * * *

Wisdom for Today Nov 12

Yet another benefit that comes from working with others is learning to live in today. When talking with newcomers in the program, one forgets about their own past and also the future. You find that the focus is just in the moment. As newcomers share their fears, frustrations and despair, it becomes impossible to focus on our own issues; and we can only be with this person in that given moment. One comes to the realization that all we have is now. We help the newcomer focus on this as well. All they need do is not drink or use now. Fretting over the past only provides reasons to drink or use. Fantasizing about the future keeps us from accepting our current responsibility. Living in today is the only sane option for the addict and alcoholic.

In sharing with others I have learned to take each moment as they come. I am given choices along the way. I make these decisions for better or worse – now. Life is simply a series of "now-s." When I choose to arrive early at a meeting and make coffee, I am living in the moment of time called now. When I speak to another member of the program, I am living in the now. When I pray, I am living in the now. Working with others shows us the futility of living life in regret and in the past. Working with others shows us the disillusionment of fantasy and the future. God gives us new breath in this moment called now. This is where we find life. No one can help us understand this and live this other than another just like us. Am I living life a moment at a time?

Meditations for the Heart

"Get over yourself," my sponsor would chip at me when he grew tired of my self-centered attitude and selfish desires. The truth is that I was so full of myself that I could not even see this for a long time. I did not understand these words from my sponsor for quite a while and was so wrapped up in myself that I could not even ask him what he meant. Finally I had heard my sponsor say this one too many times and got angry enough to ask him what in the world he meant. He let me have it with both barrels. He blasted my godlike omnipotence. He pointed out my selfishness. He pointed out all the times when everything had to be about me. My ego was slapped and slapped hard. I know now that this is exactly what needed to happen. I know today that I will never fully overcome my self-centeredness. It cannot be accomplished in this life, but I have made progress in accepting my true place in the universe. I continue to battle myself and my egocentric ways. Am I working to get over myself?

Petitions to my Higher Power
God,

In my selfishness, I sometimes lose sight of my place in the universe. Help me this day to remember that I am one of many. Help me to recall that I am Your child and not the ruler of the universe. Let me strive this day to live one moment at a time – to breathe in Your goodness with each breath I take. Help me to let go of my self-centeredness each time I exhale.
Amen.

* * * *

Wisdom for Today   Nov 13
In working with others, one of the best rewards that is gained is a real and true sense of usefulness. In my active addiction I really felt like I was a useless piece of junk. There was little that I did about which I felt good. Most of what I did left me feeling empty inside. But this has not been the case with sharing with others and helping them through by sharing my own experiences in recovery. I have found myself filled with the joy that comes from knowing that something I shared has genuinely helped another. When someone comes back to me and says that something I told them actually aided them in their recovery, I feel that I have done something to help another. Nothing I know of makes one feel more useful.

These opportunities to assist others in their recovery happen in many ways. Perhaps it is simply sharing my story at a meeting. Perhaps someone will approach me after a meeting and ask for help with some specific issue. Sometimes I find out I have helped others simply through my example. This in part is why it is important for me to live the program in all that I do. Regardless of how the opportunity to assist others happens in my life, I can rest assured that I never face this alone. My Higher Power walks with me in my interactions with all whom I meet. He will guide my words. So in truth, it is God who gives me this feeling of usefulness. Have I stopped feeling like a useless piece of junk?

Meditations for the Heart
One step at a time! This is how we walk with others on the path of recovery. Often times walking these steps through the fear, or pain or anger in early recovery can be arduous steps. It is easy to walk with someone only a short distance and then go back. It is far more of a challenge for us to walk with someone the entire distance. But think back to those who have provided you with support in your own journey, and you will see that those who walked with you each step of the way provided you with what you needed most. Think

about how your Higher Power supports you. Does He not take each step with you? We must be ready to go the distance with others in need. We will know we have gone this distance when the individual offers their gratitude and moves onward in their journey with another to guide them in the next portion of their journey. Am I willing to go the whole distance?

Petitions to my Higher Power
God,

You have walked each and every step of this journey with me. Your encouragement and wisdom guided my steps. Now You have brought me to a place where I can feel of use to others. Give me the courage to walk with them the entire distance. Help me this day to remain open to Your will for me and others.

Amen.

* * * *

Wisdom for Today   Nov 14
The rewards of the program are great. Each person I talk with in the program that works the steps has described to me in his own words how the program has changed his life for the better. As I have listened to them talk, they describe how the promises of the program have come true in their lives. My life certainly has been changed and continues to change with the recovery process. My relationship with my family has been impacted, and the rewards of my relationships with my children are great. The closeness I have been able to develop with those that really matter most to me cannot be described in any other word but awesome. The changes that I have experienced in how I view myself are truly staggering. I can look at myself through eyes of forgiveness, and I can see someone that I really like.

Most of the blocks that I had in my relationship with a Higher Power have vanished. None of my relationships with family, or friends or even God is perfect; but the progress that has been made in the recovery process could not have been predicted when I first started out. The warmth and love that I experience from others is also something that I can now return. The value that these relationships have for me cannot be counted. In truth, I do not fully understand how all this has happened; but I do know that none of it would be possible if I were not clean and sober. Perhaps what has been most astounding in all of this is to see how others have responded to me and how they value having a relationship with me. Do I feel that others value their relationship with me?

Meditations for the Heart

One piece of information that I was given by a wise man that has proven to be true is this - "God's way IS the easier, softer way." I struggled with this concept for a long, long time. I found that I was frequently frustrated by my efforts to follow His will. My will always kept coming back into the equation of life, and invariably I would mess things up. I did not see this as the easier, softer way. In fact, I found following His will extremely hard. But over time I had more and more days that I could look back on and say that for the most part I had followed His path for me that particular day. I began to understand what this wise man had told me. When I was not fighting with God and trying to run the world the way I wanted it run, my days indeed were easier. When I was not hardening my heart to His will, I found that my heart was softer. I began to see that as difficult as it seemed sometimes to follow the will of my Higher Power, this truly was the easier, softer way. Am I making progress with following my Higher Power's path for me?

Petitions to my Higher Power

God,

When I look into the eyes of others with whom I am close and see the warmth and love that is there for me, I am truly amazed. This program and Your grace are solely responsible for this wonderful reward. Keep me willing to follow Your path, and give me the wisdom I need for this day. Help me to return the warmth and love that I receive and to open new doors to new relationships with those people to whom You lead me.

Amen.

* * * *

Wisdom for Today   Nov 15

Since coming into the program, my whole concept of what friendship means has changed dramatically. I thought that I was surrounded by a large group of friends when I was drinking and using drugs, but nothing could be farther from the truth. Oh, I had plenty of acquaintances, but none were truly my friends. I had party pals, and I had bar buddies, but I did not understand the concept of friendship until I had people who accepted me for who I was. I did not understand friendship until I had people who were willing to sit with me through the long and painful nights of early recovery simply to help me get through one more day.

No I didn't understand friendship until I had real friends who would be honest with me and tell me the truth about myself. I didn't understand real friendship until I understood that these individuals would stand by me, and I knew in my heart they could be trusted. In my active addiction I thought that friends were people that I could use to get what I wanted. Now friends are people I can help and who can help me in return. They have taught me everything they know about how to live a better life and to be a better person. I know that with my friends I do not need to hold back. I can simply turn to them and ask for help and know that it will be there. I also know that if they need help, I will be there for them. This is what the program has taught me. Do I now have true friends? Am I willing to be a friend in return?

Meditations for the Heart

Recovery trains us to develop virtues. Patience is but one of these. Patience is often a real struggle for many of us because we became so used to instant gratification in our addiction. One quick fix and we had everything we wanted, or so we thought. But recovery teaches us patience. We learn that we must do the work if we are to accomplish the goal. Nothing worth having comes easy, and this is true with patience as well. We learn to put off our need for immediate satisfaction and superficial reward in order to gain the real value in recovery. Slowly and methodically we take each step and thoroughly work each requirement to find the value behind the work. We learn to live in God's time and not our own. We discover that as long as we are willing to be patient, God will supply the answers we seek in His time and when we need them. Just because we want something now does not mean that we are yet ready. God knows this and will give us His answers in His time. Am I discovering what it means to be patient?

Petitions to my Higher Power

God,

Life is filled with many twists and turns, but You have provided me with friends I can rely on to help me along the way. Give me the wisdom to give back this friendship to any who need it. Let me this day practice patience and move at Your pace. Let me not rush to accomplish anything without first talking with You, God.

Amen.

* * * *

Wisdom for Today   Nov 16

I can't really say that life has fallen into place, but I can say that all the pieces are fitting together. Just like the pieces of a jigsaw puzzle, one piece after another seems to fit back together again. It was more like I was a clay pot that

351

had been dropped and shattered into a million pieces. One after another the pieces have been glued back together again. As time passed, the program has taught me how to live with inner peace. I am content with where I am in life. Even though I am far from putting all the pieces back together again, with the help of the program this once broken vessel is now useful again. I am not tossed around by events in my life like I used to be. In the past it seemed like I was just about able to fit another broken piece of my life back together again when something would happen, and I would drop the piece before it had been fit back into place.

The program has provided me with a place of rest – a quiet place for my heart and mind to concentrate on the best way to fit the broken pieces of my life back together again. One after another has successfully been fitted together again. It has been glued in place with the steps and faith in a Higher Power. What has been surprising is that my Higher Power has instructed me to put these broken pieces back together again in a way that I would not have expected. Slowly this new vessel has become a container for inner peace. Even in the midst of insanity going on all around me, I can still carry this inner peace. Do I carry peace inside of me in every situation?

Meditations for the Heart

In all of us there is an imprinting on our heart that tells us of God. It helps to explain God to us in a way that we can understand Him. This imprinting of our hearts also speaks to us in a still, small voice. When we are quiet and look within, we can access this voice and listen to the words of wisdom that it provides. We will hear reminders when they are needed. We will hear new ideas and new solutions to old problems if we listen. This small voice will talk with us and provide suggestions and course corrections when needed. This imprint also provides us with an inner light, so that we can explore those inner pits of darkness without fear. We are able to access this inner light to brighten our days. We are able to access this inner light to shine on the paths of others in our lives. Here is where inner peace resides. Each of us can access this inner place with only two words - "Dear God." Am I praying to God as I understand Him?

Petitions to my Higher Power

God,

I wake this morning to find the inner peace that You provide. Let me use the steps this day to continue to put the missing pieces in place. Guide me and direct me as I move through this day. Help me use this inner light and peace to shine brightly in this new day. Thank You for keeping me clean and sober. Amen.

Wisdom for Today   *Nov 17*

Hope reigns eternal for the alcoholic or addict in recovery. To move from a place of total and absolute hopelessness to a life filled with nothing but hope is a treasured gift of the program. I do not recall exactly when I crossed the line from absolute hopelessness to a life of hope, but I am glad this happened. Living in quiet desperation is the curse of addiction. It robs us of all hope. It robs us of our dreams. It robs us of our tomorrows. As I indicated before, the program is solely responsible for me receiving the gift of hope. Maybe it was the speaker at the first open meeting I attended. Maybe it was the look in the eyes of those I met after the meeting. Maybe it was the quiet prayer I said when I got home begging God for a way out of the insanity. Maybe hope happened later, I am not sure.

But hope indeed came into my life. I was able to stay clean and sober for one day and then another. The days added up, and I could begin to see that maybe, just maybe, I could remain clean and sober one day at a time. It was not always easy; but hope for a better life, a real life kept me hanging on. I began to gain hope for repair from the damage done in my addiction. I began to have hope that perhaps I was indeed salvageable. I began to live a new and different life. Gone was the preoccupation and fear. Despair vanished. Hope was reborn inside, and it grew. Hope is reborn each and every day in the program. Despite the problems of life, I have hope each new day. This is another gift of the program. Has hope become reborn in my life?

Meditations for the Heart

The Spirit is the messenger of the prayer we lift up to our Higher Power. This messenger takes our words and delivers them even when we do not know what to say. He hears the groans of our hearts and puts into words that which we do not know how to say. We do not need fear that we will not have the right words when we talk to God. Our words are presented for us in ways we cannot understand, but God understands. He knows our needs and promises to fulfill what our heart requires. His love is eternal, and He will hold us in the palm of His hand. The Spirit lifts our prayers like incense to God. He carries them and presents them to God. He carries God's answers back to us and leads us through our days. We do not always understand what these answers are, but we can be sure that God will provide. This faith is all we need have. Do I know that God will listen to the words of my heart?

Petitions to my Higher Power

God,

Each day I open my eyes to see new hope in my life. You provide for me what I need for each and every day. This hope wraps around me and comforts me in the hard or difficult times. It causes me to celebrate in the small gains I make along the way. It provides me with new perspective and brings me new life. Send Your Spirit into my heart that He may carry my words to You this day. Keep me always in the palm of Your hand.

Amen.

* * * *

Wisdom for Today   Nov 18

Jumping into recovery is like leaping into the great unknown for many of us. In fact, this is a good thing, because it is the essence of what faith is all about. For many of us it is the birth of faith; walking into a meeting for the first time is much like jumping into something about which we know nothing. We hear people talk of things we have not heard of before. But in the middle of this confusion and nothingness, we sense there is something present which draws these people to return to meetings over and over again. We have no understanding what this presence is, but we find faith to hold onto what is said at the meeting. We hear the words spoken for the first time, "Keep coming back." We are somehow drawn to what is happening in this room, and for the first time for many of us we experiment with faith.

Often times we initially have faith in the faces we see and those that we meet in the program. But as we talk with them, we are told not to put our faith in them, but to place our hopes in the program and in a Higher Power. We risk everything by doing just this. Our whole way of living is to be changed. Our whole concept of faith will grow with these changes. We come to believe that there indeed is a presence in these rooms, a Divine Presence. We place our faith in that which we cannot see, but only sense. Over time we begin to see evidence that this faith is working for us in our lives. We place our faith in that which brings us new life. Do I risk faith in that which is a great unknown?

Meditations for the Heart

God rebuilds our lives in ways that we do not expect. He takes the broken pieces of our lives and makes us a useful vessel. We keep this vessel empty for God to fill, and He does just that. We continually empty this vessel by reaching out to help others; and in doing so, we find that God refills the vessel again and again. He fills us with His Spirit; and in doing so, we are given strength, courage and wisdom for our journey in recovery. We begin

354

to understand that the more we give, the more we are filled. Some of us have tried to keep all that we have been given. In doing this, we find that we are cut off from the supply of goodness that God wishes to fill us with. Our selfishness dries up the content of the vessel, and we again feel empty inside. It is only when we become willing to share what we have been given that our supply of His love is poured out upon us. Am I emptying my vessel of knowledge, strength and courage into the lives of those that need it most in the program?

Petitions to my Higher Power
God,

I am filled with Your Spirit and desire to give away what I have been given. Show me when and how to do this. Lead me to those that need to hear my story, and grant me the courage to let go and share freely what I have been given. Increase my faith in all that I do this day. Let me go about the tasks that You want me to complete.

Amen.

* * * *

Wisdom for Today   Nov 19
Another gift from the program we receive is the ability to love. I am not talking of the selfish passion which we had for our drugs and alcohol, rather an unselfish desire to be of help to others. I genuinely want to reach out to others and give them my best efforts. I want to do what is right for them. This ability to love others in an unselfish manner begins with an acceptance that I need to do what my Higher Power wants me to do. It comes by putting the other guy first and me last. This is the exact opposite of how I would behave in my active addiction. When I was drinking and using drugs everything was about me. I attempted to control the world and those in it for my own selfish needs. Nothing came between me and my desire to get high or wasted. I came before everything else. I didn't care whom I hurt in the process.

In recovery I have learned that I do not need to behave in this way. When I put God first, I no longer need to worry about my own selfish needs. I know I will be taken care of through His love. I am free to care about and give to others. This includes those I meet in the program, as well as my family and other friends. I am no longer concerned with my agenda, for I am out to accomplish another agenda. In recovery I am given one opportunity after another truly to love others. In giving from my heart, my agenda is lost; and I serve God's agenda. Do I do this perfectly? By no means can any of us ever accomplish this in this lifetime! All I can hope for is progress. Am I making progress in loving others?

Meditations for the Heart

Man has often dreamed of an unlimited supply of power; but with all our resources available to us, they all have limits in some way. But for the addict and alcoholic, we find a source of unlimited power in the program. As we turn our lives over, we find "One who has all Power. That one is God." (*Alcoholics Anonymous, Fourth Edition*, Page 56) His power is ceaseless. To tap into this never-ending supply of power, all we need do is ask God for His help. His strength is immediately available to us. Too many of us are blocked off from this Power. We get in the way by refusing to surrender fully to His will. We are blocked by returning to an attitude of self-reliance. We get blocked by being prideful and not being willing to ask for help. Yet, in our foolishness, we discover that the Power we seek is always there for us. We may at times turn our back on God, but He never turns His back on us. Where am I today in my walk with my Higher Power?

Petitions to my Higher Power

God,

Today as always You give me Your love. Help me this day to give this kind of love back to others I meet in my day. Let me seek to do Your will as I walk though this day. Let me tap into Your never-ending supply of power. Open my heart to others as I walk this journey of recovery.

Amen.

* * *

Wisdom for Today   Nov 20

One thing that addiction robbed me of was my ambition. I lost interest in life and had no initiative to accomplish any of the goals or dreams I once had. I lost any discipline I once had to stick with a task until I finished what I started. There was no fuel in my engine; and I sat on the side of the road waiting for life to bring good things to me, which never happened. Instead life just passed me by. All my wishing did nothing, and I couldn't seem to get going on anything except my next drink or high. I became this pathetic blob that never could initiate even the first step to get anything done.

In recovery I was able to regain this part of myself that had been lost. I again gained interest in life and wanted to accomplish something. I had ambition to accomplish new goals. Early on these goals were very simple. I simply wanted to get through the day clean and sober. I would get up in the morning and make my bed, clean myself up and make a beginning at getting through the day. Later my sponsor coached me though the Twelve Steps, and I wanted to do things like finish the repair work in my life. I became motivated spiritually to expand my conscious contact with a Higher Power. My dreams for life came back to life. Out of the ashes of addiction arose a fiery hope for a new and different agenda in life. Have I regained the discipline and energy I once lost?

Meditations for the Heart

Out of the desperate despair of addiction grew a new flower of happiness. This was not accomplished all at once, but step by step as I accomplished one task after another. I found a new joy. I discovered that real happiness does not come in a bottle or in some pill. No pile of white powder ever gave me a true sense of happiness, only a brief reprieve from the stark darkness of addiction. Real happiness and joy are not only possible in recovery, but they are the outcome of using the program and the steps one day at a time. As we walk this path called recovery, new seeds are sown. The flowers of joy and happiness do grow and blossom in our lives. We discover that it comes in the little things of life that happen each day in this journey. We learn to share this happiness and joy with other people in our lives. As our lives are rebuilt by and with a Power greater than ourselves, happiness and joy blossom fully in our lives. Do I see the seeds of happiness and joy blossoming in my life?

Petitions to my Higher Power

God,

Here is another new day with which You have blessed me, and in it I know You will grant me new energy and determination. Give me this day the discipline to finish the tasks set before me. Let me follow Your lead so that I might complete the next steps in my journey of recovery. I am grateful this day for the new happiness You have bought into my life.

Amen.

* * * *

Wisdom for Today   Nov 21

In previous days we have looked at some of the gains and rewards that come through the recovery process. Perhaps just as valuable as the gains we make are the things we lose through the process. Fear used to control much of my life and affected many of the decisions I would make in my addiction. I cannot say that all my fears are lost because of sobriety, but many of the unhealthy fears I had are now gone. I do not even know how or when I lost many of these fears, but I do remember waking up one morning and being grateful because there was nothing to fear as I walked into the day. When I was drinking and using, I found that I was always looking over my shoulder. I felt that the worse was about to happen.

This changed in recovery. I no longer had to worry about what I did or did not do the day before. I can't say whether fear lost its grip on me or if I lost my grip on fear. I just know it changed and then was gone. Today I look back at this and realize that but for the grace of God I still would be walking in fear. This is not the case. But fear was not the only thing I lost in the recovery process; and in the coming days, I will describe other things that I lost simply by staying clean and sober and using the steps. Does fear still have a grip on my life? Do I still maintain a grip on fear?

Meditations for the Heart

In times past I let people use me, and I also used them in order to get wasted. This is the nature of addiction. We allow others to walk all over us as long as it does not interfere with our getting drunk or high. Often times I would use these events as another excuse to go off the deep end. I also have to be honest and say there were just as many times, if not more, that I was the one using others for my own self-gratification. I didn't care if I had to step on someone or use them to get what I wanted. Recovery has a way of getting in the way of these behaviors. In working the program, I have learned that I do not need to let others walk all over me. I have also learned that I can't just go around using others anymore. This thing called a conscience gets in the way. How has using others or allowing myself to be used changed in recovery?

Petitions to my Higher Power
God,
As I awaken this morning, my breathing is quiet, and my thoughts are at ease. Fear is no longer intrusive or controlling in my life. I have no explanation for this except for a belief that You have removed this thing called fear from me. Let me walk into this day confident that You are always near and that I have no reason to fear. Keep me on the path of working the steps and living the program.
Amen.

* * * *

Wisdom for Today   *Nov 22*
In recovery anger and resentment have also slipped away. Those things that used to drive me up a wall and leave me hot under the collar have been

lost. The thought of seeking revenge or a way to get even have not been a part of my thinking in my recovery. This did not happen right away, but this poison is not something I wish to drink any longer. There was a time when all I did was plot and scheme on ways to act on my hidden anger and rage against the world, my friends and my family. Why did they have to judge me? Who gave them the right? How would I pay them back? These questions and others just like them tore my insides apart in the past, but they are needed no longer.

Hanging on to resentments only hurt me. I was never foolish enough to really act out my rage. Instead I turned this anger inward on my self. I found ways in recovery to let go and found that as I turned things over to God, I no longer needed to carry these burdens. Hate was not something I needed anymore; it only served to provide another excuse to drink or use. In its place I was able to look at my part in the problem. I could look at what I needed to change. In its place I discovered things like forgiveness, tolerance and understanding. As the rage departed and the resentments hushed, I found something called peace. Yes, losing the burden of anger and resentment has turned out to be a good thing. Do I continue to carry the burden of anger and resentment?

Meditations for the Heart

How I react to and treat others has changed dramatically over time. This was not so much up to me as it was up to His grace. Yes, I have done much of the footwork by working the steps, but the changes that occurred as a result of this really happened not because of what I had done, but because of my Higher Power's interventions. He has changed the way I think. He has changed the way I view life. He has changed the way I interact with others. I still am called to interact with others daily. I am still called to do the next right thing. I am still called to do His will. These choices I make, but as for the outcome of these choices, I leave that all up to God. He helps me to perceive the world in a new and different light. He helps me to think before I speak. He helps me to find new ways to solve old and difficult conflicts. His grace makes this happen in my life. Am I doing the footwork and leaving the outcome up to God?

Petitions to my Higher Power
God,

In Your wisdom You show me what is needed. When I need to look in the mirror, You provide me with someone who will reflect what they see back to me. When I need to see beyond my own thinking, You provide me with another opinion. When I need to look straight ahead, You give me a straight

and narrow path. When I need to struggle with something, You provide me with a wide berth and allow me to look at things for as long as I need do so. Continue this day to show me the way.
Amen.

* * * *

Wisdom for Today   Nov 23

Gone are the days when I beat myself up. Lost is the self-hatred. How does one go from self-loathing to actually loving self and others? When did this actually occur? Somewhere in the recovery process, I stopped doing all those things, which completely violated my values. I stopped doing that which my conscience knew was wrong. This is not to say that I still don't make mistakes. I am human. But I no longer need to destroy my life and hurt others for my own selfish gain. I no longer need to get out a big stick and beat myself over the head. I no longer have to ask myself why I was so stupid. I no longer need to walk in absolute shame.

I cannot fully explain what it is like to lose this need to hate myself and actually care again. This is the miracle called recovery. You see, recovery is not just about simple abstinence. The program teaches me so much more. I have been able to sort through the piles of "yuk" in my life and find that which is truly important. I have learned to operate within my values. I have learned to admit the mistakes I make and work to change my behavior so as not to repeat destructive patterns. I have developed a sense of right and wrong and a desire to do the next right thing. I no longer need to put myself down and abuse myself. I have learned to accept my humanity. Have I lost my self-hatred?

Meditations for the Heart

Values and virtues are things we do not often speak of, but they are of utmost importance to the recovering addict and alcoholic. Values are the things we hold dear. They define what is important and where we invest our time and energy. If I value my recovery I will invest time and energy into it. The same is true with family, a spiritual life, work, self-care and our relationships with others. Virtues on the other hand determine how we go about living our lives. The program teaches us many virtues such as honesty, courage, wisdom and many others. We discover that we do not need to live in a manner of self-deceit, dishonesty, fear and stupidity. We find that we can develop healthy values and virtues. Recovery and the steps and traditions teach us how to live. Am I developing a healthy set of values and virtues?

Petitions to my Higher Power
God,

Once again this morning I can look in the mirror. There was a time that I could not do this. I avoided looking at myself because I did not want to see what was there. I am grateful for this ability to see myself and accept myself again. Thank You for this new vision not only of who I am, but also who I can become. Help me this day to use my values as a guide for living. Teach me to use the virtues of the program in my daily life.
Amen.

* * * *

Wisdom for Today   *Nov 24*

Something else that I have lost as a result of staying clean and sober is the inability to believe in myself. I had become convinced that I was just a loser. I knew that there was no way to trust myself or my ability to make good decisions. I had no self-confidence. There was ample proof that if given the opportunity, I would find a way to screw everything up. This did not change simply because I stopped drinking and using. However, the longer I stayed clean and sober and the more I used the tools of the program, the more I was able to begin to make rational healthy choices in my life.

At first my self-confidence remained very low, but the program gave me something else to rely on. I could rely on the people I saw at meetings. I could rely on a Higher Power. I could rely on the steps. Today I still rely heavily on each of these supports, but I also have developed a healthy ability to make good decisions again. I found out that I am not a loser; I simply behaved like one when I was drinking and using drugs. I have learned that I no longer need to self-destruct and screw up my life. I can believe in myself again, and I can trust my gut. I do not rely solely on myself as this would be foolish, but I can now make an informed decision on when to trust my gut and when I need to ask for help. Am I regaining self-confidence?

Meditations for the Heart

In my addiction my gut was constantly tossing and turning. My anxiety would increase when I knew that what I was doing was wrong, but I would not listen to my gut. Instead I would listen to my disease, which talked to me in ways that were impossible to resist. "Go ahead; no one will know," it would say to me. "Just one more; it's okay; you can handle it." Addiction has many different voices and has a way of screaming louder so that I could hear no other voice. In recovery I have learned to listen to other voices - the voice of my sponsor, the voice of my Higher Power, the voice of the person sitting across from me at a meeting and the voice of my gut. When my gut begins to toss and turn now, I listen to what it has to say. It gives me the clues I need about what may be bothering me. Have I learned to listen to other voices in my recovery?

Petitions to my Higher Power
God,

Recovery has provided me with many blessings. I am truly grateful that my gut does not always toss and turn anymore. I am also grateful for the times it does, because I now know that I need to listen to what my gut is telling me. I also know that when I can't really understand what is being communicated to me, I simply need to ask for help and talk things through. Thank You for this blessing.
Amen.

*　*　*　*

Wisdom for Today   Nov 25
One thing I am very grateful to have lost in my recovery is the profound sense of inferiority I carried inside. I constantly walked around feeling like I was a loser and gave myself all kinds of self-talk messages to confirm this false belief. Day after day I would convince myself I was not good enough or talented enough. I would repeatedly tell myself not to even try something or attempt to better myself because I knew deep inside I was less than other people and didn't deserve to have a better life. My addiction seemed constantly to reinforce my own self-perception. In this state of mind it is easy to understand why it was so easy to slide into a pit of despair. I would spend days languishing in self-pity. I would avoid all responsibility and looked to blame others, including God, for my lowly status.

Recovery, being the wise teacher that it is, has changed this. I have found that I gain nothing from self-pity. I have learned to take responsibility for my own life and to be selfish with my recovery. I learned that I could quit running from life and could begin to embrace it. The program taught me about equality, and it taught me to be the best that I can be in my life. No longer do I feel like I am trapped in the prison that inferiority creates. Now I can feel positively about myself and about how I behave in my life. I am free to explore the very depths of who I am. This is the gift of the steps - to know one's self and approve of one's self. Do I know myself and like what I see?

Meditations for the Heart

Living in today is but a part of what I have learned in the program. I have also learned that it is just as important constantly to be reaching forward. I am forever reaching ahead and setting new goals for myself. Just as we move from one step to the next, we then learn that we are to practice what we have learned in all that we do. We reach out, we plan and we work toward new goals. We entrust the outcome of our efforts to our Higher Power. We develop faith that as we walk forward and reach out that God will lead us on the path to a stronger and better sobriety. We walk the walk, and He leads us on the path to a brighter tomorrow. Yes! There are struggles along the way, and there are pitfalls, but we hold onto the principles and our faith, and we find that progress occurs. Am I still reaching out while living in today?

Petitions to my Higher Power

God,

You brighten my day, and You also challenge me to keep growing. You have provided me with a unique set of tools and friends to teach me how to use them. Let me reach forward in my recovery and accept the challenges as they come. Strengthen my faith in Your presence in my life.

Amen.

* * * *

Wisdom for Today   Nov 26

I used to walk through life filled with one enormous negative attitude, but recovery has changed all that. No longer is there a big chip on my shoulder. No longer do I seek out what is negative about every situation I face. I didn't trust anyone. I thought that they all were liars and certainly were bad. I was projecting my own thoughts and feelings on to everyone I met. I looked for the ways people were two-faced and how they hid the truth about themselves, but it was really I who was hiding. Even when I went to church, I could see the hypocrisy of what people were doing, but I was the real hypocrite. This was my attitude toward life. Everything was negative; everything was bad; everything was wrong.

But I have developed a much more positive outlook in recovery. I no longer seek to be the judge and jury for the world. I don't even need to play judge with myself anymore. I am much more accepting of people and do not focus on their fallibility. I know we are all human, and we all make mistakes. I am much more forgiving than I ever was in my addiction. I try to walk into each day with a positive attitude. I seek out the good in others and in myself. I no longer perceive the world as a bad place. I see the good in the world and in God's plan for me in the world. I don't focus on what is wrong with the world, but look for the good in the world. Do I have a positive outlook now?

Meditations for the Heart

My Higher Power is my best companion. He walks with me every step I take. He is there to talk with on this journey called recovery. I know that I am working in concert with Him when I walk the path He lays before me. He does many things for me, and I do things for Him. When I reach out to others in need and offer my support or a helping hand, I work with and for my Higher Power. When I seek His guidance, strength or peace, He is right by my side and provides for my needs. What better friend could I have than this? When this relationship becomes real and close, my prayers find more and deeper meaning. I have clearer vision and can see how my prayers are indeed answered. Do I have a friend in my Higher Power?

Petitions to my Higher Power

God,

You seek me out and walk with me as I follow this path. Give me a brighter vision so that I may focus on all that is right in the world. Help me to keep a positive outlook as I walk through my days. Help me to give freely what has been given to me. Let me walk through this day knowing that You are my friend.

Amen.

* * * *

Wisdom for Today   Nov 27

I used to be so full of myself. Self-centeredness was a way of life. Today recovery has shown me how to be less self-centered. The world does not have to revolve around my desires and me. In the past all I cared about was myself and getting drunk or high. I didn't care about who I stepped on or hurt in the process. It was all about pleasure and feeding my desires. I cared more about my desires than I did anything else in my life. My family was not first. My job was not first. A relationship with God was not even in the picture. It was all about my way and control. Feeding my addiction was my priority.

Recovery has shown me a different way. It is no longer about me. Now I choose to live life the way my Higher Power wants me to lead my life. He helps me make better decisions and to value the things that are truly important. I have learned to care about others and consider their feelings. I have learned to seek out help from others, rather than rely solely on myself. Letting go of my self-centeredness has led me to a place of happiness. It has freed me from the bondage of desire. It has allowed me to walk away from isolation and into fulfilling relationships with those I care about and love. The program has taught me to care less about my self-centered desires and more about others. Have I found a way to let go of my selfish, self-centered desires?

Meditations for the Heart

Life's problems happen all the time. There is little we can do to stop this fact. Yes, we can prevent some problems from occurring, and we can even minimize the severity of other ones, but the real challenge for the alcoholic or addict is how we view our problems. We can see the difficulties in life as a roadblock or deterrent to progress, or we can see these difficulties as a test of our spiritual strength and a chance to keep growing. No matter what the difficulty or setback, we can choose to see it as an opportunity to overcome adversity and a chance to meet the struggle head on. We can know in our heart that our Higher Power is beside us, encouraging us and leading us through these troubles. Most of my growth in recovery has come during these difficult times and challenges. Here is where my spirit is strengthened, and I am nourished with a greater appreciation of just how well the program can and does work. Do I see problems as opportunities?

Petitions to my Higher Power
God,

You have freed me from the bondage of self-centeredness and shown me a new path. Let me walk forward and be willing to face any challenge or problem that arises knowing that You are with me in all that I face. Teach me to use these difficult times as an opportunity to grow more deeply in my spiritual life. Give me courage for this day.
Amen.

＊　＊　＊　＊

Wisdom for Today   Nov 28
I am not the big story of the program. When I stop and consider all the people who walked this path before me, I realize that the real story is the program itself. Truly wonderful things have happened for me in recovery, but none of this would have been possible had it not been for all those who preceded me on this path. The founders of the program discovered what worked. They borrowed from sources such as medicine, religion and psychiatry. The founders began to share what worked for them with others and found even more help for themselves. Over the years different members

have added more tools such as many of the sayings and slogans we hear at meetings.

All who have been successful will tell you that they found a spiritual base essential for the process to work. Each of us in recovery finds that a relationship with a Power Greater than ourselves is needed to establish and maintain recovery. No, I am not the big story; it is the program. This same program has restored my self-respect. It has provided me with friends. It has given me a roadmap to follow. It has instructed me in ways I cannot fully describe here. I, like the founders, have discovered the value of helping others. All of this and more tell me that I am not that important. I am but one among many. Do I understand that it is the program and not I that is most important?

Meditations for the Heart

As I look back over my life it is abundantly clear that everything, both good and bad, has happened for a reason. These reasons are not always immediately clear, but over time things begin to make sense. There has been a purpose for the tragedies as well as the victories. There has been a reason for the people I have met along the way. Most of all, it is clear that God has had a plan for my usefulness in the world. Life for me is like one large tapestry, and I am but one thread in this magnificent work. It is not until I gained some distance from the tapestry that I began to see the importance of each individual thread. I am a part of this magnificent whole. I know that God continues to weave me into this tapestry. Each and every event in my life is but a small part of the thread that is my life. Do I have the vision to see the great tapestry that God weaves?

Petitions to my Higher Power

God,

You are the great weaver of my life. You show me where the tread of my life fits into this tapestry. Today let me open my life to Your hands and follow where I am led. Let me acknowledge the work that has already been accomplished by You in the lives of so many others in this program. For Your skillful hands I am grateful.

Amen.

* * * *

Wisdom for Today   *Nov 29*

One thing I am very glad that I seem to have lost in recovery is my need to be critical. Early in my recovery process, I was very critical of others. I thought to myself, "How can a bunch of drunks help me?" I found myself putting people down, both in the program and outside of the program. I didn't understand for a long time that what I was really trying to do was build myself up by tearing down others. Fortunately, there were people in the program who taught me how to build myself up in healthy ways. I didn't have to tear down others to feel better about myself. I could begin to feel better about me if I started to make better decisions. I could feel better about me by learning to recognize the good things about me.

Name-calling is now a thing of the past for the most part. No, I am not perfect; there is still the occasional time when someone will cut me off in traffic and a few choice words emanate from my mouth. For the most part now, I can even choose not to open my mouth in these situations, even though I still have the thoughts. I am still working on those and probably will be for some time to come. But even here God reminds me to have a forgiving heart. He reminds me not to be critical of others until there is no more room for criticism of my behavior. The program teaches me how to live without needing to berate others. I can choose simply to feel good about what I do and leave the rest up to my Higher Power. Am I making progress in being less critical of others?

Meditations for the Heart

God can choose to help us with any of our problems if we only bring them to Him. For me this is often times the hard part, because it means that I actually have to admit that I still have problems. It also requires that I humble myself enough to ask for help with these problems. I can't even begin to tell you how many times, I get into a mindset that I can handle my problems on my own. While it is true that some minor issues I can indeed address on my own, there are still plenty of times that I need to ask for help. First, we must recognize our needs and our inability to meet all of them on our own. Next we learn that we need to carry these needs to God, as we understand Him, and ask for help. Finally, we need to become willing to accept the help that is offered. This too can be a problem, particularly if we do not like the kind of help that we are offered. God does not always build a wall for us; frequently He shows us how it is done. Am I willing to accept my need for help and reach out to get it?

Petitions to my Higher Power

God,

In this day I will cross paths with many different people. Give me patience in my interactions with them. Teach me to be tolerant and understanding. Lead me to a place where I no longer need to put others down and can find

healthy ways to build myself up. Let me walk through this day with a willing heart and risk asking for help whenever I need it.
Amen.

* * * *

Wisdom for Today   *Nov 30*
When I was active in my addiction I worked hard to hold things together. One place this was especially true was on the job. I thought that if I kept my business in tact, then my life was okay. I worked in construction and took pride in many of the jobs I worked on. As a builder I thought I was doing a good job and could take pride in my work. But there was one construction project I was involved in that I took no pride in at all.

This was the wall that I built. Slowly stone by stone and brick by brick I built this wall. It got so tall that it fully surrounded me. It cut me off from family and friends. I was also walled off from God. It doesn't matter what my beliefs were then. The fact was that I was doing things to hide from my Higher Power. I did not want to be seen. This wall had many bricks - shame, remorse, anger, guilt and fear. Do I see clearly the wall that I have built up in the past?

Meditations for the Heart
When I looked at this wall it seemed too big a project to tear down. I didn't even know where to start. In truth I had made a very strong wall. Fortunately I did not have to take this wall down by myself. In coming to believe in a Power Greater than myself again, I found help in tearing down the wall. What surprised me most was to see that God was right there beside me all along taking down the stones and bricks I had so skillfully piled up. Now I can start each day new, and now I work on building bridges rather than walls. Am I willing to follow God's plan for construction in my own life?

Petitions to my Higher Power
God,
You provide me with a new set of blueprints for my life. Teach me to use the stones and bricks to build a strong foundation in my recovery. Let me find places in my life to build bridges in the relationships harmed by my addiction. Let me each day cross these bridges without fear.
Amen.

* * * *

Wisdom for Today   Dec 1

I used to love the process of getting high. The anticipation of the rush and the feeling of euphoria always kept me coming back. I chased after the exhilaration and excitement. I always wanted to find that perfect high again. At least I tried to make the world seem right again. But there was always the morning after. The incredible feeling of regret and remorse! Waking up and feeling like my head was two sizes too big. Some mornings I could not even remember what I had done the night before.

In the AA program I no longer seek after a rush. It is not exhilaration and excitement I need. Now I seek after satisfaction with myself. I seek to live life to its fullest and without regret. Today I am making memories that count. So much has changed with this simple program. Today I can find happiness. Today I can find inner peace. Today I can find and hang onto serenity. Am I finding happiness in the reality of life in the program?

Meditations for the Heart

I used to be filled with envy and jealousy when I looked at others. I was angry that they could have a normal life and I could not. It took some time but I stopped looking at others through eyes of comparison and judgment. I began to look for the good in others and tried to see past my judgment. I work to see that all people have struggles and all people have strengths. I look to see the good in others and myself. I no longer carry the shroud of shame. I know that this new vision I have received comes only through the program and from my Higher Power. Do I look for the good in others? Do I see the good that is now a part of my life? Am I grateful for this new vision?

Petitions to my Higher Power
God,

In this new day let me seek to share Your vision for my life. Let me cast aside my need to judge others. Let me find the inner strength to see my life in a new way. Help me to create new memories with which I can find ongoing satisfaction. Let this satisfaction continue to grow in me always.
Amen.

* * * *

Wisdom for Today   Dec 2

The Twelve Step program is a whole lot more that simply learning not to drink or use drugs. It is a way of living life. If all that were involved would be abstinence, it would only require one step – stop using. Before coming into the program, many of us tried that program. Most of us quit drinking and using drugs many times only to return to our old ways once again. The program is more like walking up a down escalator. We have to keep moving at a pace faster than our disease if we are ever going to reach the top. Going to meetings, talking with sponsors, working the steps and faith – all help us to make it to the top, a stable and secure recovery. Am I working a program that will get me to that top?

Meditation for the Heart

Obedience is a concept with which many of us struggle. We want to make the rules or break the rules. The program has no rules, only suggestions. However, in my recovery I have learned that being obedient to the will of my "Higher Power" is the easier way. While it is true that I can freely choose to do what I want, when I do what God wants, I find that life is actually easier. I am not always trying to cover up, hide or lie about what I have done. When I walk along the path with God leading me, I am safe; I am secure Am I willing to be obedient?

Petitions to my Higher Power

God,

Today let me walk along the path upon which You lead me. Should I stray away, call me back. Grant me the courage I need to be obedient and follow Your will for me.

Amen.

* * * *

Wisdom for Today   Dec 3

It seemed that I was always in conflict with someone when I was actively drinking and using. Generally I would start the conflict. It was like I had to stand in rigid opposition to whatever the other person's opinion was. In fact, being rigid seemed to be my mode of operation in many aspects of my life. I was always ready to stand up to someone. If I was challenged, I accepted the call. Sometimes I would stand up just so I cold push others around.

In recovery there are times when we indeed need to stand up for our opinions; but the reality is that being rigid in recovery doesn't work. In fact, being rigid often means we risk breaking. I have learned that it is equally, if not more important, to be flexible. Flexible means that I am open to hearing other people's opinions. Have I sought to be more open to others? Am I convinced that I am not always right? Am I more flexible in my relationships with others?

Meditations for the Heart

When I walked through the doors of the program I really needed help. More help than I needed, more help than I would have guessed at first! What really surprised me was the fact that help was there for me. All I needed to do was ask. Soon after joining the fellowship I was faced with the reality that others in the program were asking for help as well. I recall sitting on the sidelines afraid to speak up and offer my opinion. I didn't think I could say anything that might be of help to others. I was so wrong. Today I recognize just how important the newcomer is. Many a new member has said things that I have found helpful. In truth, much of what I have learned along the way has come from newer voices in the program. This is not to say that the old-timers are not important as well. Am I willing to stand up and give my opinion to others? Do I offer to help others in need?

Petitions to my Higher Power
God,

In this new day let me learn when to be rigid and when to be flexible. Help me always to be open to listening to other people's opinions. Let me seek to have courage to share with others and wisdom to know when to be quiet. Help me to trust that Your vision for my life is always right.
Amen.

* * * *

Wisdom for Today   *Dec 4*

There is a song I like that the words go as follows, "Got to admit I love these chains; crawling around this cage sometimes has its advantages. Perhaps one day this could get old..." While these words probably were not written about addiction, I believe they do describe what addiction was like for me.

I really loved the chains of addiction for a while. Then I began to feel like all I did was live in and crawl around in a cage with the delusion that somehow it had its advantages. Then one day it just got old. Day after day I was stuck in a frenzied darkness. Day after day I found myself empty, alone and crazy. I wanted to stop the insanity but didn't know how. Do I want the insanity to stop?

Meditations for the Heart

Step Two tells us that the insanity of addiction can stop. We have already admitted that we cannot make it stop; but there is One who has all power that can relieve us of the insanity. Not only can we be relieved of the insanity, but we can also have the chains of bondage broken. We find that we no longer have to wander around in a cage. We begin to understand that there is no advantage to living in this manner. Yes, it is possible; and all we have to do is believe that a Power outside of us can and will show us the way out. Am I willing to give up my old beliefs and trust in a Higher Power?

Petitions to my Higher Power
God,

In this new day let me come to believe that You can and will show me a way out of the insanity of my disease. Help me to see the chains of addiction for what they were. Let me begin to enjoy a new life outside of the cage to which I had grown so accustomed. Help me to see that true recovery never gets old. Amen.

* * * *

Wisdom for Today   Dec 5
I think each of us had had the experience of the bright lights outside of the tavern calling to us. We think about how inviting an atmosphere it is. We think about the camaraderie we once knew in these places. It doesn't take long with this kind of thinking to begin to think about drinking and using. And we all know where that can lead.

In the program this is called "stinking thinking;" and yet I have to wonder if so many of us have this experience, isn't this just a normal part of recovery? I think temptation will always be around. It is what we do or don't do with temptation that gets us in trouble. I can choose to think the drink through till the end and remember what waking up with a hangover was all about. I can choose to call my sponsor to talk things out. I can choose to recall my ever-present need for a Higher Power. Yes, today I have choices that I never had before. Am I making wise choices for my recovery?

Meditations for the Heart
In early recovery I really was overwhelmed frequently. I would go to meetings just to be in the presence of other recovering people. It was where I felt safest. Looking back, there was a much deeper reason I needed to be at those meetings. This was where my strength came from. This is where I first began to search for a new relationship with God. Each of us in the recovery process has the same inner desire – to be in the presence of God, as we understand Him. I did not know this early on, but over time I have come to believe that this inner desire is what I was seeking after. It is what I continue to seek after. Do I see my need for this relationship with a Power Greater? Do I feel an inner calm when I am in His presence?

God,

Here in this place of quiet, I seek You out. In the busy and crazy times, I also seek You out. In the passing thoughts of my day, I seek you out. Help me to feel Your presence in my life this day. Let me know that I can always turn to You. Guide my thoughts to Your wisdom when I am faced with choices today. Amen.

* * * *

Wisdom for Today   *Dec 6*

No longer do I wake up in the morning with my head feeling two sizes too big. Can't say I jump out of bed like I did in my youth, but I no longer awaken with feelings of regret and emptiness. Now there is something new. There is an inner feeling of calm and knowing that I can find happiness in my day. I used to turn to alcohol and drugs to find happiness but was continually disappointed. Sure, there were good times; but as time went on, I had fewer and fewer of these experiences. I began to see trouble and grief.

Somewhere I crossed the line and became addicted. Somewhere I lost my ability to control my use, and it began to control me. Somewhere I began to use just to feel normal. I no longer sought happiness and found myself searching for escape. Time after time I was given opportunities to change my ways but kept looking for the magic again. This magic never returned. Have I stopped looking for the magic?

Meditations for the Heart

Learning to wait for God's guidance can be difficult. I was used to the immediate gratification that alcohol and drugs gave me. In recovery I have had to learn to wait. I needed to wait for direction before making any important decision. I needed to wait for His guidance before I made any significant changes. I needed to wait with hope, and I needed to wait with trust that the answers would indeed come. Indeed the answers have come, and I am sure there are still others for which I must wait. Parts of recovery require action, and parts of recovery require us to wait. Yet neither action nor waiting can be accomplished without His grace. It is this grace that allows us to find our way. Am I willing to wait for the answers I seek?

Petitions to my Higher Power

God,

It is with gratitude that I wake this morning. I may never fully understand Your grace in this lifetime, but I now can see that it is only through Your help

and guidance that I am able to wait for the answers I seek. Help me this day to seek Your guidance in all that I do. Let me put away any wishes for a magic fix. Instead, teach me the next right thing to do.
Amen.

* * * *

Wisdom for Today   Dec 7
I can remember telling myself over and over again, "I can't handle it anymore." I would get so frustrated with everything that was happening in my life, I just wanted to quit. I can even remember thinking that I should end my life. I felt hopeless, alone, and saw no other option. At meetings, I sometimes hear newcomers sounding just like I used to sound.

Fortunately, in the program we learn how to stay clean and sober. Our thinking begins to become clearer. Our feelings slowly become more manageable. Even our behavior begins to improve. We can begin to experience this thing called hope. It even seems like even our lives are worth living. Do I reach out to newcomers and help them to see things differently? Do I help to instill hope in their life just as I was helped to see things differently?

Meditations for the Heart
Life can come at you from many different directions all at once. It can even feel overwhelming at times. Recovery is no different. In fact, one of the best definitions of recovery I have ever heard goes like this: "Recovery means that you take your current set of problems and trade them in for a better set of problems. Then you take that set of problems and trade them in for an even better set of problems." In other words, we will always have problems, just better ones than we used to have.

In the promises of the Twelve Step Program, the AA writer talks about how, "we will intuitively know how to handle situations" (Alcoholics Anonymous, Fourth Edition, Page 84) even when they used to baffle us. Am I still as baffled by life's problems, or am I starting to make sense out of recovery?

Petitions to my Higher Power
God,
Today let me stop and count all my blessings. Help me to recognize all the wonderful gifts that the program can bring my way. Most of all let me not forget to thank You for all you have done for me.
Amen

* * * *

Wisdom for Today   Dec 8

Toward the end of my drinking and using career, I kept on drinking and using despite the fact that it gave me nothing but trouble. In those times nothing much mattered anymore, that is, except for keeping myself supplied with enough to get high the next day. I knew what would happen if I ever ran out. It would not take long, and I would be sick. Still I kept using. I remember thinking I must be crazy. Why would anyone behave in the way that I was? Everyone else still seemed to have a good time, but I was too busy thinking about the next day to have a good time.

In recovery I no longer need to be focused on tomorrow. I have learned to live life one day at a time. I have learned that I was not crazy, at least any crazier than the other people I see at meetings. I no longer feel alone. I feel empowered by the fellowship of the program and the Twelve Steps. So much good is happening to me living life in the here and now. No more need to worry about tomorrow! Have I learned that I am not alone? Do I work at living life to its fullest each day?

Meditations for the Heart

Years ago before my addiction took over, I worked as a lifeguard. I knew how important it was to keep a watchful eye on those under my care. I knew what to do in case there was trouble, and I knew that I had a lifeline I could throw to those in need. The program is like this; and so is God, as I understand Him. He watches out for me, and He knows what to do if I get into trouble. I have faith in His lifeline. All I need do is call out to Him when I get into trouble, and His power and care are there for me. Do I know that God watches over me?

Petitions to my Higher Power
God,

Help me this day to live my life to the fullest. Give me the inner peace that comes from knowing that You are always watching over me. Let me be filled with a grateful heart as I walk through this day. Let me seek You out whenever I am in need. Grant me courage in this new day.
Amen.

*　*　*　*

Wisdom for Today   Dec 9

I would like to say that it was commonsense that finally got me to stop drinking and using, but it was not. Instead, just like many others before me, it was one consequence after another that finally convinced me that I needed to stop. Even after all these consequences, I wanted to stop but did not know how. Commonsense told me that my way would not work. Commonsense took me down a path to the front doors of the program.

Today I know that God helped me find these doors. At the time I thought that I just stumbled on in. Here I listen to others tell of their experiences with booze and drugs. Here I heard others talk of the help they found in the steps. Here I learned that I could call on a Higher Power to help me accomplish something I could not do for myself. Here I learned I could live a sober, useful and happy life. Do I see the grace that has guided my steps to the program?

Meditations for the Heart

I remember early in recovery I planted an apple tree in my back yard. I watched this tree grow, but year after year it bore no fruit. Finally I went back to the nursery where I purchased the tree and asked for help. Here I was shown the proper way to prune the tree to allow for new growth. The next spring I was surprised to see many blossoms. That fall I was able to harvest the first apple from the tree. I also realized for the first time that I was just like this tree. I needed to be pruned back. I needed the deadwood to be stripped away in my life. Then quietly and secretly the sap began to flow in me allowing new growth. Today I am fortunate to see blossoms in my life. I see new fruit growing. Am I willing to prune back the deadwood in my life in order to see new growth?

Petitions to my Higher Power
God,

Your grace surrounds me. Help me to accept this precious gift. Let me find the courage to prune out the deadwood of my life, in order to see the new growth You have planned for me. Let me bring forth good fruit in all that I do today.
Amen.

* * * *

Wisdom for Today   Dec 10

The ship is sinking, and we want to get out of this situation alive. Our only hope is to make it to the lifeboats. We hurry to get in and breathe a sigh of relief when we realize we are safe. But then reality sets in… Twelve Step groups are like our lifeboat. When we first get there, we are still scared; but soon we breathe a sigh of relief. At least we are safe. At least we are alive. But then reality sets in. When it does, we have some choices to make. We can grumble and complain that we don't have enough room in the boat. We can insist on steering the boat. We can cry and feel like it is still hopeless. Or we can do our part to help out.

Helping others is a way to help ourselves, and asking for help is a way of helping ourselves. Can I rejoice in the fact that I have made it into the boat? Do I do my part to help others or do service work in the group? Do I trust that as long as I stay with the boat that eventually I will make it to "dry" land?

Meditations for the Heart

Having a seat in the lifeboat of the Twelve Step Program is something for which we should try to be grateful. Many addicts and alcoholics go down to the murky depths of despair or die in the raging sea of addiction as the ship sinks. Often times we are tempted to ask, "Why Me?" Why did I even get on this ship? Why am I stuck out here? The "Why me?" question is a good question to ask. We need to ask, "Why me; why am I one of the few that got a seat in this lifeboat?" Am I truly grateful to be one of the "chosen ones" to get a seat?

Petitions to my Higher Power
God,

Today I pray that I may walk in God's grace. It is given freely each day. God, help me to know that it is enough for today. Help me to trust that if I stay in the boat, You will see me safely to dry land.
Amen.

* * * *

Wisdom for Today   Dec 11

When I look back at the life I had when I was drinking and using, it was not a pretty picture. There were the repeated failures, the letting people down, the lies, the time in jail and hospitals. None of these things made my addiction pretty. Sure there were the good times; but when I look back honestly, I wonder how I ever could have wanted that life. I know now that it was not the life I truly wanted. I just wanted a good time.

But I am different. I cannot process alcohol or drugs in my system the same way other people do. I know people that drink normally, and I did not drink like they do. In the program of AA I have learned that nothing I could do could change the way I respond to alcohol or drugs. Physically, psychologically and emotionally I respond differently and negatively to my drugs of choice. I am an addict, and I now have a choice to make. Will I choose recovery?

Meditations for the Heart

My spiritual life depends on two things. One is God Himself. I surely can have no spiritual life without a Higher Power. The second thing my spiritual life depends on is maintaining a conscious awareness of God, as I understand Him. All roads I travel must lead me back to this inner consciousness of God. Every decision I make needs to be with His help and guidance. Every breath I take should lead me to gratitude for the chance at recovery He has given me. It is here in this inner consciousness that I will find peace. It is here that I will find serenity. It is here I will find strength. Am I doing all that I can to maintain this inner consciousness?

Petitions to my Higher Power

God,

So I am made differently than others. I can accept this. Help me also to accept that this difference does not mean that I am inferior or damaged products. Let me find the peace and serenity that the program promises in a relationship with You. Keep me conscious of Your presence in my life. Amen.

* * * *

Wisdom for Today   Dec 12

I don't know exactly when I crossed the line. I just know I did. I think all alcoholics and addicts in recovery eventually recognize this fact. But even though I know I crossed this line, it does not mean that I am cured. Some times I still have messed up thinking. I still catch myself thinking that I should be able to drink if I want to. I still catch myself thinking about the "good old days."

Yet it is this very fact - that I catch myself – which enables me to stay sober. The program has given me back the power to choose. I can choose to stay in my messed up thinking, or I can choose to tell on my disease and get back on track. This power to choose was not something I had when I was active in my disease process. The booze and the drugs made the choices for me. Today I can see my disease for what it really is – cunning, baffling and powerful. Do I see my disease for what it is?

Meditations for the Heart

I must take time to be with my Higher Power each and every day. It is in this quiet solitude that I find inner peace. It is in this relationship that I find strength and courage. It is in this relationship that I am given wisdom. I know that I need to be transformed mentally and spiritually. It is only in this relationship that this transformation can take place. So I need to seek out time with God. I find time to talk to Him, and I find time to listen. Will I take time to foster this relationship each day?

Petitions to my Higher Power
God,

Your wisdom is above my wisdom. Let me seek you out in all that I do today. Help me to stay on track and make good choices for my recovery today. Let me see my disease when it tries to sneak back into my thinking, my life and my heart. Grant me courage when I need it.
Amen.

* * * *

Wisdom for Today   Dec 13
I remember as a child in elementary school running a relay race. I was running the final leg of the race and heading toward the finish line when I dropped the baton with just a few steps to go. As a result my team did not win; we were disqualified.

Recovery is like this. We spend a lot of time in practice with our coaches, our sponsors and other recovering people learning the rules and how to run a good race. We enter into a competition for our lives, and we run the race. If we drop the baton we get disqualified. Am I willing to follow the guidelines of the program? Am I running a good race?

Meditations for the Heart
Practice, practice, practice! It seems that this is all I do. Sometimes I want to grumble when my coach says take another lap. Yet I know that all the sweat will be worth it someday. The longer I stick around in the program, the more suggestions my sponsor gives me. Do I understand that he or she is simply trying to get me ready to compete? I have had to run many races in recovery, races against this disease. Each time I run a race, I am relieved to find that following the suggestions of my coaches pays off.

Petitions to my Higher Power
God,

This day I will practice the principles of the program so that I can run a good race. Help me to gain a full understanding of the rules of recovery so that I don't get disqualified. Help me to trust and have faith that with Your guidance, I can finish this race a winner.
Amen.

* * *

Wisdom for Today   Dec 14

Be careful! The temptation to drink or use again never leaves. The temptation will always be there, but know that when we face the urge to get high, many have gone before us. They have had to face these same urges and made it. The program does not promise to eliminate our desire to use alcohol or drugs – just that by using the tools we will have the courage to say no to our desires. Gratefully old-timers say that it does get easier over time. Yet all of them can relate times when the desire to use raises its ugly head again. Sometimes it is just a passing thought, and at other times it may be more difficult. Do I trust that my Higher Power will give me the needed strength and wisdom to walk away from my unhealthy desires?

Meditations for the Heart

I know that my life in recovery is not trouble free and that I will have to face difficulties along the path of life. The program gives me the ability to face these difficulties with an inner peace. Serenity comes from following God's will. This is a hard lesson to learn but over time it becomes apparent that by following the will of God I have no worries. The struggles I have last for only a moment when I continually turn them over to God. All I need to do is the next right thing. Do I trust God to give me what I need in the face of trouble?

Petitions to my Higher Power

God,

Should I face difficulties today, God help me to trust that You are with me. Help me to be wise in the decisions I face. Strengthen my faith and guide me to the people who will help me along the way.

Amen.

* * *

Wisdom for Today   Dec 15

Sometimes it just seems easier to blame others or focus on them instead of myself. It is a natural defense to make others responsible for our plight in life. Yet as long as I focus on others and their responsibility for my problems, I remain sick. I have to look at my part in whatever the situation or problem is. My sponsor once told me that, "The problem is not your disease; the problem is you." He was right! The problem usually was me. Blaming others got me nowhere. It was only when I would take responsibility for my problems that I would make progress. Learning to change the things I can is a necessary lesson in recovery. Am I willing to take responsibility for my part rather than blaming others?

Meditations for the Heart

In silence I can learn the meaning of God's will for my life. Learning to listen for that still, small voice that exists within can lead me to make wise decisions. But listening without action leads no where. Knowledge alone does not produce change. Change occurs when I am willing to put it into action. Simply knowing I am an addict or alcoholic does not mean anything. Simply knowing I have character defects does not lead to change. I must take what I learn and put it to use. Am I willing to use the knowledge I gain from others and from God to better myself? Do I really listen?

Petitions to my Higher Power

God,

This day, oh, God, help me to be quiet and listen to Your guidance. Help me to listen to those who have more experience in recovery than I. Give me the courage to change the things I can.

Amen.

* * * *

Wisdom for Today   Dec 16

Very early in the program I started to receive gifts from others – gifts of hope, a sense of relief, direction. I fit in. I began to hear slogans like, "It works if you work it." It took me a while to begin to understand what that meant. I don't know if it was because my brain was so cloudy from years of alcohol and drug abuse or it was because I simply wanted an easier, softer way; but it took some time before I became willing to use the tools I was being given. I could see that it worked for others who were willing, yet I resisted.

Finally, it began to sink in. Acceptance and surrender to a Power outside of me is what I had to do. So I got to work and began to use the tools. Have I been using the tools the way I have been shown? Have I surrendered to a Higher Power?

Meditations for the Heart

The program provides us with seeds of hope, truth and faith. We are given the tools. Yet we must use the tools to nurture the seeds and keep the weeds out of our garden. There are sunny days, and other days that are filled with rain. Both are needed to grow the seeds of sobriety. Am I using the tools, or am I waiting for someone else to do the work for me?

Petitions to my Higher Power
God,

I don't know whether today will be filled with sunshine or rain, but I can trust that You will walk this path with me. Give me the wisdom and strength I need to use the tools so that I may reap a bountiful harvest.
Amen.

* * * *

Wisdom for Today   Dec 17
Desperate measures require desperate action – right? When I first walked through the doors of the program, I was desperate. I was desperate to find a way out. I wasn't really sure that my substance use was the cause of all my problems. I just knew I wanted to find a way out of all my pain. I was running around frantically looking for the answer. I wanted to find the magic. I could see in the eyes of the people at meetings that many of them had found what I was looking for. Why was it so difficult to find the answer? All I wanted was a way out!

Then one day an old-timer looked at me and said, "Quit running!" I didn't understand what he had said. "Quit running; you will never find a way out like that." He was right I had to quit running. It was only when I slowed down that I began to realize that no one had found a way out, but they had found peace in the middle of the storm. Have I quit running?

Meditation for the Heart
Sooner or later all recovering addicts and alcoholics realize that the program is not a cure for their disease, but it can teach them a new way of living. Addiction continues to raise its ugly head from time to time even in recovery. It affects our thinking, our emotional response to situations and our behavior. Our initial response may be to want run. In fellowship with others in the program and in turning our life over to "a Power Greater" than ourselves, we begin to realize that there is peace in the storm. Rather than desperately trying to find a way out, we begin to look for "His" guidance and peace in the middle of our pain and fear. Do I believe that I can find this peace if I stop running?

Petitions to my Higher Power
God,

The program tells me to take it one step at a time. It does not tell me to run. Lord, help me this day to look for You in all that I do. Grant me the

peace and serenity that is promised. Help me to know that nothing You ask
is too hard.
Amen.

* * * *

Wisdom for Today   *Dec 18*

Wrestling, struggling and fighting with the idea that I was an alcoholic or
drug addict was my nature. Even when I first started attending meetings I was
fully convinced that I was done fighting. At first I spent a lot of time trying
to prove that I was different. I wanted to show others and myself that I was
unique. But, slowly over time, I began to see more and more evidence that I
too had this disease. When I was finally convinced that I indeed was addicted
to both alcohol and drugs, I began to look for the answers to recovery. I
had a lot to learn, and I had a lot to unlearn. I began to open my ears to the
knowledge of others in the program. I picked up one resource after another.
The more I read, the more I heard, the more I asked questions, the more I
began to develop a sense of hope. I found myself fighting less often. I became
more accepting of the "suggestions" given to me.

Today I still find that I can drift back into that state of terminal uniqueness.
I still find there are times that I feel like my story is different. Fortunately the
fellowship of the program brings me back to reality. Am I still fighting?

Meditations for the Heart

There are things that are worth fighting for. Am I fighting for the right
things? God has helped me recognize that I am worth fighting for. I did not
always believe that. There was a time that I felt totally worthless. When I
do have to go into "battle," I need to remember to put my helmet on. I have
to carry my shield. The wisdom of the program is my helmet; openness and
willingness is my shield; truth is my sword. I have found these things do
protect me from harm when I go into battle. I no longer have to run in fear
and hide. Do I pick my battles wisely? When I do go into battle, do I strap
my helmet on tight? Do I remember to carry my shield and sword?

Petitions to my Higher Power
God,

Help me this day to be open to the wisdom of others. Help me to choose
my battles wisely, and help me to know that I do not need to go into any battle
alone. God help me to trust that You are with me each step of the way.
Amen

Wisdom for Today   Dec 19

We all traveled different paths to arrive at the door of opportunity that recovery offers. The same is true regarding our concept of "God, as we understand Him." (*Alcoholics Anonymous,* Fourth Edition. Page 59) Many of us claimed to believe and have faith when we were active in our addiction, but our behavior did not match our words. We may have asked for God's help, but we did not accept it when His hand reached out to offer help.

As we enter the Twelve Step program, we all start in different places with regard to our spiritual faith. Yet one thing is sure; we all need to grow in this area. Some of us can crawl, others walk, and still others may be able to run spiritually right from the start.

Do I realize that I need to grow spiritually if I am to succeed at abstinence?

Meditations for the Heart

Our journey toward spiritual health often begins in a place of weakness. Yet it is in this place of weakness that we are most receptive to grow in faith. The program offers plenty of evidence that it works. We can see that many before us have used the steps to grow and stay in recovery. Faith begins with a willingness to accept this reality and to begin to trust that the steps indeed can lead me out of insanity. Opening ourselves to the concept of "God, as we understand Him," can indeed be where we find hope in the middle of hopelessness. Do I recognize that I can no longer be my own Higher Power? Am I willing to open myself to the spiritual principles of the program?

Petitions to my Higher Power
God,

It seems strange to call out to You this way. I always looked for a quick fix. Help me today to be open to the spiritual principles of the program. Increase my willingness to have faith. Help me to continue to grow.
Amen.

* * * *

Wisdom for Today   Dec 20

In a song, a singer, writes, "God weeps, too." Sometimes our experiences along the path of recovery bring us to a place where we find ourselves filled with grief and despair. Tears may well up inside of us or may flow freely. At times like this it is helpful to know that we are not alone. God may cry with us, for us or even because of us; but He is always there with us. Do I believe that I am not alone? Do I trust that God will give me strength at the times I need it most?

When I find myself filled with despair, loneliness or grief, I can be assured that someone in the program will listen, comfort and guide me to a place of acceptance. I believe that God puts these people in our lives because He cares for us. Do I believe that God cares for me?

Meditations for the Heart

Sometimes I want to cry because of the things I have done. At other times I want to cry because of what has been done to me. Regardless of the reason, I have learned that the sadness, loss or self-disgust that I experience are only temporary. Each day that I use the steps and each day that I follow the principles of the program bring healing. It is not a cure, but it is healing. Can I trust and believe that God wants to bring healing into my life?

Petitions to my Higher Power

God,

Walk with me this day, and help me to know and trust that You will provide everything I need for me. I know I can never have everything I want in this life, but You continue to show me that I can have everything I need. For this I am grateful today.

Amen.

* * * *

Wisdom for Today   Dec 21

Good and bad things happen in recovery. Life is like that. The trick is finding a way to be content, serene, and at peace regardless of the cards you are dealt. It would seem easy to do this when things are going well, but that isn't as easy as it looks. When everything is great, it becomes easy to become grandiose, cocky or arrogant, claiming credit for the good things that are happening. On the other side of the coin, it is easy to get remorseful, resentful or "on the pity pot" when everything is going badly.

Finding the inner calm and serenity requires that we acknowledge God's handiwork in our lives. When things are good, we need to thank God for the blessings and gifts we receive. And when things look the worst, we need to recognize that God's hand is there to help us along the way. Do I give credit where credit is due?

Meditations for the Heart

The longer I stay clean and sober the more I recognize God's presence in my life. I have become convinced that nothing I have achieved and nothing

I have survived were done without His presence and help. At meetings I not only hear the "Promises" of the program read, but I see them become reality in my life and in the lives of many others who walk the walk. Things that used to absolutely baffle me now seem simple because of the Twelve Steps. It is simple, but no one said it would be easy. Have I come to believe that a Power greater than I is working for and with me in my recovery? Do I look for evidence that this is true in my life and in the lives of others?

Petitions to my Higher Power

God,

Today let me see the evidence that You are active in my life. Fill me with gratitude and help me remain focused. Walk with me step by step one moment to the next. Help me to encourage others who walk the same path. Let me accept encouragement from others.

Amen.

* * * *

Wisdom for Today   Dec 22

When I walked into my first meeting, I was carrying a heavy load – all the years of dishonesty, guilt, shame and pain. I had been foolish enough to carry that load everywhere I went. It had gotten so heavy that I was slumped over from the burden. I could not look at myself in the mirror. As time passed, I began to learn from others in the program that not only did I not need to carry the burdens from the past, but I also did not need to carry the fears associated with the future. All I needed to carry were the burdens of the day. Man is only strong enough to carry today, and he does not need to carry that weight alone. With the help of a Higher Power and other recovering addicts, I have found that the burdens of life are much easier to carry. By working the steps and following the advice and wisdom of others on the path of life, I can find it possible to stand up straight again.

Meditation for the Heart

Each day brings new possibilities and new challenges. Not every day is pain free. Yet the longer I stay clean and sober, the more I trust that God will only give me what I can carry. The load I carry today is much lighter than the one I used to carry. This is not to say that I don't have problems. Recovery is all about exchanging my current problems for a better set of problems. Then I must take those problems and exchange them for a new set of problems. Recovery does not eliminate problems, it just makes it much easier to deal with the ones I have today. Have I found it easier to carry the burdens I have this day? Am I still trying to carry the past and the future?

Staying in close contact with my Higher Power is one of the easiest ways to lighten my load. Turning over the burdens of the past and the fears of the future to God makes it possible to deal with the burdens of this day. Am I willing to let go of the past and not fear the future?

Petitions to my Higher Power
God,

As I begin this day, help me to be rid of the past and trust that You will guide my footsteps into the future. Help me to focus on just this day and to accept the burdens I am given. Help me make the choices to keep my load light. Guide my footsteps into the future. Help me walk through this day with courage.
Amen.

* * * *

Wisdom for Today   Dec 23
When I was drinking and using, I liked to buy people drinks and turn others on. It made me feel important and accepted. I was using them for my own gain. It helped me hide what I was really feeling. The thought of being helpful to others never occurred to me. At the time helping others seemed like a game, a way to make friends. I really didn't want friends; I just wanted to hide behind the mask of self-pleasure.

When I came into the Twelve Step program, I found out that helping others was really a way of helping myself. I began to experience genuine happiness and felt needed. I found a new humility in recognizing that I was no different than the people I was helping. I needed their help, too. Am I willing to help others?

Meditations for the Heart
In recovery I have found it necessary to constantly restore my energy and my faith. I have found out that God, as I understand Him, is the storehouse of this energy. By following His will for me, I have found that not only is life easier, but I am also restored. Today I will work to recognize that I am on a journey and that God provides the direction. I have to walk the path of recovery, and God points the way. Along the path He gives me opportunity to help others. Am I willing to follow God's direction?

God,

Today let me walk with You. Show me and point the way so that I avoid the pitfalls that may exist along the way. When I am given the opportunity to help others, guide me in a way to be truly helpful. Keep me in Your presence.

Amen.

* * * *

Wisdom for Today   *Dec 24*

When I was most active in my addiction to alcohol and drugs, I would joke around and tell others and myself that I liked being "abnormal." Being normal was not something I desired. This was a part of my own denial and dishonesty with myself. As my disease progressed, I became more and more abnormal. It became quite frightening.

When I started the recovery process, not drinking or using seemed abnormal to me. As time went by recovery began to seem more and more normal to me. I began to enjoy life even when there were bumps in the road. I found a healthy humility that provided me with courage and wisdom I did not know I had. Do I believe that being "normal" is okay?

Meditations for the Heart

In recovery I have been given many gifts. I have also experienced some difficult situations. Over time I have learned that all things I experience in life are for me to draw in closer contact with my Higher Power. When I experience the good things in life and receive the "gifts" of recovery, I need to have gratitude for the grace that my Higher Power has offered me. When I am walking through great struggles, and there are those, I need to know that my Higher Power is right there with me each step of the way. In these times He provides me with strength, courage and wisdom – the very things I need most in my struggle. Do I live life as an example to others? Do I express gratitude for the help I receive?

Petitions to my Higher Power

God,

Sometimes I forget to be grateful for all that You have done in my life. I know that I would not even be in this world had You not protected me from myself. Let me be reminded of all that You do in my life today. Help me to trust that You will continue to help me when I need it.

Amen.

* * * *

Many of us will be celebrating today. Exchanging gifts, spending time with family, etc. is a good time for most. As addicts and alcoholics we often remember when Christmas was not always a time to celebrate. Then we walked into the day with guilt and remorse or sadness. Today is indeed a day to celebrate, for we have been given the wonderful gift of sobriety. It is a day when we can be especially grateful. Although this gift does not come all wrapped up with ribbons and bows, it certainly is the most precious gift an addict can have, for without sobriety we have nothing. Take time to acknowledge this gift today, and look to your Higher Power with gratitude.

For some of us the holidays are not always easy. Memories can be painful. For some of us the holidays mean interacting with family, which can trigger all kinds of emotions and struggles even in recovery. Still we need to focus on the gift we have received. I find that asking myself what God wants me to do with this gift helps me even through any holiday struggles. Today I believe He just wants me to be the best person I can be regardless of my circumstances. I also believe He wants me to look for His peace and joy in this day. Do I treasure the gift that I am given this day?

Meditations for the Heart

Today is a day to experience God's heaven here on earth. With each smiling face and glimmering light in this day, I can experience joy. With each quiet moment and each deep thought I can experience peace. All that is around me may hustle and bustle with the excitement of the day, but I can carry this peace and joy inside of me. I can know God's closeness to me and rest in His arms today. I can feel His comfort in my heart as I walk through this day. This day in many ways is just like any other in recovery. Yes, there may be all the glitter and glitz and the fancy packages, but this day I am gifted with sobriety just like all the other twenty-four hours I am given. Yet it is also different because it is a holiday. So today I will be conscious of each breath I am given and seek out the inner peace and joy in my heart. Do I seek after joy and peace in my recovery?

Petitions to my Higher Power

God,

You give me only one day at a time. For this I am grateful. Help me to make this a joyful holiday and to know Your peace. Walk through this day with me, and guide me away from the pitfalls or struggles I may encounter without Your help. Let me rest in Your arms this day.

Amen.

* * * *

When I first walked through the doors of AA, I really could not imagine wanting anything more than I wanted alcohol and drugs. I felt completely empty on the inside, and I didn't know with what I could fill this emptiness. Even though I knew I had to stop, abstinence really didn't seem like a viable option. I recall thinking that maybe the program could teach me how to drink again and soon learned this was not the case.

I had to trust what I was being told. "Don't drink and don't use and your life will get better." It came down to simple faith -- faith that somehow my life would get better -- faith that the emptiness I carried around could be filled. I didn't start to even think about happiness for a while. I just wanted the pain to go away. I still wanted to escape. I didn't like the reality of my world. It was this faith that carried me for a while. I needed to find a new reality, and this is exactly what I found in the program. Am I finding a new reality?

Meditations for the Heart

I struggled a lot in the beginning. Staying sober did get easier, but I continued to struggle. I was not good at waiting, and yet this was exactly what I was being asked to do. There were no easy answers. There only were the Twelve Steps and the people I met at meetings. Waiting for the answers to my problems was not easy, but God did help me to find the answers I sought. This Higher Power not only helped me in those early days, but He continues to guide me to the answers I need today. I still have to wait for this guidance, but I have learned that God will only give me the answers when I am ready for them. Am I willing to wait for the answers I seek?

Petitions to my Higher Power

God,

I still have to look to simple faith to guide me through my days. I am grateful that this faith works for me as I walk through my days. Help me to be patient and to listen for the answers that are provided to me in all that I do. Give me a willingness to do the next right thing throughout my day. Amen.

* * * *

I want it now. These words are familiar to all addicts and alcoholics. Early in my recovery process I struggled a lot with impatience. I wanted everything to return to "normal" now. But the reality is that a new life cannot be built overnight. It takes time. It takes work, and it takes patience. Just because I was clean and sober did not necessarily mean that my addictive thinking stopped. Learning to think and do recovery takes time. It has to be practiced. It is too easy to get back into our old ways of thinking and behavior. That is why we must practice. Building a new life takes time, but it can be done if we follow the suggestions of the program. Am I practicing clean and sober thinking?

Meditations for the Heart

Faith is a gift from our Higher Power. In response to our prayers, we are given this gift. Faith and hope come from our willingness to trust God and the program. If I keep doing what I need to do each day, and if I practice the principles of the program, I receive these gifts. This does not mean I won't have struggles or problems along the way. We will always have problems. It does mean that I will find the strength and the wisdom along the way to deal with these problems in recovery. The more faith I have the easier life becomes. Am I willing to pray for a stronger faith?

Petitions to my Higher Power

God,

Today I need your help just as I do every other day. Walk with and give me the gift of faith. Strengthen me for the times I struggle and help me to think with a clear mind.

Amen.

* * * *

Wisdom for Today   Dec 28

Surrender is something I need to do each time I start my day. I cannot afford to start my day saying to myself, "I'm in control." I have to remind myself each day that I am an alcoholic and an addict. I have to remind myself that this is a problem that I have turned over to God. I have to remind myself that I have surrendered to His will. It is important for me to do this because it reminds me that I have given my addiction problem over to God's hands, because it certainly does not belong in my hands.

I have to remind myself that it is in this act of surrender that I have given up the option to return to drinking and drugging. The act of surrender frees me so that I do not have to worry about relapse anymore. As long as I follow the will of my Higher Power, I can be confident that I will not return to my old ways. As I have walked down the path of recovery, I have found that there are many other problems that I have needed to turn over to God. Each time

I do this, I find that I am led to a new place in my recovery process. Often times I am surprised by the outcomes. I am led to my Higher Power. Do I take the time to surrender anew each day?

Meditations for the Heart
I will try to grow a little each day, for if I am growing in my recovery, I am not wilting. In order to keep growing, I have to work the soil. I must keep the weeds of resentment, fear and arrogance out of my garden. I must water the seeds of hope and honesty. I must seek out the light of openness and willingness. It is only when I work the steps and fertilize my recovery with meetings that I can be assured that my garden will grow. I continue to be amazed by the growth I have seen in myself and in others in the program. Each time I go to a meeting, I try to remind myself that the room is filled with miracles. What astounds me the most is that I can see that I am one of those walking miracles! Today I will look for the miracles that God creates in my life.

Petitions to my Higher Power
God,
Again this day I fully surrender my will and my life to You. Help me to be confident in the care that You provide. Help not only me this day but all of the addicts and alcoholics who seek You out. Give me the tools I need to work in the garden today.
Amen.

* * * *

Wisdom for Today   Dec 29
When I first walked through the doors of the program, I thought that drinking and drugging were my only problem. I assumed that if I stopped using that my family, work, legal and financial problems would magically disappear. I was wrong. I had lots of work to do. I wanted to hurry up and fix all my problems. Soon I found out that I needed to slow down. I needed to trust the process. I was told that I really only had two problems – staying clean and sober, and all the rest. If I didn't stay clean, I had no chance of fixing any of the other problems I had.

With sobriety I soon found that my other problems were disappearing. Later I found out that in addition to my practical problems that I also had problems with my character. These defects of character continued to be problematic until I was ready to let go. I had to learn to trust that God would finish the work He started. Am I willing to trust God and His process?

Meditations for the Heart

Patience was something at which I was not at all good. I had this attitude – I want what I want, and I want it right now. Recovery has a way of teaching patience. I soon found out that all my troubles would not be fixed in one day. It would take some time to correct the problems I was experiencing. My character would not magically change. I had to be willing to work at it. I had to practice patience. Am I willing to practice the principles of the program? Am I willing to follow the directions I am given?

Petitions to my Higher Power

God,

Today teach me to be patient, and help me to trust Your process. Help me to realize that You are still at work and that You are not finished with me yet. Amen.

* * * *

Wisdom for Today   Dec 30

A fundamental concept in recovery is giving it away. We have been blessed through the program and by our Higher Power. Each of us has our own story – what it was like, what happened, and what it is like now that we have found the gift of recovery. Sharing our experience, strength and hopes helps us to keep what we have received.

None of us know exactly which words we share that may make a difference in someone else's life. At times I am surprised when another person in the program walks up to me and says, "What you said tonight really helped me." Imagine, my words helping someone else! Am I willing to share openly?

Meditations for the Heart

Carrying resentments and grudges can be extremely dangerous for individuals in the program. In addition to sharing our strengths and hopes, I also need to share my struggles. It is only in sharing these struggles that I can hope to hear some words of wisdom or receive a piece of insight from someone else that has been there. Am I willing to share my struggles and listen for suggestions that might just help?

Petitions to my Higher Power

God,

Today I may have an opportunity to share with others. Let me share my experiences, strengths, and hopes openly. Let me also be unafraid to share my struggles and to listen to the suggestions I am given. Amen.

* * * *

Wisdom for Today   *Dec 31*

Staying clean and sober is the most important decision I have ever made; my whole life depends on it. Without sobriety I have nothing. Every choice I make in recovery is important, but none is more important than not taking that first pill or first hit or first drink. Everything I have depends on this. Without sobriety I am not able to do any of the other things that I want or that my Higher Power wants for me. Forgetting this even for a moment can be disastrous.

Meditations for the Heart

Recovery has many demands. Often times when things seem to get difficult, I need to go back to the simple discipline of "First things first." God does not expect me to be able to handle more than one thing at a time. The discipline of "first things" demands that I do the next right thing. I need to stay focused on God's will for me. Discipline is part of my training in recovery. Do I welcome this training? Do I recognize that God has a plan for me even when I do not always see it?

Petitions to my Higher Power

God,

This day let me be disciplined and focus on the next right thing. Help me to make wise decisions and to use the tools You have given me. Help me always to seek my direction through You.

Amen.

* * * *

Bibliography

Alcoholics Anonymous. Fourth Edition. Alcoholics Anonymous World Services, Inc., New York, NY., 2001

Recovery Lane

The process of addiction to mood-altering chemicals (alcohol, prescription drugs, marijuana, cocaine, heroin, speed, downers, club drugs, etc.) is complex. Alcoholism and drug addiction are major problems facing society today. Many people need help if they are to recover from addiction, but where do you start? Complex problems do not always require complex solutions. Keep it simple.

When you are an alcoholic or addict, it is easy to get lost. Sometimes it is hard to find your way. Yet, for most alcoholics and addicts, asking for directions is not an easy thing to do. When you are ready to get out of your addiction, it is difficult to know which way to turn. Finding and using the right map can really help you get on to the....

Road to Recovery!

Visit my website at:
http://www.recoverylane.com